ACCESS TO JUSTICE AND LEGAL AID

This book considers how access to justice is affected by restrictions to legal aid budgets and increasingly prescriptive service guidelines. As common law jurisdictions, England and Wales and Australia, share similar ideals, policies and practices, but they differ in aspects of their legal and political culture, in the nature of the communities they serve and in their approaches to providing access to justice. These jurisdictions thus provide us with different perspectives on what constitutes justice and how we might seek to overcome the burgeoning crisis in unmet legal need. The book fills an important gap in existing scholarship as the first to bring together new empirical and theoretical knowledge examining different responses to legal aid crises both in the domestic and comparative contexts, across criminal, civil and family law. It achieves this by examining the broader social, political, legal, health and welfare impacts of legal aid cuts and prescriptive service guidelines. Across both jurisdictions, this work suggests that it is the most vulnerable groups who lose out in the way the law now operates in the twenty-first century. This book is essential reading for academics, students, practitioners and policymakers interested in criminal and civil justice, access to justice, the provision of legal assistance and legal aid.

Access to Justice and Legal Aid

Comparative Perspectives on Unmet Legal Need

Edited by
Asher Flynn and Jacqueline Hodgson

BLOOMSBURY
NEW DELHI • LONDON • OXFORD • NEW YORK • SYDNEY

BLOOMSBURY INDIA
Bloomsbury Publishing India Pvt. Ltd
Second Floor, LSC Building No. 4, DDA Complex, Pocket C–6&7,
Vasant Kunj, New Delhi 110070

BLOOMSBURY, BLOOMSBURY ACADEMIC INDIA and the Diana logo are
trademarks of Bloomsbury Publishing Plc

First published in India 2023
First published 2017

This edition published with permission from Bloomsbury Publishing Plc,
50 Bedford Square, London, WC1B3DP, UK

British Library Cataloguing-in-Publication Data
A catalogue record for this book is available from the British Library.

Library of Congress Cataloging-in-Publication Data

ISBN: 978-93-56403-79-6

Typeset by Compuscript Ltd, Shannon
Printed at Manipal Technologies Limited, Manipal

To find out more about our authors and books
visit www.bloomsbury.com and sign up for our newsletters

CONTENTS

Acknowledgements vii
Editors ix
Contributors xi
List of Abbreviations xvii
Tables and Figures xxi

1. Access to Justice and Legal Aid Cuts: A Mismatch of Concepts in the Contemporary Australian and British Legal Landscapes 1
   Asher Flynn and Jacqueline Hodgson
2. Challenges Facing the Australian Legal Aid System 23
   Mary Anne Noone
3. Rhyme and Reason in the Uncertain Development of Legal Aid in Australia 43
   Jeff Giddings
4. The Rise and Decline of Criminal Legal Aid in England and Wales 63
   Tom Smith and Ed Cape
5. A View from the Bench: A Judicial Perspective on Legal Representation, Court Excellence and Therapeutic Jurisprudence 87
   Pauline Spencer
6. Face-to-interface Communication: Accessing Justice by Video Link from Prison 103
   Carolyn McKay
7. The Rise of 'DIY' Law: Implications for Legal Aid 123
   Kathy Laster and Ryan Kornhauser
8. Community Lawyers, Law Reform and Systemic Change: Is the End in Sight? 141
   Liana Buchanan
9. What if There Is Nowhere to Get Advice? 161
   James Organ and Jennifer Sigafoos

10. The End of 'Tea and Sympathy'? The Changing Role of Voluntary Advice Services in Enabling 'Access to Justice' 179
Samuel Kirwan

11. Reasoning a Human Right to Legal Aid 195
Simon Rice

12. Cuts to Civil Legal Aid and the Identity Crisis in Lawyering: Lessons from the Experience of England and Wales 221
Natalie Byrom

13. Access to What? LASPO and Mediation 239
Rosemary Hunter, Anne Barlow, Janet Smithson and Jan Ewing

14. Insights into Inequality: Women's Access to Legal Aid in Victoria 255
Pasanna Mutha-Merennege

15. Indigenous People and Access to Justice in Civil and Family Law 269
Melanie Schwartz

16. Austerity and Justice in the Age of Migration 287
Ana Aliverti

Index 305

ACKNOWLEDGEMENTS

This collection is drawn from the international collaboration that has been developed between Monash University and the University of Warwick (funded by the Monash Warwick Alliance). The idea for the collection arose from the *Access to Justice: A Comparative Analysis of Cuts to Legal Aid in England, Wales and Victoria Project*, in which two conferences were hosted—the first at the University of Warwick in March 2014 and the second at Monash University in July 2014—with participants from law centres, third-sector organisations, the legal profession, judges and academics. We would like to thank our two institutions for their support in developing this collaboration, and, in particular, we would like to thank our co-investigators on the aforementioned project—Natalie Byrom, Arie Freiberg, James Harrison, Jude McCulloch and Bronwyn Naylor. It was a pleasure working with this team of inspiring colleagues, and having the opportunity to do so while visiting our respective institutions in England and Australia.

The collection brings together expertise from across Australia and the United Kingdom to reflect critically on access to justice and legal aid. Working with these scholars, practitioners and advocates, whose research and practice reveal the limits and possibilities of justice, has been a highly rewarding experience. We would like to thank each of our contributing authors for their diligence and patience, for responding so graciously and positively to critical feedback on earlier drafts, and for the tremendous contributions that their work makes, both within and beyond this book, to advance access to justice for some of the most vulnerable members of society.

We would also like to express our gratitude to the editorial team at Hart Publishing and to Bill Asquith for his support in developing the project to publication. Thank you also to Julia Farrell for her magnificent editorial assistance. We are also very grateful to our peers and colleagues who have provided advice and guidance on the content of this book.

Finally, we would like to thank our partners, families and friends for their patience, support and encouragement. In particular, Asher would like to thank Pamela, Allen and Michael for their continuing love and support, and for keeping her company on various visits to the United Kingdom during this project—even if that meant watching Australia lose the Ashes series! She would also like to thank her wonderful, loving partner, Mark. There is no doubt that it can be challenging supporting an academic whose work never seems to stay at work, and it means so much to have such a proud and caring partner who supports every endeavour and new project without hesitation. Finally, Asher would like to dedicate this book to their son Henry Maxwell. Jackie would like to thank the practitioners in legal aid firms and the advice sector (amongst them David Fanson, Nick Hodgkinson, Lisa Metherell and Paul Needham) for reminding her of the importance of this project. And, of course, Mark, Ella and Lotte for helping to make the Australia trip such fun.

Asher Flynn and Jacqueline Hodgson
May 2016

EDITORS

Dr Asher Flynn is a Senior Lecturer in Criminology at Monash University. Her research applies a critical, socio-legal framework to understand, critique and transform legal policy and practice. Informed by national and international context, her research focuses on how access to justice is negotiated; and the gendered, class-based application and practice of law. Asher has published widely in the areas of sexual violence, access to justice, plea negotiations and prosecutorial discretion, and has contributed to policy-specific research and legal change in early resolution procedures, as well as influencing reforms in homicide and rape laws. Her latest book (with Dr Anastasia Powell and Dr Nicola Henry) *Rape Justice: Beyond the Criminal Law* (Palgrave Macmillan, 2015) examines the potentials and limitations of the law and its processes for responding to experiences of sexual violence.

Asher has been awarded a number of prestigious research fellowships in recognition of her work, which have allowed her to spend time in several Law and Criminology departments in Australia and England. This includes a Monash University Emerging Researcher Fellowship and a three-year Research Fellowship in Law at the Criminal Justice Centre at the University of Warwick. She has received several prizes including the Australian and New Zealand Society of Criminology New Scholar Prize (2013) and the Monash University Excellence in Research by Early Career Researchers Award (2014). She is also an elected member of the executive committee of the Australian and New Zealand Society of Criminology. Asher is currently Chief Investigator on two Criminology Research Council-funded projects—*Negotiated Guilty Pleas: An Empirical Analysis* (CRG 51/14-16), with Emeritus Professor Arie Freiberg (Monash University), and *Responding to Revenge Pornography: The Scope, Nature and Impact of Australian Criminal Laws* (CRG 08/16-17), with Dr Nicola Henry (La Trobe University) and Dr Anastasia Powell (RMIT University).

Professor Jacqueline Hodgson holds an LLB and PhD and has researched and written in the areas of UK, French, comparative and European criminal justice. Adopting a contextual and socio-legal approach, much of her work draws upon her own empirical projects funded by the ESRC, Nuffield Foundation, British Academy, Leverhume Trust, AHRC, the European Commission and the Home Office. She has written extensively on the role of the defence, the prosecution, the trial and sentencing, as well as on miscarriages of justice and terrorism. Key monographs include *Custodial Legal Advice and the Right to Silence* (1993), *Stand-*

ing Accused (1994), *Criminal Injustice* (2000), *French Criminal Justice* (2005), *Suspects in Europe* (2007) and *Inside Police Custody* (2014). She has recently completed a major comparative empirical project on safeguards for juveniles during police interrogation, *Interrogating Young Suspects* (2016). She has also researched the work of the Criminal Cases Review Commission (the body that investigates miscarriages of justice) and Prisoners' Penfriends. She has contributed to policy reform through her research for the Royal Commission on Criminal Justice, her evidence to Parliamentary Select Committees (on Europe and on Justice) and a range of EU legislation Impact Assessments. Her expertise has also been sought in the Special Immigration Appeals Commission, a number of European Arrest Warrant cases and the Canadian extradition case of *Diab*. She held a British Academy/Leverhulme Senior Research Fellowship for 2009–10 and was awarded the Social Science Faculty Impact Prize in 2013. In 2013 she was elected to the Council of JUSTICE, and in 2014 she was elected a Fellow of the Academy of Social Sciences.

CONTRIBUTORS

Dr Ana Aliverti is Associate Professor at Warwick Law School, University of Warwick. She holds a DPhil in Law (University of Oxford, 2011), an MSc (Distinction) in Criminology and Criminal Justice (University of Oxford, 2008), an MA in Sociology of Law (Oñati International Institute for the Sociology of Law, 2005) and a BA (Hons) in Law (University of Buenos Aires, 2002). Before joining Warwick, she was the Oxford Howard League Post-doctoral Research Fellow (2012–13) at the Centre for Criminology, University of Oxford. Her work examines the intersections of immigration and criminal law regulation in Britain; in particular, the functioning of criminal law in the policing of non-citizens. Her research has focused on the criminal courts. Her book *Crimes of Mobility*, an empirical and theoretical examination of immigration crimes, was co-awarded the 2014 British Society of Criminology Book Prize.

Professor Anne Barlow is Professor of Family Law and Policy and Associate Dean for Research for Social Sciences at the University of Exeter. Having previously practised as a solicitor in London, her academic research takes a socio-legal approach and has had a particular focus on the regulation and financial consequences of adult relationships, such as cohabitation and marriage. She has published widely in the field of family law and led the three-year Mapping Paths to Family Justice project on out-of-court family dispute resolution, funded by the Economic and Social Research Council. Anne was appointed a Fellow of the Academy of Social Sciences in 2013 and was a member of the Government Task Force on Family Mediation in 2014. She was also the academic member of the Family Justice Council until 2015 and her work aims to link academic research with the needs of policy and practice.

Liana Buchanan was appointed Commissioner for Children and Young People in April 2016 and is a part-time Commissioner of the Victorian Law Reform Commission. Prior to her appointment, Liana was the Executive Officer of the Federation of Community Legal Centres, the 'peak' body for Victoria's 50 community legal centres. Liana has previously worked in a range of legal and policy roles, including at the Women's Legal Service (South Australia) and the Equal Opportunity Commission. She was also responsible for monitoring and reviewing Victoria's corrections system as Director, Office of Correctional Services Review, from 2009 to 2013.

Natalie Byrom is Director of Research and Learning at the Legal Education Foundation, a grant-making trust that exists to promote legal education in order to improve people's understanding of the law and their ability to use it to secure fair treatment. Natalie is currently completing a PhD, examining the impact of cuts to legal aid in England and Wales on the ability of vulnerable individuals to access justice, focusing on Law Centres. This research is funded by the Economic and Social Research Council and supervised at the University of Warwick. In 2014, Natalie was awarded the early career research impact award for her work with civil society organisations around the cuts to legal aid. Her work has received coverage in the national and trade press.

Professor Ed Cape is Professor of Criminal Law and Practice at the University of the West of England, Bristol. A former criminal defence solicitor, he has a special interest in criminal justice, criminal procedure, police powers, defence lawyers and access to justice. He is the author of the leading practitioner text *Defending Suspects at Police Stations* (Legal Action Group, 7th edn, forthcoming), and is a contributing author of *Blackstone's Criminal Practice* (Oxford University Press, published annually). Ed has conducted empirical research in England and overseas, including *Evaluation of the Public Defender Service in England and Wales* (2007), *Suspects in Europe: Procedural Rights at the Investigative Stage of the Criminal Process in the European Union* (2007), *Effective Criminal Defence in Europe* (2010), *Effective Criminal Defence in Eastern Europe* (2012), *Inside Police Custody: An Empirical Account of Suspects' Rights in Four Jurisdictions* (2014) and *Effective Criminal Defence in Latin America* (2015). He co-authored with Richard Edwards, 'Police Bail without Charge: The Human Rights Implications' (2013), which appeared in the *Cambridge Law Journal*, and he has recently published a major pamphlet, *What if Police Bail Was Abolished?*, which was commissioned and published by the Howard League for Penal Reform. He was commissioned by the United Nations Office on Drugs and Crime to write a handbook on implementing the UN Principles and Guidelines on Access to Legal Aid in Criminal Justice Systems, entitled *Early Access to Legal Aid in Criminal Justice Processes: A Handbook for Policymakers and Practitioners* (2014). He has recently completed, with Tom Smith, an empirical study of pre-trial detention decision-making, which was published as *The Practice of Pre-trial Detention in England and Wales* (2016).

Dr Jan Ewing is a Research Fellow at the University of Exeter on the Creating Paths to Family Justice research project, working with a number of agencies to draw on research findings to develop online and offline family mediation services. She was a Research Associate on the preceding Mapping Paths to Family Justice project, and prior to that, worked as a family law solicitor in private practice for 20 years. She is also a Family Law Lecturer on the Legal Practice Course at BPP University. For her PhD at the University of Cambridge, she interviewed 52 couples three times over the first four years of marriage to examine what drives thriving marriages and what leads to the erosion of marital satisfaction in the first few years after marriage. Her research interests are in family law and policy, particularly in strengthening couple relationships.

Professor Jeff Giddings has extensive practice experience as a solicitor and mediator in Victoria and Queensland. He teaches and researches in areas related to legal education, dispute resolution, access to justice and legal ethics. He has written extensively on legal aid and clinical legal education and established the Griffith Law School clinical programme in 1995. In 2010 he completed his PhD on the sustainability of clinical legal education programmes. His thesis was subsequently published as a book, *Promoting Justice through Clinical Legal Education*. Jeff received a National Teaching Fellowship from the Australian Office for Learning and Teaching in 2013 for the Effective Law Student Supervision Project. He also received the Australian Award for University Teaching in Law and Legal Studies in 1999, along with multiple awards from Griffith University (Queensland). For the period 2013–15, he served as an International Scholar for the Academic Fellows Program of the Open Society Foundation, working extensively with the American University of Central Asia in Bishkek, Kyrgyzstan.

Professor Rosemary Hunter is Professor of Law and Socio-Legal Studies at Queen Mary, University of London, where she teaches family law, jurisprudence and research methods. Her research includes feminist socio-legal work on family court processes and out-of-court dispute resolution, access to justice and domestic violence. She has recently completed the Mapping Paths to Family Justice project, an Economic and Social Research Council-funded project with colleagues at the University of Exeter, which examined public awareness, experiences and outcomes of different forms of family dispute resolution; and she has also been involved in studies of mediation and litigants-in-person in private family law cases commissioned by the Ministry of Justice.

Dr Samuel Kirwan is a Research Associate working on the New Sites of Legal Consciousness project. His research examines the process of money advice and the moral language of debt and credit that surrounds it. Samuel has a longstanding interest in the concept of the commons and has recently co-edited a book on the subject entitled *Space, Power and Commons: The Struggle for Alternative Futures.*

Ryan Kornhauser is a Research Associate at Victoria University and a government lawyer. Previously, he practised as a solicitor at a commercial law firm and at a community legal centre. Ryan's research interests include criminal law policy and, in particular, sentencing and attitudes towards punishment. He has published articles in the *Australian and New Zealand Journal of Criminology*, *Punishment & Society* and *Crime, Law & Social Change*, and holds degrees in law and criminology.

Professor Kathy Laster is the Director of the Sir Zelman Cowen Centre, and Professor in the College of Law and Justice at Victoria University in Melbourne. The Sir Zelman Cowen Centre is the home of the Courts and Tribunals Academy and also conducts 'community governance' training for leaders exercising decision-making responsibility, as well as community outreach and engagement activities for diverse Victorian community groups. Trained in both law and social science (LLB, MA [University of Melbourne], JSD [Columbia Law School]), Kathy has published extensively in law, history, criminology and social policy. Kathy has held a number of leadership positions in law reform and public policy including as adviser to the Federal Attorney-General on pro bono policy, the Executive Director of the Victoria Law Foundation and the CEO of the Institute of Public Administration Australia.

Carolyn McKay is a Lecturer at the University of Sydney. She recently completed her doctoral thesis in Criminology, *Audio Visual Links from Prison: Prisoners' Experiences of Video Technologies for Accessing Justice*, at Sydney Law School. Her thesis draws on fieldwork undertaken in two prisons and has been funded by the John O'Brien Memorial Research Scholarship in Criminal Law and Criminology, and the Cooke, Cooke, Coghlan, Godfrey and Littlejohn Top-Up Scholarship. Carolyn has completed a BCom/LLB at the University of New South Wales as well as a Master of Studio Art and a Master of Visual Arts at Sydney College of the Arts (University of Sydney). In 2014 she was a Visiting Scholar at the Oñati International Institute for the Sociology of Law, Basque Country.

Pasanna Mutha-Merennege worked as a senior lawyer and the Policy and Projects Manager at the Women's Legal Service Victoria (WLSV) between 2011 and 2016. WLSV is a State-wide specialist community legal centre that assists women experiencing family violence and relationship breakdown. Pasanna has previously worked in legal policy in state government and as a lawyer in private practice and community legal centres.

Professor Mary Anne Noone is a Professor in the School of Law, La Trobe University. Linking Mary Anne's research, teaching, professional and community service activities is a passion for improving access to justice. Her current research focuses on ethics in mediation and integrated legal and health services. She is a specialist on the Australian legal aid system and an authority in clinical legal education. She co-authored the only history of the Australian legal aid system, *Lawyers in Conflict*, and the recent *Best Practices in Australian Clinical Legal Education*. Mary Anne was one of Australia's first community lawyers and was the National Representative for Community Legal Centres and a member of the National Legal Aid Advisory Committee. She served 12 years as a part-time member of the Social Security Appeals Tribunal, 11 years as a Director of Victoria Legal Aid and many years as a member of the management committee of West Heidelberg Community Legal Service (Victoria).

Dr James Organ is a Lecturer in Law at the University of Liverpool, School of Law and Social Justice, having been awarded his PhD from the same institution. Prior to his academic career, James worked for Citizens Advice for over a decade, which is the largest third-sector organisation providing legal advice in the UK.

Professor Simon Rice is Professor of Law at the ANU College of Law at the Australian National University. He also chairs the Law Reform Advisory Council of the Australian Capital Territory. Simon has been a poverty lawyer, a board member in community legal centres, a board member of the New South Wales Legal Aid Commission, and legal adviser to the Australian Parliamentary Joint Committee on Human Rights. Simon researches, writes and teaches on access to justice issues. He has been a lawyer, trainer and consultant in human rights and anti-discrimination law—areas in which he also researches and writes. His co-authored books include *The International Law of Human Rights* and *Australian Anti-Discrimination Law*.

Dr Jennifer Sigafoos is a Leverhulme Early Career Fellow at the University of Liverpool, School of Law and Social Justice. Jennifer was awarded a DPhil from the University of Oxford and a Juris Doctor at the University of California, Hastings College of the Law. She is admitted to the Bar in the State of California. Prior to relocating to the UK, she was Director of Public Policy for a large charity.

Dr Tom Smith is a Lecturer in Law at the University of the West of England, Bristol. His research interests include the role of criminal defence lawyers (the subject of his doctoral thesis), criminal procedure, access to justice and legal aid. He has been involved in a variety of research projects, including a cross-jurisdictional examination of defence rights in Europe, and a recent empirical study of pre-trial detention practice in England and Wales (*The Practice of Pre-trial Detention in England and Wales: Research Report* (2016)), which was part of a ten-country European study. He has published a number of articles, including '"Justice for Sale": An Empirical Examination of the Attitudes of Criminal Defence Lawyers Towards Legal Aid Reform' in the *Plymouth Law and Criminal Justice Review*; 'Trust, Choice and Money: Why the Legal Aid Reform "U-Turn" is Essential for Effective Criminal Defence' in the *Criminal Law Review*; and 'The "Quiet Revolution" in Criminal Defence: How the Zealous Advocate Slipped into the Shadow' in the *International Journal of the Legal Profession*.

Dr Janet Smithson is a researcher in social psychology. She has worked on a variety of United Kingdom- and European-funded research projects, using both qualitative and quantitative research methods. Current research projects include the use of online forums and interventions for health and mental health support, and interactions in therapy and mediation sessions. Other research interests include gender and discourse, life course transitions, qualitative methodologies, and internet-mediated discourse and communication.

Her Honour Pauline Spencer was appointed a Judicial Officer to the Magistrates' Court of Victoria in 2006. Pauline currently sits at the Dandenong Magistrates' Court. This is a busy mainstream court in the south-east outer suburbs of Melbourne (Victoria), which deals with criminal, family violence and civil cases. Prior to her appointment, Pauline worked in the community legal sector including as a lawyer with Fitzroy Legal Service and as Executive Officer of the Federation of

Community Legal Centres (Victoria), the 'peak' body for over 50 community legal centres in Victoria. She has a long-term interest in access to justice and therapeutic jurisprudence.

Melanie Schwartz is a Senior Lecturer at UNSW Law. She is a Chief Investigator on the Indigenous Legal Needs Project (ILNP), a three-year Australian Research Council Linkage Grant. The ILNP includes a legal needs assessment for civil and family law issues for Indigenous people in five Australian jurisdictions, and a detailed discussion of access to justice issues for this cohort. It has as its partners the legal aid commissions and Aboriginal and Torres Strait Islander Legal Services in each focus jurisdiction. The work of the ILNP has been cited by the Productivity Commission and the Senate Legal and Constitutional Affairs Committee.

LIST OF ABBREVIATIONS

ABS	Australian Bureau of Statistics
ACOSS	Australian Council for Social Services
ACT	Australian Capital Territory
ADR	Alternative Dispute Resolution
AJAC	Access to Justice Advisory Committee
ALAO	Australian Legal Aid Office
ALSWA	Aboriginal Legal Service of Western Australia
ATO	Australian Taxation Office
ATSILS	Aboriginal and Torres Strait Islander Legal Services
AVL	Audiovisual link
BAME	Black, Asian and minority ethnic
BVT	Best Value Tendering
CAB	Citizens Advice Bureau
CABx	Citizens Advice Bureaux
CBA	Criminal Bar Association
CERD	Convention on the Elimination of All Forms of Racial Discrimination
CLC	Community legal centre
CLSA	Criminal Law Solicitors Association
CNS	Custody Notification Service
CPR	Collaborative Planning Resource
CPS	Crown Prosecution Service
CRPD	Convention on the Rights of Persons with Disabilities
CSA	Child Support Agency
DIY	Do-it-yourself
DLA	Disability Living Allowance

DoJ	Department of Justice
DWP	Department for Work and Pensions
ECHR	European Convention on Human Rights
ECtHR	European Court of Human Rights
ESA	Employment and Support Allowance
EU	European Union
GMMAP	Greater Merseyside Money Advice Project
GP	General practitioner
ICCPR	International Covenant on Civil and Political Rights
ICESCR	International Covenant on Economic, Social and Cultural Rights
IFVPLS	Indigenous Family Violence Prevention and Legal Services
ILNP	Indigenous Legal Needs Project
JD	Jurisdictional Data
JSA	Jobseeker's Allowance
LA	Local authority
LAA	Legal Aid Agency
LAB	Legal Aid Board
LAC	Legal Aid Commission
LACV	Legal Aid Commission of Victoria
LANSW	Legal Aid New South Wales
LASPO	*Legal Aid, Sentencing and Punishment of Offenders Act 2012*
LAQ	Legal Aid Queensland
LCCSA	London Criminal Courts Solicitors Association
LSB	Legal Service Bureaux
LSC	Legal Services Commission
LSOA	Lower layer super output area
MCA	*Magistrates' Courts Act 1980*
MIAM	Mediation Information and Assessment Meeting
MNCC	Mid North Coast Correction Centre
MoJ	Ministry of Justice

NAO	National Audit Office
NGOs	Non-Governmental Organisations
NHS	National Health Service
NLAAC	National Legal Aid Advisory Committee
NPA	National Partnership Agreement on Legal Assistance Services
NSW	New South Wales
NSWALS	New South Wales Aboriginal Legal Service
NT	Northern Territory
PCT	Price-Competitive Tendering
PDS	Public Defender Service
PIP	Personal Independence Payment
PLP	Public Law Project
PSO	Protective Service Officer
PSOs	Public Solicitors Offices
PTSD	Post-Traumatic Stress Disorder
QC	Queen's Counsel
QLD	Queensland
SP	Service Planning
TJ	Therapeutic jurisprudence
UC	Universal Credit
UDHR	Universal Declaration of Human Rights
UK	United Kingdom
UN	United Nations
US	United States
VHCC	Very high cost cases
VLA	Victoria Legal Aid
WA	Western Australia
WLSV	Women's Legal Service Victoria
WRA	*Welfare Reform Act 2012*

TABLES AND FIGURES

Table 1: Top five legal information service matters
Figure 1: Nexus between unmet legal need and social/economic problems
Figure 2: Poor outcomes for women unable to access the justice system

1

Access to Justice and Legal Aid Cuts: A Mismatch of Concepts in the Contemporary Australian and British Legal Landscapes

ASHER FLYNN AND JACQUELINE HODGSON

Significant reductions in spending and changes to the eligibility requirements of government-funded welfare services in Australia and the United Kingdom (UK) have impacted considerably on the provision of support in the areas of housing, employment, disability, health, education and the law. In the context of legal aid, there have been extensive cuts in the overall amounts of funding available to the users and providers of legal services; changes to the types of legal assistance, programmes and services that remain eligible for government funding; and alterations to the ways in which providers can access or apply for funding. These cuts have been felt across all legal sectors—criminal, civil and family.

In England and Wales, de-investment in legal aid has been rising since the mid-2000s. This has been fuelled partly by concerns voiced in the 1980s and 1990s (McConville and Hodgson 1993; McConville et al 1994)—particularly in the context of the criminal law—that defence lawyers were manipulating aspects of a poorly regulated system. In response, there was a marked increase in regulation and compliance requirements, without any commensurate increase in remuneration. Between 2006 and 2009, legal aid was subjected to a new fixed-fee regime by the government. This was followed in 2011 by a 10 per cent cut in fee rates across all legal aid services (Flynn et al 2015).

The most devastating cuts to legal aid in England and Wales began in 2013 following the introduction of the *Legal Aid, Sentencing and Punishment of Offenders Act 2012* (LASPO), which sought to reduce the legal aid budget by £350 million (AU$615 million), mainly in the areas of family law, immigration, welfare benefits, employment and clinical negligence. According to the figures of the Ministry of Justice (MoJ), after introducing LASPO, 62 per cent of those entitled to access legal aid in 2012 were no longer entitled to access that same assistance in 2013 (Howard 2014). Shortly after its introduction, further reforms were announced by the Justice Secretary in a consultation document entitled *Transforming Legal Aid: Next Steps* (MoJ 2013b). This chapter outlined a series of proposals, which, in addition to affecting the remaining areas of law funded through civil legal aid, focused on reducing criminal legal aid funding and services. To date, this has resulted in cuts of approximately £120 million (AU$211 million) to criminal legal aid—around 8.75 per cent of the total 17 per cent forecast—and in just one year (2013–14), there was a 5 per cent fall in the criminal workload of the magistrates' courts (MoJ 2014).

In January 2016, after 99 separate legal challenges to the proposals, the MoJ announced that it would suspend the remaining 8.75 per cent of legal aid cuts, which would have reduced the number of firms awarded duty contracts to provide criminal legal aid work by two-thirds, from 1600 to 527. The position will be reviewed again in April 2017 (MoJ 2016). While aimed at consolidation and economies of scale, this degree of centralisation in the provision of legal services would have left large areas of the country without access to adequate representation. In contrast to many European countries where lawyers typically work across a range of areas, criminal defence work is highly specialised in England and Wales, encouraged by the regulation requirements governing legal aid contracts. The proposed reduction in legal aid firms would not, therefore, be simply a matter of shifting the focus of lawyers' work to other areas such as family or commercial law. It would require firms either to merge—a lengthy, costly and unappealing prospect for many—or to close down altogether.

Reporting on the impact of cuts in civil legal aid, the House of Commons Justice Committee (2015) found that, while the government had succeeded in making substantial cuts to the civil legal aid budget, it had failed to target the remaining legal aid budget to those who need it most (resulting in a significant underspend) and could not demonstrate that it was delivering better overall value for money for the taxpayer. The Report noted that those eligible for legal aid were unable to access it due to a lack of public information about the services available, such as the Civil Legal Advice telephone gateway for debt advice. Domestic violence victims continue to experience problems obtaining evidence from healthcare professionals, which is necessary in order to trigger their eligibility for legal aid. Some of these failings have been the result of the government's own short-sightedness and poor strategy, as it rushed through changes without any adequate underpinning evidence (National Audit Office [NAO] 2014). For example, it did not research the geographical spread of legal provision and so, as the capacity of the legal advice and assistance sectors has reduced, legal 'advice deserts' have been created.[1] The government also did not anticipate the knock-on costs of the reforms. Courts and

[1] This phenomenon is now widely recognised and the Law Society has produced an interactive map of England and Wales showing the number of providers with legal aid contracts for housing advice in each region, indicating the location of 'legal aid deserts'. Available at http://www.lawsociety.org.uk/policy-campaigns/campaigns/access-to-justice/end-legal-aid-deserts/

tribunals expend more resources on assisting litigants in person,[2] and many problems are no longer prevented by early intervention, resulting in the escalation of cases such that eligibility for legal aid is then triggered, or costs are simply shifted across to other public services (House of Commons Justice Committee 2015). In this respect, the Committee (2015: 61) found compelling the analogy of Lord Low that 'it makes more sense to put the fence at the top of the cliff than to call the expensive ambulance when the person has fallen to the bottom'.

In Australia, a mix of Commonwealth and State government funds are provided annually to State-based statutory bodies—legal aid commissions (LACs)—and to community legal centres (CLCs). While governments control the amount of funding received by each State-based LAC, traditionally, accessibility, eligibility and policy decisions around which legal services to fund have been made by the LACs and CLCs themselves. Since 1997, there have been consistent decreases in the Commonwealth level of funding for LACs, reducing annually from around 55 per cent of each LAC's budget to approximately one-third (33 per cent). This culminated in the 2014 federal budget, which cut AU$6 million (£3.4 million) from CLCs, AU$15 million (£8.5 million) from LACs and AU$43 million (£24.47 million) from advocacy services over a four-year period, including from the Indigenous Policy Reform Program which funds Aboriginal and Torres Strait Islander Legal Services across Australia.

The impacts of these proposed cuts were immediately felt, with staff redundancies, the creation of 'advice deserts', the merger of CLCs and the (forced) imposition of new, stringent eligibility policies which removed the capacity for vulnerable individuals who would previously have met the means and merit criteria of LACs to now apply for assistance. In Victoria and New South Wales (NSW), for example, individuals facing summary criminal charges where imprisonment or detention order outcomes were unlikely were no longer able to apply for legally aided representation. In addition, Victoria Legal Aid (VLA) limited funding of parents in family law matters to trial preparation, and to advice on how to conduct oneself in court. While the government 'asserted that the cuts would not impact frontline services—and were only focused on law reform, which shouldn't be funded when there is a budget "crisis"' (Farrell 2015), the pressures being felt by frontline agencies resulted in staff and service cuts. As Farrell (2015) explains, 'as these cuts were starting to bite, the Abbott [federal] government soon realised that its decision to cut funding conflicted with its commitment to services and strategies to stop

[2] For example, the NAO (2014: 15) reports 30 per cent year-on-year increases in family court cases where neither party is represented. Judges estimate that these cases take 50 per cent longer than those with representation, and that cases that would formerly have been filtered out by focused advice on the legal merits are now continuing through to court hearings (NAO 2014: 14). There has also been an increase in unrepresented parties in cases involving contact with children (NAO 2014: 15), and while 64 per cent of these were contested in 2012–13, this rose to 89 per cent in the corresponding quarter in 2013–14 (NAO 2014: 15). The NAO estimates that the reforms cost the HM Courts and Tribunals Service an additional £3 million (AU$5.27 million) each year (NAO 2014: 17).

family violence'. Following strong lobbying from legal stakeholders and also to support its own focus on addressing family violence in Australia, the Commonwealth Government reversed some aspects of its 2014 budget. This included restoring AU$25.5 million (£14.5 million) to the sector over the next two-year period, of which AU$15 million (£8.8 million) was specifically to be used for women's legal services. This restoration of funding, however, was conditional upon new government requirements stipulating how its funding could be spent, which included preventing CLCs from using government money for policy or campaign work.[3]

These significant shifts in government-funded provisions and legal services have fuelled a robust debate over the allocation of resources, with a specific focus on the priorities that should be accorded to government-funded serious criminal cases, pre-trial representation, criminal representation in the lower courts, and civil, administrative and family law matters. This debate has raised some important questions for practitioners, recipients of legal aid, courts, academics, society, governments and providers of legal aid funding and services, namely, who deserves legal aid? In the context of finite funding and expanding demands, on what criteria are priorities decided, and who decides those criteria? Who should determine the scope and policies of legally aided services—parliament (and so, government), or LACs, CLCs and/or the courts through judicial intervention? To what extent is the right to legal assistance dependent on the right to legal aid? And, perhaps most importantly, what are the consequences of leaving many of the most vulnerable in society without representation in the assertion of their rights? These questions are answered in part by the courts and international conventions, but in practice their scope is being determined by government policy and economic austerity.

To date, much of the excellent work examining access to justice in light of legal aid cuts, while paying some attention to the implications across criminal, civil and family law areas, has focused almost exclusively on one area of the law and the associated problems in that specific context. Likewise, existing work has considered these emerging issues within one jurisdiction, or only in relation to jurisdictions located within their immediate region. Through our own research collaborations, however (Byrom et al 2014; Flynn et al 2015; Flynn et al 2016), it became clear that the key questions outlined above were being asked simultaneously across Australian and British jurisdictions, where we were witnessing some common themes and concerns emerging, but also quite different approaches and responses. This current collection is thus situated in the context of a burgeoning interest in access to justice and legal aid, bringing together the perspectives of a range of interdisciplinary British and Australian socio-legal scholars, legal practitioners, cross-sector stakeholders and advocates, with recognised expertise in criminal, civil and family law, legal aid, and access to justice, to critically examine

[3] Similar restrictions were introduced in England and Wales in May 2016 which prevented UK charities from using government funding for activity intended to influence—or attempt to influence—parliament, government or political parties.

the diverse assemblage of experiences and consequences of legal aid cuts across Australia, and England and Wales.

As common law jurisdictions, our countries share similar ideals, policies and practices; yet, they also differ in aspects of their legal and political culture, in the nature of the communities they serve and in the approaches adopted by their respective judiciaries. Accordingly, they provide us with different perspectives on accessing justice and how we might seek to overcome the crisis in unmet legal need across civil, criminal and family law in relation to a broad range of individuals, including the profession, client advice workers, legal centres, legal aid clients, Indigenous Australians, refugees, women and other vulnerable groups.

This book engages with key debates regarding the false assumption that cutting funds to government-funded social and welfare services will equate with savings either in the long or short term, by demonstrating the many adverse consequences of the various policy and funding shifts across Australia, and England and Wales, not only for the most vulnerable, but also for the courts, the legal profession and more broadly in relation to other state-based services (health, unemployment, immigration, housing and so on). A clear message also emerges in relation to changes in the professionalisation of justice. In both the Australian and British contexts, it is stressed that volunteers cannot replace lawyers and the devaluing of legally aided work has the strong potential to alter the shape and future of the legal profession, with losses of experienced professionals at one end, and a reduction in law students entering the field at the other. This book also addresses the important role of efficiencies and new technologies within the current financial climate, but recognises the changes such advancements make in social understandings and expectations of the way we access justice, and the ways justice 'should' be done. In doing so, it considers how the successful neoliberal rhetoric of the anti-welfare state has combined with an absence of community to demonise those most in need, creating a new 'other' within the legal realm (Garland 1996, 2001).

This book details the stark outcomes of recent policy and funding changes in legal aid across Australia, and England and Wales, which can make for a depressing and confronting read. But within the discussions of injustice, vulnerability, marginalisation and disadvantage, the chapters contain considered recommendations to address the seemingly bleak future of legal services across and possibly beyond the focus jurisdictions. These recommendations involve highlighting the innovative responses of various advocates, practitioners and services to the changes; identifying suggestions for further innovation that seeks to compensate for a reduction in frontline services; prioritising a comprehensive response that avoids silo-ing the issues experienced in criminal and civil law sectors away from their broader social, environmental and structural contexts; and, as Mary Anne Noone (Chapter 2) discusses, recognising the vital need for the completion of 'legal aid impact statements' to accompany any proposed changes to legally aided services and funds. These statements would require detailed and comprehensive pre-planning of the potential consequences of any shifts in legal policy for LACs, the courts and their clients, CLCs and so on, *before* changes are made.[4]

While it is likely that there will always be unmet legal need and some contention over legal aid funds, government restrictions to legal aid services, budgets and policies bring into sharp focus concerns about human rights, due process, the rule of law and the ability of vulnerable and marginalised groups to access justice; and it is these issues with which this collection is concerned.

In the first three sections of this chapter, we address key themes arising from the collection as a whole and provide a context for understanding how the various austerity measures have been introduced. We also highlight what the broader (perhaps more hidden) consequences of the changes have been. The second section provides an overview of each chapter.

I. Access to Justice

Within the legal setting, justice is traditionally equated with equality, fairness and respect for individual rights. It falls under the rule of law framework, which encompasses procedural justice ideals (measured by perceptions of fairness within the legal *processes* used) and substantive justice ideals (measured by perceptions of fairness in the *outcomes* of those legal processes) (Flynn and Fitz-Gibbon 2013; Henry et al 2015). In this sense, justice is the pinnacle of our legal system—it informs our social moral consensus, it keeps the legal process and related services operating in line with community expectations and values, and it is the essential link between 'the law' and society. When engaging with any form of law—criminal, civil or family—the definitive outcome may therefore be considered the attainment of justice. But what exactly does justice mean and what does 'accessing justice' look like?

As Robert Sackville (2002: 19) observed, 'like other catchphrases, such as "fairness" and "accountability" (if not "democracy" itself), the expression "access to justice" survives in political and legal discourse because it is capable of meaning different things to different people'. Justice is thus 'a slippery concept' (Easton and Piper 2012: 86). In his foreword to the *Access to Justice Taskforce Report*, then Australian Federal Attorney-General, Robert McClelland (2009: 1), equated an effective justice system with being accessible 'in all parts' for all members of the community. He further noted that access to justice extends beyond the provision of legal advice, to having a system that demonstrates 'an appreciation and understanding of the needs of those who require the assistance of the legal system'. Similar views were voiced by former English Justice Secretary, Chris Grayling,

[4] As noted above, the House of Commons Justice Committee (2015) criticised the government's failure to consider the broader impact of the legal aid cuts it so rapidly implemented.

when introducing LASPO: 'access to justice should not be determined by your ability to pay, and I am clear that legal aid is the hallmark of a fair, open justice system' (MoJ 2013a). Yet as the costs and expectations in relation to government-funded legal aid have grown, and unmet legal need has subsequently increased, such statements could not be further from the reality of the legal aid systems and legal landscapes currently operating in Australia, and England and Wales.

In the Australian context, this is evident in the comments of the Chief Justice of Western Australia, Wayne Martin (2012: 3), who notes:

> The hard reality is that the cost of legal representation is beyond the reach of many, probably most, ordinary Australians … In theory, access to that legal system is available to all. In practice, access is limited to substantial business enterprises, the very wealthy, and those who are provided with some form of assistance.

Australian Federal Senator, Penny Wright (2013), has similarly expressed her concerns that, 'increasingly, ordinary Australians are being priced out of the court system because they cannot afford legal representation and court fees'. Parallel sentiments echoed across England and Wales in the lead-up to and following the implementation of LASPO; as Jo Renshaw (2012) observed, LASPO means 'to all intents and purposes, the concept of equal access to justice will be dead'. Similarly, the President of the Supreme Court, Lord Neuberger, forewarned that 'if you start cutting legal aid, you start cutting people off from justice … and that's dangerous' (cited in Bowcott 2013a). These concerns were further evidenced in the successful passing of three motions of regret pertaining to LASPO in the House of Commons. In putting forward one of these motions, Lord Bach stated that LASPO would 'demean the reputation of our legal system', adding that 'the behaviour of the Government towards Parliament, towards this House in particular and towards its citizens is unacceptable' (HC Hansard 27 March 2013: Col 1088). Chantal-Aimée Doerries QC, Chair of the England and Wales Bar Council, similarly argued that, in previous times, the British justice system was the 'envy of the world. However … the reputation of our courts and their ability to serve the public is under threat … Justice is not a luxury, and everyone should be able to defend their rights through the legal system' (cited in Bowcott 2016). This is an outcome that is evidently becoming less and less possible—as the Lord Chief Justice (2015: 5) reported in 2015: 'our system of justice has become unaffordable to most'.

II. An Environment Susceptible to and Accepting of Legal Aid Cuts

As the chapters in this collection demonstrate, de-investment in legal services has and will continue to have serious implications for already vulnerable and disadvantaged individuals coming before the law. In its 2014–15 annual report, VLA (2015: 3–4) highlighted these tensions, claiming: 'We value a society that aspires to fairness and opportunity, and we work towards reimagining injustice where it exists … [But] without further investment or changes to services, we will again be in deficit by 2018'.

Under a justification of austerity, we have witnessed an almost irreparable shift in priorities away from welfare, towards neoliberal forms of governance, which is reshaping the operation of justice and raising questions about the values and procedures once considered normative legal practice. Today, access to justice is problematically transforming in response to government funding cuts, to the point where accessing the law is becoming a contested privilege rather than a fundamental right. This is perhaps most evident in relation to the civil law, where there is an emerging social consensus that civil law matters are a private issue—presented as a 'wants', not a 'needs' matter. As examined by Simon Rice (Chapter 11), this argument draws strength from the (often misconceived) perception of voluntariness in civil law matters as compared to criminal law matters, where the accused is 'an involuntary participant … whose presence in court is mandatory and, if necessary, forced'. Further to this, Rice explores how the persistent use of the 'incarceration is more serious argument' allows for the criminal law to be considered the more serious legal issue and therefore a matter of greater priority, despite the fact that a person involved in a civil dispute may be at risk of losing 'their home, their livelihood, their children, their reputation, their earning capacity, their freedom of expression, their right to vote, and so on'.

As various chapters in this volume show (see Aliverti Chapter 16, Byrom Chapter 12, Mutha-Merennege Chapter 14, and Schwartz Chapter 15), this simplistic view of the civil law, and the idea of accessing civil law remedies or justice being a *want* rather than a *need*, is not reflective of the reality. According to the Law and Justice Foundation of NSW's most recent comprehensive survey of legal need (Coumarelos et al 2012), almost half of the 20,000 plus respondents had experienced one or more civil legal problems in the 12-month period leading up to the survey. This common occurrence of civil law problems is because civil law comprises 'a rag-bag of matters and participants'. As Genn (1997: 160) explains:

> There are disputes relating to the performance or non-performance of contracts involving businessmen [sic] suing each other, individuals suing businesses, and businesses suing individuals. There are claims for compensation resulting from accidental injury in which individuals sue institutions. There is the use of the courts by lenders who realise their security by evicting individual mortgage defaulters. Civil justice also involves attempts by citizens to challenge decisions of central and local government bureaucrats, a rapidly growing field that includes immigration, housing, mental health, child welfare, and the like … Finally, there are the acrimonious and often heartbreaking struggles between men and women following the breakdown of family relationships, as property and children become the subject of legal disputes.

As discussed below, the implications of not addressing civil law issues expand well beyond each individual matter, to also have significant ramifications for society, health, education, social services and the criminal law. Yet this simplistic view of civil law as an individualised want of only some sections of the community allows for cuts to civil legal aid to be more readily accepted.

Further to promoting civil law as a wants not a needs issue, the governments of the focus jurisdictions have been quite clever in some regards in framing their cuts, drawing on populist perceptions of legal aid and social exclusion, and targeting the reforms at already demonised groups in society. For example, in England and Wales we have seen this in relation to policies focused on non-UK citizens, prisoners and welfare recipients. Attention has also been placed on the amount of money awarded to those working in the legal aid field, thus exploiting the idea that 'fat-cat lawyers' who abuse the system for profit are going to be the most effected, so we should have minimal sympathy for them and in turn support the cuts. As the then Justice Secretary of England and Wales stated in the Ministerial Foreword to the *Transforming Legal Aid* consultation paper:

> Taxpayers' money has been used to pay for frivolous claims, to foot the legal bills of wealthy criminals, and to cover cases which run on and on racking up large fees for … lawyers … Under these reforms, those with significantly higher than average incomes will no longer be eligible for financial support … those who have no strong connection with the UK will cease to have their … legal costs covered too. Prisoners … will have recourse to the prisoner complaints procedures rather than accessing a lawyer … Lawyers who bring weak cases [to judicial review] will no longer be reimbursed. (MoJ 2013a: 3)

Similar comments were voiced in November 2013 by Courts and Legal Aid Minister Shailesh Vara, who claimed:

> The Government is trying to make the legal aid system fairer for the taxpayers who pay for it … We will stop criminal legal aid being given to prisoners unnecessarily—such as those using legal aid to seek an easier ride elsewhere … To make the legal aid system fairer for the taxpayers who pay for it, we are also planning to introduce a residence test for civil legal aid next year. Why should those without a strong connection to the UK, such as those who have barely stepped over the border or are here illegally, be eligible for civil legal aid? (Vara 2013)

These comments play to the populist right-wing concerns of the British public—views reflected in a YouGov (2013) survey in April 2013, which found that 64 per cent of the almost 2000 people surveyed believed that legal aid should not be available for immigration claims.

A similar approach has been taken in Australia by some politicians and sections of the media who have focused on 'undeserving criminals', such as 'rapists, paedophiles [and] thugs … who use tax payer funds' (Crawford 2013), and 'drug king-pins' who allegedly hide their resources to make them eligible for legal aid.[5] Likewise, media outlets have highlighted the total annual monetary

[5] Media-driven outrage around legal aid funding was particularly strong in Victoria (Australia) in relation to the cases of Adrian Bayley, who was tried for the rape and murder of Jill Meagher in 2013, and Tony Mokbel, who was tried for drug trafficking offences in 2013.

figures awarded to private practitioners who act on behalf of legal aid, as if to suggest that they are unfairly profiting from representing disadvantaged people in legal matters (Johnston and Smethurst 2013). In response to VLA funding the appeal of a convicted murderer in 2013,[6] the Victorian State Government went so far as to publicly ask VLA to 'think about what they've done and … explain themselves' (cited in Johnston and Smethurst 2013). This view emerged despite the findings of the Australian Commonwealth Productivity Commission's (2014: 30) *Access to Justice Report*, which noted that the means tests of LACs were so restrictive, and in fact 'sat below those of other government benefits due to underfunding', that in contrast to populist perceptions 'it is not the case that people are "too wealthy" to be eligible for legal assistance, but rather that they are not sufficiently impoverished'.

With the use of such tools, the tightening of legal aid budgets and implementation of strict policy provisions can be more successfully accepted in the public realm through the creation of what Garland (1996) terms the 'criminology of other'. This means that, despite crime-cutting across class, ethnic and gendered boundaries, we seek to construct accused persons, welfare recipients and those who find themselves in civil and criminal disputes as 'not like us'. In this rhetoric, those accessing legal aid can be treated as 'a different species … for whom we can have no sympathy' (Garland 1996: 461). This approach reflects changes in crime control and social welfare policies more generally, where we have seen a clear shift away from social acceptance and recognition of injustice and support for governments to respond with a combination of welfare-enhancing measures of social reform, such as education, housing, job creation and welfare services, to instead viewing legal and social need as the fault of the individual. In this way, state responsibility to assist 'those who had been deprived of the economic, social, and psychological provision necessary for proper social adjustment and law-abiding conduct' (Garland 2001: 15) has been replaced by individual responsibility to 'fix' the problem themselves. This approach perpetuates a neoliberal society and anti-welfare attitudes, and fuels the creation of a social order based on class, race and gender. It also perpetuates ineffective solutions to complex crime and social problems, including changes in legal aid priorities and resourcing.

III. Bigger Picture Consequences

The types of state resource-driven decisions discussed within this collection are unlikely to result in the delivery of significant savings, because they fail to take into account the broader picture implications, such as higher levels of incarceration, fewer quality lawyers working in legal aid areas, increased numbers of

[6] This statement was made in relation to Adrian Bayley's appeal against sentence severity.

self-represented defendants and litigants, and issues that might have been prevented by recourse to legal assistance being instead escalated to major problems requiring public resources. There are also likely to be increases in the use of court resources and costs, and decreased services and access to justice for already vulnerable and marginalised groups:

> Cuts to legal aid have resulted in the courts being flooded with people representing themselves without legal advice or representation, including those in emotionally difficult circumstances such as losing access to their children, facing the loss of their home, or fighting deportation to a country where they might be persecuted. (Bowcott 2016)

As explored throughout this collection, the impact of these changes is being felt by the most vulnerable, with the funding cuts and policy changes meaning 'greater levels of injustice when you're already dealing with people who experience injustice in every facet of their lives' (Perkins and Lee 2015).

In 2013, prior to the introduction of LASPO, the Warwick University Centre for Human Rights in Practice evaluated the possible implications of the legislation, finding that in addition to impacting on the most vulnerable people—mainly those located in rural areas, women and those with a disability—almost one-third of the 674 legal practitioner respondents believed that they were at risk of redundancy (Byrom 2013). As the chapters in this collection show, there are a number of consequences arising from the cuts that extend well beyond 'fat-cat lawyers' and 'undeserving' legal aid clients. These include the creation of geographic gaps in the availability of advice; limited focus on early interventions, particularly in civil law matters; sharp increases in the number of unrepresented accused and litigants in person, alongside an increased burden on the already congested court system; difficulties for persons navigating increasingly complex systems of law; a risk that financial imperatives will push firms towards corporatisation of policies and practices, undermining the individual professional lawyer–client relationship; changes in the accessibility and existence of not-for-profit organisations; and an overall increase in unmet demand for services, placing further pressure on those services that remain and the individuals that provide them.

The broader social consequences include affecting the degree of diversity and the level of expertise within the legal profession. As Natalie Byrom explains in Chapter 12, these effects will perhaps be most felt in relation to lawyers from black and ethnic minority backgrounds, and women. Additionally, as Rosemary Hunter et al (Chapter 13), Pasanna Mutha-Merennege (Chapter 14) and Ana Aliverti (Chapter 16) discuss, new provisions requiring applicants for legal aid in family violence proceedings to provide documentary proof in support of their application (England and Wales), and changes to the funding policies of family law cases (Australia), have had a detrimental impact on victims of family violence. A survey carried out in 2013 by the Rights of Women, Women's Aid and Welsh Women's Aid (2013) showed that half of all women surveyed who had experienced or were experiencing family violence did not have the prescribed forms of evidence to access family law legal aid. Of these, 61 per cent took no action in relation to their family law problem as a result of not being able to get legally aided assistance. In Chapter 14, Mutha-Merennege identifies similar concerns in the Australian context, examining how changes in legal aid funding policies may force women and children to stay in violent, volatile relationships, due to the lack of available assistance.

The changes implemented in England and Wales and the new restrictions enforced on CLCs in Australia to stop advocacy and campaigning work are also likely to result in significant miscarriages of justice going unnoticed. As Liana Buchanan argues in Chapter 8, the campaign work of CLCs across Australia has resulted in improvements to all Australians' access to justice and basic rights. But the new requirements 'deprive the Australian community of a force for change that has brought the experience of the disadvantaged, marginalised and vulnerable to light and improved our laws and justice system in a myriad of ways'. Similar concerns can be seen in England and Wales, where the exposure of significant miscarriages of justice such as the case of Stephen Lawrence would be unlikely to occur in the current LASPO climate:[7]

> If a grieving family in the same situation as the Lawrences were in 1993 called on [legal aid] now, [they] would turn them away … If the planned legal aid cuts were in place at the time, no one other than his family and friends would now even remember Stephen Lawrence. (Bawdon 2013)

As reported by the Australian Productivity Commission (2014: 6), there are 'good reasons for governments to seek to improve the functioning and accessibility' of the justice system, not simply to address individuals' interests, but also for the potential wider societal benefits. As the Commission explains (2014: 6), in the civil law context 'a well-functioning civil justice system … promotes social order, and communicates and reinforces civic values and norms … [which] contributes to Australia's economic performance'. Additionally, as Melanie Schwartz argues in Chapter 15, if left unaddressed: 'Civil law issues such as unpaid debts, housing problems or social security disputes can escalate to become full-blown legal matters … Unaddressed legal issues not related to the criminal law can also escalate to become criminal matters'.

This view is strengthened by the findings of the Law and Justice Foundation of NSW's legal need survey (Coumarelos et al 2012: xvi), which found that 55 per cent of respondents acknowledged that their legal problem had a 'severe' or 'moderate' impact on their lives, including income loss or financial strain (29 per cent), a stress-related illness (20 per cent), physical ill health (19 per cent), relationship breakdown (10 per cent) and moving home (5 per cent)—problems that ultimately create an increased economic burden for the community.

[7] Stephen Lawrence was killed in a racially motivated murder in England in 1996. There were a range of substantial injustices relating to the police investigation and the trial of those accused of the crime. In 2012, double jeopardy exceptions allowed for one of the alleged murderers, Gary Dobson, to be re-tried. He was found guilty (*R v Dobson* [2011] EWCA Crim 1255).

These broader monetary concerns are significant, as the key rationale underpinning the reforms to legal aid has been the potential financial savings. In England and Wales, the MoJ has argued that the LASPO reforms will result in a saving of £220 million (AU$386 million) annually by the 2018–19 financial year. However, Armstrong's (2013) financial analysis of the proposed cuts to prison law, the resident's test and judicial review indicated that the on-costs of the funding changes would actually cost the government around £30 million (AU$52.7 million) each year. In addition, he found that the changes proposed would not deliver significant savings, and would cost more in terms of court time, resources and taxpayer contributions (Armstrong 2013). Likewise, the analysis completed by the NAO in 2014 noted that, despite some potential short-term financial savings:

> In implementing the reforms, the Ministry did not think through the impact of the changes on the wider system early enough … The Ministry needs to improve its understanding of the impact of the reforms on the ability of providers to meet demand for services. Without this, implementation of the reforms to civil legal aid cannot be said to have delivered better overall value for money for the taxpayer. (NAO 2014: 8)

The potential costs to the taxpayer as a result of reduced court efficiency and standards are examined across numerous chapters in this collection. In particular, as Pauline Spencer (Chapter 5) and Rosemary Hunter et al (Chapter 13) argue, the costs of representing accused persons in criminal matters and providing representation and advice in civil and family law are simply transferring to other areas of the court, as a result of significant increases in self-representation. The implications of this have been identified by the Judicial Executive Board in England and Wales, which claims that such cases will 'occupy more court time and take longer to come to a conclusion, while simultaneously increasing the risk of mistakes and miscarriages of justice' (cited in Bowcott 2013b). Such concerns were likewise summarised in a letter to *The Times* signed by nine professors working in universities across England:

> The long-term effects [of the legal aid reforms] will be devastating and once the damage has been done it will be extremely hard to put right. The legal profession will be decimated, and defendants, the police and the courts—and ultimately the taxpayer—will pay the price. (Law Society 2013)

IV. Structure of the Book

In this final section, we summarise briefly the themes of each of the contributions in chronological order, in order to enable the reader to navigate the collection more easily.

In Chapter 2, Mary Anne Noone outlines the background and context to legal aid funding in Australia before examining the sometimes competing objectives of increased demand for legal services, with a desire to improve both the quality and efficiency of legal assistance, and the need for a more joined-up approach to the provision of legal services. She focuses in particular on the impact of legal aid changes and reforms, including for the legal profession itself. Running through her analysis is an awareness of the need to take a more systemic approach to understanding and improving access to justice, taking account of the intertwined nature of public services. In her chapter, Noone clearly demonstrates that access to justice depends on health and welfare services, as well as those providing legal assistance.

In Chapter 3, Jeff Giddings takes an historical look at the development of legal aid and access to justice in Australia, examining the range of providers, their interrelationships and their sources of funding—be it State and Territories, or Commonwealth (federal) funds. He discusses the establishment of the Australian Legal Aid Office (ALAO), which, although extending the provision of legal services, was challenged by the legal profession, who feared that a model of salaried lawyers might compromise the independence of legal assistance. LACs replaced the ALAO, operating as part of a mixed model of legal provision, together with CLCs and the private profession. However, LACs have been unable to resist funding cuts and they continue to face conflict-of-interest concerns, especially in duty lawyer services.

Moving to England and Wales, in Chapter 4, Tom Smith and Ed Cape document the growth in criminal legal aid and the roots of its decline, which can be located within the removal of real terms fee increases from 1994 onwards. They also chart the various challenges faced by the profession, such as the establishment of the Public Defender Service (PDS) and the quality assurance and accreditation measures that were adopted in response to research demonstrating that lawyers were failing to ensure the provision of high-quality legal assistance (McConville and Hodgson 1993; McConville et al 1994). In addition to financial cuts, there has been a shift from hourly rates to fixed fees and systems of competitive tendering designed to reform the market of legal providers. The authors argue that the reduction in the criminal legal aid budget reflects a broader antipathy to state welfare provision and a lack of concern for procedural justice and the right to a fair trial. They have little room for optimism, despite international measures recognising the importance of the right to legal aid as a measure of a fair trial.

In Chapter 5, Pauline Spencer provides a view from the bench of a busy magistrates' court in Melbourne (Victoria, Australia). Using a hypothetical case scenario based on the many cases she hears each day, Spencer focuses on the ways in which legal representation can improve the efficiency and effectiveness of the court and help to guide the client through a legal process that is often difficult to comprehend. She argues that lawyers can provide the missing social information that the court needs to ensure that interventions are timely and appropriate, enabling them to draw on therapeutic justice approaches and saving money by avoiding unnecessary adjournments. Spencer also highlights the challenges defendants face, as they are often unaware of the consequences of their choices and so can inadvertently make their situation worse. In this regard, she argues that lawyers can help to prevent the escalation of problems by translating the requirements of legal decisions to align with the personal situation of the client's case. This better understanding of the process gives the client a greater sense of agency and thus a belief in the legitimacy of the process.

In Chapter 6, Carolyn McKay discusses the growing use of video-link technology in prisons and courtrooms in Australia and the impact that this reduction in face-to-face contact has on the nature of the lawyer–client relationship from the perspective of those held on remand and serving time in prison custody. McKay draws on empirical data gathered through 31 prisoner interviews in NSW with individuals who had experienced court hearings through video link. While McKay argues that there are clear advantages in avoiding prisoners and lawyers having to travel between courts and prisons, and that videoconferencing sometimes provides a better experience than telephone consultation, she identifies a range of concerns, in particular around maintaining the confidentiality of the lawyer–client relationship. McKay notes that there has been significant financial investment in videoconferencing facilities, as this is seen as a way of saving money without compromising quality, but she questions the extent to which prisoners, especially those most disadvantaged, enjoy 'access to justice' when their needs are complex and the camera represents a barrier to establishing emotional empathy.

In Chapter 7, Kathy Laster and Ryan Kornhauser argue that, arising out of the television and online culture in which everyone can refashion themselves as an expert, the institution and provision of legal aid is being undermined by 'DIY law'. They discuss the shift from the consumer movement of the 1970s, which emphasised the value of access to justice, provided in practice by a professional elite, and where legal aid ensured the protection of the most vulnerable and marginalised in society, to the current climate where direct access to legal information and self-help resources, together with a dominant ideology of public sector managerialism and a focus on reducing costs, now encourages consumers to take responsibility for addressing and resolving their own problems. In examining this shift, Laster and Kornhauser argue that it has de-skilled the law in some respects, but it has also deprived those without the technological know-how of the opportunity to access legal assistance or to assist themselves.

In Chapter 8, Liana Buchanan examines the history of CLCs in Australia, their social ethos and the important legal changes that they have helped initiate. Often working in areas of law that affect those who are most marginalised in society, CLCs, Buchanan demonstrates, aspire to use the law as an agent of social change, focusing on substantive as well as procedural justice. She explains that the wider social ethos of CLCs includes providing not only legal advice and representation, but also community legal education, and law and policy reform. In discussing the multifaceted role of CLCs, Buchanan shows that their innovative approach to improving access to justice includes developing integrated multi-agency responses to identifying and resolving legal needs and that they are committed to forms of 'systemic' advocacy, focusing on broader underlying problems that affect groups of people beyond the immediate litigant, such as family violence and police racial profiling. In doing so, Buchanan reflects on the responses of CLCs as their funding is cut and their legal activism curtailed.

In Chapter 9, James Organ and Jennifer Sigafoos assess the impact of recent funding cuts and policy changes to third-sector advice agencies in the English city of Liverpool—an area of high social and economic deprivation. They describe the perfect storm that is created by cuts to welfare benefits and to the funding of non-profit legal advice agencies (the largest providers of welfare benefits advice) following LASPO. This includes demonstrating how advice agencies have lost specialist advice services and so have to rely on volunteers, telephone advice services, and client self-help and online information. Unsurprisingly, respondents in Organ and Sigafoos' empirical research reported that the quality of their service provision has fallen, as has the number of clients they are able to assist, resulting in growing unmet legal need. Additionally, their findings show that some agencies have sought to ameliorate the impact of these changes by merging with other organisations, but even larger bodies are not immune to funding reductions. Organ and Sigafoos conclude that these short-term savings are unlikely to deliver long-term gains, as the preventive benefits of legal assistance are lost, and increases in anxiety and mental health problems create costs elsewhere in the public sector.

In Chapter 10, Samuel Kirwan considers the changing funding for the organisation and provision of advice by Citizens' Advice Bureaux (CABx) in England and Wales, with a particular focus on the experience of advisers. Drawing on the author's own qualitative empirical data, he considers two principal areas of concern. The first is the voluntary nature of this work and the emotional connection with advice provision as practice—a connection which is under threat as a result of funding cuts that place pressure on advisers' time and responsibility. Second is the complex nature of 'advising' clients, a process which—more than the simple conveying of information—also encompasses practices that enable CAB clients to understand, process and act upon the information and advice provided. This analysis is used to critique funding cuts, which Kirwan argues ignore the human and emotional context of CAB workers, treating volunteer 'advice' as practical and non-legal, and therefore as something that can simply be made more productive when required.

In Chapter 11, Simon Rice examines the nature of the relationship between human rights and legal aid in non-criminal matters, posing the question of whether legal aid is a necessary part of our understanding and enjoyment of some substantive human rights. After a detailed analysis of the nature of human rights and the international and European human rights jurisprudence around legal aid, he notes that the right to legal aid is less well established in non-criminal matters (where it centres on access to the courts), than in criminal matters (where it is more closely tied to the right to a fair trial). In conclusion, he casts doubt on the idea of legal aid as a right in itself, arguing that a more fruitful approach is to identify the right to legal aid as an aspect of pre-existing substantive human rights.

In Chapter 12, Natalie Byrom considers the extent and impact of cuts to civil legal aid in England and Wales, and the context within which such drastic funding reductions have been possible. Drawing on a range of official reports as well as her own research, Byrom notes the resulting uneven geographic distribution of civil law advice now available (resulting in what have been termed 'advice deserts') and the loss of expertise, as firms and agencies are unable to retain experienced advisers. She highlights the fact that black, Asian and minority ethnic lawyers are more likely to work in legal aid practices and so have been disproportionately affected by the cuts, reducing diversity within the profession. She goes on to examine the low visibility of civil legal aid and poor public perceptions of lawyers, both of which formed part of the context in which these cuts were possible. Byrom concludes by proposing more creative ways of thinking about the role of lawyers in society in the post-LASPO funding landscape, and how lawyers should best approach protecting what remains of public funding for civil legal aid.

In Chapter 13, Rosemary Hunter, Anne Barlow, Janet Smithson and Jan Ewing argue that LASPO's removal of legal aid funding for the majority of private family law disputes in England and Wales, and the expectation that all such matters will now be resolved through mediation, reflects a moral as well as an economic ideology. Mediation is cheaper than legal advice and representation, but it is also promoted by a government rhetoric that deems parties responsible for resolving their own 'private' disputes concerning separation, divorce and child custody. Drawing on their extensive qualitative empirical research, Hunter et al conclude that mediation—the only option available to those with limited means—does not represent justice; it is not appropriate for all cases; and in the one-third of cases where it is unsuccessful, there is no alternative procedure available to the parties. This privatisation of family disputes reduces access to justice, and allows the state to abdicate responsibility for child welfare.

In Chapter 14, Pasanna Mutha-Merennege examines the impact of cuts to family law legal aid for the women of the Australian State of Victoria, bringing insights from her time working at the Women's Legal Service Victoria. Mutha-Merennege discusses how domestic violence and separation are growing areas of unmet legal need (recorded family violence increased by more than 80 per cent between 2010 and 2014 in Victoria), and as women are most likely to be the victims of domestic abuse, often leading to separation and child custody disputes, they are disproportionately affected by the cuts. In line with the arguments presented in several other chapters in this volume, Mutha-Merennege argues that removing access to legal advice and representation can lead to wider social and economic harms, as well as health consequences, as related problems are not dealt with and so escalate. She demonstrates how self-representation is not a realistic alternative for women with long histories of family violence, as they find it difficult to cross-examine violent ex-partners and prepare technical affidavits under pressure of time. Mutha-Merennege concludes that, without adequate legal aid funding, women experiencing family violence risk losing their children, their homes and even their lives.

In Chapter 15, Melanie Schwartz examines civil law access to justice issues for Aboriginal and Torres Strait Islanders, drawing on government inquiries and qualitative data from her large-scale empirical project conducted across five jurisdictions, which included 800 Indigenous focus group participants and nearly 3500 interviews with organisations and agencies providing legal and welfare services. She notes that geographical remoteness is a major disadvantage for Indigenous people, often leading to negative socioeconomic consequences, as well as difficulties in accessing legal assistance, which is most often located in urban areas. Schwartz argues that a lack of knowledge of how civil and family law might provide solutions for Aboriginal and Torres Strait Islander people is a key obstacle to overcome, along with how to ensure effective communication (by both clients and lawyers) that takes into account the complex and culturally sensitive needs of Indigenous clients. Schwartz discusses how Indigenous women in particular have low levels of trust and confidence in the legal system, and concludes by warning of the necessity for wide-ranging reforms in order to address the structural disadvantages facing Aboriginal and Torres Strait Islanders. She also highlights the need to see civil and family law funding as essential in preventing the criminal offending that often results when these problems are not addressed.

The collection closes with Chapter 16, in which Ana Aliverti considers legal aid in the context of migration control, played out through a proposed UK Government policy to restrict legal aid eligibility to those who have resided in England and Wales for more than 12 months, which she critiques as part of a wider reconstituting of social citizenship. While the High Court ruled that, in assessing on the basis of residence rather than need, the proposed test was unlawful, Aliverti is critical of the court's failure to tackle the underlying broader questions of fairness and inequality in the immigration sphere, and so the less overt sources of discrimination that reduce the ability of lower-class foreign nationals to access justice. Although the test relates to residence and so might equally apply to non-resident British nationals, she argues that in practice this fulfils the less palatable objective of targeting foreigners. Aliverti also argues that legal aid reform reflects social hierarchies of who is deserving of state assistance and who is not, concluding that, while on the face of it, the High Court ruling was favourable, it also left unquestioned the state's presumed right to treat people differently on the grounds of 'foreignness'.

V. Conclusion

In this book, each chapter drives home the need for a new narrative around access to justice to counter the current dominant view that legal advice is unnecessary, and that legal aid cuts are unavoidable. This collection seeks to rebuild belief in the value and necessity of accessing and understanding law; and in the value of the quality of justice through legal assistance—civil, family and criminal. Without this, we run the risk of irreversibly damaging the legal system, and hiding the true extent of unmet legal need.

References

Access to Justice Taskforce (2009) *A Strategic Framework for Access to Justice in the Federal Civil Justice System*, available at: www.ag.gov.au/LegalSystem/Documents/A%20Strategic%20Framework%20for%20Access%20to%20Justice%20in%20the%20Federal%20Civil%20Justice%20System.pdf.

Armstrong, N (2013) *Costing the Legal Aid Transforming Justice Proposals*, available at: detentionaction.org.uk/wordpress/wp-content/uploads/2013/06/Nick-Armstrong-Costing-the-civil-legal-aid-proposals-130624.pdf.

Bawdon, F (2013) 'For Legal Aid Lawyers, It's All about the Clients', *The Guardian*, 10 July 2013, available at: www.theguardian.com/law/guardian-law-blog/2013/jul/10/legal-aid-lawyer-awards-clients.

Bowcott, O (2013a) 'Legal Aid Cuts Will Create Advice Deserts', *The Guardian*, 1 April 2013, available at: www.theguardian.com/law/2013/apr/01/legal-aid-cuts.

—— (2013b) 'Legal Aid Cuts Will Lead to More Miscarriages of Justice, Judges War', *The Guardian*, 5 July 2013, available at: www.theguardian.com/law/2013/jul/05/legal-aid-cuts-miscarriages-of-justice.

—— (2016) 'Top Judge Says Justice Is Now Unaffordable to Most', *The Guardian*, 14 January 2016, available at: www.theguardian.com/law/2016/jan/13/uk-most-senior-judge-says-justice-has-become-unaffordable-to-most.

Byrom, N (2013) *The State of the Sector: The Impact of Cuts to Civil Legal Aid on Practitioners and Their Clients*, available at: www2.warwick.ac.uk/fac/soc/law/research/centres/chrp/projects/legalaidcuts/153064_statesector_report-final.pdf.

Byrom, N, Flynn, A, Harrison, J and Hodgson, J (2014) *Access to Justice: A Comparative Analysis of Cuts to Legal Aid: Report I* (Coventry, University of Warwick), available at: www2.warwick.ac.uk/fac/soc/law/research/centres/cjc/researchstreams/comparative/warwick_monash_conf_march.pdf.

Coumarelos, C, Macourt, D, People, J, McDonald, H, Wei, Z, Iriana, R and Ramsey, S (2012) *Legal Australia-Wide Survey: Legal Need in Australia* (Sydney, Law and Justice Foundation of New South Wales).

Crawford, C (2013) 'Calls to Improve Flawed Legal Aid System', *Herald Sun*, 21 October 2013, available at: www.heraldsun.com.au/news/law-order/call-to-improve-flawed-legal-aid-system/story-fni0fee2-1226743451514.

Easton, S and Piper, C (2012) *Sentencing and Punishment: The Quest for Justice*, 3rd edn (Oxford, Oxford University Press).

Farrell, J (2015) 'Reversing Legal Aid Cuts Isn't Enough to Ensure Justice', *The Conversation*, 31 March 2015, available at: theconversation.com/reversing-legal-aid-cuts-isnt-enough-to-ensure-access-to-justice-39463.

Flynn, A and Fitz-Gibbon, K (2013) *A Second Chance for Justice: The Prosecutions of Gabe Watson for the Death of Tina Thomas* (Newcastle-upon-Tyne, Cambridge Scholars Publishing).

Flynn, A, Freiberg, A, McCulloch, J, Naylor, B, Byrom, N and Hodgson, J (2015) *Access to Justice: A Comparative Analysis of Cuts to Legal Aid—Report II* (Melbourne, Monash University).

Flynn, A, Hodgson, J, McCulloch, J and Naylor, B (2016) 'Legal Aid and Access to Legal Representation: Re-Defining the Right to a Fair Trial' 40 *Melbourne University Law Review* 207.

Garland, D (1996) 'The Limits of the Sovereign State: Strategies of Crime Control in Contemporary Society' 36 *British Journal of Criminology* 445.

—— (2001) *The Culture of Control: Crime and Social order in Contemporary Society* (Oxford, Oxford University Press).

Genn, H (1997) 'Understanding Civil Justice' 50 *Current Legal Problems* 155.

HC Hansard (2013) *House of Commons Debate: Hansard*, 27 March (Col 1088).

Henry, N, Flynn, A and Powell, A (2015) 'The Promise and Paradox of Justice: Rape Justice Beyond the Realm of Criminal Law' in A Powell, N Henry and A Flynn (eds), *Rape Justice: Beyond the Criminal Law* (Basingstoke, Palgrave Macmillan).

House of Commons Justice Committee (2015) *Impact of changes to civil legal aid under Part 1 of the Legal Aid, Sentencing and Punishment of Offenders Act 2012* Eighth Report of Session 2014–15, HC 311 (London, The Stationery Office), available at: www.publications.parliament.uk/pa/cm201415/cmselect/cmjust/311/311.pdf.

Howard, E (2014) 'Legal Aid Cuts: The "Forgotten Pillar of the Welfare State"—A Special Report', *The Guardian*, 25 September 2014, available at: www.theguardian.com/law/2014/sep/25/-sp-legal-aid-forgotten-pillar-welfare-state-special-report-impact-cuts.

Johnston, M and Smethurst, A (2013) 'Legal Aid Rethink after Outcry', *Herald Sun*, 27 September 2013, available at: www.heraldsun.com.au/news/law-order/legal-aid-rethink-after-outcry/story-fni0ffnk-1226728832369.

Judiciary of England and Wales (2015) *Lord Chief Justice's Annual Report 2015*, available at: www.judiciary.gov.uk/wp-content/uploads/2016/01/lcj_report_2015-final.pdf.

Law Society (2013) *Leading Academics Warn Legal Aid Cuts Could Have Devastating Effects*, available at: www.lawsociety.org.uk/news/stories/leading-academics-warn-legal-aid-cuts-could-have-devastating-effects/.

Martin, W (2012) 'Creating a Just Future by Improving Access to Justice', Paper presented at the *Community Legal Centres Association WA Annual Conference 2012*, available at: www.supremecourt.wa.gov.au/_files/Creating%20a%20Just%20Future%20by%20Improving%20Access%20to%20Justice%20Martin%20CJ%2024%20Oct%202012%20v.2.pdf.

McConville, M and Hodgson, J (1993) *Custodial Legal Advice and the Right to Silence* (London, HMSO).

McConville, M, Hodgson, J, Bridges, L and Pavlovic, A (1994) *Standing Accused: The Organisation and Practices of Defence Lawyers in Britain* (Oxford, Clarendon Press).

Ministry of Justice (2013a) *Transforming Legal Aid: Delivering a More Credible and Efficient System*, available at: www.justice.gov.uk/downloads/consultations/transforming-legal-aid.pdf.

—— (2013b) *Transforming Legal Aid: Next Steps* available at: consult.justice.gov.uk/digital-communications/transforming-legal-aid-next-steps/supporting_documents/transforminglegalaidnextsteps.pdf.

—— (2014) *Legal Aid Statistics in England and Wales 2013–14* available at: www.gov.uk/government/uploads/system/uploads/attachment_data/file/366575/legal-aid-statistics-2013-14.pdf.

—— (2016) *Changes to Criminal Legal Aid Contracting*, Written statement to Parliament, 28 January 2016, available at: www.gov.uk/government/speeches/changes-to-criminal-legal-aid-contracting.

National Audit Office (2014) *Implementing Reforms to Civil Legal Aid*, available at: www.nao.org.uk/wp-content/uploads/2014/11/Implementing-reforms-to-civil-legal-aid1.pdf.

Perkins, M and Lee, J (2015) 'Aboriginal Legal Services Call on Federal Government to Reverse Funding Cuts', *The Age*, 25 March 2015, available at: www.theage.com.au/federal-politics/political-news/aboriginal-legal-services-call-on-federal-government-to-reverse-funding-cuts-20150325-1m7j9u.html.

Productivity Commission (2014) *Access to Justice Arrangements Inquiry*, Report No 72, 5 September 2014 (Canberra, Productivity Commission).

Renshaw, J (2012) 'April Fools: The Quiet Demolition of Legal Aid', *Oxford Human Rights Hub*, 16 November 2012, available at: ohrh.law.ox.ac.uk/april-fools-the-quiet-demolition-of-legal-aid/.

Rights of Women, Women's Aid and Welsh Women's Aid (2013) *Statistics and Research*, available at: www.welshwomensaid.org.uk/index.php?option=com_content&view=article&id=49&Itemid=55.

Sackville, R (2002) 'Access to Justice: Assumptions and Reality Checks', *Access to Justice Roundtable: Proceedings of a Workshop* (Sydney, Law and Justice Foundation of New South Wales).

Vara, S (2013) 'We Are Trying to Reform Legal Aid, Not Destroy It', *The Telegraph*, 22 November 2013, available at: www.telegraph.co.uk/news/uknews/law-and-order/10468093/We-are-trying-to-reform-legal-aid-not-destroy-it.html.

Victoria Legal Aid (2015) *Twentieth Statutory Annual Report 2014–15* (Melbourne), available at: www.legalaid.vic.gov.au/about-us/our-organisation/annual-reports.

Wright, P (2013) *Labor Ignores Legal Service Crisis*, available at: penny-wright.greensmps.org.au/content/media-releases/labor-ignores-legal-services-crisis.

YouGov (2013) *Legal Aid Survey Results*, available at: cdn.yougov.com/cumulus_uploads/document/x1vwbrs8zj/YG-Archive-Legal-Aid-results-030413.pdf.

2

Challenges Facing the Australian Legal Aid System

MARY ANNE NOONE

I. Introduction

At several stages in the history of the Australian legal aid system, it has been suggested that legal aid policy was at a crossroads (Churchman 1988; Giddings 1998). For many people concerned about access to justice, it might seem that, rather than a crossroads, the Australian legal aid system is currently heading down a road that continues to get narrower, and more pot-holed and poorly signposted. Australian legal aid organisations (legal aid commissions [LACs], community legal centres [CLCs] and Indigenous legal services) face significant challenges that impact on their future viability. In this chapter, critical challenges are detailed, including increasing demand for services, the quest to improve the efficiency and quality of legal aid practice, and attempts to provide joined-up services. The provision of legal aid services is placed in context before the potential impact of these challenges on the legal aid infrastructure, including the relationship between legal aid organisations and the private legal profession, is discussed. Finally, these many challenges highlight the importance of taking a systemic approach to improving access to justice—one that includes not only the justice system, but also the health and welfare systems, as well as the need for legal aid impact statements arising from government policy implementation.

II. The Australian Legal Aid System

Australia is a federation comprised of seven States and Territories. Legal aid is funded both by the federal government (the Commonwealth) and the State governments (Productivity Commission 2014). There is no national legal aid scheme. Instead, there are a variety of legal aid organisations providing legal information, advice, assistance and legal representation for the poor and disadvantaged.[1] Australia's legal aid system is described as a mixed model.[2] It comprises salaried lawyers working in statutory LACs; independent CLCs and Indigenous Legal Services; and private lawyers providing services under a 'judicare' scheme, as well as on a pro bono basis. Additionally, there is a large volunteer base that provides services in CLCs. The range of legal aid organisations includes: state-based statutory LACs; independent, not-for-profit CLCs (both generalist and specialist; see Buchanan, Chapter 8, this volume); Aboriginal and Torres Strait Islander Legal Services (ATSILS; see Schwartz, Chapter 15, this volume); Family Violence Prevention and Legal Services (see Mutha-Merennege, Chapter 14, this volume); a range of Commonwealth statutory schemes;[3] and university-run Clinical Legal Education programmes (Gibson and Noone 2013).

There are also a large number of pro bono schemes, through which the private legal profession provides services for free or at a reduced rate. These include Law Society and Bar Council schemes such as the Law Society of New South Wales (NSW) Pro Bono Scheme; not-for-profit organisations like Justice Connect (formerly the Public Interest Law Clearing House) and the Queensland Public Interest Law Clearing House; and court-related schemes, like the Federal Court of Australia Court Referral Legal Assistance.[4] These pro bono schemes remain largely uncoordinated nationally.[5]

The Australian Productivity Commission (2014: 724–25) identified the following benefits of the Australian mixed model: harnessing private sector expertise; LAC in-house lawyers specialising where the private sector is unable or unwilling to provide services; flexibility—offering a choice of provider while avoiding issues of quality and information asymmetry (between lawyer and consumer); enabling conflict of interest situations to be managed; creating competition between public and private lawyers; and cost control.

A. Funding of Legal Aid

Australian legal aid has always been poorly funded compared to that of the United Kingdom (UK). In 1992–93 it was estimated that Australia spent US$7 per head of population while the UK spent US$32 (Regan 1997). In 1996 there were unexpected and severe funding cutbacks and, ever since, the Australian legal aid

[1] For further detail, see Giddings, Chapter 3, this volume, and Gibson and Noone (2013); for a history of the Australian legal aid system, see Noone and Tomsen (2006).

[2] There are four principal models of providing legal aid: charitable, 'judicare', salaried and mixed. In the 'Judicare' model, the state funds the private profession to provide legal services to individuals. This model is common in the United Kingdom (UK), the Netherlands and Canada. For further discussion see Paterson (1996).

[3] For more details on these schemes, see: https://www.ag.gov.au/LegalSystem/Legalaidprogrammes/Commonwealthlegalfinancialassistance/Pages/default.aspx.

[4] For details of this scheme, see: www.federalcourt.gov.au/attending-court/court-referral-assistance.

[5] For details of various programmes, see: www.nationalprobono.org.au/home.asp.

system has been trying to at least get back to the pre-1996 level (in real terms) (Noone and Tomsen 2006; Productivity Commission 2014). The latest series of funding issues in the Australian context are outlined throughout this collection (see Buchanan, Chapter 8, Flynn and Hodgson, Chapter 1, Mutha-Merennege Chapter 14, Schwartz, Chapter 15, and Spencer, Chapter 5). In 2014, the Productivity Commission recommended that legal assistance services be subject to an urgent, interim investment of AU$200 million (£113 million) per year (see recommendation 21.4, Volume 1).

The low levels of government funding to Australian LACs have meant that they have always had restrictions on whom and for what legal assistance is provided. This chronic underfunding of legal aid means that restrictive guidelines and the determination of priority areas of law to receive assistance are used as a budgetary measure to ensure organisations remain solvent (Productivity Commission 2014).

The boards of LACs have the difficult task of deciding who and what legal issues are eligible for legal aid (*Legal Aid Act 1978* [Vic] section 8). They must weigh up competing factors affecting priority for services. Most State-funded legal aid expenditure is targeted at criminal law, whereas most Commonwealth legal aid funding is directed at providing assistance in family law. There is minimal funding for civil law matters. This privileging of criminal law matters over family and civil law has an ongoing impact on the poor's social exclusion and access to justice(for the Australian context, see Mutha-Merennege, Chapter 14 and Schwartz, Chapter 15, this volume; for the UK context, see Aliverti, Chapter 16, Byrom, Chapter 12, and Hunter et al, Chapter 13, this volume).[6] Additionally the boards of LACs have to decide on the 'allocation of work between officers of VLA [LAC] and private legal practitioners' (*Legal Aid Act 1978* [Vic] section 8(2)).

III. Legal Aid Services in Context

In order to understand the challenges facing Australian legal aid services, it is helpful to discuss briefly several contextual matters. These include the changes occurring within the legal services industry and legal practice, growing inequality and diminished government funding for all welfare services, and the National Partnership Agreement on Legal Assistance Services (NPA).

[6] For further discussion of this issue, see Cunneen and Schwartz (2009); Gibson (2006) (2010); Hunter and De Simone (2009).

A. Changes to Legal Practice

It is predicted that legal institutions and the work of lawyers will change more radically in the next two decades than they have over the past two centuries (Susskind 2013). In Australia, the demand for commercial legal services has steadily declined, while productivity has increased (Melbourne University Law School & Thomson Reuters 2015). Simultaneously, the number of law graduates continues to increase, while available positions decline (Tadros and Walsh 2015; see similar trends in the UK context outlined in Smith and Cape, Chapter 4, this volume). Another influential trend is globalisation, which continues to have a significant impact on legal practice. In 1989–90, Australia's export market for legal services was worth AU$67 million (£38.1 million) and by 2006–07 it had increased to AU$675 million (£384 million) (Coumarelos et al 2012).

Susskind (2013: 3) argues that the three main drivers of change in the legal services industry will be 'the "more for-less" challenge, liberalization, and information technology'. Although he focuses primarily on the delivery of legal services by commercial firms in civil matters, he also discusses the implications for access to justice. Susskind suggests that technology, the changing role of lawyers and the court process itself will all provide a range of ways in which the citizen can be empowered to manage their own legal problems (see also Laster and Kornhauser, Chapter 7, this volume). He argues that the concept of access to justice should include 'embrac[ing] improvements not just to dispute resolution but also to … dispute containment, dispute avoidance and legal health promotion' (2013: 85). The 'disruptions' in technology will enhance the capabilities of virtual operations and accessibility of legal information and resources. There will be more virtual and semi-virtual law practices established, offering web-based legal solutions, particularly for clients. As an example, larger firms are increasing their outsourced workloads to overseas vendors as a cost-saving measure. As courts gain momentum in their use of technology, there will be a continued expansion of 'e-procedures' such as e-discovery and e-trials in a wider variety of matters (Susskind 2013; see also McKay, Chapter 6, this volume).

IV. Growing Inequality in Australia

A 2015 report by the Australian Council for Social Services (ACOSS) analysed the level of inequality in Australia and identified a trend of growing inequality. The Report identified a big gap in incomes and wealth between different groups in society. A person in the top 20 per cent income group receives around five times as much income as a person in the bottom 20 per cent. Over the past 20 years, the share of income going to those at the top has risen, while the share flowing to those in the middle and at the bottom has declined. Additionally, a person in the top 20 per cent wealth group has a staggering 70 times as much overall wealth as a person in the bottom 20 per cent. The wealth of the top 20 per cent group increased by 28 per cent over the period from 2004 to 2012, while the wealth of the bottom group increased by just three per cent (ACOSS 2015). The ACOSS report also found that these gaps are widening.

Inequality has economic consequences that will also impact on the clients of legal aid organisations. Not only does it lead to greater demand for legal aid services, but there are also more people eligible and the range of problems and issues becomes more complex. As Dr Anne Holmes (2015) states:

> At a microeconomic level, inequality increases ill health and health spending and reduces the educational performance of the poor. These two factors lead to a reduction in the productive potential of the work force. At a macroeconomic level, inequality can be a brake on growth and can lead to instability.

V. The National Partnership Agreement on Legal Assistance Services

The NPA is an agreement between the Commonwealth of Australia and the State and Territory governments that sets out the funding provided by the federal government to the States and Territories, and the criteria for legal assistance funded under this agreement. In contrast to the previous NPA (2012–15), the 2015 version includes funding arrangements for CLCs, in addition to LACs. This inclusion provides some stability for CLCs but also places further restrictions on what type of work this funding can be used for; for example, it prohibits using this funding for 'lobbying' purposes (see Buchanan, Chapter 8, this volume, for an expansive discussion of how CLCs' work has been fundamentally changed in this regard).

The objective of the current NPA is 'a national legal assistance sector that is integrated, efficient and effective, focused on improving access to justice for disadvantaged people and maximising service delivery within available resources' (Council of Australian Governments [COAG] 2015: 4). Optimistically, the NPA aims to facilitate the following outcomes:

(a) legal assistance services are targeted to priority clients with the greatest legal need;
(b) legal assistance service providers collaborate with each other, governments, the private legal profession and other services, to provide joined-up services to address people's legal and related problems;
(c) legal assistance services are appropriate, proportionate and tailored to people's legal needs and levels of capability;

(d) legal assistance services help people to identify their legal problems and facilitate the resolution of those problems in a timely manner before they escalate; and

(e) legal assistance services help empower people to understand and assert their legal rights and responsibilities and to address, or prevent, legal problems. (COAG 2015: B-2).

However, CLCs are very concerned about the agreement as they claim it contains a 30 per cent funding cut to them in 2017. Additionally, as argued by Buchanan (Chapter 8, this volume), the NPA prevents legal aid organisations from using Commonwealth funds for lobbying or public campaigns. The restrictions on lobbying are contained in the General Principles of Commonwealth Priorities and include that:

> Commonwealth funding should not be used to lobby governments or to engage in public campaigns. Lobbying does *not* include community legal education or where a legal assistance service provider makes a submission to a government or parliamentary body to provide factual information and/or advice with a focus on systemic issues affecting access to justice. (COAG 2015: B 7)

This is a specific concern for CLCs, as systemic advocacy and law reform work has been an integral aspect of their work since they began in the 1970s (Federation of Community Legal Centres 2015; Noone and Tomsen 2006).

VI. Challenges for Legal Aid Services in Australia

Legal aid organisations around the globe are facing difficult times and numerous challenges. Prior to the current diminution of legal aid in the UK (see Byrom, Chapter 12, and Smith and Cape, Chapter 4, this volume), Paterson (2012: 72) outlined three key challenges for legal aid services: 'the role for strategic planning; questions of affordability, rationing and prioritisation; and the problem of integrating supply and demand'. More recently, Susskind (2013: 87) has posited that the UK cuts in legal aid will lead to 'legal and court services that are less affordable and less accessible'. As a consequence, he states that a 'major and urgent social challenge is to find new ways of providing legal help, not least to citizens and to small businesses' (Susskind 2013: 87).

Clearly, the need to maintain and increase funding levels as well as diversify funding sources is a critical challenge for all legal aid organisations and those concerned with improving access to justice. However, in this chapter, I discuss three related challenges in the Australian context: (1) increasing demand and related policy decisions, (2) the maintenance of an efficient and effective mixed model legal aid infrastructure, and (3) the provision of legal services that are joined up.

VII. Increasing Demand For Legal Aid Services

Despite significant developments in access to justice, including legal assistance services, many people are unable to access legal advice and assistance when experiencing a legal problem. The Law and Justice Foundation of NSW's LAW Survey (Coumarelos et al 2012) revealed that 50 per cent of the Australian population experienced a legal issue in the past 12 months, yet only 51 per cent of these people sought any advice. The LAW Survey indicates significant pockets of unmet legal need, particularly in civil law (Coumarelos et al 2012).

Since the LAW Survey was conducted, legal aid organisations have experienced continued growth in demand for their services. Factors such as an economic downturn, significant demographic changes, new policy initiatives and natural disasters have affected demand for legal assistance (Warner 2013). Another indicator of increased demand is that there is growing inequality (see above) and more people are reliant on social security and in low-paid, part-time work (ACOSS 2014). Due to these factors, more individuals are in need of legal assistance, and are unable to pay for legal services and satisfy the means test eligibility criteria of LACs.

While natural disasters are unpredictable, the impact of other factors, like changes to government policies and practices, can be anticipated and should be planned for. As an example, in its 2011–12 Annual Report, Victoria Legal Aid (VLA) predicted that the key drivers for future demand for services would be the increase in number of police officers and child protection workers; the incidence and severity of family breakdown; the widening gap between the working poor and those able to fend for themselves; the policies of government departments and prosecutorial agencies; and population growth, particularly in areas of disadvantage (ACOSS 2012; VLA 2012).

In the first half of the 2012–13 financial year, the increased demand for VLA services did intensify and it was estimated that the organisation would face a financial deficit of between AU$10 and AU$13 million (£5.69 and £7.4 million), if the same level of services continued to be provided. As a consequence, VLA severely curtailed its services in a variety of ways—by narrowing types of legal matters and aspects of legal work eligible for legal assistance, closing a regional VLA office and implementing staff reductions (Noone 2014). This resulted in a significant reduction of legal services provided, as well as increased acrimony between the private legal profession and VLA (see discussion below).

In the intervening two years, VLA has been able to record a budgetary surplus; however, in its 2014–15 Annual Report the ongoing concern with increased demand was again reported, 'particularly in the areas of family violence, child protection and criminal matters, where demand has increased 19 per cent over the past two years' (VLA 2015). The Report predicted that:

> [D]emand is forecast to further grow in response to an additional 88 child protection officers, increases in police and child protection notifications and reporting of family violence. Without further investment or changes to services we will again be in deficit by 2018. (VLA 2015)

VIII. Legal Aid Impact Statements

One response to shifts in government policy and practice that generate increased legal aid demand is to require the inclusion of legal aid impact statements in any new government announcement. Unremarkably, increased demand for legal aid can be directly related to shifts in government policy. Multiple government policies, relating to social security, immigration, employment, family and crime, impact on the demand for legal aid services. Yet no allowance is made by government for the 'downstream' impact of these policy changes on demand for legal aid services. Despite the recognition of the need for impact statements in many other areas of policy development, it is still not standard practice to prepare impact statements when formulating government justice sector policy.

In 1990, the National Legal Aid Advisory Committee recommended that 'all government policy proposals include consideration of the likely impact on the cost and need for legal aid programs'. At the time, the Commonwealth Government agreed to include the impact on legal services of any new policy proposal being considered by the Cabinet. It was also proposed that the State and Territory governments adopt a legal aid impact statement protocol (NLAAC 1990). However, the recent funding crisis at VLA, partly caused by increased demand due to increases in the numbers of police and child protection officers, suggests that this is definitely not occurring at a State level (Noone 2014). Government policy changes can have a dramatic impact on demand for legal aid services. This is most clearly illustrated by the ongoing focus of governments on 'law and order' and a recent focus on reducing family violence, which are discussed in turn below.

A. Law and Order

All changes to government policies should include a legal aid impact statement and, where an increase in demand for legal services is anticipated, appropriate funding should be provided. It is most obvious within the criminal justice sector not only for legal aid but also for prisons and courts. For instance, an increase in the number of police officers and criminal prosecutions not only leads to an increase in demand for legal aid, but also overcrowding in police cells and increased workload for courts. The need for impact statements for justice sector policy changes should include the impact on legal aid, the courts, prisons, prosecutions and a range of related services.

All Australian State governments have an ongoing focus on 'law and order'; this usually translates into increasing the numbers of police and the severity of sentences. Across Australia, since 2002–03, expenditure on criminal justice has increased by 49 per cent overall and by an average of 10 per cent each year. Police services represent the largest component of the criminal justice system, accounting for approximately 71 per cent of total expenditure. Corrective services account for a further 23 per cent, while criminal courts administration accounts for the remaining six per cent (Australian Institute of Criminology 2014).

An example of the impact of government policy changes on legal aid demand can be seen in the changes introduced by the Victorian Government that came into power in November 2010. As part of its law and order agenda, the government committed to an extra 1700 police officers and 940 Protective Service Officers (PSOs) on train stations by November 2014 (Savage 2014).[7] This increase in police officers and the introduction of PSOs were identified as two factors that led to a significant increase in demand for VLA services. The 2011–12 Victoria Police crime statistics showed a 10.3 per cent increase in recorded violent crime and 6.8 per cent increase in recorded crime overall. The reporting of assaults was up by 41.3 per cent, rapes by 39.6 per cent and abduction and kidnapping by 31.8 per cent. These figures were reported as reflecting the improved reporting of domestic violence and additional police resources dedicated to responding to complainants and investigating crime. In March 2013, the Victorian Acting Police Commissioner, Lucinda Nolan, noted that there had been an increase in the number of offenders proceeded against by police in Victoria over the previous three years (Bucci 2013). Consequently, the demand for legal aid representation and legal advice in relation to these prosecutions also increased.

B. Family Violence and Child Protection Matters

The federal and State governments are equally concerned about the high levels of family violence in the community and have implemented a range of inquiries

[7] PSOs are a quasi-form of police officer who receive 12 weeks of training, compared to a Victoria Police member who receives 33 weeks of (initial) training. PSOs are responsible solely for protecting the Victorian railway network and some public buildings.

and new policies aimed at improving safety for women and children.[8] In 2008, the *Australian Policing Strategy for Preventing and Reducing Family Violence* was launched by Police Commissioners across Australia. Although there had been legislative reforms in the late 1980s and 1990s that strengthened police powers to deal with domestic violence, it is only recently that the trend towards pro-arrest policies has begun to influence operational policing. In general, Australian police agencies have adopted policies that promote arrest as the primary intervention where there is a belief on reasonable grounds that an offence has been committed.

In February 2012, Victoria Police announced a doubling of existing family violence units over the next three years, an increase in the number of family violence court liaison officers to help victims with police-initiated intervention order applications and an expansion of the civil advocacy unit which runs police intervention order applications at the Victorian Children's Court and Melbourne Magistrates' Court (Le Grand and Ferguson 2012).

As an example of the impact of government policy shifts, policies aimed at eliminating family violence and better protecting children have led to a 45 per cent increase in substantiations of child abuse and neglect nationally since 1997–98; an 82 per cent increase in family violence incidents reported to Victoria Police between 1999–2000 and 2009–10; a 341 per cent increase in the number of children identified as 'affected by family matters' in court data relating to family violence matters between 1999–2000 and 2009–10 in Victoria; and an 89 per cent increase in the number of family violence intervention orders that have been finalised in the Victorian magistrates' courts over the past 10 years (Warner 2013). For VLA, this translated into an 11.5 per cent increase in family law grants of aid in 2011–12, a 20 per cent increase in child protection substantiations and a 43.3 per cent increase in the reporting of family violence-related assaults (Warner 2013).

Given the current focus by governments on family violence, such as the Royal Commission into Family Violence (Victoria), additional government resources are being mooted. At the time of writing, the Royal Commission has yet to report its findings, but following the release of its report (anticipated early 2016),[9] the government will be under the spotlight to provide additional resources. However, for legal aid service providers, the challenge remains in how to ensure that

[8] Most recent examples are the Senate Finance and Public Administration References Committee inquiry into Family Violence in Australia, which reported in August 2015, available at: http://www.aph.gov.au/Parliamentary_Business/Committees/Senate/Finance_and_Public_Administration/Domestic_Violence, and the Victorian Royal Commission into Family Violence, which released its report in April 2016 (see Neave, Faulkner and Nicholson 2016). For a detailed discussion, also see Mitchell (2011).

[9] The Royal Commission released its report into family violence in April 2016. See Neave, M, Faulkner, P and Nicholson, T (2016) *Royal Commission into Family Violence: Summary and Recommendations* available at: files.rcfv.com.au/Reports/Final/RCFV-All-Volumes.pdf.

governments consider the legal aid implications of all policy changes and allocate additional funds accordingly.

C. Maintenance of Efficient and Effective Mixed-model Legal Aid Infrastructure

In the context of changes to how legal practice is conducted, the impact of technology, and the need to improve the efficiency of legal aid service provision, the sustainability of Australia's legal aid infrastructure is under challenge. The quest of LACs to improve the efficiency of legal aid practice risks damaging the mixed model of legal aid service delivery and the relationship between LACs and the private profession. Any suggestions to improve (change) how the private profession provides legal aid services are normally met with hostility and concerns about the level of payment. As discussed in Giddings (Chapter 3, this volume), this is not a new issue, but the 2013 VLA crisis (resulting in a number of restrictive changes to VLA funding policies and guidelines for the allocation of work to the private profession) highlights these challenges and illustrates the difficulties faced by LACs in seeking greater efficiencies in the provision of legal representation while also aiming to improve the quality of services (Noone 2014).

Idealistically, the NPA seeks collaboration between the various legal aid service providers; however, the latent tensions and competition for funding between the private legal profession, LACs and CLCs pose a significant challenge. One of the outcomes sought by the NPA is that 'legal assistance service providers collaborate with each other, governments, the private legal profession and other services, to provide joined-up services to address people's legal and related problems'. Two aspects of this aim are the focus on collaboration between stakeholders in legal aid infrastructure and the provision of a 'joined-up service' to address legal and related problems. The NPA wants collaboration with government and other services, and not merely among legal aid service providers.

Although there are recent examples of successful collaboration, such as the New South Wales Cooperative Legal Service Delivery Program,[10] the nature of government funding arrangements militates against sustainable collaboration (Pleasence et al 2014). With a limited (and decreasing in real terms) budget allocation for legal aid funding, ongoing competition exists between LACs and the private legal profession, between LACs and CLCs, and between governments.

[10] The Cooperative Legal Service Delivery Program is a regionally based approach to legal service delivery in NSW. It aims to improve outcomes for economically and socially disadvantaged people by building cooperative and strategic networks of key legal services and community organisations. See: www.legalaid.nsw.gov.au/what-we-do/community-partnerships/cooperative-legal-services-delivery-clsd-program.

Specifically, the history of the Australian private legal profession's relationship with legal aid is a complex one. Despite the legal professional bodies being key advocates for increased legal aid funding, there is a lack of clarity among the stakeholders, including government, about what the aims and objectives of legal aid should be and there is latent conflict about who should manage legal aid and provide the legal services. This tension manifests itself in debates about the role of the private legal profession on the boards of LACs, and the benefits of using private lawyers compared to salaried lawyers (Noone and Tomsen 2006).

Although the private legal profession has a limited role in the administration of legal aid organisations, it remains an integral part of the legal aid service provision model. Between 60 and 70 per cent of legal aid funds are paid to the private legal profession in grants from LACs as part of a judicare model (Productivity Commission 2014). Consequently, any changes by LACs to eligibility guidelines impact on private practitioners' clients and often their income. The 2013 'legal aid crisis' in Victoria illustrates the latent tensions between the private profession and LACs, and the rhetoric used in that conflict resonates with decades-old debates about the management and purposes of legal aid (Noone 2014; see also Giddings, Chapter 3, this volume).

The private legal professional bodies, namely the Law Institute of Victoria and Victorian Bar Council, criticised the decision of VLA to limit eligibility and the funding of lawyers' involvement in criminal trials (Flynn et al 2016). The professional bodies called for an independent review of the legal aid organisations and sought to intervene in court cases. The legal aid organisations countered with accusations that lawyers were only concerned with missing out on taxpayer dollars. It was also claimed that changes were intended to abolish abuse of legal aid funding by private practitioners and ensure the quality of representation for clients. As the Victorian experience illustrates, in the context of ongoing limited funding, the task of reviewing the merits and efficiency of certain legal practices is warranted, but any changes to the status quo are likely to cause significant tensions between LACs and the private legal profession (Noone 2014; PricewaterhouseCoopers 2015). The Productivity Commission report acknowledged these issues, and the terms of reference of the current Access to Justice Review by the Victorian Government also indicate an awareness of the complexity involved.[11]

[11] The terms of reference of the Access to Justice Review include: 'the availability and distribution of funding amongst legal assistance providers by the Victorian and Commonwealth governments to best meet legal need; … whether there is any duplication in services provided by legal assistance providers, and options for reducing that duplication, including the development of legal education material; … the resourcing of Victoria Legal Aid (VLA) to ensure that Government funding is used as effectively and efficiently as possible and services are directed to Victorians most in need, including within the total funding envelope, the types of matters funded by VLA, eligibility criteria for legal assistance and the level of assistance provided; VLA's current service delivery model, including the use of panel arrangements and internal lawyers, and spending on allied support services'. See: https://myviews.justice.vic.gov.au/accesstojustice.

Including governments in the collaborative process (as required by the NPA) is also challenging because in the Australian federal system there are inherent tensions between State and federal governments, who often blame the other for a lack of funding for legal aid. The State governments argue that the federal share of funding has dropped from 50 per cent to 30 per cent over the past decade, while the State governments have substantially increased their contributions (Productivity Commission 2014: 694). The Commonwealth Government argues that the State governments should increase their funding, as it is their policy changes that are responsible for the increase in demand for legal aid services (see discussion above)—changes such as increases in police numbers, the introduction of PSOs, minimum sentences for gross violence and changes to suspended sentences, including their abolition in Victoria (Lee 2013).

For collaboration to have a chance at success, resources need to be allocated to the task and heed paid to lessons learnt from other areas—like health, which has been engaged in collaborative efforts to improve patient wellbeing. In a positive example, the Law and Justice Foundation of NSW (the Foundation), in a project (partially funded by the Attorney-General's office) and in anticipation of the focus of the NPA, has drawn together empirical research evidence in a *Collaborative Planning Resource* (CPR). The CPR is intended to support the planning of legal assistance services across Australia (Coumarelos et al 2015), and has two elements: a Service Planning (SP) resource and Jurisdictional Data (JD) resource. The SP resource summarises the research evidence on legal need and access to justice and the implications for planning legal service delivery. It provides useful information for designing appropriate legal services for specific priority demographic groups: 'who' priority clients are, 'what' types of services are appropriate to their legal needs and capabilities, and 'how' these services might be delivered. The JD data covers the geographic distribution of the Commonwealth's priority groups for services, the prevalence of legal problems for each priority group, and the geographic distribution of those most likely to be in need of legal assistance services for financial or other reasons.[12]

Clearly, the CPR will be an invaluable resource for those seeking to collaborate on the provision of legal aid services. This approach is to be applauded and replicated as appropriate. However, there needs to be ongoing systemic support, from both levels of government, to enable the identification and development of programme responses to local community justice needs. Without additional resources, legal aid service providers who are facing increased demand and declining funds will have little capacity to be actively engaged in these processes.

[12] The Foundation will issue new versions of the CPR-JD as new information becomes available. The data provided is available for a range of geographical boundaries. For details of jurisdictional reports, see: www.lawfoundation.net.au/ljf/app/B6DC9E05711F044CCA257EF5000E995F.html.

D. The Challenge of 'Joined-up' Services

International and Australian research has established links between legal and health problems, links between clusters of legal need and social disadvantage and the prevalence of non-legal services as the first port of call for assistance with legal problems (Clarke and Forell 2007; see also Organ and Sigafoos Chapter 9, this volume). These research findings provide strong support for integrating the provision of legal services with health and welfare services, for establishing good referral practices between legal services and non-legal community and health services, and for developing joined-up services (Coumarelos et al 2012).

Studies that establish the link between legal, health and social need suggest that a holistic approach to service delivery between legal, health and other community services could help to meet the needs of people and communities facing significant levels of social exclusion. It is suggested that legal assistance services for disadvantaged people will be most efficient and effective when they are, as far as practicable:

— *targeted* to those most in need
— *joined-up* with other services (non-legal and legal) likely to be needed
— *timely* to minimise the impact of problems and maximise utility of the service, and
— *appropriate* to the needs and capabilities of users. (Pleasence et al 2014)

The NPA has replicated some of this language in its anticipated outcomes. For example, there is a clear focus on joined-up services.

There are many elements required to ensure successful joined-up services. Integration needs to occur at many levels, including across sectors (whole-of-government), between organisations and across service delivery (professional) approaches. Consequently, the challenges to joined-up legal services occur at all of these levels (Noone 2012). In this regard, Darlington, Feeney and Rixon (2005) noted five common barriers to collaborative practice: (i) inadequate resources, (ii) the confidentiality practices of workers, (iii) gaps in agency-level processes, (iv) unrealistic expectations, and (v) workers protecting professional identities and working narrowly to theoretical constructs.

Additionally, joined-up service solutions to problems are often concerned with finding a solution to a recognised systemic problem, and are focused on defining the complexities of a problem. Many partnership theories centre on the service system itself—how sectors, organisations and professionals can better communicate, capacity build and integrate to achieve solutions for complex problems (Noone 2012).

The complexity within individuals and communities experiencing the problem is often overlooked for the complexity within the problem. Individuals and communities come with a unique set of characteristics and issues that impact on their engagement with service solutions. Research demonstrates that recognising the needs of the local community, and then working with them to address problems, is essential for targeted, timely and appropriate solutions to complex problems (Noone 2012; Pleasence et al 2014).

Research also confirms that the success of a solution is determined by how the government system and community organisation interact, how the community organisation and staff/service delivery model interact, how the service delivery model/staff and government system interact, and how the individual or community interacts with all of these levels (Noone 2012).

This last set of interactions—how the community or individual interacts—is the most important for successful joined-up services. If the individual or community will not, or cannot, engage in problem-solving, there will be no solution. Consequently, a critical challenge lies in how best to develop processes that enable understanding of individuals' and communities' advice-seeking behaviour (Noone 2014; Pleasence et al 2014).

The changes to the way legal services are delivered (as outlined briefly above) and the development of virtual legal practice and a wide range of internet-based information and services present many opportunities to enhance current legal aid services (Smith 2014; see also McKay Chapter 6, this volume). However, research looking at legal aid service innovations in the 1990s provides a note of caution (Banks, Hunter and Giddings 2006; see also Giddings Chapter 3, this volume). Many of the services evaluated were designed more to satisfy the needs of the legal aid service providers than those of their consumers. The research concluded that new services should be designed in consultation with prospective users in order to ensure that their legal needs are most appropriately addressed. This should involve identification of the intended target groups, determination of how those target groups can best be assisted and realistic negotiation of an achievable service (Banks et al 2006: 234). This most significant challenge—how to ensure that the most disadvantaged continue to receive appropriate and targeted legal services (Pleasence et al 2014)—must remain at the forefront of all new development in legal aid.

There is also a challenge in seeking to understand 'what works?' (Law and Justice Foundation of New South Wales 2015). The Law and Justice Foundation of NSW (2015) is undertaking systematic reviews of evidence to identify what is currently known about effective ways to assist people to meet their legal needs and evaluations of new projects aimed at assisting people to access the justice system, in order to learn new lessons. However, as various government inquiries have noted, there is inadequate funding for such research and evaluation (Productivity Commission 2014). In order to understand what works best and to have continued improvement of services, ideally additional funding needs to be allocated to research and evaluation. Although governments are unlikely to provide funds for substantial research, legal aid organisations need to think creatively about how to conduct research and consider it an essential aspect of their strategic planning. The Law and Justice Foundation of NSW work provides a solid foundation but there are also opportunities with universities and social research institutes.[13]

IX. Conclusion

The current challenges posed by increasing levels of demand and the need to ensure effective and efficient forms of legal service delivery and to expand joined-up services are significant, and could threaten aspects of the unique Australian cooperative mixed model of legal aid service delivery. However, despite poor levels of funding, the Australian legal aid system is vibrant and creative.[14]

In 2014, the Australian Productivity Commission acknowledged that legal assistance is an integral part of ensuring that the justice system is accessible to all. It affirmed that government involvement in legal assistance services is justified (at least, at a conceptual level). However, the Commission also affirmed the importance, in an environment of constrained resources, of being able to establish 'that legal assistance providers are providing the "right" mix of services, to the "right" clients, in the "right" areas of law and in the "right" locations' (Productivity Commission 2014).

These issues raise challenging questions that those concerned about access to justice should continue to ask. Those involved in the collaborative process—governments, the private legal profession, LACs, CLCs, Indigenous services and the community—should be focused on how best to deliver access to justice to the poor and disadvantaged. Those involved in the legal aid service delivery process must rise above their own self-interests and partisan concerns. The ultimate challenge for the Australian legal aid system is how to consistently and genuinely put the individual in need of legal assistance at the centre of the legal aid process.

References

Australian Council of Social Service [ACOSS] (2012) *One in Eight People Living in Poverty in Australia: New Report* available at: http://www.acoss.org.au/poverty/.

—— (2014) *Poverty in Australia: ACOSS Paper 194*, available at: acoss.org.au/images/uploads/ACOSS_Poverty_in_Australia_2014.pdf.

—— (2015) *Inequality in Australia 2015: A Nation Divided* (Sydney, ACOSS).

[13] As illustrated by a number of the references in this chapter and other chapters in this book, the research in access to justice is often conducted by academics within universities.

[14] Recent developments in health-justice partnerships are an illustration of this innovation. For recent examples, see: healthjusticecop.wordpress.com/, and https://healthjustice.org.au/.

Australian Institute of Criminology (2014) 'Chapter 7: Criminal Justice Resources' in *Australian Crime: Facts and Figures 2013*, available at: www.aic.gov.au/publications/current%20series/facts/1-20/2013.html.

Banks, C, Hunter, R and Giddings, J (2006) *Australian Innovations in Legal Aid Services: Balancing Cost and Client Needs* (Brisbane, Socio-Legal Research Centre, Griffith University).

Bucci, N (2013) 'Police Grapple with Challenges as Crime Rate Rises', *The Age*, 1 March 2013.

Churchman, S (1988) 'Legal Aid at the Crossroad' 13 *Legal Services Bulletin* 191.

Clarke, S and Forell, L (2007) *Pathways to Justice: The Role of Non-legal Services* (Sydney, Law and Justice Foundation of NSW).

Coumarelos, C, Macourt, D, People, J, McDonald, H, Wei, Z, Iriana, R and Ramsey, S (2012) *Legal Australia-Wide Survey: Legal Need in Australia* (Sydney, Law and Justice Foundation of New South Wales).

Coumarelos, C, McDonald, H, Forell, S and Wei, Z (2015) *Collaborative Planning Resource—Service Planning* (Sydney, Law and Justice Foundation of New South Wales).

Council of Australian Governments [COAG] (2015) *National Partnership Agreement on Legal Assistance Services.*

Cunneen, C and Schwartz, M (2009) 'Civil and Family Law Needs of Indigenous People in New South Wales: The Priority Areas' 32 *University of New South Wales Law Journal* 725.

Darlington, Y, Feeney, J and Rixon, K (2005) 'Interagency Collaboration between Child Protection and Mental Health Services: Practices, Attitudes and Barriers' 29 *Child Abuse and Neglect* 1085.

Federation of Community Legal Centres (2015) *The Facts about Federal Cuts: Community Law Blog*, available at: communitylawblog.wordpress.com/the-facts-about-federal-cuts/.

Flynn, A, Hodgson, J, McCulloch, J and Naylor, B (2016) 'Legal Aid and Access to Legal Representation: Re-Defining the Right to a Fair Trial' 40 *Melbourne University Law Review* 207.

Gibson, F (2006) 'Extending Aid to the Unrepresented' 80 *Law Institute Journal* 59.

—— (2010) 'Article 13 of the Convention on the Rights of Persons With Disabilities: A Right to Legal Aid?' 15 *Australian Journal of Human Rights* 123.

Gibson, F and Noone, MA (2013) 'Going to Court: Access to Legal Assistance in Australia' in *Australian Courts: Serving Democracy and its Publics* (Canberra, Australian Institute of Judicial Administration Incorporated).

Giddings, J (ed) (1998) *Legal Aid in Victoria: At the Crossroads Again* (Melbourne, Fitzroy Legal Service Publishing).

Holmes, A (2015) *Some Economic Effects of Inequality*, available at: http://www.aph.gov.au/About_Parliament/Parliamentary_Departments/Parliamentary_Library/pubs/BriefingBook44p/EconEffects.

Hunter, R and De Simone, T (2009) 'Women, Legal Aid and Social Inclusion' 44 *Australian Journal of Social Issues* 379.

Law and Justice Foundation of New South Wales (2015) *What Works?*, available at: http://www.lawfoundation.net.au/ljf/app/&id=7B11620ED3302A0CCA257464001880F4.

Lee, J (2013) 'State Has 1950s Law and Order Policies: Dreyfus', *The Age*, 18 April 2013, available at: www.theage.com.au/victoria/state-has-1950s--lawandorder-policies-dreyfus-20130418-2i2g3.html.

Le Grand, C and Ferguson, J (2012) 'Soaring Family-related Violence Linked with Drugs and Poverty', *The Australian*, 4 September 2012.

Melbourne University Law School & Thomson Reuters (2015) *Australia: State of the Legal Market 2015 (Whitepaper)*, available at: insight.thomsonreuters.com.au/files/2015/11/Australia-State-of-the-Legal-Market-2015-report.pdf.

Mitchell, L (2011) *Domestic Violence in Australia: An Overview of the Issues*, available at: http://www.aph.gov.au/About_Parliament/Parliamentary_Departments/Parliamentary_Library/pubs/BN/2011-2012/DVAustralia.

National Legal Aid Advisory Committee [NLAAC] (1990) *Legal Aid for the Australian Community* (Canberra, Australian Government Printing Service).

Neave, M, Faulkner, P and Nicholson, T (2016) *Royal Commission into Family Violence: Summary and Recommendations*, available at: files.rcfv.com.au/Reports/Final/RCFV-All-Volumes.pdf.

Noone, MA (2012) 'Key Features of Integrated Legal Services: Lessons from West Heidelberg Community Legal Service' 37 *Alternative Law Journal* 26.

—— (2014) 'Legal Aid Crisis: Lessons from Victoria's Response' 39 *Alternative Law Journal* 40.

Noone, MA and Tomsen, S (2006) *Lawyers in Conflict: Australian Legal Aid* (Annandale NSW, Federation Press).

Paterson, A (1996) 'Financing Legal Services: A Comparative Perspective' in A Paterson and T Goriely (eds), *A Reader on Resourcing Civil Justice* (Oxford, Oxford University Press).

—— (2012) *The Hamlyn Lectures 2010: Lawyers and the Public Good: Democracy in Action?* (Cambridge, Cambridge University Press).

Pleasence, P, Coumarelos, C, Forell, S and McDonald, HM (2014) *Reshaping Legal Assistance Services: Building on the Evidence Base—A Discussion Paper* (Sydney, Law and Justice Foundation of New South Wales).

PricewaterhouseCoopers Australia (2015) *Criminal and Family Law Private Practitioner Service Delivery Model* (Melbourne, Law Institute of Victoria).

Productivity Commission (2014) *Access to Justice Arrangements Inquiry*, Report No 72, 5 September 2014 (Canberra, Productivity Commission).

Regan, F (1997) 'Rolls-Royce or Rundown 1970s Kingswood?' 22 *Alternative Law Journal* 225.

Royal Commission (2015) *Royal Commission into Family Violence* available at: www.rcfv.com.au/.

Savage, A (2014) 'PSOs: Vic Government, Police Command Appear at Odds over Roll-out of Protective Service Officers', *ABC News*, 15 July 2014, available at: www.abc.net.au/news/2014-07-14/vic-govt-and-police-appear-at-odds-over-train-pso-roll-out/5595596.

Senate Finance and Public Administration References Committee (2015) *Domestic Violence in Australia: Report*, available at: www.aph.gov.au/Parliamentary_Business/Committees/Senate/Finance_and_Public_Administration.

Smith, R (2014) *Digital Delivery of Legal Services to People on Low Incomes* (London, Legal Education Foundation).

Susskind, R (2013) *Tomorrow's Lawyers* (Oxford, Oxford University Press).

Tadros, E and Walsh, K (2015) 'Too Many Law Graduates and Not Enough Jobs' *Financial Review*, 22 October 2015.

Victoria Legal Aid (2012) *Seventeenth Statutory Annual Report 2011–12* (Melbourne), available at: www.legalaid.vic.gov.au/about-us/our-organisation/annual-reports.

—— (2015) *Twentieth Statutory Annual Report 2014–15* (Melbourne), available at: www.legalaid.vic.gov.au/about-us/our-organisation/annual-reports.

Warner, B (2013) *Review of the National Partnership Agreement: An Opportunity to Iron Out the Creases* (Conference Paper, National Access to Justice and Pro Bono Conference, March 2013).

Treaties, Conventions, Principles, Directives, Rules and Legislation

Legal Aid Act 1978 (Vic)

3

Rhyme and Reason in the Uncertain Development of Legal Aid in Australia

JEFF GIDDINGS[1]

I. Introduction

The phrase 'History does not repeat but it does rhyme', attributed to Mark Twain,[2] could be said to apply to Australian legal aid, as many of the issues faced by Australia's legal aid system in the 1980s and 1990s have resurfaced and are prominent today. Until the late 1960s, legal aid and concerns around access to justice were bit-players in Australian public policy discussions. In the 1970s, the emergence of community legal centres (CLCs) and the reformist zeal of the Whitlam Labor government and its Attorney-General, Lionel Murphy, led to a greater emphasis on the accessibility of justice. This included the Commonwealth Government's attempts to extend its existing Legal Service Bureaux (LSB) by establishing the Australian Legal Aid Office (ALAO); unprecedented tensions were generated by this Commonwealth initiative, which will be discussed in terms of its enduring legacy.

The late 1970s and 1980s saw the development of a robust mixed legal aid model, with the establishment of individual State and Territory Legal Aid Commissions (LACs). Distinctive and complementary services were provided by LACs, CLCs and the private legal profession. LACs and CLCs became important players in terms of both casework and policy development (see Buchanan, Chapter 8, this volume). Given that the history of CLCs is addressed elsewhere in this collection, this chapter will focus on LACs as the larger legal aid institutions that have

[1] This chapter draws on a range of publications including work I have co-authored with various colleagues. In particular, I have drawn on collaborations with Rosemary Hunter and Cate Banks, Chris Field and Mary Anne Noone, and a series of publications on self-help legal services written with Michael Robertson and Merran Lawler. I gratefully acknowledge the contributions of the various co-authors involved in those projects.

[2] Doubts have been raised regarding this attribution, see: quoteinvestigator.com/2014/01/12/history-rhymes/.

numerous service responsibilities, including providing a wide range of casework services to eligible clients, administering grants of legal assistance involving work completed by private legal practitioners and working with and administering government funding for CLCs.

Having inherited frameworks that saw the provision of legal assistance limited to the defence of serious criminal offences, LACs have made major contributions to the provision of a broad range of services to people needing to defend their liberty or assert their rights in a range of contexts. Legal aid arrangements in Australia have been framed by a set of key relationships, with the most important being that between the legal profession and governments—both State and federal. The profession resisted efforts to bureaucratise legal aid, emphasising the importance of preserving professional independence. The relationship between State and federal governments has also been crucial to shaping the work of LACs.

The growing realisation that legal aid funding could support the work of local law firms, especially in suburban and regional Australia, saw the private profession lobby for improvements in legal aid. While the private profession's support for legal aid has endured, its relationship with legal aid has changed with the development of preferred supplier models that see fewer firms taking on legal aid work, but doing so in larger volumes.

The Productivity Commission's (2014) *Access to Justice Arrangements* report identified LACs as receiving the majority of government access to justice funding. In the 2012–13 financial year, LACs received AU$609.5 million (£346.8 million) of the AU$786.4 million (£447.4 million) distributed among the four government-funded legal assistance providers (Productivity Commission 2014). Clearly, LACs play a key role in the discharge of a range of functions directed by government; yet they are not *part* of government. They have had to navigate a wide range of challenges related to representing the interests of marginalised clients in an increasingly challenging public policy environment.

This chapter examines the history of legal aid arrangements in Australia. It focuses on the work of LACs, as the statutory authorities responsible for overseeing the administration and delivery of legal services to those unable to secure their own private advice and representation. A brief account of the limited services that were available to those in need of legal representation prior to the development of more comprehensive schemes in the 1970s and 1980s is provided, and the chapter also reviews research on innovations in legal aid and the effective development of self-help legal services. The chapter closes by considering the seemingly cyclical nature of many of the issues facing legal aid in Australia. The chapter draws on research conducted by a range of scholars who have examined how and why various legal aid services developed, including Don Fleming, Francis Regan, Mary Anne Noone and Steven Tomsen.

II. Early Legal Aid Arrangements

Legal aid in Australia began with the adoption of British arrangements. The *In forma pauperis* rules that had operated in England since 1494 were adopted in the various Australian colonies and continued to operate until the late twentieth century (Robertson 2001).[3] Under this framework, lawyers were considered to have a responsibility to provide free or reduced-rate services to the poor and disadvantaged in deserving cases.[4] The tradition was that members of the 'gentleman's profession' should devote up to 10 per cent of their professional time to such charitable cases. This was the arrangement that resulted in defendants at the Eureka Stockade Treason Trial held in 1855 being represented free of charge by leading members of the Victorian Bar (Field and Giddings 1998: 20).[5]

The murder trial of Ned Kelly provides a stark example of the serious limitations of legal aid arrangements in colonial Australia in the late 1800s. Tried for the murder of four police officers at Stringybark Creek, Kelly was the country's most infamous outlaw and the most famous person to receive a Crown assignment of legal assistance (Phillips 1987). Crown assignments of legal assistance were available to people charged with capital crimes and to Indigenous Australians charged with indictable offences (Lynch 2001: 139). The perceived inadequacy of the Crown assignment and the availability of more lucrative alternative work meant that Kelly was represented by the least experienced barrister in Victoria, Henry Bindon, who had never previously appeared in the Supreme Court and who only met Kelly for the first time two days before the trial commenced (Phillips 1987: 33).

After being found guilty, following a trial lasting two days, Kelly was invited to address the court. He stated, in part:

> Well, it is rather too late for me to speak now. I thought of speaking this morning and all day, but there was little use and there is little use blaming anyone now. Nobody knew about my case except myself and I wish I had insisted upon being allowed to examine the witnesses myself. If I had examined them, I am confident I would have thrown a different light on the case. It is not that I fear death; I fear it as little as to drink a cup of tea … I lay blame on myself that I did not get up yesterday and examine the witnesses, but I thought that if I did so it would look bravado and flashness. (Phillips 1987: 97)

[3] Donald Robertson (2001) provides a very helpful account of the development of arrangements for the delivery of legal services to the economically and politically disadvantaged.

[4] Cases were considered deserving where they raised issues of equity, injustice and the need for Christian charity (Robertson 2001).

[5] The Eureka Rebellion involved miners on the Ballarat gold field (a town located approximately 72 miles or 116 kilometres from Melbourne, Victoria) rebelling against the levying of a substantial mining licence fee by the British colonial authorities. After a period of civil disobedience, growing militancy among the miners resulted in the establishment of a stockade that was overrun by colonial forces. Some 30 miners died, along with six soldiers and police officers. Some 120 'diggers' were detained after the rebellion, with 13 brought to trial for high treason. All were found not guilty (Dunn and Darby 1977).

This early concern with legal aid representation is reflective of recent critiques of the system in terms of the inadequacy of legal aid fees and the challenges generated by self-represented defendants, discussed in more detail below.

While the paupers' rules regarding access to legal services for civil matters were codified in Australia in the 1880s, they were rarely used in the early twentieth century. In 1927, the Victorian Attorney-General described the arrangements as 'utterly ineffective, noting that the rules had only been used twice in the previous 20 years, in the divorce jurisdiction'. Indeed, the rules had never been used in the general civil jurisdiction (Lynch 2001: 138). And there was no formal structure that addressed what types of cases were appropriate for free and reduced-fee legal services. In response, legislatures created schemes making legal assistance available in criminal appeals and indictable criminal trials, representing an extension beyond the previous focus on capital offences (Lynch 2001: 139).

Australia's first government-funded, salaried solicitors' practices were the Public Solicitor Offices (PSOs) established in South Australia (1925), Victoria (1928) and New South Wales (NSW) (1943) (Lynch 2001: 142). The PSOs' statutory monopoly over legal aid for indictable criminal trials and criminal appeals, together with their exclusive jurisdiction over civil matters involving the paupers' rules scheme, prompted tension with the private profession. In 1928, the president of the Law Institute of Victoria described the PSOs as open to abuse by the public, arguing that private litigants could be left facing unenforceable costs orders due to capricious funding decisions by the PSOs (Lynch 2001: 143).

The establishment of the NSW PSO in 1943 took salaried legal aid arrangements a step further by abandoning the paupers' rules for civil and matrimonial claims and removing the requirement for judges to issue a certificate in criminal matters. The Public Solicitor was instead empowered to grant legal assistance to applicants who had a reasonable case and met the means test. However, this drew criticism for representing the first step towards the nationalisation of the legal profession (Lynch 2001: 145).

The Australian Constitution did not confer responsibility for legal aid to the Commonwealth Parliament. The *Judiciary Act 1903* (Cth), passed by the newly established Commonwealth Parliament, enabled a person charged with an indictable offence against a Commonwealth law to apply to a judge in chambers for the appointment of defence counsel (Lynch 2001: 139–40). However, there were strict time-limits on the making of such an application and no application could be made if the offence was triable summarily or if the accused was charged pursuant to State laws. Further, the relevant section (section 69[3]) contained key phrases that were not clearly defined—for example, 'adequate means' and 'interests of justice' (Lynch 2001: 140).

One notable exception to the Commonwealth's limited engagement in legal aid service delivery was the Commonwealth LSB. The LSB was established in 1941 within the Attorney-General's Department to address the needs of the wives and children of servicemen serving overseas (Fleming and Regan 2006: 71). The programme was popular and effective during and after the Second World War, with its staffing complement peaking at more than 100 in 1946, before gradually declining. Following the war, unsuccessful attempts were made to extend the scheme to include social security recipients. By 1973, the LSB was estimated to have assisted more than 1.5 million clients from the armed services, including former service personnel and their families (Fleming and Regan 2006: 71).

Various developed nations established publicly funded legal aid schemes in the post-Second World War era and Australia was part of that trend. The 1950s and 1960s saw the development of 'judicare' schemes involving service delivery contributions from the private legal profession.[6] These schemes were the primary means of guaranteeing equality before the law and equal access to justice for all citizens, regardless of means (Regan 1999: 1). These welfare state schemes involved the provision of paid legal advice and representation to eligible people, either through in-house (staff) lawyers or payment schemes for the private legal profession (Regan 1999: 185).

One reason why legal aid in Australia has faced ongoing challenges in securing appropriate levels of support has been its ambivalent place in relation to the arrangements between different tiers of government. Since the Second World War, Australia's federation has become characterised by an 'unusually high degree of vertical fiscal imbalance' (Fenna 2008: 509) in favour of the Commonwealth. LACs and the services they run and support have always been closely tied to institutions managed by the various States and Territories, particularly the courts, the police and corrective services, yet Commonwealth (federal) funds are increasingly important to the legal assistance schemes administered by LACs. Unlike some key areas of human service provision such as health and education that form the focus of Commonwealth government departments, legal aid has been a secondary responsibility of the Attorney-General's Department. The department's main focus continues to be on the provision of legal advice to the government through the Australian Government Solicitor. This focus generated particular challenges for legal aid when the Department was given the task of developing the ALAO in 1973 and again when major funding cuts were imposed on the Department in 1996 and 2014. These challenges are addressed in the following parts of this chapter.

III. New Providers: A Broader Vision of Legal Aid

The late 1960s and early 1970s saw radicals and progressives engage with a range of access to justice issues. New legal service providers, in the form of CLCs, emerged during this period. There is a sizeable literature on the emergence and

[6] Judicare schemes involve decentralised arrangements whereby private legal practitioners deliver services to legal aid clients. See Fleming and Regan (2006) and Menkel-Meadow (1984).

development of CLCs in Australia (Basten 1987; Basten, Graycar and Neal 1983; Chesterman 1996; Giddings and Noone 2004; McCulloch and Blair 2012; Neal 1984; Noone and Tomsen 2006; Rice 1993; Smith 2015). CLCs are the subject of Buchanan (Chapter 8, this volume), and so will not be addressed in detail here, but a brief discussion of Aboriginal Legal Services follows.

The first CLC established in Australia was the NSW Aboriginal Legal Service (NSWALS). Police harassment of local Aboriginals in the Redfern area of Sydney saw the NSWALS start in 1969 as a voluntary service, involving a panel of lawyers prepared to represent Aboriginal people in the Sydney region. Public funding was then offered to the service in 1971, enabling the employment of a solicitor, an Aboriginal field officer and an Aboriginal secretary/receptionist. The NSWALS provided the basis for similar independent services in the various Australian States and Territories (Noone and Tomsen 2006: 66–67). The Aboriginal legal services were seen as having 'a more overtly political agenda' than other CLCs as 'they represented a significantly disadvantaged minority group which was notably troubled with police and legal problems' (Noone and Tomsen 2006: 232).[7]

Those seeking to reform access to justice arrangements were assisted by changing demographics, expanding social welfare systems and the actions of some in the legal profession. Additionally, from late 1972, the presence of a reformist Commonwealth Attorney-General, Lionel Murphy, with 'an unprecedented commitment to law reform' (Fleming and Regan 2006: 70), influenced significant legal aid developments. Murphy was interested in a wide range of access to justice initiatives. Along with the establishment of the Family Court and the Australian Law Reform Commission, Murphy was responsible for the implementation of the *Trade Practices Act 1974* (Cth) and the *Racial Discrimination Act 1975* (Cth). He also fostered the development of alternative dispute resolution, as well as driving the establishment of the ALAO (Fleming and Regan 2006: 69; Hocking 1997). Fleming and Regan (2006: 71) refer to the Whitlam government's decision to engage in national legal aid reform as a 'watershed event'.

Murphy was enthused by the grassroots models of legal service delivery he encountered in discussions with activists in the United States early in 1973, his visit to the recently established Fitzroy Legal Service (in Melbourne) and developments in Canada (Fleming and Regan 2006: 78; Noone and Tomsen 2006: 52). In a speech to the Australian Senate in December 1973, Murphy explained the decision to develop the ALAO in the following terms: '[The] government has taken action because it believes that one of the basic causes of inequality before the law is the absence of adequate and comprehensive legal aid arrangements throughout Australia'. (Fleming and Regan 2006: 74) Murphy faced resistance from the private legal profession, which since the 1960s had lobbied for the establishment of a

[7] The literature on the development and operation of Aboriginal Legal Services is less comprehensive than that for CLCs more generally (see Chapman 1984; Eggleston 1977; Faine 1993; Lyons 1984; Potter 1974).

judicare legal aid scheme that would be run by the profession, but subsidised by the state in line with 'the English scheme of Legal Aid' (Fleming and Regan 2006: 71). But Murphy argued instead for a Commonwealth-funded and managed approach to legal aid (Fleming and Regan 2006: 76). Making use of the existing LSB structure provided the Whitlam government with an alternative to permanently funding the various State judicare schemes. This administrative approach also avoided the possibility of the federal opposition blocking the legislation required to establish the ALAO as a new statutory authority (Fleming and Regan 2006: 76–77).

The establishment of the ALAO in 1973 was designed to enable the provision of assistance in matters arising from Commonwealth legislation. Key areas of Commonwealth law included social security, certain drug and customs offences, taxation offences, bankruptcy and divorce. The ALAO was also aimed at assisting people from groups for which the Commonwealth was viewed as having a special responsibility—these groups included Aboriginals and Torres Strait Islanders, newly arrived migrants, social security recipients and defence personnel who had served their country. These people became known in legal aid circles as 'Commonwealth persons' (Noone 1998: 191). For such 'Commonwealth persons', the federal government would pay for the legal work carried out on these 'Commonwealth matters'.

The ALAO was intended to involve an Australia-wide network of shopfront law offices, providing legal services with a dual emphasis on preventative law and impact litigation. This goal was chosen partly in recognition of the growing concern about low-income and disadvantaged people having very limited access to justice. There was seen to be a real benefit in all members of society having the opportunity to make use of the law and legal processes to assert their rights. Judicare schemes had focused on representation services and rarely provided non-litigation services such as legal advice and minor assistance, yet these latter services were to become a major part of the casework undertaken by ALAO staff (Fleming and Regan 2006: 78). Significantly, regional ALAO offices commenced visits to isolated areas that were not being serviced by private practitioners, and the ALAO also addressed areas of law that had previously not been covered by legal aid, such as environmental and conservation cases, racial discrimination and administrative review (Fleming and Regan 2006: 79).

However, the proposal to create the ALAO raised constitutional issues and the professional bodies representing the private legal profession initiated a legal challenge to its establishment. At an extraordinary general meeting in February 1975, the Law Institute of Victoria resolved to commence High Court proceedings. The issue of establishment of the ALAO was viewed as representing a conflict between 'the future of an independent and decent legal profession versus Marxist-socialist type state control' over the legal profession (Field and Giddings 1998: 27). The salaried employment of lawyers as public servants was characterised as undermining the legal profession's independence. It was asserted that the interests of clients would be best protected by maintaining the independence of lawyers, and that private lawyers would provide a superior service (Tomsen 1992: 314).

Following its election in November 1975, the Liberal–National Coalition government led by Malcolm Fraser did not proceed with further development of the ALAO. With its 'new federalism' policy, the incoming government entered negotiations with a view to encouraging each State to establish its own LAC, combining their various legal aid services. The new Attorney-General, Robert Ellicott, sought to involve the private profession in shaping policy development and delivery, and recognised the rights and responsibilities of the States in determining legal aid arrangements (Fleming and Regan 2006: 86). Western Australia was the first State to establish an LAC in 1976, followed by South Australia and the Australian Capital Territory in 1977, Victoria and Queensland in 1978 and NSW in 1979. The Northern Territory and Tasmanian ALAO offices were merged with new LACs in 1990 and 1991, respectively.

Divergent views exist regarding the success of the ALAO. In an excellent article, Fleming and Regan (2006) refer to many commentators having described the ALAO as a failure, with some referring to the lack of planning and haste with which the organisation was established. They particularly note Armstrong's analysis that the ALAO proposal suffered from three further limitations. First, there was a lack of support from the States in a context in which the Commonwealth faced constitutional limitations on its right to legislate regarding legal aid. Secondly, the Whitlam government's inability to control the Senate meant that the ALAO was not established as an independent authority outside the control of the Commonwealth Attorney-General's Department. Further, the legal profession was hostile to the ALAO proposal. In view of these impediments, it is important to recognise the significant contributions made by the ALAO in making a broader range of legal services available to people, with a focus on delivering services beyond litigation (Fleming and Regan 2006: 89). Indeed, the push to develop the ALAO appears to have also played an important part in the development of the mixed legal aid service delivery model that has served Australia well.

A. The Law and Poverty in Australia Inquiry

A Commission of Inquiry into Poverty was established in 1972 by the McMahon Liberal government. The Commission's broad terms of reference prompted a group of academics to meet to discuss problems relating to law and social justice. This led to the establishment of a special inquiry into the relationship between law and poverty, chaired by Professor Ronald Sackville (Partington 1977: 201–2). In November 1974, Sackville released a discussion paper on legal aid that referred to 'grave deficiencies in the present system' that could 'only be overcome by the establishment and development of a network of neighbourhood or local law centres, employing salaried lawyers' along with paralegals and specialist non-lawyers (Australian Commission of Inquiry into Poverty 1974). Sackville saw the ALAO as only an interim solution and noted that its operation within the

Attorney-General's Department left its salaried lawyers without an 'effectively and demonstrably guaranteed' independence (Fleming and Regan 2006: 80).

The Sackville Inquiry Report 'Law and Poverty in Australia' (1975) was submitted to the Whitlam government in October 1975 shortly before the government was dismissed by the Governor-General. The Report proposed a wide range of reforms across areas of law that impacted significantly on disadvantaged Australians, noting the harsh impacts of such laws on non-English-speaking migrants, Aboriginal people, homeless people and juvenile offenders (Sackville 1995: 212). Sackville (1995: 213) and others subsequently identified that the Report contained insufficient coverage of certain issues, such as the impact of the legal system on women and the elderly, the role of the legal profession and the operation of adversarial justice (Field and Giddings 1998: 28). Nonetheless, in 1990 the National Legal Aid Advisory Committee (NLAAC) described the Sackville report as 'an important research document for its examination of the major legal aid schemes, the role of governments and legal aid agencies and legal aid strategies' (NLAAC 1990: 31–32). Sackville then chaired the Commonwealth Government's Access to Justice Advisory Committee that presented a very comprehensive report in 1994, laying the platform for the *Justice Statement* delivered by the Keating Labor Commonwealth Government in early 1995. From the mid-1980s, legal aid schemes began to be cut back for both cost and ideological reasons (Banks, Hunter and Giddings 2006: 2). The next section sets out some of the impacts of these cuts on legal aid and LACs during the 1990s.

IV. Targeting Legal Aid: Focusing on Efficiency

The late 1980s and early 1990s was a dynamic period that saw legal aid policy issues raised and addressed by a number of interested parties. The start of this period can be marked by the 1985 publication of the *Legal Aid Task Force Report*. The Task Force was made up of five public servants—a narrow membership that saw the Report criticised by the LACs, the private profession, legal professional associations and CLCs (Noone and Tomsen 2006: 153). Subsequently, a more consultative approach was taken in efforts to develop legal aid policy. The NLAAC and the National Legal Aid Representative Council were both established by the Commonwealth Government in 1986 and sought to involve the private profession, LACs and CLCs in examining a range of legal aid issues. In 1990, the NLAAC released a major report, *Legal Aid for the Australian Community*. The key features of the Report were the endorsement of Australia's mixed model of legal aid service delivery, involving LACs and CLCs, as well as the private profession, arguing for a 'solution-oriented' approach to programme management to replace the existing 'services-orientation' and calling for a set of national legal aid principles and guidelines.

The capacity of interested parties to actively pursue changes to legal aid arrangements following the release of the NLAAC report was limited by the difficult financial times generated by what then Federal Treasurer Paul Keating described as 'a recession that Australia had to have'.[8] The collapse of several financial institutions, including the State Banks of Victoria and South Australia, understandably preoccupied governments during this period. While the Commonwealth contributed 55 per cent of legal aid funding, State governments were able to reduce the direct contributions they made to legal aid by legislating to direct that interest earned on funds held in lawyers trust accounts would be used for purposes including legal aid funding. While interest rates were at record levels in the late 1980s and early 1990s, trust account interest covered much of the 45 per cent of legal aid funding that each State was expected to provide (Field 1998; Noone and Tomsen 2006: 155–6). However, once interest rates dropped significantly in 1991–92, State governments were obliged to contribute to legal aid at unprecedented levels. For example, in Victoria, the Solicitors Guarantee Fund's contribution to legal aid fell by 90 per cent between 1992 and 1994, from AU$17 million (£9.67 million) to AU$1.5 million (£850,000), leaving the State government to meet the shortfall (Field 1998: 92).

The early 1990s also saw court judgments that impacted directly on the capacity of LACs to determine priorities for the granting of legal assistance. The High Court's 1992 judgment in *Dietrich v The Queen* (1992) 177 CLR 292 extended the importance attached to legal representation in terms of courts meeting their duty to ensure that accused persons are not tried unfairly (Zdenkowski 1994). To facilitate this, trial judges were held to have discretion to stay or adjourn a criminal trial to ensure fairness. Five of the seven members of the Court held that, where an unrepresented accused is facing a serious charge, the discretion to grant a stay or adjournment should be exercised in their favour unless there are exceptional circumstances (Giddings 1998: 9).

The Dietrich judgment generated significant tension between LACs and their respective State governments. Sackville (1995: 214) described the case as having 'fundamentally altered the balance between the authority of the trial court and government or legal aid bodies responsible for financing legal aid'. The Victorian Government chose not to provide additional funds to enable the State LAC to provide representation in all affected cases. Instead, it legislated to give judges the power to order that legal aid be granted in circumstances where they were satisfied that the Court would otherwise be unable to ensure that an accused, not being able to afford the full cost of legal representation, would receive a fair trial (Giddings and Noone 1998: 40).

The 1994 judgment of the Full Family Court in *Re K* saw a similar broadening of the circumstances in which the Court could order that separate legal

[8] Keating made this now famous statement on 29 November 1990. See: www.uow.edu.au/~bmartin/pubs/92freedom.html.

representation be provided for children involved in proceedings before the Family Court. The Court specified 13 circumstances in which a separate child representative should be appointed. While some States, such as Queensland, were already paying for substantial numbers of separate child representatives, others, such as Victoria, faced increased costs in this area (Giddings 1998: 9).

The mid-1990s saw a series of moves to make Australia's legal processes more accessible. In 1994, the Law Council of Australia called for the Commonwealth Government to raise its legal aid funding by AU$50 million (£28.45 million) in order to restore legal aid eligibility to 1987–88 levels. The same year saw the release of landmark reports from the Access to Justice Advisory Committee (AJAC) and the Australian Law Reform Commission's reference on legal equality for women. The AJAC report identified a series of matters impacting on the demand for legal aid services, including: economic conditions (poor economic conditions could result in more people meeting the legal aid means test); population changes; law enforcement (greater resources being directed to particular areas of law); the extent of legislative activity and change; the growth of more flexible legal rules; changes in community behaviour, such as greater levels of family breakdown; recognition of broader legal obligations related to legal assistance; greater community expectations; and cost increases beyond the rate of inflation (AJAC 1994: 240–42).

In response to the AJAC report and in the lead-up to a federal election, the Keating government released the *Justice Statement* (1995). The *Justice Statement* addressed a broad range of issues affecting access to justice, including alternative dispute resolution, reform of the legal profession, crime prevention, a National Women's Justice Strategy and a commitment to the promotion of human rights. The statement also indicated the Commonwealth's intention to take a more active role in the setting of legal aid policies and priorities. Legal aid funding was to be increased by almost AU$70 million (£39.83 million) nationally over a four-year period, with a focus on civil and family law, as well as providing non-means-tested legal advice (Giddings and Noone 1998: 47). Unfortunately, much of this funding never materialised following the election of the Howard government in early 1996. Instead, the 1996 federal budget earmarked legal aid for a AU$100 million (£57 million) funding cut to be implemented between 1997–98 and 2000–01 (Giddings 1998: 3; Noone 2001: 40). Legal aid ended up bearing the brunt of the funding cuts imposed on the Attorney-General's Department, leading Regan (1997: 226) to suggest that this targeting was symbolic of ongoing internal hostility towards legal aid.

By the mid-1990s, Australian LACs were operating under capped budgets, levied substantial contributions from clients (Giddings and Field 1998: 51) and, in some cases, limited the authority of some private lawyers to undertake legal aid work (Giddings 1998: 69). Legal aid for civil matters other than family law was not widely available. Franchising and competitive tendering arrangements were introduced for the first time with a view to improving the quality of legal work undertaken on legally assisted cases. Legal Aid Queensland (LAQ) first tendered out duty lawyer services in 1992 (Noone 2001: 47), while Victoria drew on developments in England and Wales, where a comprehensive and systematic approach was under way to develop and test new frameworks to define, measure and monitor the quality of legal aid services (Giddings 1996: 361). A small-scale franchising pilot was conducted in Victoria in 1994, and in 1995, LAQ tendered out the conduct of prescribed criminal cases. LAQ then implemented a preferred supplier scheme in 1998 (Noone 2001: 47–48). Preferred supplier schemes are now more comprehensive and LACs have closer integration of services with those firms that have the authority to take on legal aid cases.

The mid-1990s also saw LACs introduce fee caps that limited the amount of legal aid expenditure for any one applicant's involvement in a case (Noone 2001: 52). This was justified on the basis of encouraging the more efficient conduct of legal aid cases and spreading available legal aid funds further. South Australia was the first LAC to introduce such caps, in 1991, while NSW, Queensland and Victoria all followed suit in 1996. 'Fee ceilings' were incorporated into the Commonwealth–State legal aid funding agreements that came into effect in mid-1997. Particular concerns were raised regarding the impact of these caps on women involved in family law-related legal processes because the retrospective application of caps meant that no further assistance was available for those assisted persons who had already reached the cap (Noone 2001: 52–53).

In keeping with the growing public sector focus on targeting and efficiency, LACs also had their governance arrangements altered. The organisational structure of various LACs was changed to reflect a more corporate ethos, with Victoria taking the lead in 1995. The broadly representative 11-member LAC was replaced by a five-member Board of Management for Victoria Legal Aid (VLA) (Noone 2001: 42–43). The independence of LACs was also fettered by provisions enabling the responsible government minister to direct the LAC in relation to the performance of its functions or exercise of its duties (Giddings 1998: 1; Noone 2001: 42).

LACs also moved from a 'service orientation' (concerned with the provision of particular types of services) to a 'solution-oriented' approach that was designed to assist consumers to find their own solutions to problems by less expensive means, particularly by accessing information rather than representation. This move was hastened by a number of factors, including the 20 per cent cut to the legal aid funds contributed by the Commonwealth government from 1 July 1997, and the targeting of Commonwealth funding towards matters involving Commonwealth law, thereby leaving the States with responsibility for the provision of legal aid for most criminal cases (Fleming 2000: 347).

The more cooperative approach to legal aid funding between Commonwealth and State levels of government was replaced by a purchaser–provider model under which State LACs became contracted providers of services purchased by the Commonwealth as principal (Fleming 2000: 358; Noone 2001: 44). The availability of new technologies also enabled the delivery of legal information and advice via methods such as the internet, interactive computer systems and videoconferencing, which depart from the traditional, face-to-face lawyer–client relationship (see McKay Chapter 6, this volume, for a discussion of more recent technological advancements in this realm). LACs in Victoria and Queensland took the lead in making use of new technology. There was also increased promotion of alternative dispute resolution mechanisms, and the associated philosophy that people with legal problems are better served by avoiding rather than engaging in litigation (Hunter 2003).

V. The Potential and Limitations of Legal Aid Services

In the face of this challenging policy environment, LACs were encouraged and supported by the Commonwealth to develop new modes of service delivery. A key criticism of these developments has been that some such services have been offered not as a supplement to, but as a substitute for, traditional individual casework in circumstances where representation services were needed. Greater breadth of service provision has not always been coupled with an appreciation of the limits of the various forms of service.

These new, non-traditional forms of legal aid services have included the use of videoconferencing and other technology to provide legal advice and community legal education to clients in remote areas, along with expanded telephone advice and information services. LAC websites became much more extensive, providing legal information and kits designed to support people to manage their own legal work. Information kiosks were also developed and placed in courts and other public places. There has also been a new focus on collective rather than individual forms of service delivery, such as child support forums and divorce workshops, along with the introduction of alternative dispute resolution (conferencing) processes as a precondition, and in some instances, a substitute, for litigation legal aid. These service innovations have been particularly prominent in the family law area, with greater reliance on duty lawyer schemes providing limited, one-off legal assistance at court (Banks et al 2006: 4).

A major research project conducted at Griffith University from 2003–06, the Australian Legal Aid Innovations Research Project, examined the suitability and effectiveness of various innovative services (duty lawyer services, group-based services, self-help kits and technology-based services) and found that alternative approaches to legal service provision can work effectively where full legal representation is not necessary or economically viable (Banks et al 2006: 233). The findings in relation to duty lawyer services, for example, illustrated how an advocacy service provided in court can ameliorate some of the immediate challenges of self-representation. While group-based services can be highly effective in disseminating generic information, they need to be augmented by a complementary service that includes legal advice. The Child Support Forum offered by Legal Aid Western Australia provided an exemplar of how such augmented service delivery can work very well (Banks et al 2006: 233). It provided participants with useful information on a specific legal issue and had a well-designed feedback mechanism in place, and its performance was monitored regularly. The forum also acknowledged and sought to address participants' unmet need for individual legal advice by specifically building in an appointment process to enable them to obtain that advice. The forum, therefore, was designed to augment individual advice, by giving clients basic information about the child support scheme before they saw a lawyer (Banks et al 2006: 92).

Trialling different types of services and modes of delivery is an obvious function of large-scale legal service providers seeking to address the needs of disadvantaged groups in the most cost-effective way, and it is inevitable that not all of these experiments will succeed. However, all new services need to be planned with clear and achievable objectives in mind. In some instances, the objectives of the services studied in the Australian Legal Aid Innovations Research Project appear never to have been clear, to have been forgotten or to have been so broad as to provide little guidance to service providers (Banks et al 2006). The goals and objectives of any service should provide the basis for its detailed design and implementation, and for subsequent evaluation of its effectiveness (Banks et al 2006: 234).

The Australian Legal Aid Innovations Research Project further found that many legal aid service innovations were designed more to satisfy the needs of their providers than those of their consumers. The desire to respond to a perceived crisis, to deploy a particular technology or to take advantage of a particular source of funding sometimes appeared to take priority over meeting the actual needs of intended users. To avoid this, Banks et al (2006: 234) recommended that new services be designed in consultation with prospective users in order to ensure that their legal needs are appropriately addressed. This should involve identification of the intended target groups, determination of how those target groups can best be assisted, and realistic negotiation of an achievable service (Banks et al 2006: 234).

VI. Community Legal Education, Self-Help and Legal Literacy

The development of the ALAO and CLCs has meant that, since the 1970s, Australian legal aid services have included a range of 'outside litigation' options, such as free legal information and advice, community legal education and do-it-yourself kits, in place of a sole focus on litigation support (Giddings and Robertson 2001). Such 'outside litigation' options were strongly promoted by CLC workers during the 1970s and 1980s on the basis that they would empower citizens to use the law for themselves, and were important in reducing reliance on lawyers (Regan 1999: 199). LACs also became increasingly prominent in the provision of community legal education, with Victoria, South Australia and Queensland taking a significant lead in this area. For example, in NSW, the Legal Information Access Centre operated by the State Library became a prominent provider of legal information through its network of local libraries.

But the late 1990s saw increased scepticism among CLC workers and others regarding the over-reliance on self-help and similar outside litigation options, especially for disadvantaged clients. The concern expressed was particularly related to the replacement of more substantial legal aid services with self-help mechanisms, which many people may find relatively inaccessible and difficult to use (Robertson and Giddings 2002: 68–69; see also Laster and Kornhauser, Chapter 7, this volume). Regan (1999) and Hunter (2003) have both identified that litigation and outside litigation legal aid services should be viewed as complementary, and that legal aid schemes need to balance their provision of these different types of services; but the Commonwealth Government has actively encouraged LACs to develop alternative services to litigation legal aid, and to adopt service innovations developed by other Commissions. Within this culture, innovations have been invested with a high symbolic value, but, as noted earlier, less attention has been paid to assessing their quality, effectiveness and efficiency (Banks et al 2006: 5).

The Legal Self-Help Research Project I conducted with colleagues between 2006 and 2008 found that self-help legal resources can assist those who either choose or are obliged to engage in the resolution of their own legal problems. However, the utility of these resources is heavily dependent upon a clear and close alignment between the goals and motivations of the providers and the immediate practical needs of the users. Three key variables appear to influence the effectiveness of legal self-help resources: (1) the nature and complexity of the legal work to be attempted; (2) the context in which self-help legal work is to be performed, including whether it is adversarial and litigious in nature; and (3) the variable characteristics of the self-helpers themselves (Robertson and Giddings 2014: 124–25). Equipping legal self helpers with relevant information, guidance and know-how, so that they become effective self-helpers, is often, but not always, possible. Printed materials in kit- and guide-form tend to work best when users already possess certain relevant skills (including adequate literacy skills to enable completion of forms) and at least a basic knowledge of the relevant legal domain. We also found that when the producers of self-help resources are motivated by a concern to create 'informed citizens' rather than 'effective legal self-helpers', there is a risk that such resources may hinder rather than help those in need (Lawler, Giddings and Robertson 2012). For example, they may present a complex legal task as straightforward, based on assumed knowledge. Self-help resources that focus on explaining the procedural steps associated with a legal process or transaction are likely to encourage users to draw on existing skills and legal knowledge to achieve worthwhile and helpful legal outcomes. Likewise, we argue that the design of self-help resources should focus on the user and the legal tasks at hand rather than on the wider reaches of the law and what it means for citizens in general (Lawler et al 2012).

VII. Conclusion: The Rhyme in the History of Australian Legal Aid

As noted in the introduction, Mark Twain's phrase 'History does not repeat but it does rhyme' appears to resonate with the history of Australian legal aid. Many of the issues faced by Australia's legal aid system in the early twentieth century and again in the 1980s and 1990s have resurfaced today. These issues revolve around the key relationships between government, the legal profession, LACs and CLCs. Tension between government and the profession emerged as early as the 1920s in relation to the PSOs' statutory monopoly on legal aid for serious criminal matters. The profession strongly resisted the Whitlam government's move to establish the ALAO in the early 1970s and subsequently sought to maintain and increase its share of the legal aid 'pie'.

The history of legal aid in Australia shows the value of a mixed model of service delivery involving LACs, CLCs and the private profession. The services these providers contribute should be viewed as complementary. LAC staff have developed significant expertise in particular legal areas, while CLCs have focused their attention on harnessing the involvement of community volunteers and providing information and advice services. LACs and CLCs should both be involved in harnessing new technology to make legal information and advice provision as accessible as possible. They also have a particularly important role to play in supporting effective and equitable access to legal services for people living in rural and regional areas, where private legal services are less accessible. The different roles of CLCs and LACs can be seen to extend to their advocacy in relation to the broader justice system. The National Association of Community Legal Centres, for example, has a stronger focus on submissions and advocacy than does National Legal Aid.

The private profession continues to be the largest provider of legal aid services and plays an important role in ensuring that the profession remains closely engaged with fostering the accessibility of the law and legal processes across the community. Private practitioners have the capacity to provide the representation services required by many people facing legal problems. Like CLCs, suburban law firms also play a vital role in providing people with access to advice in order to prepare them to effectively address their legal issues.

In 1995–96, Prime Minister John Howard's Liberal–National Coalition government instituted cuts to Commonwealth spending on legal aid as part of its response to a federal funding 'black hole'. In 2014–15, the Federal Coalition Government led by then Prime Minister Tony Abbott proposed similar cuts as part of its response to a federal 'budget emergency'. While CLCs have had some success in resisting the most recent cuts, LACs have not received the same level of support for their efforts to resist these changes. LACs continue to lack the champions and advocates they need to publicise and promote their contributions to access to justice, and this is problematic for them moving forward.

Like all legal service providers, LACs have long faced challenges in relation to conflict-of-interest concerns. This has been a particular difficulty in relation to duty lawyer services, with parties unable to access LAC services because other LAC staff have already advised the other party involved. The *Australian Innovations in Legal Aid Services Report* highlighted these issues in 2006 and emphasised the need for action (Banks et al 2006). It is encouraging to see that information protocols are now being used to address this continuing limitation on the availability of some legal aid services, but LACs also need to respond to continuing challenges in relation to increasing numbers of court users who are wholly or partially self-represented (see Laster and Kornhauser, Chapter 7, and Spencer, Chapter 5, this volume, for a discussion of these concerns in the Australian context; and Byrom Chapter 12, this volume, for a discussion in the UK context).

Delivering on the promise of legal aid in the 1970s and 1980s was always going to be a great challenge. Partnerships and collaborations with law firms, CLCs, universities and non-government organisations can be important in building the support base for LACs and legal aid more generally. In this regard, it is worth noting that LAQ played a leading role in the establishment of the Queensland Public Interest Law Clearing House in 2002 and that partnerships involving different legal service providers have been important in providing responses to the legal needs generated by natural disasters, such as the 2009 Black Saturday fires in Victoria and the 2011 floods in South-East Queensland.[9] Working collaboratively has thus enabled legal aid service providers to make more effective contributions and is an important way to move forward in responding to 'history-repeating' challenges.

References

Access to Justice Advisory Committee [AJAC] (1994) *Access to Justice: An Action Plan* (Canberra, AJAC).

Australian Commission of Inquiry into Poverty (1974) *Discussion Paper: Law and Poverty in Australia* (Commissioner: R Sackville) (Canberra, Australian Government Printing Service).

Banks, C, Hunter, R and Giddings, J (2006) *Australian Innovations in Legal Aid Services: Balancing Cost and Client Needs* (Brisbane, Socio-Legal Research Centre, Griffith University).

Basten, J (1987) 'Legal Aid and Community Legal Centres' 61 *Australian Law Journal* 714.

[9] The Black Saturday fires of 7 February 2009 burnt across much of the State of Victoria, causing the deaths of 173 people and displacing 7,500 people. The South-East Queensland floods of January 2011 caused 21 deaths and inundated more than 25,000 homes.

Basten, J, Graycar, R and Neal, D (1983) 'Legal Centres in Australia' 6 *University of New South Wales Law Journal* 163.

Chapman, M (1984) 'Aboriginal Legal Service: A Black Perspective' in D Neal (ed), *On Tap, Not on Top: Legal Centres in Australia 1972–1982* (Melbourne, Legal Service Bulletin Cooperative).

Chesterman, J (1996) *Poverty Law and Social Change: The Story of the Fitzroy Legal Service* (Oxford, Oxford University Press).

Commonwealth Attorney-General's Department (1995) *Justice Statement* (Barton, The Department).

Dunn, M and Darby, R (1977) 'The Aftermath' in G Gold (ed), *Eureka: Rebellion beneath the Southern Cross* (Melbourne, Rigby).

Eggleston, E (1977) 'Aboriginal Legal Services' in R Berndt (ed), *Aborigines and Change: Australia in the 1970s* (Canberra, Australian Institute of Aboriginal Studies).

Faine, J (1993) *Lawyers in the Alice: Aboriginals and Whitefellas' Law* (Annandale NSW, Federation Press).

Fenna, A (2008) *Commonwealth Fiscal Power and Australian Federalism* 31 *University of New South Wales Law Journal* 509.

Field, C (1998) 'Interest on Trust Accounts: Declining Legal Aid Funds' in J Giddings (ed), *Legal Aid in Victoria: At the Crossroads Again* (Melbourne, Fitzroy Legal Service Publishing).

Field, C and Giddings J (1998) 'A History of Legal Aid in Victoria' in J Giddings (ed), *Legal Aid in Victoria: At the Crossroads Again* (Melbourne, Fitzroy Legal Service Publishing).

Fleming, D (2000) 'Australian Legal Aid under the First Howard Government' 33 *University of British Colombia Law Review* 343.

Fleming, D and Regan, F (2006) 'Revisiting the Origins, Rise and Demise of the Australian Legal Aid Office' 13 *International Journal of the Legal Profession* 69.

Giddings, J (1996) 'Legal Aid Franchising: Food for Thought or Production Line Legal Services' 22 *Monash Law Review* 344.

—— (1998) 'Legal Aid: At the Crossroads Again' in J Giddings (ed), *Legal Aid in Victoria: At the Crossroads Again* (Melbourne, Fitzroy Legal Service Publishing).

Giddings J and Field, C (1998) 'Client Contributions: Lawyers on Hire Purchases' in J Giddings (ed), *Legal Aid in Victoria: At the Crossroads Again* (Melbourne, Fitzroy Legal Service Publishing).

Giddings, J and Noone, MA (1998) 'Recent Developments in Legal Aid in Victoria' in J Giddings (ed), *Legal Aid in Victoria: At the Crossroads Again* (Melbourne, Fitzroy Legal Service Publishing).

—— (2004) 'Australian Community Legal Centres Move into the 21st Century' 11 *International Journal of the Legal Profession* 215.

Giddings, J and Robertson, M (2001) '"Informed Litigants with Nowhere to Go": Self-help Legal Aid Services in Australia' 26 *Alternative Law Journal* 184.

Hocking, J (1997) *Lionel Murphy: A Political Biography* (Cambridge, Cambridge University Press).

Hunter, R (2003) 'Adversarial Mythologies: Policy Assumptions and Research Evidence in Family Law' 30 *Journal of Law and Society* 156.

Lawler, M, Giddings, J and Robertson, M (2012) 'Opportunities and Limitations in the Provision of Self-Help Legal Resources to Citizens in Need' 30 *Windsor Yearbook of Access to Justice* 187.

Lynch, J (2001) 'Early Australian Statutory Legal Aid Scheme and the Legal Profession' 19 *Law in Context* 138.

Lyons, G (1984) 'Aboriginal Legal Services' in P Hanks and B Keon-Cohen (eds), *Aborigines and the Law* (Melbourne, George Allen and Unwin).

McCulloch, J and Blair, M (2012) 'From Maverick to Mainstream: Forty Years of Community Legal Centres' 37 *Alternative Law Journal* 12.

Menkel-Meadow, C (1984) 'Legal Aid in the United States: The Professionalization and Politicization of Legal Services in the 1980's' 22 *Osgoode Hall Law Journal* 29.

National Legal Aid Advisory Committee (1990) *Legal Aid for the Australian Community* (Canberra, Australian Government Publishing Service).

Neal, D (ed) (1984) *On Tap, Not on Top: Legal Centres in Australia 1972–1982* (Melbourne, Legal Service Bulletin Cooperative).

Noone, MA (1998) 'The Future of Legal Aid' in J Giddings (ed), *Legal Aid in Victoria: At the Crossroads Again* (Melbourne, Fitzroy Legal Service Publishing).

—— (2001) 'The State of Australian Legal Aid' 29 *Federal Law Review* 37.

Noone, MA and Tomsen, S (2006) *Lawyers in Conflict: Australian Lawyers and Legal Aid* (Annandale NSW, Federation Press).

Partington, M (1977) 'Reports of Committees: Australian Government Commission of Inquiry Into Poverty—Law and Poverty Series' 40 *Modern Law Review* 201.

Phillips, J (1987) *The Trial of Ned Kelly* (Melbourne, Law Books).

Potter, C (1974) 'Poverty Law Practice: The Aboriginal Legal Service in New South Wales' 7 *Sydney Law Review* 237.

Productivity Commission (2014) *Access to Justice Arrangements Inquiry*, Report No. 72, 5 September (Canberra, Productivity Commission).

Regan, F (1997) 'Rolls Royce or Rundown 1970s Kingswood?' 22 *Alternative Law Journal* 225.

—— (1999) 'Why Do Legal Aid Services Vary between Societies? Re-examining the Impact of Welfare States and Legal Families' in F Regan, A Paterson, T Goriely and D Fleming (eds), *The Transformation of Legal Aid: Comparative and Historical Studies* (Oxford, Oxford University Press).

Rice, S (1993) 'Community Legal Centres, Steam Trains and Bourgeois Management' 18 *Alternative Law Journal* 86.

Robertson, D (2001) 'Pro Bono as a Professional Legacy' 19 *Law in Context* 97.

Robertson, M and Giddings, J (2002) 'Legal Consumers as Co-producers: The Changing Face of Legal Service Delivery in Australia' 40 *Family Court Review* 63.

—— (2014) 'Self-Advocates in Civil Legal Disputes: How Personal and Other Factors Influence the Handling of Their Cases' 38 *Melbourne University Law Review* 1, 119.

Sackville, R (1995) 'From Law and Poverty to Access to Justice' 20 *Alternative Law Journal* 212.

Smith, S (2015) 'Springvale Legal Service: The Coming of a Community Legal Centres Movement' in S Blackburn (ed), *Breaking Out: Memories of Melbourne in the 1970s* (Sydney, Hale & Iremonger).

Tomsen, S (1992) 'Professionalism and State Engagement: Lawyers and Legal Aid Policy in Australia in the 1970s and 1980s' 28 *Australian and New Zealand Journal of Sociology* 307.

Zdenkowski, G (1994) 'Defending the Indigent Accused in Serious Cases: A Legal Right to Counsel?' 18 *Criminal Law Journal* 135.

Treaties, Conventions, Principles, Directives, Rules and Legislation

Judiciary Act 1903 (Cth)
Trade Practices Act 1974 (Cth) and the *Racial Discrimination Act 1975* (Cth)

Cases

R v Dietrich (1992) 177 CLR 292

4

The Rise and Decline of Criminal Legal Aid in England and Wales

TOM SMITH AND ED CAPE

I. Introduction

England and Wales comprised one of the first jurisdictions to introduce a comprehensive criminal legal aid system. In less than three decades, from the 1970s, criminal legal aid was developed so that all suspects arrested and held in custody by the police were entitled to non-means-tested legal aid, and most defendants appearing in criminal courts (other than in respect of minor offences) could rely on state support to cover the costs of their defence. Criminal defence came to be a specialist branch of the legal profession, with solicitors' practices devoted to it, and a range of strategies were adopted that were designed to improve and assure quality. The criminal justice system came to rely on defendants being represented by a lawyer, adopting procedures designed to save time and costs that were reliant on legal representation. Yet, by the middle of the 1990s, even as lawyers were being encouraged to adopt specialist, legal aided practices and to assure the quality of the services that they provided, the seeds of decline were already being sown. Remuneration for legal aid work began to decline in real terms, and relationships between the Ministry of Justice (MoJ) and the legal aid authorities on the one hand, and legal aid lawyers and their professional bodies on the other—a relationship that was always likely to be tense—became increasingly fractious. Most importantly, governments increasingly failed to recognise the essential role of legal aid in ensuring a fair and just criminal justice system and ultimately determined that legal aid should suffer the same fate as other parts of the welfare state.

In this chapter we argue, with regret, that the prospects for criminal legal aid in England and Wales are bleak. We begin by tracing the development of the modern system of criminal legal aid from its inception as an essential element of the welfare state following the Second World War, to its peak in the 1990s. We then describe and analyse its decline, arguing that, while the need for economy and efficiency, especially following the global financial crisis of 2007–08, has been used to rationalise government policy in the first decade and a half of the twenty-first century, the roots of that decline are deeper, and reflect an antipathy not only to state welfare provision but also to procedural justice and fair trial. This is followed by an examination of the likely impact of both budget cuts and changes to the arrangements for managing and delivering criminal legal aid. While there are grounds for optimism at the international level, with both the United Nations (UN) and the European Union (EU) recognising the fundamental importance of legal aid in underpinning justice and fair trial, successive British governments have lacked a commitment to developing and sustaining a high-quality criminal legal aid system.

II. The Rise of Criminal Legal Aid

Schemes for assisting indigent defendants appearing before the criminal courts have existed in England and Wales since at least the early part of the twentieth century.[1] The Rushcliffe Committee, reporting in 1945 in the same month as the war in Europe ended, made relatively modest recommendations regarding criminal legal aid. While these were broadly accepted by the government, it was not until the 1960s, when the relevant provisions of the *Legal Aid and Advice Act 1949* were implemented, that the expansion of the criminal legal aid scheme really began. In the 1950s, very few defendants appearing in magistrates' courts received legal aid: in 1955, 0.3 per cent of defendants dealt with summarily in magistrates' court and less than 10 per cent of those appearing in committal proceedings were granted legal aid (Report of the Departmental Committee on Legal Aid in Criminal Proceedings 1966). However, by 1980, there were 330,000 grants of legal aid annually in magistrates' courts, a twofold increase compared to 1970 (McConville et al 1994: 300). By 2002–03, the number of grants of legal aid in magistrates' courts had increased to nearly 600,000 (Legal Services Commission [LSC] 2003: 50).[2] This expansion was mirrored by an increase in criminal legal aid expenditure. In 1966–67, less than £600,000 (AU$1 million) were spent on magistrates' court legal aid, but by 1982–83 expenditure had risen to £54 million (AU$95 million), increasing to £169 million (AU$297 million) in 1990, while in 2002–03 the cost of magistrates' court legal aid amounted to more than £300 million (AU$527.2 million). In that year, the cost of all forms of criminal legal aid was over £1 billion (AU$1.76 billion), a quarter of which was accounted for by Crown Court and higher courts' representation (LSC 2003: 50).

[1] See, for example, the *Poor Prisoners' Defence Act 1930*. For an account of the history of criminal legal aid in England and Wales, see Goriely (1996) and Hynes (2012).

[2] The numbers are not directly comparable since the LSC figures include only orders in respect of which a claim for payment was made, and a further 100,000 defendants were represented under other forms of legal aid, such as the duty solicitor scheme and the advocacy assistance scheme.

The significant expansion of criminal legal aid during this period was the result of a number of factors (some of which are discussed in more detail in the section below), including the increase in crime over much of this period, accompanied by an increase in the number of defendants appearing before the courts. The formal scope of criminal legal aid remained largely the same, although a non-means-tested scheme for legal advice for suspects held in police custody was introduced in 1986; and while it was projected that this would cost £6 million (AU$10.5 million) annually, by the early years of the twenty-first century the scheme was costing over £170 million (AU$32987 million) a year (Department for Constitutional Affairs 2005a: 9). However, a significant factor in the expansion of legal aid was that magistrates' courts, which had primary responsibility for determining legal aid applications, became more willing to grant them. Dissatisfaction with the inconsistent approach taken by the courts in determining applications led to the establishment of the Widgery Committee in 1964.[3] The Committee's recommendations regarding the criteria to be applied in deciding whether the merits test was satisfied, which came to be called the Widgery Criteria, were accepted and have remained more or less the same since they were introduced in the mid-1960s.[4] However, a notable feature of the criteria is that they allow for a great deal of flexibility in interpretation, and it would seem that as legal representation became more routine, courts came to interpret the criteria more generously—a process that was mutually reinforcing (Young 1996; Young and Wilcox 2007). Legal representation for defendants became the norm for all but the least serious allegations, and came to be relied upon to facilitate procedures designed to make criminal proceedings quicker and more efficient.[5]

While the Rushcliffe Committee favoured a salaried advice scheme, it rejected proposals for a public defender service, and the model adopted for the delivery of legal aid services was that legal aid should be provided by private law firms (sometimes referred to as a 'judicare' model). Solicitors would provide legal advice and assistance, and representation in magistrates' courts, and would instruct barristers on an ad hoc basis for cases requiring representation in the higher courts. Legal aid was an important element in the growth of the legal profession, which increased in size five-fold in the latter half of the twentieth century (Zander 2003).[6] Initially,

[3] See *Report of the Departmental Committee on Legal Aid in Criminal Proceedings* (1966).

[4] See now the *Legal Aid, Sentencing and Punishment of Offenders Act 2012* (LASPO), s 17(2). The criteria are: likely loss of liberty or serious damage to reputation; the case may involve the consideration of a substantial question of law; the defendant may be unable to understand the proceedings or to state his or her own case; the proceedings may involve the tracing, interviewing or expert cross-examination of witnesses; and whether it is in the interests of another person that the defendant be represented.

[5] For example, 'paper' committals under the *Magistrates' Courts Act 1980* (MCA), s 6(2), required a defendant to be legally represented, and complex procedures such as 'plea before venue' under the MCA 1980, s 17A, would make little sense to defendants without explanation by a lawyer.

[6] The number of barristers increased from about 2,000 to in excess of 10,000, and the number of solicitors rose from under 20,000 to nearly 90,000.

any firm of solicitors could provide legal aid services, and by 1999–2000, over 13 per cent of the gross income of solicitors' firms was derived from civil and criminal legal aid (Law Society 2001: 40). However, from the mid-1980s onwards, law firms became more specialised, and while most solicitors' firms initially carried out some magistrates' court work, by 1991–92 the number of firms performing such work had declined to just under 7500 (from 8716 in 1986–87) (Bridges 1992). The introduction of legal aid contracting in 2001 led to a dramatic fall in the number of firms engaged in legal aid work, so that by 2002–03 the number of such firms with a criminal law contract was 2900 (LSC 2003: 46). This was a deliberate policy objective of the LSC, which signalled its intention to reduce the number of contracts by as much as a further two-thirds—a somewhat limited ambition given the more recent developments explored later in this chapter.

While the decision over whether to grant legal aid for court representation was the responsibility of the courts, the administration of legal aid was initially in the hands of the legal profession itself in the form of the Law Society. When the *Legal Aid Act 1988* was implemented in 1989, responsibility for the administration of legal aid was transferred to a new institution—the Legal Aid Board (LAB)—on which the solicitors' profession only had two representatives, with half of the Board being drawn from the business sector. Responsibility for determining legal aid remuneration, which had previously been based on a discounted market rate, was given to the Lord Chancellor, who was given a free hand in this regard. The LAB introduced a system of legal aid franchising which was, in part, an attempt to establish and assure minimum standards, but this had a relatively limited impact on criminal legal aid work. However, it laid the foundation for the introduction of legal aid contracting, which restricted legal aid work to those solicitors' firms with a contract—contracts being awarded for specific practice areas, including criminal law. The LAB was to have a relatively short life, and it was replaced by the LSC in 2000 which had an expanded remit for planning and funding legal aid services. While commissioners were appointed by the Lord Chancellor—who also had the statutory power to provide guidance to the Commission, which it was required to consider—the LSC had a significant degree of autonomy; although crucially, it had a capped budget (Lord Chancellor's Department 1998).[7] Civil and criminal legal aid were divided between a Community Legal Service and a Criminal Defence Service, respectively, and the LSC was empowered to determine how legal aid services were to be delivered, and who should deliver them.

Two early initiatives of the LSC were the introduction of legal aid contracting in 2000, and the piloting of a Public Defender Service (PDS). Ironically, given the relative independence of the new LSC, the LAB had already piloted legal aid contracting,[8] and the creation of a PDS had been enthusiastically backed by

[7] See the *Access to Justice Act 1999*.

[8] For an account of the contracting pilot, see Bridges et al (2000).

a government minister in the Lord Chancellor's Department and announced in a White Paper in 1998 (Lord Chancellor's Department 1998: paragraphs 6.18–6.19).[9] Under contracting, firms were paid in respect of work done, rather than in accordance with a contract price, but contracting enabled the LSC to have a significant influence, if not control, over the nature and extent of work carried out, and also to establish minimum quality requirements that could be monitored and controlled via contractual mechanisms. Research carried out following the introduction of the right of suspects held in police custody to consult a solicitor showed that the legal assistance provided was often inadequate. Solicitors were sometimes slow to respond to requests for assistance, advice was frequently given over the telephone where the circumstances warranted personal attendance, some firms made significant use of unqualified advisers and many lawyers took a passive approach to providing advice and assistance (Brown 1997; McConville et al 1994; McConville and Hodgson 1993).[10] This research, and the need to pre-empt criticism of the profession by the Royal Commission on Criminal Justice (1993), resulted in a number of initiatives including the introduction of an accreditation scheme for police station representatives, in 1995.[11] This was extended to cover all lawyers providing legally aided advice at police stations in 2001 and, together with a magistrates' court duty lawyer accreditation scheme, was included as a contractual obligation in the legal aid contract. In addition, the contract incorporated a number of quality assurance requirements including minimum response times, minimum obligations regarding police station attendance, recording obligations and regular supervision of both solicitors and representatives providing services under the contract.

The PDS, which at its peak had eight offices, proved to be a short-lived experiment as a significant provider of criminal defence services, although it continues to operate through five offices. It was never intended that the PDS should replace the judicare model. Rather, the government believed that a mixed system would enable the costs of providing criminal legal aid services to be 'benchmarked', and that the PDS could fill gaps in provision (Lord Chancellor's Department 1998). Evaluation of the PDS, conducted in the first couple of years following its establishment, showed that it was able to provide a generalist criminal defence service 'that is of good quality, equal and in many respects better than the general standard of service provided by private practitioners' (Bridges et al 2007: 261). However, overall its average cost-per-case was higher than that of private practice. The authors of the pilot evaluation argued that there were a number of reasons why this was the case, some of which resulted from the way in which the PDS had been

[9] For an account of the policy context, see Bridges et al (2007).

[10] For example, many lawyers were found to be reluctant to intervene during police interviews of their clients.

[11] Research demonstrated that this resulted in an improvement in quality of the work of police station representatives and the solicitors who supervised them. See Bridges and Choongh (1998).

set up, and that the PDS could have 'an important role in the continuing development of quality standards and service innovation' (Bridges et al 2007: 268). However, although the PDS was subsequently used by the government to try to break resistance by the private profession to the introduction of competitive tendering, no government has seriously suggested that it be expanded (Baksi 2015).

III. The Decline of Criminal Legal Aid

It is difficult to define a precise point in time when the rising tide of criminal legal aid turned. One point could be in 1994—the last time there was a 'real terms' increase in legal aid fees (Deloitte 2013). Another could arguably be the passage of the *Access to Justice Act 1999*, which overhauled the structure of criminal legal aid provision and engendered heated public debate between the government and its opponents (Abel 2004). Yet another could be the peak in criminal legal aid expenditure, at approximately £1.4 billion (AU$2.46 billion) in 2003–04, which was followed by a steady decrease of 12 per cent in real terms over the subsequent five years (National Audit Office 2009). Whichever event is identified, there was a critical decade between the mid-1990s and mid-2000s, during which a decline in financial investment and returns to the legal profession—and an increasingly negative view of criminal legal aid by successive governments—emerged and became mutually reinforcing. During this period, a now well-established narrative developed, espoused by government ministers and significant sections of the media, that the criminal legal aid system in England and Wales was one of the most expensive in Europe, and that spending had 'spiralled out of control' in a manner that was 'unsustainable' (MoJ 2013). Both of these assertions are misleading.

With regard to the first element of this narrative, any comparison with other jurisdictions is complicated by the different procedural traditions in European jurisdictions. Most countries in continental Europe have an inquisitorial criminal procedure tradition, in contrast to the adversarial tradition of England and Wales. Compared to adversarial jurisdictions, judges and prosecutors in inquisitorial jurisdictions have a much more substantial role in criminal proceedings—including both supervising criminal investigations and proceedings, and protecting the rights of suspects and defendants[12]—while defence lawyers have had, at least until recently, a less significant role. As a result, inquisitorial jurisdictions spend a much greater proportion of their criminal justice budgets on the prosecution and courts, and much less on legal aid, rendering a direct comparison of legal aid expenditure unjustified. Bowles and Perry (2009: 36), relying on the evidence

[12] This is true in a formal sense, although in practice the level of supervision and engagement is often less significant. See, generally, Cape et al (2010) and Hodgson (2005).

of the European Commission's CEPEJ report (European Commission for the Efficiency of Justice 2006), point out that comparing legal aid costs in isolation 'risked missing important structural differences between justice systems'.

The second element of the dominant narrative—that expenditure on legal aid is out of control—also needs to be contextualised. Between 1997–98 and 2005, the criminal legal aid budget rose by 37 per cent (Department for Constitutional Affairs 2005b: 13), part of which can be attributed to inflation, but other factors were also instrumental. One such factor was the generally accepted notion of increased criminalisation. In 2010, it was estimated that around 70 Acts of Parliament relating to criminal justice had been passed since the late 1990s (Faulkner 2010), and that between 1997 and 2010, approximately 3000 new criminal offences were created by primary and secondary legislation (Chalmers 2014). While questions can be raised about the absolute accuracy and reliability of these figures, 'the huge increase in the number of incidents criminalised is indisputable' (Silvestri 2011). The implication is that this generated work for the criminal justice system, driving up costs. Indeed, after a slight drop in workload (including committals for trial/sentence and appeals) between 1997 and 2000, the Crown Court saw an eight per cent rise in the number of cases disposed of between 2000 and 2004 (Department for Constitutional Affairs 2005a: 85). Over the same period, there was a six per cent increase in the number of defendants proceeded against in magistrates' courts (MoJ 2007: 134). There was also substantial growth in the prison population (an increase of 15 per cent between 2001 and 2005), suggesting that a greater number of cases in respect of which the legal aid merits test was satisfied were dealt with by the courts (Home Office 2001, 2006).

The rise in the criminal legal aid budget should also be compared with the increase in the budgets of other criminal justice institutions. There was an increase in expenditure on policing of around 30 per cent between 1998–99 and 2004–05 (Mills, Silvestri and Grimshaw 2010: 68). Between 2001–02 and 2005–06, the Crown Prosecution Service's (CPS) request for resources increased by 50 per cent (CPS 2002, 2006), and between 1997 and 2005 the Serious Fraud Office's expenditure increased by 110 per cent (Serious Fraud Office 2003, 2007). It has, therefore, been argued that 'the upward pressures [on criminal legal aid] are due to external cost drivers' (Constitutional Affairs Committee 2007: 224). Cape and Moorhead (2005) also identified a number of external factors driving legal aid costs, including an increase in arrests (and thus in volumes of police station work), an increase in the uptake of police station advice, an increase in the number of complex investigations and more serious cases, and the high cost of a small number of Crown Court cases.

By contrast, governments have favoured the 'supplier-induced demand' theory: that the *providers* of legal aid services were driving demand for their work and thus increasing costs (Bevan 1996). This may be seen as being based on an ideological objection to criminal legal aid, a general desire to curb state spending and, ultimately, hostility to welfare spending. Despite evidence to the contrary, successive governments and significant sections of the media have, at various times, caricatured legal aid lawyers as 'fat cats' who exploit taxpayers in order to grow wealthy (Baksi 2014; Slack 2013).[13] Yet, this is contradicted by the stagnancy of the market at the time. Between 2001 and 2005, fees for criminal legal aid providers remained virtually static (Grindley 2006). Over the same period, the number of providers contracted to supply criminal legal aid reduced by 14 per cent, and by a further 23 per cent by 2010 (Carter 2006; LSC 2001, 2010). Yet, despite the fact that spending began to decline in the mid-2000s, the argument that expenditure on criminal legal aid is 'unsustainable' has persisted (Grayling 2013). As Cape and Moorhead (2005) argued, the supplier-induced demand theory provides 'a convenient political justification' for reducing the criminal legal aid budget.

The decline of criminal legal aid accelerated following the election of the Coalition government in 2010 and still further after the election in 2015 in which a Conservative government came to power. The decline can be partially explained by reference to the economic context of the past decade. Throughout the late 1990s and early 2000s, the United Kingdom (UK) experienced unprecedented economic growth accompanied by substantial investment in public services. Following the global financial crisis of 2007–08, 'austerity' and the desire to reduce the 'footprint' of the state have been central to both economic and social policy. The result was swingeing cuts across the public sector, from which the criminal justice system has not been exempt.[14] Following the 2010 election, the Home Office sought to cut the police budget substantially, with the number of police officers reduced to pre-2003 levels in just three years (Home Office 2015). The MoJ was required to find nearly £2 billion (AU$3.5billion) of savings from its £9 billion (AU$15.8 billion) budget over five years (HM Treasury 2010). The net expenditure of the CPS reduced by nearly a quarter between 2010 and 2015 (CPS 2015), and 146 courts were closed over the same period (Caird 2015). Legal aid, both civil and criminal, was considered by the government to represent a prime source of potential savings, with significant cuts and cost-saving reforms implemented or proposed.[15] The Coalition government planned to cut approximately £220 million (AU$386.6 million) per year from the criminal legal aid budget by 2018–19 (MoJ 2013: 5), justified on the basis of similar arguments to those posited by previous governments, despite the markedly different economic climate they faced.

After the election of the Conservative government in 2015, the austerity agenda continued unabated, with the MoJ proposing to meet Treasury demands for a further £1 billion (AU$1.76 billion) of savings in 2015–16 through the closure of another 91 courts (MoJ 2015a)—amounting to a reduction of nearly 40 per cent of the court estate in five years (Public and Commercial Services Union 2015)—and

[13] It should be noted that government ministers have always been careful to avoid explicitly using terms such as 'fat cats', while characterising criminal legal aid lawyers in this manner.

[14] See the Chancellor of the Exchequer's Emergency Budget speech of June 2010 available at: www.telegraph.co.uk/finance/budget/7846849/Budget-2010-Full-text-of-George-Osbornes-statement.html.

[15] See the changes implemented by LASPO.

the continued implementation of market reforms and fee reductions for criminal legal aid. Clearly, the austerity context has been highly influential in accelerating the decline of criminal legal aid, yet the perceived problem of disproportionate spending on criminal legal aid had existed for some years prior to the 2007–08 global financial crisis. We can, therefore, conclude that the austerity context is only one relatively recent factor influencing the decline of criminal legal aid.

Before the global financial crisis, the New Labour government had offered a number of responses to the assertion that criminal legal aid expenditure was out of control. In 2006, following the Carter Review, it proposed to 'marketise' criminal legal aid (Carter 2006). This was to be achieved by introducing fixed fees for police station work, revising the fixed-fee and graduated fee schemes for litigation and advocacy and introducing competitive tendering for legal aid work. In most circumstances, lawyers would not be paid an hourly rate for criminal legal aid work, meaning that the more time a lawyer spent on a case, the less profitable it would become. The policy was rationalised on the basis that lawyers would be encouraged to focus on cost-effective and efficient work practices and would be deterred from wasting time (for which, incidentally, no evidence was produced). Additionally, it was argued that lawyers would benefit from 'swings and roundabouts'—they might lose money on some cases, but would profit from others. In the same year in which the Carter Review (2006) was published, the government reintroduced means testing for criminal legal aid (initially for magistrates' court cases, and subsequently for Crown Court cases). The means test for criminal legal aid had been abolished in 2001 on the grounds that it was costly and bureaucratic, and raised little by way of contributions:

> The value of contributions collected scarcely paid for the direct costs of the system. Less than 1% of applications were refused legal aid on grounds of means and only 5% of defendants were ordered to make any contribution towards the cost of their legal aid. (Department for Constitutional Affairs 2004: 7)

However, by 2004, the government was explicitly proposing its reintroduction as a way of limiting demand, and these proposals were implemented in the *Criminal Defence Services Act 2006*.[16]

Successive governments have also sought to reduce expenditure on criminal legal aid by reforming the 'market' of providers. As noted earlier, criminal legal aid is primarily delivered by a variety of private entities—either firms of solicitors or self-employed barristers—using public funds, supplemented by a small number of PDS offices (Cape 2004: 401). Since the *Access to Justice Act 1999* came into force, solicitors' firms have only been able to provide criminal legal aid services if they have a contract (initially with the LSC, and subsequently with the Legal Aid Agency [LAA]). Both the previous Labour government and the Coalition government sought to reduce the size of the market, and therefore the cost to the

[16] The Act was repealed by LASPO, but the means test provisions remained the same.

state, through competitive tendering—in essence, by conducting an auction in which each provider would 'bid' for a contract. In 2009, the Labour government proposed a scheme entitled Best Value Tendering (BVT), which required providers to submit bids for work that would ensure a 'sustainable profit margin' (LSC 2009: 11). However, this scheme was widely criticised on the basis of fears that providers desperate to secure work would be encouraged to enter unsustainable 'suicide' bids, and that the quality of service would be compromised (Criminal Bar Association 2009). After substantial opposition from the legal profession, BVT was abandoned. In 2013, the Coalition government resurrected the idea, renamed Price-Competitive Tendering (PCT)—a similar scheme, but one requiring that bids be at least 17.5 per cent lower than the then current levels and capping the number of contracts to be awarded (MoJ 2013). The legal profession (and many other organisations) strongly opposed this, and again it was abandoned (Smith 2013: 906).

A third attempt to introduce a competitive tendering scheme was initiated in September 2014 with the publication of a consultation on a 'two-tier' system of contracting for criminal legal aid (MoJ 2014c). The first tier would allow an unlimited number of law firms to offer 'own client' services: that is, to provide legal representation to 'an individual who selects you, at the point of request' (LAA 2015a). The second tier would allow a maximum of 527 law firms to offer 'duty solicitor' services at police stations.

The fear of many, and no doubt the intention of the government, was that the number of firms providing criminal legal aid services would be drastically reduced.[17] Duty solicitor cases form a substantial proportion of legally aided criminal defence work. The Carter Review (2006: 24) estimated that half of police station representation was delivered under the duty solicitor scheme, and research by Otterburn in 2013 suggested a figure of 43 per cent (Otterburn 2014: 14). Duty solicitor work is also an important method by which solicitors' firms attract new clients, described as 'critical to future revenue streams' and 'integral to medium term viability' (Otterburn 2014: 59). Generally, if a firm represents a suspect as a duty solicitor, it will continue to act for them if they are charged with a criminal offence throughout the criminal justice process. Moreover, this can lead to 'duty conversions'—in short, a 'duty' client becomes familiar with the firm and becomes an 'own' client in the longer term (Otterburn 2014: 59). Since there are approximately 1600 solicitors' firms with a criminal legal aid contract, the limitation on the number of firms with a duty solicitor contract would lead to a large

[17] The MoJ stated that the 'principal objective' of the reform process was 'to deliver a sustainable service through encouraging consolidation of the provider base', which it justified on the basis that 'current providers are chasing too little work' in a market that was 'extremely fragmented' (MoJ 2014a: 7, 10). Representative groups, including the Law Society, the London Criminal Courts Solicitors Association (LCCSA) and the Criminal Law Solicitors Association (CLSA), argued that this artificial reduction in the size of the supplier base would seriously damage the delivery of criminal legal aid, challenging the proposals in court (see Van Der Luit-Drummon 2015).

forced contraction in the size of the supplier base, resulting in several potential problems for providers and legal aid recipients alike. By limiting the number of 'duty' contracts, a major source of new clients for providers would be restricted, reducing the possibility for firms without a contract to remain viable businesses, and ultimately reducing the level of choice for suspects and defendants generally. This would be a particular problem for legal aid recipients in areas with small numbers of existing providers (such as rural locations) or for communities with specific needs (for example, black and minority ethnic groups). Additionally, the two-tier model would have an indirect impact on barristers, who would not be contracted under it, since solicitor firms would be likely to make greater use of in-house advocates.

The impact of the introduction of the two-tier contracting model would have been exacerbated by the parallel introduction of reduced legal aid fees. In April 2013, the then Lord Chancellor, Chris Grayling, announced cuts of at least 17.5 per cent to criminal legal aid fees for solicitors and barristers, to be implemented in two tranches (MoJ 2013).[18] The government subsequently postponed the reduction of fees for barristers, leaving only solicitors subjected to the reduction (MoJ 2014b). The first cut of 8.75 per cent took effect in March 2014, and the second was implemented in July 2015, prompting widespread direct action by solicitors and barristers. The introduction of reduced fees meant that many solicitors' firms, including those that would have secured a duty contract under the two-tier system, would be on the cusp of profitability, with some becoming unprofitable. Legal aid firms were generally not highly profitable before the reduction in fees; in 2013, such firms were achieving an average 5 per cent net profit margin for criminal legal aid work (Otterburn 2014: 5). Coupled with the consistent decline in fee levels in real terms over the previous 20 years, the fee reductions presented a serious threat to the long-term survival of many firms (Deloitte 2013: 23). Since criminal legal aid providers tend to be specialised rather than generalist law firms (a long-term trend encouraged by successive governments and legal aid authorities), they cannot easily offset losses in legal aid work with alternative work (Deloitte 2013; Otterburn 2014). Yet, the LAA did not appear to have undertaken any analysis of the impact of the two-tier scheme on either providers or legal aid recipients, beyond predicting an 11 per cent drop in the number of providers between April 2012 and April 2015 (LAA 2015b).

After the conclusion of the two-tier contract bidding process in the summer of 2015, the government planned to implement the scheme in January 2016. However, a large number of firms launched legal challenges, largely on the basis of the arbitrary way in which the contracts appeared to have been awarded.[19] As a

[18] The fee cuts would also apply to solicitor advocates.

[19] According to Michael Gove, who replaced Chris Grayling as Lord Chancellor, the MoJ faced 99 separate legal challenges to the tender for contracts and a judicial review (Bowcott 2016). In a letter before claim to the LAA, those firms challenging the tender process argued that it had been 'vitiated by serious structural flaws giving rise to an unacceptable risk of unlawful decision-making' (Fouzder 2015).

result, the LAA announced that introduction of the scheme was to be delayed until Spring 2016 (LAA 2015b); and in February 2016, the government announced that it would not go ahead with the two-tier scheme, and would also suspend the fee cut that had been introduced in July 2015 (MoJ 2016). On the face of it, this appears to have been a victory for lawyers and others who opposed the introduction of the scheme. However, in making the announcement, the Lord Chancellor made clear that the primary reason for the decision not to implement the scheme was pragmatic; the large number of legal challenges meant that implementation would be problematic. Furthermore, the suspension of the reduction in fees was temporary—for a period of 12 months—and the Lord Chancellor indicated that he would return to the issue of 'the second fee reduction and market consolidation before April 2017' (MoJ 2016). It is highly likely, therefore, that the long-term contraction of the supplier base, and real-terms reduction in the legal aid budget, will continue.

IV. An Uncertain Future for Criminal Legal Aid

While the latest attempt to reduce the number of criminal legal aid suppliers, and fee levels, has been temporarily halted, criminal legal aid in England and Wales has an uncertain future, in terms of both scope of provision and delivery of service to clients, and this has implications for the criminal justice system as a whole. Government policy has become increasingly focused on reducing expenditure, and the austerity agenda has de-prioritised criminal legal aid—and many other public services—in favour of deficit reduction and public debt management. Government rhetoric continues to emphasise the importance of access to justice in principle, but in practice it is a secondary consideration. The assertion that criminal legal aid expenditure is 'out of control' and 'unsustainable' persists as a rationalisation for government policy even though this is an increasingly untenable justification given the consistent decline in expenditure since 2003–04. The introduction of comprehensive criminal legal aid was a product of post-war welfarism, founded on the concept that all citizens should be able to equitably access public services.[20] While criminal legal aid remains theoretically available to a significant proportion of the population, it now bears little resemblance to the model developed as part of the foundations of the welfare state.

This new culture—what might be termed 'minimalism'—is ideologically driven, reflecting the approach of the government to the responsibilities of the state in general, and to the criminal justice system in particular (see Laster and Kornhauser, Chapter 7, this volume, for a discussion of this in the Australian

[20] Although there is some debate about this—see, for example, Wilmot-Smith (2014).

context). The cuts to the budgets of other criminal justice agencies have been accompanied by a series of measures designed to maximise throughput at minimum cost. The *Criminal Procedure Rules*, which were introduced at the turn of the century and emphasise 'efficient and expeditious' criminal proceedings (Rule 1.1(2)(e), the 'Overriding Objective'), exemplify this culture (Smith 2013). Suspects and defendants are co-opted into assisting with the achievement of this objective of efficiency and cost cutting via a mixture of 'carrot and stick', with an emphasis on the 'stick'. The primary 'carrot' is the sentence discount scheme for an early guilty plea, designed to encourage swift resolution, save time and reduce costs.[21]

There are many 'sticks'. In addition to the sanctions set out in the *Criminal Procedure Rules* (which may apply to both defendants and their lawyers), defendants who do not cooperate with the police following their arrest by telling them the basis of their defence face 'adverse inferences' at trial (*Criminal Justice and Public Order Act 1994* sections 34–38). Limitations have been placed on the recovery of defendants' costs in criminal proceedings, encouraging a limited approach to defence preparation (LASPO Schedule 7). Most recently, the government introduced the *Criminal Court Charge*,[22] requiring courts to impose a charge on all defendants irrespective of financial means. The charge was increased in the event of a conviction following a not guilty plea, and further increased if the defendant chose to be tried in the Crown Court.[23] Following a vigorous campaign by, among others, the Howard League for Penal Reform (2015) and the Magistrates' Association (2015), who argued that the charge encouraged inappropriate guilty pleas, the government scrapped the charge in December 2015 (HC Debate 3 December 2015: Column 26WS). While the *Criminal Court Charge* was short-lived, it provides just one example of a longer-term trend encouraging, cajoling and inducing defendants (and their lawyers) to cooperate in the 'speedy and efficient' processing of their cases through the criminal justice system.[24]

[21] The Sentencing Guidelines Council has issued a consultation on revising the guidelines so that the maximum reduction in sentence would only apply if a defendant pleads guilty no later than the first hearing, with the level of the sentence reduction falling more rapidly for a guilty plea entered thereafter (Sentencing Guidelines Council 2016).

[22] Introduced in April 2015 by the *Prosecution of Offences Act 1985 (Criminal Court Charge) Regulations 2015* (SI 796/2015), the charge was the last act of Chris Grayling, the Justice Secretary, prior to the General Election.

[23] In fact, the enhanced charge applied irrespective of whether the defendant elected or the Court directed trial in the Crown Court, but arguably it would affect defendants' decisions where they did have a choice. The charge ranged from £150 (AU$263) for a guilty plea to a summary offence in a magistrates' court to £1,200 (AU$2108) following conviction for an indictable offence in the Crown Court. The charge was in addition to an order that the defendant pay the prosecution costs, compensation, the victims' surcharge and any legal aid contribution, as well as any financial penalty imposed as, or as part of, the sentence.

[24] For an extensive analysis of how the 'process of State-induced guilty pleas is *intended to replace* in whole or part the promise of adversary justice', see McConville and Marsh (2014). Also see Flynn (2016) for a discussion in the Australian context.

The policy choices made will have a long-term impact not only on the legal profession, but also on legal aid recipients and other aspects of the criminal justice system. With the number of solicitors' firms that are able to offer legal aid services having been reduced, and likely to be reduced still further, client choice will inevitably be limited. Outside major conurbations and particularly in less populous areas, suspects and defendants will be unlikely to have any real choice, since there may be only a small number of firms with a contract covering such locations (Otterburn 2014: 46). Defendants who do not perceive that they have a choice will likely be less trusting of their lawyer (Smith 2013), which in turn will be likely to diminish their trust in the criminal justice system more generally (Hough et al 2010; Tyler 2007, 2009).

The quality of criminal defence services is also likely to be a casualty. Quality is the product of an interaction between professional ethics, competition, and financial and other incentives, mediated by any applicable quality assurance measures. A smaller market of providers will reduce competition. Indeed, in some locations that have few providers there will be no effective competitive market. With reduced remuneration, and business models focused on economies of scale rather than quality of service, surviving providers will need to improve efficiencies in both the range and level of service that they offer. The consultation paper that inaugurated the recent reform process explicitly encouraged the 'economies of scale' approach and the achievement of 'efficiencies' (MoJ 2013: para 5.6.4). Law firms that do not focus on reducing costs and providing services in greater volume will be unlikely to survive. The nature of criminal defence services is such that lawyers have a great deal of discretion in determining the level of service that they provide. As Tata (2007) has argued, faced with a number of choices each of which 'may' benefit the client, lawyers will tend to advise clients to adopt the option that benefits the lawyer. Kemp (2010) found that the fixed-fee regime for police station advice resulted in some police station lawyers spending the minimum amount of time on advising suspects in person, or providing advice by telephone rather than in person. Faced with a contract that is on the borderline of profitability, lawyers will be likely to spend less time on client consultations and case preparation, considering disclosure and investigating evidence. If an early guilty plea is likely to be the most profitable option from the lawyer's perspective, it may be difficult for the lawyer to resist the temptation to emphasise to their client the systemic incentives of sentence discount and reduced costs, particularly when combined with the system incentives for defendants to plead guilty that were referred to earlier. McConville and Marsh (2014: 167) argue that defence lawyers have been co-opted into inducing clients to plead guilty, and that the *Criminal Procedure Rules* are 'a tool for bringing the defence bar into line'. Such nuanced practices, carried out by lawyers working for larger, less personalised firms, will be almost impossible to register or capture in any conceivable quality assurance scheme.

The potential long-term impact on the future of the criminal legal profession is also troubling, with increasing costs of qualification, reduced remuneration, lack of job security and limited career progression offering 'little incentive for debt-saddled graduates to opt for a career in legal aid work' (HC Committee of Public Accounts 2010: 19). Indeed, a report released in December 2015 suggested that fees for junior barristers have decreased by eight per cent since 2012 (MoJ 2015b), with the chair of the Bar Council arguing that 'the payment structure provides little scope for career progression for criminal barristers' (Smith 2015a). This raises questions about who will deliver criminal legal aid services in the future. In 2009, the National Audit Office conducted a survey of criminal legal aid solicitors, finding that the profile of the profession was ageing and that 15 per cent of respondents would be unlikely to be conducting legal aid work in five years' time due to impending retirement (NAO 2009). The issue is not simply whether suitable lawyers can be recruited to the criminal defence profession, but whether it will be possible for new law firms dedicated to criminal legal aid to emerge. Criminal defence work is largely carried out under legal aid. There is relatively little privately paid criminal defence work, and such work as currently exists is largely concentrated in firms that do little, if any, legal aid work, and have little appetite for moving into the legal aid market. Since there is only a small privately-paying client base, there will likely be no firms that rely largely on private clients that would wish to extend their client base to those funded by legal aid, and start-up practices will not have the capacity to move into a market dominated by relatively large firms. This will have a greater impact on firms that wish to specialise in working for particular communities or socio-demographic groups, or in providing specialist services such as those for young or vulnerable people. Thus the criminal defence supplier base will not be entrepreneurial, dynamic or inventive in developing new ways of providing criminal defence services. Rather, it will be static, rigid and ossified.

The reduction in the number of suppliers, and their increasingly commercialised business ethic, will also have adverse consequences for other areas of the criminal justice system. The police will likely have to wait longer for the arrival of a lawyer who has a larger caseload of police station cases, and who may be based some distance from the station. At court, defence lawyers will have to balance higher caseloads, and the number of unrepresented suspects and defendants will likely increase, which will limit court efficiency and increase the time spent on cases in court. No systematic research has been conducted on litigants in person in criminal cases, but surveys undertaken in February and November 2014 suggest that legal aid reforms have already increased their number (Bureau of Investigative Journalism 2015). There is also concern regarding the future of the criminal judiciary, which is primarily drawn from the ranks of criminal practitioners (particularly the Bar). As Sir Bill Jeffrey (2014: 62) commented in his review of independent criminal advocacy: 'as the present generation of experienced criminal barristers moves towards retirement, concerns about the future "talent pipeline" for criminal Queen's Counsel (QCs) and judges are not, in my view, fanciful'. A decline in the number of providers, the likely departure of experienced lawyers from criminal practice and a lack of new entrants will combine to reduce the pool of lawyers with expertise in criminal law from which new judges can be drawn. Less choice may result in a reduction of the overall numbers of criminal law judges, and risks lowering their quality, seriously affecting the administration of criminal justice.

It is not too strong to conclude that criminal legal aid and the criminal defence profession are in crisis. It is difficult to see, at this juncture, how (if at all) that crisis will be resolved. Yet the fast-moving context—the rise of crime associated with social media, other technological developments and the ease of cross-border criminal activity—demands enterprise and innovation in approaches to the investigation and prosecution of crime, and also in the delivery of criminal legal aid services. Where is such enterprise and innovation to come from? The significance of the abolition of the LSC, and its replacement by the LAA located within the MoJ, has not been sufficiently appreciated. The LAB and the LSC—both with a measure of independence from government—piloted and introduced franchising, contracting, accreditation and new forms of legal aid delivery, and also conducted research on the demand for and supply of legal aid. The LAA, while functionally independent in respect of individual decisions around whether to grant legal aid, is fully part of the MoJ in all other respects, and has no independent members on its board. The Director of Legal Aid Casework must comply with directions given by the Lord Chancellor (LASPO s 4(3)), and one of the primary objectives of the LAA (no date) is to 'support the strategic aims of Ministers and the Department'. The LAA carries out almost no research, and therefore has limited knowledge of the impact of its policies. Indeed, the agency has been the subject of strident criticism. Its lack of independence from the MoJ has led to suggestions that both its specific funding decisions and general strategy for delivering legal aid are influenced by the government's austerity agenda. For example, in July 2015, the High Court ruled that the LAA's exceptional funding scheme for civil legal aid was unlawful, with a 'very low' number of successful applications (*IS v Director of Legal Aid Casework* [2015] EWHC 1965 (Admin)). In another case, involving family law, the agency was described by the High Court as 'wasteful and inefficient' (*Re R* [2014] EWHC 643 (Fam): 95), and it has been accused of being in 'institutional denial' over problems with its Client and Cost Management System (Association of Costs Lawyers 2015). In his assessment of the LAA's approach to analysis in its most recent Annual Report, Martin Partington—a former Law Commissioner—suggested that it was 'very narrowly focused on corporate concerns' rather than examining 'the robustness of the scheme for delivering legal aid services'. He concluded, 'the report is thus about administrative and operational outcomes, rather than giving a view of how citizens are (or are not) being assisted by legal aid' (Partington 2015). As a mechanism for managing and delivering legal aid in a dynamic and innovative manner, the LAA has patently failed. However, since the LAA was the product of a bi-partisan policy, the prospects for re-establishing an independent legal aid agency are minimal.

The professional associations of lawyers, principally the Law Society and the Bar Council,[25] have been vigorous in their opposition to fee reductions and dual contracting.[26] However, as representatives of their respective professions, they have a vested interest in protecting their members or, rather, the majority of their members who are in private practice.[27] The professional bodies appear to be implacably opposed to a public defender service, yet they have not sought to develop ideas about alternative ways of delivering legal aid services in the context of a radically reduced legal aid budget.

The PDS itself, as part of the LAA, is not in a position to independently develop a concept of a national service. While, as noted earlier, the evaluation of the PDS pilot suggested that it could play a role in developing quality standards and covering localities in need of criminal legal aid services, opponents have latched onto the tentative conclusion that the PDS was more expensive than private practice.[28] Opposition was, unfortunately, strengthened when the government implicitly threatened the private profession with an expansion of the service if it did not desist in its opposition to fee cuts.[29] The PDS could provide a basis for developing alternative methods of delivering legal aid services if legal aid contracting results in gaps in supply geographically, or in terms of the needs of particular client groups, or if—which remains a distinct possibility—a radically reduced supplier base leads to upward pressure on legal aid fees in future. However, it is doubtful that any party that is likely to form a government in the foreseeable future would adopt such a policy.

[25] Even more active have been the CLSA, the LCCSA and the Criminal Bar Association (CBA).

[26] The Law Society and Bar Council have lobbied the government directly and through consultations. In reaction to the government decision to proceed with its proposed reforms in February 2014, the Bar Council stated that 'our worst fears have been confirmed' and that barristers would be 'dismayed and demoralised' (Bar Council 2014). In June 2015, Law Society President Andrew Caplen (2015) wrote to the Lord Chancellor to express 'disappointment and concern' about the decision to implement cuts and two-tier contracting. The CLSA, LCCSA and CBA have led more proactive resistance, balloting members on various forms of direct action tantamount to 'strikes' (for example, the refusal of barristers to undertake very high cost cases (VHCC) and 'returns' work, and the refusal of solicitors to represent clients in criminal proceedings in Summer 2015).

[27] Lawyers who work for the PDS are regulated by their respective professions, but their particular interests have not been represented by the professional associations.

[28] For example, the use of highly paid PDS QCs in junior-level crime trials during the legal aid 'strikes' (Smith 2015b).

[29] In December 2013, the MoJ imposed 30 per cent cuts to fees for VHCC. As a result, barristers refused to accept such cases. A high-profile victim of this action was a serious fraud case (*R v Crawley and others* [2014] EWCA Crim 1028), in which insufficient advocates were available to represent the defendants. After a number of adjournments, the Court of Appeal overturned the stay on proceedings in May 2014. Sir Brian Leveson (who delivered the judgment) commented that, during the dispute between the MoJ and the Bar, 'the Public Defender Service … began actively to recruit a pool of employed advocates to take on work that might otherwise have been done by independent advocates', suggesting that this was 'a response to the impasse which had arisen between the Bar and the Lord Chancellor'. A number of commentators interpreted this expansion of the PDS as a veiled threat that the PDS could replace the private Bar should it refuse to accept cuts (McCabe 2014).

V. Conclusion

The approach of successive governments over the past two decades suggests a very distinct direction of travel for criminal legal aid policy in England and Wales. The consistent downward trend in real-terms levels of funding, together with repeated attempts to reduce and limit the size and cost of the criminal legal aid market, encouragement of economy and speed over quality of delivery and just results, and repeated failures to engage in meaningful consultation with the legal profession and other stakeholders on reform all suggest a disinclination to strengthen the provision of criminal legal aid. By contrast, the EU has been pursuing an agenda of positive reform through its 'procedural rights roadmap' and consequent legislation, developing clearly defined procedural rights for suspects and defendants, underpinned by legal aid (Flynn et al 2016).[30] With two exceptions, the UK Government has opted out of this programme of reform, including a proposed directive on criminal legal aid,[31] describing the proposed legislation as 'unnecessary and unwelcome'.[32] In 2012, the United Nations (UN) unanimously adopted *Principles and Guidelines on Access to Legal Aid in Criminal Justice Systems*, but the UK Government has completely ignored them. In adopting the Principles and Guidelines, the UN General Assembly declared that 'legal aid is an essential element of a fair, humane and efficient criminal justice system that is based on the rule of law', which is a 'foundation' for the right to fair trial.[33] Since the turn of the century, successive UK governments have not only failed to provide a lead in the development of criminal legal aid globally, but have also set about weakening and undermining a system that, while imperfect, has provided good-quality legal services to the majority of suspects and defendants who cannot pay for a lawyer from their own resources.

References

Abel, R (2004) *English Lawyers between Market and State* (Oxford, Oxford University Press).

Association of Costs Lawyers (2015) *Report on the Legal Aid Agency's Client and Cost Management System (CCMS)* (Diss, Association of Cost Lawyers).

[30] *Roadmap with a view to fostering protection of suspected and accused persons in criminal proceedings*. 1 July 2009, 11457/09 DROIPEN 53 COPEN 120.

[31] *Proposal for a Directive of the European Parliament and of the Council on provisional legal aid for suspects and accused persons deprived of liberty and legal aid in European arrest warrant proceedings*, 27 November 2013 COM(2013) 824 final, 2013/0409 (COD).

[32] The government opted into the EU Directive on the right to interpretation and translation (2010/64/EU), and to the Directive on the right to information (2012/13/EU). For the government's response to other proposed directives, see: europeanmemoranda.cabinetoffice.gov.uk/files/2014/09/17633-13_Min_Cor_29_July_2014_Grayling-Cash (2).pdf.

[33] UN General Assembly Resolution 67/187, 20 December 2012.

Baksi, C (2014) 'Ministry Ticked Off over Barrister Earning Claim' *The Law Society Gazette*, 18 March 2014, available at: www.lawgazette.co.uk/practice/ministry-ticked-off-over-barrister-earnings-claim/5040420.fullarticle.

—— (2014) 'PDS Accused of Trying to Break Strike Action', *Law Society Gazette*, 12 May 2014.

Bar Council (2014) *Unsustainable and Unnecessary Legal Aid Cuts Confirm Our Worst Fears*, 27 February 2014, available at: www.barcouncil.org.uk/media-centre/news-and-press-releases/2014/february/bar-chairman-unsustainable-and-unnecessary-legal-aid-cuts-confirm-our-worst-fears.

Bevan, G (1996) 'Has There Been Supplier-induced Demand for Legal Aid?' 15 *Civil Justice Quarterly* 98.

Bowcott, O (2016) 'Michael Gove in U-Turn over Legal Aid Fund', *The Guardian*, 29 January 2016, available at: www.theguardian.com/politics/2016/jan/28/michael-gove-in-u-turn-over-legal-aid-fund.

Bowles, R and Perry, A (2009) *International Comparison of Publicly Funded Legal Services and Justice Systems* Ministry of Justice 14/09 (London, Ministry of Justice).

Bridges, L (1992) 'The Professionalisation of Criminal Justice', (August 1992) *Legal Action* p 7.

Bridges, L, Cape, E, Abubaker, A and Bennett, C (2000) *Quality in Criminal Defence Services: A Report on the Evaluation of the Legal Service Commission's Pilot Project on Contracting Criminal Legal Advice and Assistance* (London, Legal Services Commission).

Bridges, L, Cape, E, Fenn, P, Mitchell, A, Moorhead, R and Sherr, A (2007) *Evaluation of the Public Defender Service in England and Wales* (London, TSO).

Bridges, L and Choongh, S (1998) *Improving Police Station Legal Advice: The Impact of the Accreditation Scheme for Police Station Legal Advisers* (London, Law Society and Legal Aid Board).

Brown, D (1997) *PACE Ten Years on: A Review of the Research*, Home Office Research Study 155 (London, Home Office).

Bureau of Investigative Journalism (2015) *Magistrates in New Legal Aid Warning to Grayling as Survey Shows Growing Fears over Justice System*, 15 January 2015, available at: www.thebureauinvestigates.com/2015/01/18/magistrates-warn-chris-grayling-legal-aid-new-survey/.

Caird, J (2015) *Briefing Paper: Court and Tribunal Closures* CBP 7346 (London, House of Commons Library).

Cape, E (2004) 'The Rise (and Fall?) of a Criminal Defence Profession' [2004] *Criminal Law Review* 401.

Cape, E and Moorhead, R (2005) *Demand Induced Supply? Identifying Cost Drivers in Criminal Defence Work* (London, Legal Services Research Centre).

Cape, E, Namoradze, Z, Smith, R and Spronken, T (2010) *Effective Criminal Defence in Europe* (Antwerp, Intersentia).

Caplen, A (2015) *From the President: Letter to the Secretary of State*, 10 June 2015, available at: www.lawsociety.org.uk/news/documents/Letter-to-secretary-of-state-on-duty-contract-tender-process/.

Carter, Lord (2006) *Legal Aid: A Market-based Approach to Reform* (London, Lord Carter's Review of Legal Aid Procurement).

Chalmers, J (2014) '"Frenzied law making": Overcriminalisation by Numbers' 67 *Current Legal Problems* 483.

Constitutional Affairs Committee (2007) *Implementation of the Carter Review of Legal Aid: Third Report of Session 2006–07* HC 223-II (London, TSO).

Criminal Bar Association (2009) *Criminal Bar Association Response to Ministry of Justice Consultation Paper Dated August 2009 'Legal Aid: Funding Reforms'*, available at: www.criminalbar.com/resources/cba-responses/?page=8&.

Crown Prosecution Service (2002) *Crown Prosecution Service Resource Accounts 2001–02* HC 1239 (London, TSO).

—— (2006) *Crown Prosecution Resource Accounts 2005–06* HC 1203 (London, TSO).

—— (2015) *Annual Report and Accounts 2014–15* HC 20 (London, TSO).

Deloitte (2013) *The Government's Proposed Legal Aid Reforms: A Report for the Law Society* (London, Deloitte).

Department for Constitutional Affairs (2004) *Criminal Defence Services Bill Consultation Paper* CP 17/04 (Cm 6194) (London, DCA).

—— (2005a) *Judicial Statistics Annual Report 2004* (Cm 6565) (London, HMSO).

—— (2005b) *A Fairer Deal For Legal Aid* (Cm 6591) (London, HMSO).

European Commission for the Efficiency of Justice [CEPEJ] (2006) *Report on European Judicial Systems Edition 2006 (2004 data): An Overview* (CEPEJ).

Faulkner, D (2010) *Criminal Justice and Government at a Time of Austerity* (London, Criminal Justice Alliance).

Flynn, A (2016) 'Plea-negotiations, Prosecutors and Discretion: An Argument for Legal Reform', 49 *Australian and New Zealand Journal of Criminology* 564.

Flynn, A, Hodgson, J, McCulloch, J and Naylor, B (2016) 'Legal Aid and Access to Legal Representation: Re-Defining the Right to a Fair Trial' 40 *Melbourne University Law Review* 207.

Fouzder, M (2015) 'Agency Faces Two-Pronged Attack over Tenders', *The Law Society Gazette*, 3 November 2015, available at: www.lawgazette.co.uk/law/laa-faces-two-pronged-attack-over-legal-aid-contracts/5051972.article.

Goriely, T (1996) 'The Development of Criminal Legal Aid in England and Wales' in Young, R and Wall, D (eds), *Access to Criminal Justice: Legal Aid, Lawyers and the Defence of Liberty* (London, Blackstone).

Grayling, C (2013) 'Letters: Britain's Legal Aid Costs Are Unsustainable', *The Guardian*, 7 October 2013.

Grindley, P (2006) *Legal Aid Reforms Proposed by Lord Carter: Analysis and Commentary* (London, LECG).

HC Committee of Public Accounts (2010) 'The Procurement of Legal Aid in England and Wales by the Legal Services Commission', Ninth Report of Session 2009–10, HC322 (London, TSO).

HC Debate (2015) *House of Commons Debate*, 3 December (Col 26WS).

HM Treasury (2010) *Spending Review 2010* (Cm 7942) (London, TSO).

Hodgson, J (2005) *French Criminal Justice* (Oxford, Hart Publishing).

Home Office (2001) *Prison Statistics England and Wales* (Cm 5743) (London, Home Office).

—— (2006) *Offender Management Caseload Statistics 2005* (London, Home Office).

—— (2015) *Police Workforce, England and Wales: 31 March 2015—Data Tables*, available at: www.gov.uk/government/statistics/police-workforce-england-and-wales-31-march-2015-data-tables.

Hough, M, Jackson, J, Bradford, B, Myhill, A and Quinton, P (2010) 'Procedural Justice, Trust, and Institutional Legitimacy' 4 *Policing: A Journal of Policy and Practice* 203.

Howard League for Penal Reform (2015) 'Howard League Launches Campaign for Urgent Criminal Courts Charge Review', Press Release, 5 August 2015, available at: www.howardleague.org/criminal-courts-charge/.

Hynes, S (2012) *Austerity Justice* (London, Legal Action Group).

Jeffrey, B (2014) *Independent Criminal Advocacy in England and Wales* (London, Review by Sir Bill Jeffery).

Kemp, V (2010) *Transforming Legal Aid: Access to Criminal Defence Services* (London, Legal Services Research Centre).

Law Society (2001) *Annual Statistics* (London, Law Society).

Legal Aid Agency [LAA] (2015a) *Own Client Contract 2015 Standard Terms*, available at: www.gov.uk/government/publications/own-client-crime-contract-2015.

——(2015b) 'Crime News: Provision of Criminal Legal Aid Services from 11 January 2016', *Gov. UK*, 13 November 2015, available at: www.gov.uk/government/news/crime-news-provision-of-criminal-legal-aid-services-from-11-january-2016.

—— (no date) *Legal Aid Agency Framework Document*: para 1.2, available at: www.gov.uk/government/organisations/legal-aid-agency/about/our-governance.

Legal Services Commission (2001) *Annual Report 2000/01* (London, TSO).

—— (2003) *Annual Report 2002/03* (London, TSO).

—— (2009) *Best Value Tendering for CDS Contracts: A Consultation Paper* (London, Legal Services Commission).

—— (2010) *Annual Report and Accounts 2009/10* HC 575 (London, TSO).

Lord Chancellor's Department (1998) *Modernising Justice* (Cm 4155) (London, TSO).

Magistrates Association (2015) *MA Chairman Voices Concern on Criminal Courts Charge*, available at: magistrates-association.org.uk/news/ma-chairman-voices-concern-criminal-courts-charges-–-27-march-2015-0.

McCabe, R (2014) 'MoJ Criticised over Public Defender Service Expansion' *Legal Aid Voice*, 22 January 2014, available at: www.legalvoice.org.uk/2014/01/22/moj-recruits-lawyers-for-public-defender-service/.

McConville, M and Hodgson, J (1993) *Custodial Legal Advice and the Right to Silence*, RCCJ Research Study No 16 (London, HMSO).

McConville, M, Hodgson, J, Bridges, L and Pavlovic, A (1994) *Standing Accused* (Oxford, Clarendon).

McConville, M and Marsh, L (2014) *Criminal Judges: Legitimacy, Courts and State-Induced Guilty Pleas in Britain* (Cheltenham Edward Elgar).

Mills, H, Silvestri, A and Grimshaw, R (2010) *Police Expenditure 1999–2009* (London, Centre for Crime and Justice Studies).

Ministry of Justice [MoJ] (2007) *Judicial and Court Statistics 2006* (Cm 7273) (London, MoJ).

—— (2013) *Transforming Legal Aid: Delivering a More Credible and Efficient System* CP14/2013 (London, MoJ).

—— (2014a) *Transforming Legal Aid: Next Steps—Government Response* (London, MoJ).

—— (2014b) 'Agreement between Ministry of Justice, Bar Council and Criminal Bar Association' (27 March 2014).

—— (2014c) *Transforming Legal Aid: Crime Duty Contracts*, available at: consult.justice.gov.uk/digital-communications/transforming-legal-aid-crime-duty-contracts.

—— (2015a) *Proposal on the Provision of Court and Tribunal Estate in England and Wales* (London, MoJ).

—— (2015b) *The Composition and Remuneration of Junior Barristers under the Advocates' Graduated Fee Scheme in Criminal Legal Aid*, available at: www.gov.uk/government/publications/composition-and-remuneration-of-junior-barristers-under-the-advocates-graduated-fee-scheme-in-criminal-legal-aid.

—— (2016) 'Changes to Criminal Legal Aid' *Gov.UK*, 28 January 2016, available at: www.gov.uk/government/speeches/changes-to-criminal-legal-aid-contracting.

National Audit Office (2009) *The Procurement of Criminal Legal Aid in England and Wales by the Legal Services Commission* HC 29 (London, TSO).

Otterburn Legal Consulting (2014) *Transforming Legal Aid: Next Steps, A Report for the Law Society of England and Wales and the Ministry of Justice* (London, Otterburn Legal Consulting).

Partington, M (2015) 'Who Is Doing Legal Aid? The Statistical Evidence', *Blog by Martin Partington*, available at: martinpartington.com/2015/08/04/who-is-doing-legal-aid-the-statistical-evidence/.

Public and Commercial Services Union (2015) 'New Court Closures Will Further Restrict Access to Justice' *Press Release*, 16 July 2015, available at: www.pcs.org.uk/en/ministry_of_justice/moj-news.cfm/new-courts-closures-will-further-restrict-access-to-justice.

Report of the Departmental Committee on Legal Aid in Criminal Proceedings (1966) (Cmnd 2934) (London, HMSO).

Royal Commission on Criminal Justice (1993) *Report* Cm 2263 (London, HMSO).

Sentencing Guidelines Council (2016) *Reduction in Sentence for a Guilty Plea Guideline: Consultation*, 11 February 2016, available at: www.sentencingcouncil.org.uk/wp-content/uploads/Reduction-in-sentence-for-a-guilty-plea-consultation-paper-web.pdf.

Serious Fraud Office (2003) *Annual Report 2001–2002*, available at: data.gov.uk/dataset/annual-reports-sfo.

—— (2007) *Annual Report 2005–2006*, available at: data.gov.uk/dataset/annual-reports-sfo.

Silvestri, A (2011) *Lessons for the Coalition: An End of Term Report on New Labour and Criminal Justice* (London, Centre for Crime and Justice Studies).

Slack, J (2013) 'Legal Aid Payouts to Fat Cat Lawyers Will Be Slashed by a Third, Says Justice Secretary', *Daily Mail*, 13 April 2013, available at: www.dailymail.co.uk/news/article-2306630/Legal-aid-payouts-fat-cat-lawyers-slashed-says-Justice-Secretary.html.

Smith, C (2015a) 'Crime Work "Unaffordable" for Young Barristers, Warns Bar' *Law Society Gazette*, 17 December 2015.

—— (2015b) 'Action Day 51: PDS Silks Cover Junior-Level Trials', *The Law Society Gazette*, 20 August 2015, available at: www.lawgazette.co.uk/practice/action-day-51-pds-silks-cover-junior-level-trials/5050625.fullarticle.

Smith, T (2013) 'Trust, Choice and Money: Why the Aid Reform "U-turn" Is Essential for Effective Criminal Defence' [2013] *Criminal Law Review* 906.

Tata, C (2007) 'In the Interests of Clients or Commerce? Legal Aid, Supply, Demand, and "Ethical Indeterminacy" in Criminal Defence Work' 34 *Journal of Law and Society* 489.

Tyler, T (2007) *Legitimacy and Criminal Justice: An International Perspective* (New York, Russell Sage Foundation).

—— (2009) 'Legitimacy and Criminal Justice: The Benefits of Self-regulation' 7 *Ohio State Journal of Criminal Law* 307.

Van Der Luit-Drummon, J (2015) 'Grayling Back in Court over Duty Contract Process', *Solicitors Journal*, 15 January 2015, www.solicitorsjournal.com/news/crime/funding-legal-aid/grayling-back-court-over-duty-contract-process.

Wilmot-Smith, F (2014) 'Necessity or Ideology?' 36 *London Review of Books* 21, 15.

Young, R (1996) 'Will Widgery Do?: Court Clerks, Discretion, and the Determination of Legal Aid Applications' in Young, R and Wall, D (eds), *Access to Criminal Justice: Legal Aid, Lawyers and the Defence of Liberty* (London, Blackstone).

Young, R and Wilcox, A (2007) 'The Merits of Legal Aid in the Magistrates' Courts Revisited' [2007] *Criminal Law Review* 109.

Zander, M (2003) *Cases and Materials on the English Legal System* (London, LexisNexis).

Treaties, Conventions, Principles, Directives, Rules and Legislation

Access to Justice Act 1999
Criminal Defence Services Act 2006
Criminal Justice and Public Order Act 1994
Legal Aid Act 1988
Legal Aid and Advice Act 1949
Legal Aid, Sentencing and Punishment of Offenders Act 2012
Magistrates' Courts Act 1980 (MCA)
Poor Prisoners' Defence Act 1930

Proposal for a Directive of the European Parliament and of the Council on provisional legal aid for suspects and accused persons deprived of liberty and legal aid in European arrest warrant proceedings, 27 November 2013 COM(2013) 824 final 2013/0409 (COD).
Prosecution of Offences Act 1985 (Criminal Court Charge) Regulations 2015 (SI 796: 2015)
Roadmap with a view to fostering protection of suspected and accused persons in criminal proceedings, 1 July 2009, 11457/09 DROIPEN 53 COPEN 120.
United Nations Principles and Guidelines on Access to Legal Aid in Criminal Justice Systems 2012

Cases

IS v Director of Legal Aid Casework [2015] EWHC 1965 (Admin)
Re R [2014] EWHC 643 (Fam)
R v Crawley and others [2014] EWCA Crim 1028

5

A View from the Bench: A Judicial Perspective on Legal Representation, Court Excellence and Therapeutic Jurisprudence

PAULINE SPENCER[1]

Steve walks into a busy courtroom clutching a bundle of papers. He knows that he did something wrong the night he got really drunk and fought with his wife, Sylvia.[2] He remembers yelling and smashing things, but not a lot else. The police were called; he was removed from the house. He does not, however, understand all the charges that he is now facing, as his reading skills are not great. He is worried that he might go to jail, and then lose his job and end up homeless. He works as a security guard. He is angry that Sylvia called the police on him and even angrier that she is not letting him come home or see the kids. After the incident, he was contacted by a men's support service but he feels he doesn't need that kind of help. He just needs to sort out this legal problem and get his family back. He is pretty sure he cannot afford a private lawyer. He gets in the queue to see the legal aid duty lawyer at court, but by 1pm he still has not met with the lawyer, and he needs to get to his afternoon work shift. He goes into court and asks for an adjournment, which is granted. He is relieved. At least he can forget about this mess for a while.

Four weeks pass and Steve has to go back to court. He has still not seen a lawyer. It has now been over two months since the night of the incident. Lately, he has been getting drunk and calling Sylvia to try and get her to allow him to see their kids. The police have questioned him again about contravening the intervention order that was put in place. He thought that the order allowed him to contact Sylvia to organise to see the kids, but the police say he is mistaken. It has been

[1] The author would like to acknowledge Philip Christidis, Law Student, Monash University, for his contributions to this chapter.

[2] This scenario is based on a series of cases that have appeared before the author. The names and details have been altered to ensure anonymity.

so long since the intervention order was processed and he can't find his copy. He meets with the legal aid duty lawyer at court, who says that he will not qualify for legal aid because he earns too much money. The duty lawyer gives him a list of private lawyers and he goes into court, asks for, and is granted, another adjournment.

The following week, Steve phones a lawyer's office and gets an appointment for two weeks' time. When he meets with the lawyer they say they will need AU$2000 (£1138) up front. A day before the next court date he still does not have the money and the lawyer says he will need to ask for another adjournment. On the next court date, the magistrate is unhappy about the number of adjournments. Steve is too embarrassed to admit that he cannot afford the money for the lawyer, yet he says he will get the money together and he is granted one further adjournment.

At the next court appearance, Steve still does not have the money for a private lawyer. He tells the magistrate that he is representing himself and wishes to plead guilty. He pleads guilty to one count of recklessly causing injury and two counts of contravening an intervention order. The magistrate hears first from the prosecutor what is alleged to have occurred and then hears from Steve. Steve does not tell the magistrate that he works in security, as he doesn't think this is relevant. The magistrate sentences him to a Community Corrections Order with a recorded conviction,[3] and a requirement that he complete 100 hours community work. Steve leaves the court feeling angry about the whole thing. He feels that he was forced to represent himself because he could not afford a lawyer and that the whole system is against him. He is still not sure how he is going to see his children, as he knows he cannot afford a family lawyer.

Over the next few months these feelings of anger and frustration build, and he drinks more and more. Steve applies to renew his security licence for work and is told that he is no longer eligible because he has a conviction for an indictable violent offence. He loses his job. That night Steve goes around to Sylvia's house drunk, demanding to see his children. He is arrested, and remanded in custody to await his court date.

For a person in contact with the law, legal advice and representation are necessary to understand their options and make decisions on how to proceed. The availability of legal advice and representation can make all the difference in terms of whether a person feels that a process and outcome are just and fair. From the perspective of a judicial officer, the availability of competent legal counsel also plays an important role in the legal process. Unrepresented people often struggle to understand the complexities of law and legal procedure. In such cases, judicial officers struggle to strike the balance between assisting the person and independent adjudication. In most cases, judicial officers would prefer to have a person represented by competent legal counsel.

[3] A Community Corrections Order is a probation-type order under s 37 of the *Sentencing Act 1991* (Vic) that is served in the community under the supervision of Community Correctional Services.

In times of fiscal restraint—like those currently being experienced in Australia's social and welfare support systems—legal aid is forced to compete for government funding allocation with other areas such as health and education. And while the cost of private legal representation remains out of reach for many working people, the effect is a large number of unrepresented persons turning up daily in the court system.

As argued by Smith and Cape (Chapter 4, this volume), in the criminal courts, the lack of access to timely and affordable legal advice and representation impacts on the quality of the court system. The International Consortium for Court Excellence (2013: 3) recognised that:

> Fair, accessible, and efficient courts create positive relations among citizens and between the individual citizen and the State. Public trust and confidence that a court will provide accessible, fair and accountable processing is, in turn, naturally enhanced by an effective and efficient court system. Confidence within the business community and therefore in business investment are likewise heightened. A sound justice system enables positive economic growth and healthy social development.

In this chapter's opening scenario, the lack of timely and affordable legal advice and representation undermined the quality of the court intervention in two key ways. First, it resulted in a range of inefficiencies in the processing of the criminal case and contributed to additional charges as a result of delay and failure to intervene in a timely manner. Secondly, it reduced the effectiveness of the court intervention, missing opportunities for early and positive therapeutic intervention with the accused, resulting in the deterioration in the accused's mental health and wellbeing and increased risk to the victim of (repeat) family violence.

This chapter draws on my experiences on the bench of a busy magistrates' court in Melbourne (Victoria, Australia) to consider how access to legal advice and representation impacts on court excellence in terms of both efficiency and quality. The impact of legal representation on the quality of courts is also explored through consideration of sentencing and therapeutic jurisprudence principles.

I. Legal Aid and Court Efficiency

Given the limited resources available, it is crucial that courts, particularly high-volume courts (usually those handling the bulk of summary offences), operate in an efficient manner. Timeliness, the balance between the time required to properly deal with a case and unreasonable delay due to inefficient processes or insufficient resources, has been recognised as a core value for court excellence (International Consortium for Court Excellence 2013: 3).

A criminal court is part of a system that has a range of inputs, including the work of various legal actors such as the judiciary, court staff, police and prosecutors, defence lawyers, correctional services personnel and staff from other support services both internal and external to the court (such as mental health workers, drug and alcohol workers and family violence workers). Court efficiency is affected, directly and indirectly, by the availability and actions of these legal actors.

The defence lawyer, as the interface between the person who is the subject of the proceedings and the system, is a fundamental part of the system. In Australia, and many other jurisdictions, counsel include lawyers in the employment of legal aid organisations and the private profession, funded by legal aid or privately, or at times acting pro bono. The capacity of each of these types of lawyer to provide representation in a timely and effective manner impacts on the operation of the court. Likewise, the paucity of legal aid funding not only impacts on the lawyers and the people they seek to represent, but also results in inefficiencies in the court system.

In the opening scenario, the case described had three unproductive court hearings, and additional consequences resulted from a failure of the system to intervene effectively at the earliest opportunity. Costs were shifted onto the court system. The Productivity Commission (2014: 30) identified this form of 'cost shifting' in its 2014 report, in respect of the civil justice system, noting that 'advocating for increases in funding (however modest) in a time of fiscal tightening is challenging. However, not providing legal assistance in these instances can be a false economy'. The Commission (2014: 30–31) went on to note that 'the costs of unresolved problems are often shifted to other areas of government spending such as healthcare, housing and child protection. Numerous Australian and overseas studies show that there are net public benefits from legal assistance expenditure'. Citing former Chief Justice Gleeson, the Law Council of Australia submission to the Commission (2014: 31) similarly noted:

> The expense which governments incur in funding legal aid is obvious and measurable. What is not so obvious, and not so easily measurable, but what is real and substantial, is the cost of the delay, disruption and inefficiency, which results from absence or denial of legal representation. Much of that cost is also borne, directly or indirectly, by governments. Providing legal aid is costly. So is not providing legal aid.

Inefficiencies are clear in circumstances in which a person is unrepresented. Unrepresented people struggle to navigate the system. In the courtroom, arguably one of the most expensive parts of the system, judicial officers are required to take time to explain the law and legal processes. In complex cases, one unrepresented person alone can take up a significant amount of court time, but even in very simple cases court time can add up. In a high-volume criminal court, like the one I work in, there will be approximately 100 mention court cases listed daily;[4]

[4] All summary matters begin as a Mention Hearing. This is 'the first date on which the matter is listed before the court. If the accused pleads guilty the matter can be heard and determined at the mention hearing' (Magistrates' Court of Victoria 2016); if not, it proceeds to a Contest Mention Hearing to see if matters or issues can be resolved prior to a Contested Summary Hearing. See also Flynn (2010) for a breakdown of Victoria's pre-trial process.

if one-third of those cases are unrepresented and take even an extra three to five minutes for the judicial officer per case, this can add several hours to the duration of a court hearing day.

Inefficiencies also occur where the pathway to someone obtaining legal representation is not clear. The Productivity Commission (2014: 9–10) noted that people can find it hard to 'shop around' for legal services, judge the quality of legal services and discern whether or not such services make them 'better off'. In the criminal law courts, people often attend court unsure about how to access legal representation. A common courtroom interaction (and one that, in my experience, occurs multiple times daily) involves an unrepresented person requesting an adjournment, followed by the judicial officer enquiring about the reason for the adjournment and then taking time to explore whether the person knows how to access representation, whether they will be able to afford a private lawyer, whether they might qualify for the legal aid means and merits test and how they will go about sorting this all out. This all takes precious court time. Furthermore, in the absence of this type of active judicial case management, there will often be multiple adjournments while a person endeavours to secure representation. While adjournments are individually quick to deal with, in a high-volume court dealing with tens of thousands of cases per year, these unproductive court listings add up. This means that even when a person is *eventually* able to access representation, the delay in determining the representation pathway can cause considerable inefficiencies.

Difficulty in navigating the system and securing representation is a particular problem for those that the Productivity Commission (2014: 20) has described as the 'missing middle'. This group comprises working people who earn too much to qualify by the legal aid means test but not enough to be able to find several thousand dollars to pay for private representation at short notice. The Productivity Commission (2014: 20) estimated that only eight per cent of Australian households would likely meet the income and asset tests for legal aid, 'leaving the majority of low and middle income earners with limited capacity for managing large and unexpected legal costs'.[5] This large cohort regularly seek court adjournments as they attempt to pull together funding for a private lawyer. Often, despite multiple adjournments, they are still not able to find the money, leaving them unrepresented and often months past their initial hearing date no closer to a resolution.

Where a person navigates the system and ultimately qualifies for a grant of legal aid, court inefficiencies can be driven by the inadequacies of grants of aid or the ways in which the grant of aid is structured. If legal aid funding is inadequate, private lawyers may take on large caseloads, resulting in them juggling multiple cases on one day and having limited time in the office to take instructions,

[5] For an example of a legal aid income and assets test refer to the *Victoria Legal Aid Lawyers Handbook*, available at: handbook.vla.vic.gov.au/handbook/12-means-test.

prepare cases and negotiate resolutions (Flynn 2010: 48). This can result in inefficiencies at court—for example, when a plea hearing is adjourned because a necessary medical report has not been obtained, or a case is resolved on the day of a one-day hearing listing.

II. Access to Justice Principles for Court Efficiency

Given the importance of legal advice and representation to court systems, as well as to accused persons, there is a need for advice and representation to be adequately funded and designed in such a way as to minimise 'cost-shifting' to courts. Consideration needs to be given to the levels of funding, the models of funding and the access to justice pathways. A system that promotes court efficiency would require a number of specific features, and I outline these in the subsections below.

A. Adequate Levels of Legal Aid Funding Based on Evidence of Legal Need

As noted, the Productivity Commission (2014: 20) estimated that only eight per cent of Australian households would likely meet the income and assets test for legal aid. This highlights the significant shortfalls in legal aid funding. There needs to be an acknowledgement that inadequacies in legal aid funding are not cost-neutral but result in cost-shifting to other parts of the system, including expensive court processes. A detailed examination of these costs and of the benefits of providing more extensive and timely access to legal advice and representation is required and this should inform changes to funding and decision-making about the allocation of funding.

B. Funding Structures Promoting Early Resolution and for those Matters that Should Go to a Full Hearing, a Funding Structure Promoting Adequate Preparation

Funding structures need to promote the early and comprehensive assessment of the prospects of a successful defence and/or the early identification of issues—those in dispute and those that could possibly be resolved. Structures should also encourage early negotiations and discussions with the prosecution, with a view to identifying those matters that could be resolved without a contest at the earliest possible opportunity (Flynn 2016). Yet, care needs to be taken not to skew the system in favour of early resolution where this is not an appropriate outcome

(Flynn 2016). Those cases that can be resolved early should do so, and those that need to go on to full hearing should be funded appropriately, to permit early consideration and preparation of the issues (Flynn 2010).

C. Active Judicial Case Management, Coupled with Investment in Early Identification of a Representation Pathway

There is certainly a role for more active case management by judicial officers with the aim of ensuring that people who are seeking adjournments are aware of the pathways to representation. Bearing in mind, however, that the role of the judicial officer is one of the more expensive components of the system, it would be more efficient to have as much of this work performed outside the courtroom as possible. It may be more efficient for the representation pathway to be identified by a legal aid representative and for this to be presented to the court with an adjournment date that is informed by the actual steps a person will need to take to secure representation, so that the future court date is a productive one. This triage role could be performed by duty lawyers; however, it may be more efficient for this role to be carried out by a suitably qualified and trained administrator, working collaboratively with duty lawyers.

D. Strategies to Assist the 'Missing Middle'

Even with increases to legal aid funding, it is likely that the 'missing middle' will remain a large cohort in the longer term. It is also the case that many in this cohort are able to undertake certain tasks associated with their legal case. There is certainly room for innovations in this area to ensure that resources go towards those most in need, while at the same time minimising cost shifting through inefficiencies in the court system. On this point, the Productivity Commission (2014: 20) has suggested that there is potential for the 'unbundling' of legal services—that is, 'a half-way house between full representation and no representation … making costs more manageable and predictable'. The Commission explains:

> Unbundling means that the lawyer and the client agree that the lawyer will undertake some, but not all, of the legal work involved. Sometimes called 'discrete task assistance' or 'limited scope representation', it differs from traditional 'full-service' representation as clients perform some tasks on their own. Where clients cannot afford full representation they at least have the option of *some* level of assistance, rather than none at all. While this practice runs counter to the convention of engaging a lawyer for the duration of a legal problem—a convention that is supported by a range of professional conduct rules—the practice of unbundling has been a common feature of the legal assistance landscape for some time. Unbundling has also become more common in some sectors of corporate practice. Given the potential benefits of unbundling legal services, the Commission considers that changes to court and professional conduct rules are warranted to facili-

> tate a shift towards more unbundling of legal services. (Productivity Commission 2014: 20–21)

In a high-volume criminal court that deals with driving matters, for example, many people are, with some information, quite capable of making a decision about whether to plead guilty or not guilty and, particularly if they decide to plead guilty, to speak on their own behalf in the courtroom. Rather than giving this advice one-on-one, legal aid could conduct group information sessions at which people are given information on the basic defences; and then once they have decided how they wish to proceed, information could be offered as to what they would need to cover in their plea hearing.

For Steve (the subject of the opening scenario), the availability of an information session about family law options soon after he had been served with the intervention order would likely have helped him to understand the appropriate pathways for exploring child contact arrangements, rather than taking matters into his own hands by harassing Sylvia in breach of the intervention order. At certain points in the family law process, individual assistance could be provided—for example, help completing documents required to initiate a case in court. Care needs to be taken that these types of unbundled services do not become a substitute for individual legal advice or representation (see Laster and Kornhauser, Chapter 7, this volume). They could, however, be used to assist those who do need some assistance, but not comprehensive assistance, and also operate to triage those cases that do require more comprehensive individual advice and representation.

III. The Role of the Lawyer in Maximising the Quality of Criminal Court

The core values of the International Consortium for Court Excellence (2013: 3) encourage courts to not just focus on timeliness or efficiency, but also to work towards improving the quality of the court intervention. In this chapter, the impact of legal representation on the quality of courts will now be explored through the example of the sentencing of offenders in criminal courts.

In most jurisdictions, courts are required to strike a balance with respect to various sentencing principles. In Victoria, section 5 of the *Sentencing Act 1991* (Vic) provides that the only purposes for which sentences may be imposed are to punish, to deter the offender or other persons from committing offences, to establish conditions for the rehabilitation of the offender, to manifest the denunciation by the court of the offending, to protect the community from the offender, or a combination of two or more of those purposes. The application of the concepts of specific deterrence, rehabilitation and, ultimately, community protection requires some consideration of how the offender will change their future behaviour. This is particularly the case when there are underlying causes of offending such as substance abuse, poor mental health and/or the choice to use violence against women and children.

In an increasing number of courts around the world, the legal philosophy of therapeutic jurisprudence (TJ) is providing a lens through which courts are seeking to improve the effectiveness of sentencing interventions and the quality of justice. TJ is the multidisciplinary study of law as a 'healing' profession and 'therapeutic agent' with a focus on the emotional, psychological and social effects, both therapeutic and anti-therapeutic, that the law has on people (Wexler 2008: 3). TJ invites us to explore the laws themselves ('the bottles') as well as the legal processes and the roles of legal actors ('the wine') to identify what can be changed or done differently to maximise therapeutic outcomes (Wexler 2014). TJ invites legal actors to draw on the social sciences for guidance, including psychology, social work and criminology (Wexler 2008: 3).

TJ approaches have underpinned the work of specialist courts such as drug courts, mental health courts, Indigenous courts, family violence courts and community courts (King 2009: 25–26). TJ thinking has also informed many innovations in mainstream criminal courts throughout the world and there is a growing international movement in this regard.[6]

IV. The Defence Lawyer's Role in Addressing the Underlying Causes of Offending

As courts shift towards applying diverse TJ approaches to effect behavioural change and reduce recidivism, all parts of the system have a role to play. Of all the legal actors involved in a criminal court—judges, defence lawyers, prosecutors, court staff, security and support services—defence lawyers are arguably one of the most important, as they are the interface between the participant and the system that is seeking to support their process of change.

The majority of offenders have underlying issues that are contributing to their offending in some way. Social science tells us that if these underlying risks and needs can be identified and sentences tailored to respond to such needs, recidivism risk can be lowered (Centre for Court Innovation 2014). Courts that apply a TJ approach take this knowledge from social science and translate it into sentencing practice. Accordingly, judicial officers increasingly need information about any underlying issues and what steps, if any, can be taken to respond to those risks and needs. Defence lawyers, as actors who are independent of the system and have the trust of their clients, are in a prime position to identify these issues, to investigate further (for example, by obtaining expert reports), to raise them in a sensitive way

[6] For examples, see: www.mainstreamtj.wordpress.com.

in open court, and to develop a rehabilitation plan in consultation with their client and in collaboration with health and social support services.

Common issues arising alongside criminal offending include substance abuse, poor mental health, cognitive impairment, poverty, unemployment, social isolation and homelessness. Often these issues are co-occurring. Sometimes presenting issues are the tip of the iceberg, such as the case of an accused who is abusing substances, who has been a victim of childhood sexual abuse, or who is stealing food because of poverty and is a victim of family violence. These issues may be underlying the current offending and/or be heightening the risk of reoffending. Sometimes these issues are quite apparent to the court even if a person is unrepresented, but often they only emerge, or their full extent only emerges, where there is a relationship of trust between a lawyer and client. The importance of this lawyer–client interaction is illustrated in the following example from the Dandenong Magistrates' Court:

> An offender was pleading guilty to a driving while suspended charge. He said he was driving so he could continue working. After some careful questioning by the lawyer he discloses that his partner was suffering from post-natal depression. He was worried about her and their finances if he didn't work, since he was the family's only source of income. It was clearly very difficult for the client to talk about these issues and initially he referred only in superficial terms to 'stuff' he 'had on'. The lawyer said that she understood that this was hard, but that 'this is the time to say it'.

Once such issues have been identified, lawyers are also able to develop a 'rehabilitation-oriented package' to present to the court (Wexler 2008). This type of preparation by lawyers is a key part of the plea process and puts the offender and the court in the best position to intervene to reduce the risk of future offending.

Looking at the scenario presented at the start of this chapter, a number of issues could have been dealt with proactively by a lawyer: the stress of the breakdown of the relationship, Steve's excessive alcohol use, the need for advice about the intervention order and family law child contact issues and the protection of Steve's job (a protective factor against future reoffending) through advocacy in favour of a non-conviction penalty. In the absence of legal representation, none of these issues were addressed, causing additional harm not only to Steve but also to Sylvia and their children.

V. The Role of the Lawyer in Facilitating Self-Determination and Autonomy

As Magistrate Michael King (2009: 26) has written:

> Self-determination has been valued as being vital for health, motivation and successful action in various traditions and disciplines over hundreds of years ... Self-determination allows a person to choose action that is personally meaningful and for which she has an

> internal commitment to perform. Choice promotes motivation, confidence, satisfaction and increased opportunities to build skills necessary for successful living.

Drawing on this understanding, courts that take a TJ approach ensure that participants are provided with a choice in terms of entering a programme, setting their goals and strategies, behavioural contracting and involvement in problem-solving around their own issues as a means of 'promoting participant self-determination, motivation and commitment to change' (King 2009: 27).

The ability to make choices is predicated upon a person understanding their options. The role of the lawyer in explaining the available options and the positives and negatives of different options is fundamental in any TJ process. Additionally, the involvement of lawyers in the design and implementation of such approaches is key to ensuring that self-determination and autonomy are promoted and protected.

VI. The Lawyer's Role as 'Change Agent'

In a TJ-informed sentencing process, the process of behavioural change should commence well before a person steps into a courtroom. The way in which a lawyer handles their client's case can affect the client's emotional and psychological wellbeing (Dewhurst 2013: 973). Therein lies the importance of therapeutic practitioners, who are commonly referred to as 'change agents' and 'effective helper[s]' (Wexler 2008: 24). TJ encourages lawyers, when interviewing and advising clients, to be aware of 'psycho-legal soft spots' (Daicoff 2005)—that is, 'certain legal issues, procedures, or interventions [that] may produce or reduce anxiety, distress, anger, depression, hard or hurt feelings, and other dimensions of [emotional] … well-being' (Daicoff 2005). Identifying and being cognisant of broader social, emotional and health concerns in a client's life allows a lawyer to minimise these sorts of negative attributes and maximise the ability of the offender to shift towards positive behavioural change.

In the scenario at the opening of this chapter, Steve had recently been separated from his wife and his children after using violence against them. He was in a state of crisis, living in a motel and facing criminal charges. He was worried about going to jail, losing his job, losing his family and becoming homeless. He was under a great deal of stress. Left without intervention, the stress manifests in anger, and he regularly drank too much and would then call Sylvia in breach of the court order. A lawyer with the confidence and trust of the client would be able to explore these issues and, acting therapeutically, would be in a position to start to problem-solve with the client in relation to his situation and make appropriate referrals to counselling and other support networks, such as counselling, alcohol treatment and men's behaviour change programmes.

Lawyers also have an important role to play in preparing a person to embark on a process of behavioural change. In a mainstream criminal court, persons charged with criminal offending may often be resistant to or ambivalent about changing behaviour or engaging in treatment. Various psychological techniques such as motivational interviewing can be used to help promote progress through the stages of change (Birgden 2002: 225). Judicial officers who apply a TJ approach draw on knowledge from behavioural science and psychology to inform the ways in which they communicate with an offender in court to maximise behavioural change.

There is, however, only so much a judicial officer can do in court. Lawyers who have a relationship of trust with their client have an important role to play in both laying the foundations for this type of approach in their preparatory meetings with the client and maximising the impact of these conversations by reinforcing the messages coming from the bench both after and in between court hearings. In taking this approach, the judicial officer and the team around the participant—including, importantly, the participant's lawyer—can help build and maintain the participant's confidence to embark upon change (King 2009: 4–5).

In the opening scenario, Steve is left feeling angry and resentful about what has happened to him, and without a lawyer to start the conversation, no one is assisting him to acknowledge the problem, take responsibility for his choice to use violence, or to do something about it.

VII. The Role of the Lawyer in Facilitating Offender Participation and 'Voice'

A court that takes a TJ approach draws on a range of tools from psychology to maximise the therapeutic outcomes of the legal process. One such tool is procedural justice. In essence, procedural justice refers to the fairness of the overall court process and how this influences the satisfaction of court users. Regardless of outcome, people see procedures as fairer and more legitimate if they are given the opportunity to be heard (Brookbanks 2015: 128). Writing for the American Judges Association, Judge Kevin Burke and Judge Steve Leben (2007: 7) provided that:

> People have a powerful urge and need to express their thoughts, experiences, or even their questions … The belief that one can go to legal authorities with a problem and receive a respectful hearing in which one's concerns are taken seriously is central to most people's definition of their rights as citizens in a democracy.

Procedural justice legitimises court decision-making and has been shown to build future compliance with the law and court orders (Tyler 2007: 28). From a participant's perspective, this means being afforded 'process control', that is, some control over the process of their hearing, rather than 'outcome control' (Tyler 1988: 104).

Burke and Leben (2007: 6) discuss procedural justice in terms of: (i) voice—the litigant's ability to participate in the case by expressing their viewpoint; (ii) neutrality—consistently applied legal principles, unbiased decision-makers and a 'transparency' about how decisions are made; (iii) respectful treatment—individuals are treated with dignity and their rights are obviously protected; and (iv) trustworthy authorities—authorities are benevolent, caring and sincerely trying to help litigants. King (2009: 191) similarly summarised the elements of procedural justice as involving voice, validation and respect.

Lawyer communication is vitally important here—a lack of communication leads to client dissatisfaction (King 2006: 138). As King (2006: 138) highlighted:

> A lawyer who encourages the client to tell their story, who is attentive in doing so, who validates that story by seeking confirmation with the client as to key aspects of the instructions given and referring to those instructions and client concerns in giving advice and who treats the client with respect can help allay client concerns and develop client faith in the lawyer.

Accordingly, a lawyer who has gained this trust, taken careful instructions and then presented their client's story to the court in a compelling way will maximise the client's perception of procedural justice and, regardless of the outcome itself, maximise the chances of the person complying with court orders. In the opening scenario, despite what would be considered a sentence that is within range for the offending (that is, a Community Corrections Order), Steve leaves his plea hearing feeling angry about the court process. This feeling builds over the ensuing months. An opportunity to possibly increase the level of his future compliance with court orders has been missed, resulting not only in poor outcomes for Steve, but also heightened risk for Sylvia and their children.

The role of the lawyer in preparing and then supporting a person to participate or have a 'voice' is becoming even more important, with judicial officers in traditional court settings adopting techniques of direct communication with the participant. In fact, this is seen as a key distinction between the traditional court process and courts that adopt a TJ approach (Bartels and Richards 2013: 31).

In court settings, a person's ability to engage in the process may be undermined by the stress of the proceedings (King 2009: 123) and/or underlying issues that may impact on their oral competence (Bartels and Richards 2013: 31). The role of the lawyer in preparing a person to participate, to raise issues that may impact on that person's ability to participate and, if necessary, advocate to have proceedings carried out in a way that facilitates their client's voice, is essential. In the absence of such representation, there is certainly a risk that approaches may become unfair and anti-therapeutic.

VIII. Conclusion

Timeliness, the balance between the time required to properly deal with a case and unreasonable delay due to inefficient processes or insufficient resources, has been recognised as a core value for court excellence. Court efficiency is dependent upon all parts of the system—courts, lawyers, prosecutors and support services—working towards that goal. Inadequate or misdirected legal aid funding results in cost-shifting to courts through inefficiencies such as adjournments, unrepresented accused persons, unproductive court hearings, delay and wasted effort. Access to timely and affordable legal advice and representation is therefore key to court efficiency. Yet the current state of legal aid funding in Victoria, and Australia more generally, lends itself to inefficiency and cost-shifting.

Court excellence is also dependent upon the quality of justice dispensed. Criminal courts throughout the world are increasingly shifting towards the use of TJ approaches to maximise the effectiveness of offender interventions. This is a dynamic area and requires ongoing attention to developments in psychology, criminology and social work, and to their integration into the legal system (Wexler 2015: 5). Lawyers, as the trusted advocate of the participant, are crucial to the success of TJ approaches in traditional courts and need to be funded to play this role. In the absence of adequate funding for legal representation, there is a real risk that the implementation of TJ approaches will be seriously undermined.

References

Bartels, L and Richards, K (2013) 'Talking the Talk: Therapeutic Jurisprudence and Oral Competence' 38 *Alternative Law Journal* 31.

Birgden, A (2002) 'Dealing with the Resistant Criminal Client: A Psychologically-minded Strategy for More Effective Legal Counseling' 38 *Criminal Law Bulletin* 225.

Brookbanks, W (2015) '# his intro' in W Brookbanks (ed), *Therapeutic Jurisprudence: New Zealand Perspectives* (New Zealand, Thomson Reuters).

Burke, K and Leben, S (2007) 'Procedural Fairness: A Key Ingredient in Public Satisfaction' 44 *Court Review: The Journal of the American Judges Association* 4.

Centre for Court Innovation (2014) *Evidence-based Strategies for Working with Offenders* (New York, Centre for Court Innovation).

Daicoff, S (2005) 'Law as a Healing Profession: The Comprehensive Law Movement' *Pepperdine Dispute Resolution Law Journal, NYLS Clinical Research Institute Paper No 05/06-12*, available at: ssrn.com/abstract=875449.

Dewhurst, D (2013) 'Understanding the Legal Client's Best Interests: Lessons from Therapeutic Jurisprudence and Comprehensive Justice' 6 *Phoenix Law Review* 973.

Flynn, A (2010) 'Victoria's Legal Aid Funding Structure: Hindering the Ideals Inherent to the Pre-Trial Process' 34 *Criminal Law Journal* 48.

—— (2016) 'Plea-negotiations, Prosecutors and Discretion: An Argument for Legal Reform' 49 *Australian and New Zealand Journal of Criminology* 564.

International Consortium for Court Excellence (2013) *International Framework for Court Excellence*, available at: www.courtexcellence.com/~/media/Microsites/Files/ICCE/The%20International%20Framework%202E%202014%20V3.ashx.

King, M (2006) 'Therapeutic Jurisprudence in Australia: New Directions in Courts, Legal Practice, Research and Legal Education' 15 *Journal of Judicial Administration* 129.

—— (2009) *Solution-Focused Bench Book* (Melbourne, Australian Institute of Judicial Administration), available at: www.aija.org.au/Solution%20Focused%20BB/SFJ%20BB.pdf.

Magistrates' Court of Victoria (2016) *Types of Hearings*, available at: www.magistratescourt.vic.gov.au/jurisdictions/criminal-and-traffic/criminal-proceedings/types-hearings.

Productivity Commission (2014) *Access to Justice Arrangements Inquiry*, Report No 72, 5 September 2014 (Canberra, Productivity Commission).

Tyler, T (1988) 'What Is Procedural Justice?: Criteria Used by Citizens to Assess the Fairness of Legal Procedures' 22 *Law and Society Review* 103.

—— (2007) 'Procedural Justice and the Courts' 44 *Court Review: The Journal of the American Judges Association* 26.

Wexler, D (2008) 'An Introduction to Therapeutic Jurisprudence' in D Wexler (ed), *Rehabilitating Lawyers: Principles of Therapeutic Jurisprudence for Criminal Law Practice* (Durham NC, Carolina Academic Press).

—— (2014) 'New Wine in New Bottles: The Need to Sketch a Therapeutic Jurisprudence "Code" of Proposed Criminal Processes and Practices', *Arizona Legal Studies Discussion Paper, No 12-16*, available at: ssrn.com/abstract=2065454.

—— (2015) 'Guiding Court Conversations along Pathways Conducive to Rehabilitation: Integrating Procedural Justice and Therapeutic Jurisprudence', *Arizona Legal Studies Discussion Paper, No 15-33*, available at: ssrn.com/abstract=2677431.

Treaties, Conventions, Principles, Directives, Rules and Legislation

Sentencing Act 1991 (Vic)

6

Face-to-interface Communication: Accessing Justice by Video Link from Prison

CAROLYN MCKAY

Audiovisual communication technologies are radically changing the criminal justice system and the concept of access to justice. Globally, remote sites such as prisons, police stations and courtrooms are interfaced into a matrix of justice and law enforcement agencies, with digital innovations facilitating legal procedure and transforming the way we 'do' justice. This chapter focuses on the shifting paradigms of legal advice, specifically the increased reliance on video links in place of face-to-face legal representation and consultation between prisoners and their lawyers. In light of successive and significant funding cuts to legal aid services, the use of video link technologies is likely to further expand. Drawing on fieldwork interviews conducted with prisoners in two New South Wales (NSW) (Australia) correctional centres, this chapter examines prisoners' experiences of using video links to access justice and legal representation. As traditional face-to-face legal conferencing transmutes into 'face-to-interface' (Richardson 2010), it is critical to contrast these forms of communication. This chapter seeks to articulate the benefits of technologies that address some efficiency concerns by replacing the transportation of prisoners to and from courtrooms with video links and lessening the need for prisoners' lawyers to visit their place of incarceration. Indeed, as a form of communication for prisoners, videoconferencing has advantages over the telephone and saves time for both prisoners and lawyers. Such benefits, however, are tempered by some potential negative repercussions, particularly compromised confidentiality in client–lawyer communications.

I. Research Methodology

In 2012, I conducted interviews with 31 prisoners in two NSW correctional centres: Dillwynia Women's Correctional Centre and Mid North Coast Correction

Centre (MNCC). The participants included 17 women (average age 35.5 years) and 14 men (average age 31.5 years). The interviews lasted between 10 and 39 minutes. Of the 31 prisoners, 18 were being held on remand, and nine identified as Aboriginal or Torres Strait Islander. All participants have been de-identified and are referred to by pseudonyms according to number and gender, such as M05 and F08. The specific focus of my fieldwork was to gather data regarding prisoners' lived experiences of appearing in court by video link from the prison studio.[1] Naturally, this included several questions relating to the prisoners' legal representation and access to legal advice before, during and following their video-linked court appearance. I treat the resulting empirical data as emerging from prisoners' constructed and mediated experiences (Bachman and Schutt 2011; Mason 2001; Miller and Glassner 2009) of using video links within a penal regime. So while the data do not represent objective knowledge, they reveal prisoners' subjective encounters with technologies.

II. The Legal Matrix

Videoconferencing technologies allow real-time interaction between two or more people located in remote sites (Bellone 2013; Wallace 2011). Given the benefits this can offer—including reducing the need for prisoner and even lawyer transport—jurisdictions around the world are integrating such technologies into a network of criminal justice agencies. This technological matrix results from a general societal uptake of digital platforms in all facets of life. The configurations, of course, differ across jurisdictions (Bellone 2013; Lederer 2004; Mulcahy 2008; Rowden et al 2013; Ward 2015) and I have only observed video links in operation in the United Kingdom (UK) and NSW. In 2012, I visited London's Camberwell Green Magistrates' Court to observe the Virtual Court system, whereby a live link between the police station and the Virtual Court allows a defendant to appear, while remaining in police custody (Ridout 2010; Susskind 2013). At a Crown Court, I also observed the Prison to Court Video Links system that operates on a similar basis.

The technological legal matrix in NSW includes courts, correctional centres and other justice agencies (Department of Justice [DoJ] NSW 2014–15: 4). There are a range of digital technologies including the Video Conferencing Scheduling System,[2] the Joined Up Justice Police Project,[3] the Online

[1] Prison video studios are typically small rooms furnished with a desk and chair and fitted with split screens to enable the prisoner to view a remote courtroom or legal conferencing space. The studio has a microphone, a telephone handset for communicating with lawyers during court hearings, and a camera focused on the prisoner to transmit his or her image to the other endpoint of the video link.

[2] This is an online collaborative database across NSW Justice Agencies that allows for the scheduling of court matters and prisoners' conferences with their lawyers.

[3] This enables 'near real-time electronic exchange of data' between courts, the police force, Corrective Services and Juvenile Justice (Department of Justice 2014–15: 24).

Registry for electronic interaction with NSW courts and JusticeLink eServices for electronic document filing (DoJ NSW 2014–15: 25). More recently, the NSW Government has trialled an online court that may eventually hear criminal matters (Whitbourn 2015).

The digital matrix in NSW can be further demonstrated by the *Evidence (Audio and Audio Visual Links) Act 1998* (NSW) ('the Act'), which legislates for the use of audiovisual links (AVL) between prisoners and courtrooms. The focus on increased technological infrastructure in the justice system is also evidenced by the State government's 2014 investment of AU$40 million (£22.76 million) in the Justice Audio Visual Link Consolidation Project (Hazzard 2014). This funding will allow for additional 'professional videoconferencing facilities' to be installed in correctional centres between 2014 and 2018, and there are plans to increase the access of 'un-sentenced inmates to legal representatives', including private legal practitioners, via AVL (Hatzistergos 2015: 44–45). This means that remand prisoners will increasingly access legal advice by AVL. An additional AU$41.9 million (£23.82 million) has also been allocated to upgrading existing technological equipment (Hazzard 2014).

Technological change in the justice system has effected a major conceptual shift, with the longstanding preference for accused persons to be physically present in court for most bail, committal, sentencing and appeal procedures being abandoned in favour of video link appearance for many criminal law procedures. In NSW, both adult and child prisoners can appear by AVL unless the court directs otherwise or the proceedings are 'physical appearance proceedings'—defined in section 3(1) of the Act as any trial, hearing or inquiry into a person's fitness to stand trial, and certain bail proceedings. In 2014–15, AVLs accounted for 44,802 of all court (63.1 per cent) and parole (100 per cent) appearances across the State (DoJ NSW 2014–15: 10).

Not only are accused persons increasingly appearing in court by video link from prison, but they are also increasingly accessing legal advice in this manner. This extension of AVL into the realm of legal advice has been described as a 'by-product' of the technological rollout between prisons and courtrooms (Forell, Laufer and Digiusto 2011: 3), and raises a number of fundamental questions around access to justice that this chapter will address.

III. Shifting Paradigms of Lawyering

Legal Aid NSW (LANSW) was established by the *Legal Aid Commission Act 1979* (NSW) to provide legal services to disadvantaged and vulnerable people (LANSW 2014–15). Video link technologies are now extensively used for communications between LANSW lawyers and their incarcerated clients (Forell et al 2011: 10), with an increase of over 2000 per cent in the use of AVLs since

2003–04.[4] AVL now represents a major portal for prisoners' access to justice, being used 'in providing advice and taking instructions from persons in custody' (LANSW 2014–15: 39). While there is an expanding use of AVL between lawyers and incarcerated clients, the efficacy of such communication in criminal justice, as discussed in the next sections, is somewhat questionable (Forell et al 2011: 2; Grunseit et al 2008).

The legal profession is not static. Over time, the legal services market has responded to a range of forces that have expanded the ambit of practice or restricted traditional monopolies, challenging accepted business models, modes of regulation and ethical frameworks. Digital information technologies represent the latest adjustment, as they become pervasive in daily legal practice and evidential court procedures, reshaping the legal modus operandi. Multidisciplinary practices and electronic law firms have arisen as the emphasis shifts to connectivity and speed (Baron and Corbin 2014; Muder [no date]; Susskind 2013; Terry, Mark and Gordon 2012). In essence, 'disruptive technologies' have radically transformed the delivery of legal services and courtroom procedures (Mezrani 2015; Susskind 2013).

Simultaneous with the rise of technologised legal practice have been dramatic government austerity measures (Smith and Paterson 2013: 6). The apparent inverse relationship between expanding technologies and tightening budgets inextricably affects the funding of legal aid programmes. Smith and Paterson have traced the growth of publicly funded legal services in countries such as the UK, the United States (US), the Netherlands and Australia, arguing that, 40 years ago, the affluence of these countries meant they could (more) readily address unmet legal need. But current economic decline has placed pressure on expenditure for essential services such as legal aid (Smith and Paterson 2013: 6). This has been seen in the UK, where the Ministry of Justice (MoJ) has been effecting major transformations to criminal and civil legal aid through stringent funding cuts (Law Society 2015; see also Byrom, Chapter 12 and Smith and Cape, Chapter 4, this volume). In NSW, successive funding cuts and persistent underfunding have impacted on the provision of legal aid services, leading to substantial unmet legal need and a growing 'justice gap': 'unless you can afford a lawyer you're on your own. Or if you're poor you can get access to Legal Aid-funded representation; that is—[if you're] really, really poor' (Blumer 2015; see also Baron and Corbin 2014). In light of the temporal coincidence of technological intervention and compounding austerity measures, we might ask: can technologies deliver justice effectively and for less money (Smith and Paterson 2013: 6–7)?

The diffusion of video link technologies into criminal justice systems has been justified on the basis of achieving economic efficiencies. For example, the UK Government's mission of 'swift and sure justice', via the Virtual Courts, has focused

[4] There were 938 AVL sessions in 2003–04 and 'almost 20,000' sessions a decade later (LANSW 2013–14: 57), an increase of over 2000 per cent.

on increasing productivity and accessibility to justice, while ensuring improved convenience and security for victims and vulnerable witnesses (MoJ 2012: 45). The system has been touted as one that will make justice faster and cheaper 'without loss of quality' (MoJ 2010: 9). However, it has been much critiqued by the UK legal profession as producing rushed justice (Atkinson 2012) and creating difficulties in communication between defendants and their legal representatives (Rowden 2011: 11–14; Ward 2015). In this Virtual Court world, individuals are being imprisoned without ever meeting their legal representative in person (Atkinson 2012). This hasty, 'stripped-back' justice has been challenged by Ward (2015: 342) for compromising fundamental principles of *fair* justice. Furthermore, Mulcahy (2011: 72) suggests that the Virtual Court system conflates dock, witness-stand and legal consultation room, so that an accused person must access justice entirely from within the prosecutorial space of a police station or prison. As discussed in detail below, the observations of the prisoners I interviewed suggest similar issues in NSW where they increasingly interact with their lawyers from a prison video studio instead of face-to-face.

IV. What is Access to Justice?

The concept of 'access to justice' implies the advancement of equity and fairness in the justice system, as well as the ability of disadvantaged populations to seek legal advice, participate in the legal system and obtain advocacy (Attorney-General's Department 2012; Baron and Corbin 2014; Grunseit et al 2008). In significantly expanding the ambit of video link technologies, the NSW Government argued that AVL provides improved access to justice (Hatzistergos 2007), especially for people in regional, rural and remote areas (Department of Attorney-General and Justice 2012; Forell et al 2011). Specifically, the Australian Attorney-General's Department (2012: 5–6) has advocated that technological initiatives promote access to justice through providing information and support as well as 'seamless and integrated service delivery' and cost-effective resolutions to disputes (LANSW 2014–15).

From the perspective of prisoners, access to justice means the ability to obtain legal advice and representation, participate in and comprehend legal proceedings, and communicate with their legal representative (Grunseit et al 2008). Their legal needs relate to their immediate situation, including what criminal charges or convictions they face, and frequently a multitude of civil law issues and personal crises, such as housing, child custody and financial matters. By reason of their loss of liberty, prisoners 'experience a unique range of barriers' and complications in seeking to resolve their legal needs (Grunseit et al 2008: iii–iv). They do not have free access to the internet and have only limited access to fixed landline telephones. Further to this, it is widely accepted that prisons are filled with people who have 'multiple vulnerabilities', including an over-representation of individuals with mental health issues or intellectual disabilities, those from Indigenous or 'over-policed' communities (Mackay 2014: 273–74), and those whose lives are shaped by poverty (Crewe 2013: 20). In prison, access to justice is inherently affected by the intersection of 'the systemic environment, the pathways to legal help and the prison culture' (Grunseit et al 2008: iv). Prisoners have complex needs that are difficult to address from closed environments. Thus, we might question whether video technologies provide an effective portal for accessing legal advice, or whether the technology acts as yet an additional barrier to the outside world.

V. The Emergent Prison Portal

Given the mass assimilation of digital technologies into society, the diffusion of communication technologies into the criminal justice system may not seem particularly controversial. However, the fact that many prisoners come from deprived backgrounds means that they may form part of the 'digital divide' (Cabral et al 2012; Hardwick 2014). Additionally, they may have had restricted opportunities for technological engagement in the outside world, be 'technologically illiterate' (Plotnikoff and Woolfson 1999: 51), leading to feelings of alienation and distance when using communication technologies, and certainly most prisons remain 'technological dead zones' (Roose and Harshaw 2015). My research found that for some prisoners, particularly those in the 20-to-29-year age group, there was a marked level of confidence with communication technologies, including feeling comfortable in front of cameras and screens. Since his time in juvenile detention, 21-year-old M05 had used AVL 'at least 100 times … [for] court, legal visits to my lawyer … bail and everything like that'. F06, a 23-year-old Aboriginal woman, had 'been in and out of the system for a couple of years' so was familiar with AVL, having used it for bail, 'court matters, legal, parole … [and] rehab'. Whether this confidence was a result of their age or increased exposure to the technological prison system was unclear. Other prisoners, like 54-year-old M08, however, had very limited technological experience, and for these prisoners entering a video suite, usually with no instructions other than to sit down, was an intimidating and daunting experience. M08 told me, 'I'm pretty much computer illiterate to be honest'. Likewise, F07—a 32-year-old Aboriginal woman who had experienced a bad concussion and suffered from memory loss—said of communication technologies in general, 'it freaks me out, yeah technology, it scares me'. Regarding AVL specifically, F07 said it was 'freaky' and 'trippy' seeing herself as if she was on television. M13, a 40-year-old prisoner, recalled his first experience using AVL:

> [T]hey walked me into a room and they sat me down in front of a computer and said, 'You've got video link' and I [said], 'I don't know how to use a fucking computer'. I'd never seen one. I've been in gaol since I was 13.

This range of diversity among prisoner experience and technological comfort indicates the disjuncture between general society and the 'pre-internet dark-age' of incarcerating environments (Begley 2015; Hardwick 2014: 5), and some of the perhaps ill-considered consequences of technological advances as an efficiency measure.

VI. Communicating with Lawyers from Prison

As flagged above, video links are increasingly the portal for prisoners' interactions with the outside world and the means for accessing legal advice and representation. While legal aid services have traditionally been delivered face-to-face, the emergent mode is 'face-to-interface' (Richardson 2010), on the basis that AVL is considered to be an efficient replacement that minimises the expense and discomfort of transporting prisoners to and from court (Hatzistergos 2008), and reduces the costs and time associated with lawyers physically visiting prisoners (Bellone 2013; Ridout 2010; Ward 2015).

In the prison context, it is important to realise that '*all* modes of communication between lawyers and inmate clients are compromised by the custodial environment' (Forell et al 2011: 13). Legal advice, whether in-person, by telephone or by AVL, is always challenged by security protocols and penal regimes. My fieldwork suggests that prisoners communicate with their legal representatives using a variety of means: telephone, postal services, video links and in-person visits. M02 explained: 'My solicitor … he's contacted me just over the gaol phones. I ring him up sometimes, and yeah he just sends me mail'. M02 noted that he also receives in-person visits from his lawyer: 'Yeah he comes up. He'll probably come up … after this [AVL] today … to talk about me sentence and what's gonna happen'. Regarding contact with his solicitor, M03 said, 'he sees me face-to-face, video link, phone, all three, I've got his mobile and that too'. In another example, I asked F06 if she had had contact with her solicitor in the days leading up to her video-linked court appearance. She replied, 'Yeah, I had contact with him, umm, he come and see me, and then I talked to him through a video link-up. He was at the courts and I was through the video link talking to him'.

Communication with legal representatives is of great importance to prisoners and M02 told me how he had 'seen boys before, like, they're a bit upset and stressed out' if their solicitor does not contact them. The worst thing for an incarcerated client is to be 'left in the dark' (M03). In light of the various modes of communication with lawyers, it is thus pertinent to consider what benefits the prisoners derive from AVL conferencing as compared with face-to-face meetings.

A. Benefits of AVL Conferences

In discussing AVL with prisoners, F01 spoke positively about the video legal conference she had just had with an LANSW lawyer, saying, 'She was very nice and very helpful and I did feel like I had a, umm, personal connection with her, as if she had been sitting here, the way you're sitting [*gesturing to me*]'. F01 appreciated the personal connection she made by AVL. She also appreciated the wider benefits of this mode of contact:

> The lady [lawyer] who was helping me was all the way in at the city and I'm just one of many that she helps today. She probably helps someone in Emu Plains, and then someone in Mulawa, and then someone in the John Morony Centre, and then someone down at Bega.[5] So she needs to be there and access us where we are, but not have to do the travelling between [us]. So I think it's not a bad idea, you know, using technology to maximise the amount of help she can give people.

In NSW, many correctional centres are located in regional locations; for example, MNCC is some 400 kilometres (248 miles) north of Sydney. As F01 observed above, she was just one of many prisoners being assisted by LANSW on the one day and recognised that technology enabled her lawyer to conference with multiple prisoners scattered across NSW.

Other prisoners appreciated how AVL saves time and told me that they had instructed their lawyers to use video links for all court appearances and communication. F10 said, 'I've told my lawyer I don't want to go on the trucks so he makes sure that I'm in video link'. F04 was similarly adamant about her preference for video link, telling me several times, 'I'd rather get video link than go to court' given the distance of over 400 kilometres (248 miles) between the prison and the courthouse: 'It's a long trip in a truck'.

Similar benefits were noted by the interviewees who, during video-linked court proceedings, felt enabled to communicate with and instruct their remote lawyers via a telephone on a desk in front of the screens. M01 said, 'there's a phone on the bench table so you can just pick the phone up, that cuts all the sound out, so you can talk to your solicitor'. M05 thought this was an acceptable form of communication with his remote lawyer, 'I can just speak up and say, look, pick up the phone or whatever, she's not doing her job or he's not doing his job, so pick up the phone … then she'll do the instructions'.

Overall, F01 expressed acceptance of the legal conference being conducted by AVL 'for this sort of thing, where I'm talking to someone who's on my side, I don't mind the video link'. However, she drew a clear distinction between this situation—where she was communicating with someone who was on *her* side—and using AVL for court appearances. With regard to the latter, she stated a firm preference for going to court physically, so that 'the judge gets to see me in the flesh'. She told me: 'to see someone face-to-face, they can get a feel for them that they can't get on the, umm, video link'.

[5] F01 was incarcerated in Dillwynia, part of the John Morony Centre, which is located approximately 53 kilometres (33 miles) from the Sydney CBD; Emu Plains is 73 kilometres (45 miles) from the CBD; Mulawa (Silverwater) is 19 kilometres (12 miles) from the CBD; and Bega Community Corrections Offices is 508 kilometres (316 miles) from the CBD.

As evidenced from the above data, there are a number of advantages of using AVL for accessing legal advice from prison. Compared to telephone, AVL enables both lawyers and their clients to see one another's responses (Forell et al 2011: 12). This is demonstrated by my discussion with F11, where she spoke of meeting her barrister for the first time: 'It was a couple of weeks ago I spoke to a barrister by video link … I'd never met him before so it was actually good to be able to see him and he could see me'. Furthermore, AVL offers relative accessibility and convenience, and possibly 'longer and uninterrupted consultation' (Forell et al 2011: 13). Interestingly, new protocols have recently been introduced to 'streamline the volume of telephone calls from prisoners' to LawAccess NSW and LANSW (LANSW 2014–15: 49, 56).[6] The volume of telephone calls to these services was, apparently, increasing at unsustainable levels. It is reported that the benefits to prisoners of the new protocols is that it will enable them to 'connect faster to their lawyer and maximize the limited amount of time they have on legal phone calls communicating directly with their lawyer' (LANSW 2014–15: 56). It is unclear at this stage how these new protocols may affect the use of AVL.

B. Benefits of Face-to-face Conferences

Without doubt, video links offered a level of convenience for prisoners and lawyers. Yet prisoners also revealed strong preferences for face-to-face meetings and a number of important drawbacks of AVL compared with face-to-face interactions. A number of prisoners expressed their preferences for in-person legal conferences either in prison or at the courthouse. I asked F04: 'Has your solicitor been to the prison at all?' and she responded: 'No they haven't. I think they should come and see you'. In response to my question about what form of communication she preferred—face-to-face, telephone or video link—F04 replied, 'Face-to-face; I prefer just to know what's going on'. A similar view was expressed by M11, who explained face-to-face as being better 'cause you get to talk to your solicitor sort of one-on-one … face-to-face yeah is always better … it's just … a bit more intimate … and you can sort of … just communicate better with them face-to-face'. M10 likewise stated his preference for face-to-face meetings with his solicitor, 'I'd rather … face-to-face, even though technology is cool, don't get me wrong, but … I'd rather talk to a person face-to-face. It … helps you understand more and gives you … a degree of … security'. M04 also spoke of the importance of meeting his lawyer face-to-face, stating, 'it's important for the lawyer to get an idea of, like, who you are … I think that you can tell a lot … by being with someone, by speaking with someone'.

[6] A free telephone service providing legal information, advice and referrals to LANSW.

M08 preferred to meet with his solicitor face-to-face, compared with telephone, because of the noise of the prison itself:

> I'm not the best with my hearing and, umm, in here it's pretty hard to hear what's going on over phones, yeah it's best to see him face-to-face. You've just got time to say what you want to say rather than being limited to the telephone you know. … There's always noise going on and it's hard to hear what they're saying on the phone you know.

M02 mentioned that physical trips to court provide opportunities for face-to-face meetings with his solicitor who will 'come down to the cells and just have a yarn to you, let you know what's happening'. Similarly, M03 observed that if he is actually in court, the solicitor can 'come down and speak to you straight away'. By video link, he has to wait 'another few hours' before being contacted by the lawyer.

C. Drawbacks of AVL Conferencing

In contrast with face-to-face legal conferences and physical court appearances, throughout video-linked sessions, prisoners remain incarcerated while their lawyers are in the remote courtroom or their office. This physical separation changes prisoners' abilities to instruct their legal representatives and to confirm legal outcomes. Prior to her AVL, F03 had not been contacted by anyone: 'I haven't spoken to anyone yet. I don't even know what's happening'. F02 told me that her solicitor had rung her on the telephone before the AVL session and she had spoken to him for only 'a minute'—an inadequate period for her to express instructions. She felt aggrieved that they had not had a longer conversation: 'You need to be able to speak one-on-one with your lawyer'. F02 thought the quality of representation was better when she was physically present in court. During video link, F02 explained that 'we're not being represented right, you know, it's totally different from being [in court]'. Furthermore, F02 felt communication was constrained by video link: 'If you went up [to court] you can at least … explain the situation. You can't do it on video link'. These comments call into question the quality of representation available through the use of video link.

F17 also felt she had been given insufficient time to communicate with her solicitor before her AVL court appearance. As a recommendation, she suggested that prisoners require 'more communication with your solicitor beforehand, not like fucking just half an hour before you go up in front of the judge. That's fucked up'. Additionally, a number of prisoners complained of having to wait for extended periods of time in a prison holding cell, only to find that their lawyers had completed processes in their absence. F15 said:

> I went up to the [AVL] court but I didn't end up using it because they just went ahead without me anyway, so … it was pretty … shitty … I was there like all day and then … my solicitor rang and said, OK you just appear next week and I was like, why did I get called up there in the first place?

> *So you spent the day waiting?*
>
> Yeah, in a cell and in the end they done it without me even going onto video link to be part of it.
>
> *How did that make you feel?*
>
> Just like I wasn't in the loop and [*laughs*] that's the last thing you want when you're in gaol, like you want to actually know what's going on with your court cases.

As these excerpts suggest, video links are not necessarily resulting in more-timely or better quality interactions between lawyers and their incarcerated clients. Furthermore, some prisoners spoke of the difficulty in recognising their lawyer in the remote courtroom. During one video link session this proved upsetting for F05: 'I got really peed off … I didn't recognise my lawyer in the courthouse and I was like: where's my lawyer?, you know, 'cause, yeah, I couldn't recognise him'. When asked how she felt about the physical separation from her lawyer in this instance, F05 replied: 'Yeah, kind of weird, umm, actually'.

An increased concern about the use of AVL for communication between lawyers and incarcerated clients is the dearth of studies evaluating the efficacy of AVL legal assistance, particularly for disadvantaged populations with complex needs (Forell et al 2011: 17–18; Kluss 2008). AVL has been found to be functional and acceptable for legal conferencing; however, the existing (albeit limited) literature in this area reveals an overwhelming preference for *in-person* legal meetings (Forell et al 2011: 2, 11). AVL inherently alters the means by which lawyers obtain instructions from their clients, and the loss of face-to-face communication may have a greater impact on Indigenous and non-English-speaking prisoners (Kluss 2008). The physical dislocation affects opportunities for privileged discussions and restricts non-verbal communication, blocking the lawyer's assessment of the client's emotional and psychological state (Poulin 2004: 1130). As such, the technology presents challenges in establishing empathy (Rowden 2013). Regarding Aboriginal Legal Services and juvenile justice, the NSW Law Society (2013) advocates face-to-face communication so that lawyers may gauge comprehension and fitness to be tried, and be enabled to receive coherent instructions. LANSW has also reported some challenges with AVL including the 'rising prison population, limited AVL suites, [and] the constant movement of prisoners' so new information and communications technology initiatives are planned to ease these difficulties (LANSW 2014–15: 39).

While AVL communication may be functional, 'prisoners have a strong preference for face to face advice because it is their only contact with the outside world' (de Simone and d'Aquino 2004: 25). In de Simone and d'Aquino's study of female prisoners' access to legal aid services, concerns were expressed regarding confidentiality, and the undesirable audio leakage from the prison video suites (McKay 2016). Grunseit et al (2008) also found that legal access via AVL can be problematic. The authors highlighted the inability of prisoners to freely speak with their lawyer and how that can impact on prisoners' comprehension (Grunseit et al 2008: 107). Given the 'profound impact' that legal processes may have upon the lives and liberty of prisoners, Grunseit et al (2008: 130–31) emphasised the need to ensure that AVL does not further compromise comprehension. In a UK evaluation of a video link pilot between a prison and a Crown Court, concerns were expressed by both judges and advocates regarding the ability of prisoners to hear, see, participate, comprehend and communicate confidentially with their legal advisers, leading to concerns regarding fairness (Plotnikoff and Woolfson 2000: 28–30, 35). In this way, video links may be seen to hamper discussions with prisoners about their plea, and act as a barrier to building rapport. Live video links also produce an additional layer of 'cognitive confusion and complexity' through spatial separation (Mulcahy 2008: 485; see also Grunseit et al 2008). Face-to-face legal conferencing remains critical in facilitating confidence and comprehension in legal representation, especially when instructions involve documents and exhibits (Kluss 2008: 51).

D. Confidentiality

The literature discussed above highlights prisoners' preferences for face-to-face meetings and the impact of video links on confidential client–lawyer communications. In my study, the principal reason why prisoners preferred their lawyers to visit them face-to-face in prison was to ensure confidentiality. The ability to hold confidential conversations with lawyers is almost always compromised by incarceration. F12 told me about a face-to-face meeting with her lawyer in prison when the prison officers insisted on the door remaining open: '[Prison officers] don't allow you privacy with your solicitor … they've got to keep the door open which even my solicitor thought was odd'. In addition, prison regimes may limit face-to-face meetings. M10 told me that his solicitor had visited him recently but the meeting was cut short: 'Time limited, yeah, 'cause [prison officers] wanted to get us back for the dinner time'.

However, the opportunities for prisoners to have confidential conversations with, and to give instructions to, their lawyers may be further compromised by video link (Bellone 2013; Hillman 2007; Kluss 2008; Poulin 2004; Ridout 2010; Rowden, Wallace and Goodman-Delahunty 2010; Ward 2015). Bellone's 2013 study investigated whether videoconferencing is detrimental to private communications between incarcerated clients and their lawyers. Referencing existing scholarship on videoconferencing and empirical data from a survey of US courts, Bellone concluded that videoconferencing has negative impacts on private communications, resulting in compromised access and inadequate representation (Bellone 2013: 47; Poulin 2004: 1129). Similarly, Davis (2001) found that 'virtual' presence lessens opportunities for private communication between an incarcerated defendant and their legal representative. In terms of access to justice and the client–lawyer relationship specifically, Poulin (2004: 1129) identified profound negative impacts, especially when the client is in prison and the lawyer is in a remote court.

Privacy issues were certainly raised by many prisoners during my interviews. F09 asked, 'How are you supposed to talk privately to your solicitor if you're video linked'? Similarly F02 said, 'You're supposed to be able to speak to your lawyer, you know, one-on-one … there's nowhere you can speak with your lawyer without them listening which is not good you know'. F08 preferred to meet her legal team face-to-face because then the authorities 'can't record conversations'. While discussing a murder charge, M13 was concerned about his restricted view of the remote legal conferencing room and whether confidentiality was being compromised:

> I did actually say to me mouthpiece: is there anyone else in the room with yah' cause we're not talking about a break and enter, you know what I mean, we're talking about the rest of me life in gaol. He says, 'there's no one in the room' … [but] I still didn't go into any details, so we just set up a date when we could go to a watch house and talk there [face-to-face].

M13 concluded that 'face-to-face, it's the only way you can have it private'.

Further to this, the soundproofing of the prison video suites in the prisons I visited appeared to be inadequate, as several prisoners complained about the infiltration of prison noises (McKay 2016). M02 said, 'it's hard to hear because there's other things like outside the room, they shut the door but you can still hear like what's going on in the cells, and all the yelling and whatnot'. Intrusive sounds and technical problems may militate against prisoners' ability to concentrate on and comprehend legal conferences. Critically, the seemingly inadequate soundproofing affects the privacy afforded to prisoners in communicating with their remote lawyers. A few prisoners were concerned with the proximity of prison officers to the video studios and the potential for 'eavesdropping' (M10) or being 'too nosy' (F14).

Difficulties in holding confidential conversations and giving instructions result in some prisoners feeling that their representation is compromised. Certainly, quiet asides during court proceedings are impossible by video link. As mentioned above, prisoners may use the telephone in the video studio to communicate with their lawyer during video-linked court hearings, but that can be problematic. F11 discussed the issues around attracting the attention of her remote lawyer:

> With the parole hearing I was going like this to the solicitor [*waving gesture*] … I'm not familiar with this solicitor, he's prison legal aid and he wasn't watching me on the screen, he was too busy watching the judges, and it was the lady next to him [who] said, 'I think your client wants to talk to you on the phone'.

Problematically, if prisoners need to attract the attention of their remote lawyer, they must often resort to waving frantically, if not histrionically, at the camera (*R v Baladjam & Others [No 41]* [2008] NSWSC 1462). F11's account highlights the problems of how easily video-linked prisoners may be ignored—even unintentionally—even by their own legal representatives.

Some prisoners were happy to make use of the video studio telephone to speak with their remote lawyers while others were suspicious; for example, M11 thought there was a possibility that someone could 'read your lips'. Both F08 and F11 could not speak freely with their remote lawyers who were in court and sitting too close to the prosecution. F11's communication with her remote lawyer was constrained, as he advised her: 'I can't elaborate; I have the prosecution sitting right next to me'. Additionally, there are suggestions that telephone calls at the bar table with prisoners are not private and are monitored 'in accordance with cross-justice agencies' specification' (Kluss 2008)—an assertion contested by the government (Hatzistergos 2008). These accounts highlight how video links in criminal justice are *transformative* technologies that radically alter the interactions between prisoners and their legal representatives (Licoppe and Dumoulin 2010; Rowden 2013: 108).

VII. Conclusion

Communication technologies have irrevocably recomposed the delivery and production of legal services (Dumoulin and Licoppe 2015), and continue to do so: 'All is changed, changed utterly by new technology' (Smith and Paterson 2013: 51, 83). Communication technologies have been increasingly installed throughout justice agencies, creating an integrated legal matrix, while funding for essential legal aid services has been cut. Video link technologies may achieve economic efficiencies, optimise business targets and represent a mainstream form of communication in the corporate and civil sector. However, the experience of incarcerated clients' access to justice is not comparable. The prison endpoint of videoconferencing is quite distinct and prisoners face significant inequalities in accessing legal services. The expansion of legal services into internet and digital platforms that are not readily available to incarcerated populations does little to address their legal needs. Modernising 'justice through new technology' cannot be achieved if prisoners' access to technologies is ignored (Hardwick 2014).

This chapter has examined some of the advantages and disadvantages of video links between prisoners and their lawyers. AVL has been used successfully by lawyers when there has been an established client–lawyer relationship based on prior face-to-face contact (Kluss 2008: 50). Indeed, the extant scholarship and my fieldwork suggest that video links may provide a level of convenience for lawyers and prisoners. However, in providing a comparison of client–lawyer communication, face-to-face versus video interactions, my fieldwork evidences weaknesses in video interactions. For some prisoners, it may diminish the quality of communication and fracture confidential discussions. As the extension of AVL into the realm of legal advice has been, in effect, a 'by-product' of the technological rollout between prisons and courtrooms (Forell et al 2011: 3), missing is a close examination of the conceptual challenges regarding access to justice in this age of digital interface and integrated criminal justice matrix. Given that 'equitable access to justice is an essential right for individuals' (Baron and Corbin 2014: 223), '*real* access to justice will only be achieved when remote [video-linked] participation does not equate to diminished participation' (Rowden 2013: 109). The multifaceted responses from my interviewees evidence that, within the taxing environment of prison, video links increasingly represent their portal for connection with the outside world. To maintain democratic standards of access to justice and 'equality of arms' (Ridout 2010), that portal needs to facilitate, not compromise, private communications between lawyer and client. However, current technologies seemingly erect new barriers, reinforcing prisoners' exclusion from the world and a loss of access to justice.

Finally, insofar as legal representatives are visiting prisons less frequently, the independent scrutiny of prisoners and their conditions is affected. Prisons are inherently closed environments (Naylor, Debeljak and Mackay 2014)—that is, breach-resistant, non-public institutions with strict security procedures determining who may enter and exit. The decrease in visits by lawyers may be reinforcing the impermeable and opaque nature of prisons. Institutions that are more permeable and transparent are 'less prone to the development of abusive practices' (Quirk, Lelliott and Seale 2006: 2114). Conversely, negative cultures may flourish where there is a lack of independent monitoring (Owers 2014: 215–16; Stevens 2014: 253). Within the closed environment of prison, individuals are susceptible to human rights violations due to the non-public nature of these sites and the inherent power imbalances (Naylor et al 2014: 8–9). The reduction in physical legal visits may make prisons even more unseen and unknowable than they are already.

References

Atkinson, R (2012) 'Virtual Courts: More Speed, Less Justice', *The Guardian*, 18 July 2012.

Attorney-General's Department (2012) 'Harnessing the benefits of technology to improve access to justice: Analysis Paper', Commonwealth of Australia, available at: www.lccsc.gov.au/agdbasev7wr/sclj/harnessing_the_power_of_technology_analysis_paper.pdf.

Bachman, R and Schutt, RK (2011) *The Practice of Research in Criminology and Criminal Justice*, 4th edn (Thousand Oaks CA, Sage).

Baron, P and Corbin, L (2014) *Ethics and Legal Professionalism in Australia* (Oxford, Oxford University Press).

Begley, P (2015) 'Social media site iexpress at centre of internet for prisoners debate' *The Sydney Morning Herald*, 4 October 2015, available at: www.smh.com.au/nsw/social-media-site-iexpress-at-centre-of-internet-for-prisoners-debate-20150924-gjtupi.html.

Bellone, ET (2013) 'Private Attorney-Client Communications and the Effect of Videoconferencing in the Courtroom' 8 *Journal of International Commercial Law and Technology* 24.

Blumer, C (2015) 'No Right to Justice', *ABC News*, available at: www.abc.net.au/news/2015-04-01/no-right-to-justice/6328790.

Cabral, JE, Chavan, A, Clarke, TM, Greacen, J, Hough, BR, Rexer, L, Ribadeneyra, J and Zorza, R (2012) 'Using Technology to Enhance Access to Justice' 26 *Harvard Journal of Law & Technology* 241.

Crewe, B (2013) 'Writing and reading a prison: making use of prisoner life stories' 91 *Criminal Justice Matters* 20.

Davis, D (2001) 'Talking heads: virtual reality and the presence of defendants in court' 75 *Florida Bar Journal* 26.

de Simone, T and d'Aquino, C (2004) *Inside Out: The Access of Women and Girls in Custody to Legal Aid Services*, available at: www.sistersinside.com.au/media/insideout.pdf.

Department of Justice of New South Wales (2014–15) *Annual Report*, available at: www.justice.nsw.gov.au/publications-research/annual-reports.

Department of Attorney-General and Justice (NSW) (2012) *Review of the delivery of legal assistance services to the NSW community*, available at: www.justice.nsw.gov.au/justicepolicy/Documents/delivery_of_legal_assistance_services_report_final.pdf.

Dumoulin, L and Licoppe, C (2015) 'Trial at a Distance: Videoconference Technology as a Policy Tool?' Paper presented at International Conference in Public Policy, 1–5 July 2015, Milan, available at: www.icpublicpolicy.org/conference/file/reponse/1435654716.pdf.

Forell, S, Laufer, M and Digiusto, E (2011) *Legal assistance by video conferencing: what is known?* Justice Issues Paper 15 (Sydney, Law and Justice Foundation of New South Wales).

Grunseit, A, McCarron, E, Forell, S and Law and Justice Foundation of New South Wales (2008) *Taking Justice into Custody: The Legal Needs of Prisoners* (Sydney, Law and Justice Foundation of New South Wales).

Hardwick, N (2014) 'Modernising justice through new technology: Improving prisoner access to new technologies', HM Chief Inspector of Prisons, 24 June 2014, available at: www.justiceinspectorates.gov.uk/hmiprisons/wp-content/uploads/sites/4/2014/02/MODERNISING-JUSTICE-THROUGH-NEW-TECHNOLOGY-FINAL.pdf.

Hatzistergos, J (2007) Attorney-General and Minister for Justice, Second Reading Speech, NSW Legislative Council, *Parliamentary Debates, (Hansard)*, 15 November 2007, available at: www.parliament.nsw.gov.au/prod/parlment/nswbills.nsf/6355a6928b367630ca256e6700008afa/0f1426500c16134bca2573930001f1c4/$FILE/LC%207507.pdf.

—— (2008) 'The virtues of audiovisual links in the courtroom' (July 2008) 46 *Law Society Journal: The official journal of the Law Society of New South Wales* 57.

—— (2015) *Review of the Bail Act 2013*, Final Report June 2015, available at: www.justice.nsw.gov.au/Documents/publications-research/jh-review-of-the-bail-act-2013-final-report-june-2015.pdf.

Hazzard, B (2014) *$81.9 million technology upgrade to slash costs and time in justice system*, available at: www.justice.nsw.gov.au/Documents/Media%20Releases/MR_14_81_million_technology_upgrade.pdf.

Hillman, ZM (2007) 'Pleading Guilty and Video Teleconference: Is a Defendant "Constitutionally Present" when Pleading Guilty by Video Teleconference?' 7 *Journal of High Technology Law* 41.

Kluss, S (2008) 'Virtual Justice: The Problems with Audiovisual Appearances in Criminal Courts' 46 *Law Society Journal* 48.

Law Society of NSW (2013) 'AVL proposal for NSW Children's Court', Letter to Department of Attorney-General & Justice, 7 June 2013, available at: www.lawsociety.com.au/cs/groups/public/documents/internetpolicysubmissions/744002.pdf.

Law Society (UK) (2015) 'Legal aid cuts: House of Lords asks further questions of the MoJ', 3 July 2015, available at: www.lawsociety.org.uk/news/stories/law-society-statement-on-criminal-legal-aid-cuts/.

Lederer, F (2004) 'Introduction: What Have We Wrought?' 12 *William & Mary Bill of Rights Journal* 637.

Legal Aid New South Wales [LANSW] (2013–14) *Annual Report*, available at: www.legalaid.nsw.gov.au/publications/annual-report.

—— (2014–15) *Annual Report*, available at: www.legalaid.nsw.gov.au/publications/annual-report.

Licoppe, C and Dumoulin, L (2010) 'The "Curious Case" of an Unspoken Opening Speech Act: A Video-Ethnography of the Use of Video Communication in Courtroom Activities' 43 *Research on Language and Social Interaction* 211.

Mackay, A (2014) 'Operationalising Human Rights Law in Australia: Establishing a Human Rights Culture in the New Canberra Prison and Transforming the Culture of Victoria Police' in B Naylor, J Debeljak and A Mackay (eds), *Human Rights in Closed Environments* (Annandale NSW, The Federation Press).

McKay, C (2016) 'Video Links from Prison: Permeability and the Carceral World' in A Flynn and M Halsey (eds), 5 *International Journal for Crime, Justice and Social Democracy* 21.

Mason, G (2001) *The Spectacle of Violence: Homophobia, Gender and Knowledge* (London, Routledge).

Mezrani, L (2015) 'Opting out of technology no longer an option', *Lawyers Weekly*, 10 March 2015, available at: www.lawyersweekly.com.au/news/16247-opting-out-of-technology-no-longer-an-option?utm_source=lawyersweekly&utm_campaign=lawyersweekly_Bulletin11_03_2015&utm_medium=email.

Miller, J and Glassner, B (2009) 'The 'inside' and the 'outside': finding realities in interviews' in D Silverman (ed), *Qualitative Research: Theory, Method and Practice* (London, Sage).

Ministry of Justice [MoJ] (UK) (2010), *Virtual Court Pilot: Outcome Evaluation*, Ministry of Justice Research Series 21/10.

—— (2012), *Swift and Sure Justice: The Government's Plans for Reform of the Criminal Justice System* (London, The Stationary Office).

Muder, J (no date) 'Technology and the Legal Profession—A Perfect Merger', available at: www.articlesphere.com/Article/Technology-and-the-Legal-Profession---A-Perfect-Merger/140759.

Mulcahy, L (2008) 'The Unbearable Lightness of Being? Shifts Towards the Virtual Trial' 35 *Journal of Law & Society* 464.

—— (2011) *Legal Architecture: Justice, Due Process and the Place of Law* (Abingdon, Routledge).

Naylor, B, Debeljak, J and Mackay, A (eds) (2014) *Human Rights in Closed Environments* (Annandale NSW, The Federation Press).

Owers, A (2014) 'Comparative Experiences of Implementing Human Rights in Closed Environments: Monitoring for Rights Protection' in B Naylor, J Debeljak and A Mackay (eds), *Human Rights in Closed Environments* (Annandale NSW, The Federation Press).

Plotnikoff, J and Woolfson, R (1999) *Preliminary Hearings: Video Links Evaluations of Pilot Projects* (London, The Home Office), available at: lexiconlimited.co.uk/wp-content/uploads/2013/01/Videolink-magistrates.pdf.

—— (2000) *Evaluation of Video Link Pilot at Manchester Crown Court* (London, The Home Office).

Poulin, AB (2004) 'Criminal justice and videoconferencing technology: the remote defendant' 78 *Tulane Law Review* 1089.

Quirk, A, Lelliott, P, and Seale, C (2006) 'The permeable institution: An ethnographic study of three acute psychiatric wards in London' 63 *Social Science & Medicine* 2105.

Richardson, I (2010) 'Faces, Interfaces, Screens: Relational Ontologies of Framing, Attention and Distraction' *Transformations* 18.

Ridout, F (2010) 'Virtual Courts—Virtual Justice?', *Criminal Law & Justice Weekly*, 24 September 2010, 603.

Roose, K and Harshaw, P (2015) 'Inside the prison system's illicit digital world' *Fusion, Tech Behind Bars Series*, available at: fusion.net/story/41931/inside-the-prison-systems-illicit-digital-world/.

Rowden, E (2011) 'Remote Participation and the Distributed Court: An approach to court architecture in the age of video-mediated communications' PhD Thesis, Architecture, Building and Planning (Victoria, The University of Melbourne).

—— (2013) 'Virtual Courts and Putting "Summary" Back into "Summary Justice": Merely Brief or Unjust?' in J Simon, N Temple and R Tobe (eds), *Architecture and Justice: Judicial Meanings in the Public Realm* (London, Ashgate).

Rowden, E, Wallace, A and Goodman-Delahunty, J (2010) 'Sentencing by videolink: up in the air?' 34 *Criminal Law Journal* 363.

Rowden, E, Wallace, A, Tait, D, Hanson, M and Jones, D (2013) *Gateways to Justice: Design and Operational Guidelines for Remote Participation in Court Proceedings*

(Sydney, University of Western Sydney), available at: www.uws.edu.au/__data/assets/pdf_file/0019/471223/Gateways_to_Justice_Guidelines.pdf.

Smith, R and Paterson, A (2013) *Face to Face Legal Services and Their Alternatives: Global Lessons from the Digital Revolution*, available at: www.strath.ac.uk/media/faculties/hass/law/cpls/Face_to_Face.pdf.

Stevens, J (2014) 'Changing Cultures in Closed Environments: What Works?' in B Naylor, J Debeljak and A Mackay (eds), *Human Rights in Closed Environments* (Annandale NSW, The Federation Press).

Susskind, R (2013) *Tomorrow's Lawyers: An Introduction to Your Future* (Oxford, Oxford University Press).

Terry, L S, Mark, S and Gordon, T (2012) 'Trends and Challenges in Lawyer Regulation: The Impact of Globalization and Technology' 80 *Fordham Law Review* 2661.

Wallace, A (2011) 'Justice and the "virtual" expert: Using remote witness technology to take scientific evidence' PhD thesis (New South Wales, The University of Sydney).

Ward, J (2015) 'Transforming "Summary Justice" Through Police-Led Prosecution and "Virtual Courts"' 55 *British Journal of Criminology* 341.

Whitbourn, M (2015) 'NSW Government trials online court for civil cases in Sydney' *The Sydney Morning Herald*, 10 August 2015, available at: www.smh.com.au/nsw/nsw-government-trials-online-court-for-civil-cases-in-sydney-20150807-giuig2.html.

Treaties, Conventions, Principles, Directives, Rules and Legislation

Evidence (Audio and Audio Visual Links) Act 1998 (NSW)
Legal Aid Commission Act 1979 (NSW)

Cases

R v Baladjam & Others [No 41] [2008] NSWSC 1462.

7

The Rise of 'DIY' Law: Implications for Legal Aid

KATHY LASTER AND RYAN KORNHAUSER

I. Introduction: Technology and the Age of the Gifted Amateur

The 'Google revolution' has given rise to the age of the gifted amateur. Individuals now have immediate access to information and skills once completely beyond their ken. People enjoy unparalleled support for their diverse, even difficult, personal quests. Everything from recipes that detail how to make the most obscure international dishes to advice from complete strangers on almost any conceivable topic is readily accessible with the click of a mouse. The wonders of consumer technology also grow exponentially as new generations of savvy machines, with ever-new capabilities, regularly come onto the market. And each night, various pop culture reality television series show ordinary people becoming elite home renovators, weight-loss and exercise experts, and culinary master chefs.[1]

The not-so-subtle message of these cultural products is that there is seemingly no aspect of human endeavour that perseverance, technology and self-directed learning cannot conquer. The technology-informed do-it-yourself (DIY) Zeitgeist has lifted the bar of social competence. The neoliberal subject—already expected to be rational and prudent (Rose 2000: 324)—is now also expected to become the skilled and knowledgeable expert (O'Malley 1996: 201).

At one level, this shift is positive, as people now have direct control over their lives in ways that were unthinkable just a decade ago. We have realised something of William Morris's nineteenth-century socialist Utopia, where work and leisure overlap through creative artisanal collaboration (Morris 1908). There is pride among the growing cadre of social DIY-ers who feel empowered to refashion themselves, create their own 'lifestyle', learn new skills, and share ideas and information with each other (see, for example, Kuznetsov and Paulos 2010).

[1] For example, reality television shows like *The Block*, *Masterchef*, and *The Biggest Loser*.

The DIY spirit, we contend, extends beyond mastery of the kitchen, home renovation or even medical self-diagnosis to now include navigation of the complexities of the legal system. In this chapter, we argue that 'DIY law' accounts, in part, for the relative ease with which the socially progressive institution of legal aid is being undermined. Our focus is on Victoria (Australia's second most populous State) and Victoria Legal Aid (VLA) as a case study of developments that, to varying degrees, are also evident in comparable jurisdictions.

We contend that influences from both the political Left and Right, spurred on by technological developments, have provided the means and the impetus for individuals to take control over their legal issues. We argue that one significant unintended consequence of this shift is a change in community support for individual access to legal aid, as legal consumers are themselves expected to play a greater role in the provision of self-directed legal services. The chapter begins by showing how community legal education and access to law opportunities have delivered on the idealistic aims of the consumerist movement of the 1970s and 1980s. To some extent, the monopoly of elites, such as lawyers, has been displaced, as ordinary people have been provided with direct access to legal information and self-help resources. But, we go on to argue, this development has neatly dovetailed with the other dominant ideological forces at play in Western democracies during this same period: neoliberalism and public sector managerialism. We demonstrate how the introduction of private sector corporate efficiency into the public sector has combined with new models of 'co-production' which increasingly expect citizens to assist and support government service delivery, rather than the other way round.

Legal aid, created as a legal safety net for the most marginalised in society, now provides an ever-receding range of services for progressively fewer people, as a result of a shift in classification from 'need' to 'status'. At the same time, the courts, already over-burdened and under-resourced, try to deal with unrepresented litigants while simultaneously becoming the unacknowledged 'help hub' that authorises and prioritises access to (diminishing) social support services more generally (see Spencer, Chapter 5, this volume).

We conclude that the net effect of these radical cultural developments is that a new version of an old social stigma attaches to those individuals deemed 'unable to cope'—with life and with the law. In an aggressively DIY culture, the inherent complexity of many tasks is seriously underestimated. Failure is implicitly ascribed to deficits of character, rather than the demands of the task. Too often, the personal and structural factors that militate against success, such as age, limited technological and English language proficiency, intellectual ability, and mental and physical health, are not accounted for.

The new 'undeserving poor' are the 'ungifted amateurs': people who lack the skills and knowledge to find their way through the complexities of the new information age and knowledge economy. Legal aid has become too easily dismissed as a problematic drain on the public purse, as the wider community of gifted amateurs—capable of adapting to significant change—has little patience or sympathy for this emerging underclass of seemingly socially incompetent, undeserving litigants and criminal defendants.

II. Making Law Accessible

'Law Week' is an annual public outreach event held in the third week of May each year in Victoria. The Victoria Law Foundation, with the statutory mandate and tag line of 'helping Victorians understand the law', coordinates this high-profile event.[2] Typically, during this week, over 100 activities are hosted by legal sector agencies—courts are opened on weekends, mock trials are held for public audiences, and there are a variety of public lectures presented on legal topics such as wills and estates, family law and privacy (Victoria Law Foundation 2015b).

The enthusiasm of legal sector agencies to participate in Law Week, and to appreciate the importance of community engagement more generally, is a relatively new phenomenon. Until 2001, Law Week was run by Victoria's professional association of lawyers, the Law Institute of Victoria, which largely viewed the event as a marketing exercise to promote the services of its membership, such as drafting wills or settling family law matters 'properly'. Many courts were also initially dubious and refused to open on weekends, citing cost, security concerns and a lack of interest among judicial officers. As one senior judge explained to the then Executive Director of the Victoria Law Foundation, 'I am a judicial officer, *not* a tour guide'.[3]

There was a sense that the law existed as the province of professionals—the realm of lawyers and judges, not the general public. This view prevailed among the legal sector establishment despite a strong movement in Australia, and other common law countries, from the 1970s onwards to improve community understanding of the law, and a concerted effort by sections of the profession to make law more accessible, particularly through community legal education.

A. The Rise of Community Legal Education

In the 1970s and 1980s, a then quite radical community legal centre (CLC) movement emerged, seeking to provide free legal advice and support to marginalised clients (see Buchanan, Chapter 8, Giddings, Chapter 3, and Noone, Chapter 2, this volume). The movement also aimed to empower individuals through better knowledge of the law and the legal system—a trend that continues today (see

[2] The Victoria Law Foundation operates under the *Victoria Law Foundation Act 2009* (Vic), and is funded primarily from the interest on solicitors' trust accounts (Victoria Law Foundation 2015a).

[3] One of the authors of this chapter was previously an Executive Director of the Victoria Law Foundation.

Buchanan, Chapter 8, this volume). As Giddings and Robertson (2001: 185, citations omitted [see also Giddings and Robertson 2002: 438]) explain:

> Improving community understanding of the law has been an important aspect of the philosophy of Australian CLCs since their establishment in the 1970s. This community legal education focus continues to be emphasised by CLCs. Sam Biondo refers to community legal education as comprising the provision of both legal information and legal education … Biondo states that the education aspect of community legal education 'is about developing a deeper understanding of legal rights and responsibilities'. Further, he endorses the view of Allan Nicoll that the vital and essential ingredient of relevant and successful community legal education is 'empowerment' which 'gives individuals and groups an ability to have a say in decisions that are likely to affect them'.

These aspirations were given concrete form in the development of the first hard-copy plain language handbooks on various aspects of 'everyday' law. The Fitzroy Legal Service's *Law Handbook*, which covers a diverse range of common legal issues, was first published in 1977. This resource—updated yearly—has been successful in demystifying the law and providing practical answers to Victorians' common legal problems. At the time of writing, an online version, launched in 2009, has attracted almost five million views (Fitzroy Legal Service 2015).

Giddings and Robertson (2001) also point to various other self-help resources and kits that flowered at this time, including the *Motor Vehicle Accident Crash Kit*, produced by the Nunawading and Eastern Suburbs Legal Service; a *Divorce Kit*, published by the Divorce Law Reform Association of Queensland; and the *Australia Party's Conveyancing Kit*, which contained annotated pro formas to assist individuals to complete straightforward private property transactions without lawyers.[4] VLA, too, is now a major publisher of self-help guides and information pamphlets on topics ranging from legal issues facing young people, to the division of property after a separation (VLA 2015a).

B. De-professionalisation and Plain Language

The expansion of community legal education and self-help legal services was part of a wider critical response to the monopolies enjoyed by the professions who, it was argued, exploited the inaccessibility of their domain expertise to maintain their power, financial privilege and elite status (Abbott 1988; Danet 1980). Indeed, during the 1960s and 1970s, 'de-professionalism' was one of the catch words of Western social protest movements against the 'disabling effects of professional elitism' (Noone and Tomsen 2006: 9). One criticism put forward at the time was that inaccessible language and legal jargon were being used by professions

[4] Such resources are hardly the domain of CLCs, legal aid and community groups alone—private sector companies also offer self-help resources to compete with traditional legal service models (Figueras 2013; Morris 2013).

to maintain their power over the laity. The 'plain language movement' sought to demystify the law to make it comprehensible to all (Danet 1980: 451–52).[5]

Nowadays, lawyers themselves are some of the strongest proponents of plain language. It has made their work easier and their businesses more efficient, and is favoured by clients and the courts. Law firms have introduced plain language writing into their training programmes for young lawyers; legal professional associations offer workshops to hone these skills; and law firms market their ability to produce accessible, plain language advice for clients (Gibson and Stella 2006).

There is also a growing acceptance that governments have an obligation to facilitate citizen comprehension of legislation and regulation through the use of plain language. In 1977, New York became the first American state to introduce plain English laws, mandating that certain agreements be written in a '"clear and coherent manner" using words which are commonly understood' (Moukad 1979: 453–54). More recently, US President Barak Obama introduced the *Plain Writing Act of 2010* (5 USC §301 note), which 'requires the federal government to write all new publications, forms, and publicly distributed documents in a "clear, concise, well-organized" manner' (Plain Language Action and Information Network 2015). In Australia, while there is no similar legislative foundation, various agencies, including the Commonwealth Office of Parliamentary Counsel, which is responsible for drafting Commonwealth legislation, have adopted plain language approaches (Office of Parliamentary Counsel 2015).

C. De-legalisation: Alternative Dispute Resolution and Self-help

Another ambitious agenda of the progressive legal movement was de-legalisation, which was based on the view that people should be empowered to resolve disputes for themselves, outside the adversarial court system. The well-documented claim was that, in formal proceedings, people lose control of their disputes and become enmeshed in counterproductive legal skirmishes that only exacerbate their problems. Advocates argued that fashioning individualised remedies quickly and cheaply without recourse to formal court processes better serves the needs of parties than protracted and expensive litigation (King et al 2009: 91–94, 104; see also Hunter et al, Chapter 13, this volume). Disputing neighbours, business people, divorcing couples and even the victims and perpetrators of some crimes could suddenly own and resolve the differences between them.

[5] This is not, of course, a new complaint (Danet 1980). Cicero bemoaned the use of complex language that obscures meaning, and there is a long history of efforts to make law more accessible to lay people. England's 1362 Statute of Pleading, for instance, required court proceedings to take place in English, rather than French (Mellinkoff 2004: 111–12). Jeremy Bentham and Napoleon pushed for the codification of laws that would be understandable by lay people, the former famously describing the language of lawyers as 'literary garbage' and 'excrementitious matter' (Bentham 1839; Schwartz 1978). And DIY law books have been around since at least the eighteenth century (Mellinkoff 2004: 198–99).

Again, these ideals have, in large measure, been realised. Alternative dispute resolution (ADR) (also commonly referred to as 'appropriate' dispute resolution: see, for example, *Civil Procedure Act 2010* (Vic) and Hunter et al, Chapter 13, this volume), which encompasses various processes from negotiation and mediation to formal arbitration, has become a mainstream process in civil disputes to the point where courts often require some attempt at ADR prior to hearing a case. In the criminal jurisdiction, restorative justice practices—such as mediation between offenders and victims—are deemed an acceptable way to restore the harm to victims and allow offenders to understand the full impact of their crimes (King et al 2009: 39–64, 88–123). Similarly, 'tribunalisation' has seen the proliferation of various specialist administrative decision-making bodies on the legal landscape (Bell 2008). Designed to deal with disputes efficiently and relatively informally (see, for example, *Administrative Appeals Tribunal Act 1975* (Cth) section 2A(b)), self-representation in tribunals is often encouraged, with, in some cases, legislative restrictions on legal representation (see, for example, *Victorian Civil and Administrative Tribunal Act 1998* (Vic) section 62).

The solutions designed to make law more accessible and overcome the existing system's often counterproductive effects—including, as we have canvassed, the rise of community legal education and self-help services, de-professionalisation and de-legalisation—have all proved to be relatively successful enablers of a 'DIY law' culture, minimising recourse to lawyers. Ironically, these reforms were probably so successful because they aligned with the other dominant ideological forces that encouraged a greater role for consumers of legal services: neoliberalism and public sector managerialism.

III. Neoliberalism: Downstream Consequences

The public sector bedfellow of neoliberalism—new public management or 'managerialism'—has encouraged governments to reduce costs along the lines of private sector corporatism and 'bring the "bottom line" economic rationality of the marketplace into the public sector' (Ward 2011: 206). This has included, for example, the privatisation of public sector service providers, as well as the contracting out of services to non-government, private sector 'partners', who compete to deliver services that were once the realm of government itself, such as prison management, healthcare or public transport (Ward 2011).

In Victoria, managerialist concerns drove the Auditor-General's 1993 Performance Audit of the then Legal Aid Commission of Victoria (LACV), which sought to review the 'effectiveness, efficiency and economy of the management and operations' of the LACV (Auditor-General of Victoria 1993: 31). The audit found that the LACV was under significant pressure to meet a greater demand for services, as the costs and complexity of the legal system increased.

It recommended measures to improve the efficiency of the LACV's operations, such as the development and implementation of a time-recording and costing system to enable the assessment of the relative cost-effectiveness of internal legal aid services compared to services provided by private solicitors (Auditor-General of Victoria 1993: 76, 78–79). In doing so, it was noted that, without increases in funding, this was the only way the LACV could continue to provide additional services to greater numbers of clients.

A year later, the Review of the Delivery of Legal Aid Services recommended that the LACV be modernised and radically reorganised (Cooper 1994). The *Legal Aid Commission (Amendment) Act 1995* (Vic) was enacted in 1995, with the stated aim of converting the LACV into 'a new and more business-like corporate body'—that of VLA (Giddings and Noone 1998: 45).

Ensuring value for money and greater accountability of public sector organisations is important. However, commentators agree that, in Victoria, the shape and speed of reforms under the conservative premiership of Jeff Kennett from 1992 to 1999 were particularly aggressive (Freiberg 2005: 16–17; see also Armstrong 1998; Fairbrother, Svensen and Teicher 1997).[6]

In the criminal justice system, managerialism has had a 'pervasive, powerful and in some cases, problematic' translation (Freiberg 2005: 13). There are clear tensions between the aims and objectives of the justice system and pressures to adopt more managerial approaches to law enforcement, court adjudication and legal representation, such as the need to ensure that human rights and other common law protections are respected, even if this is 'inefficient' and costly (Freiberg 2005; Raine and Willson 1995).

The tightening of VLA is part of this broader neoliberal agenda of 'doing more with less': the mantra of both the private and public sectors. As explored in various chapters in this collection (Buchanan, Chapter 8; Noone, Chapter 2; and Spencer, Chapter 5), while Australian legal aid funding, including that of VLA, has increased over the past decade in real terms (Productivity Commission 2014), funding growth has failed to keep pace with the growing demand for legal services (Productivity Commission 2014; see, for example, VLA 2014: 102; VLA 2013a: 96). VLA faces significant budgetary pressures and regular operating deficits.

To more efficiently allocate and utilise its scarce resources, VLA has determined that clients' entitlements to its services are based on increasingly restrictive categories of eligibility, under a 'triage'-style model that determines the individual service response. While the provision of both online and telephone call centre

[6] Aside from changes to legal aid, reforms included the selling off or corporatisation of a number of public service utility providers, the construction of a private prison, accelerating the privatisation of Victoria's public transport system and the introduction of a 'Compulsory Competitive Tendering' process in local government that required councils to put 50 per cent of their expenditure out to competitive tender (Fairbrother et al 1997: 7–8).

information has been significantly increased (see McKay, Chapter 6, this volume), growing numbers of legal matters are now deemed 'out of scope' and referred elsewhere as eligibility guidelines have been tightened and the number of grants of legal assistance has consequently fallen (including a 25 per cent decline between 2011–12 and 2013–14: VLA 2013a, 2014).

In this economic climate, only those considered to be most at legal risk—those facing significant criminal charges, or belonging to a small band of 'priority' disadvantaged groups (individuals with an intellectual disability, acquired brain injury or mental illness; those who are homeless; individuals who cannot speak, read or write well in English; and Indigenous Australians)—are eligible for duty lawyer representation in court (VLA 2015b). For relatively minor charges, duty lawyer assistance is usually restricted to generalised information, with limited, if any, personalised advice provided (VLA 2015b).

The apparent rationality underpinning this new resource allocation typically assigns services on the basis of status rather than need (Glaser and Laster 1990). In the legal aid context, 'status' is based on particular legal consequences rather than the potentially devastating personal and social consequences of being unrepresented—such as the loss of a job or family, homelessness, or the prospect of serious negative mental and physical health outcomes (see Spencer, Chapter 5, this volume). Under previously more generously funded legal aid regimes, lawyers had both an ideological and financial incentive to defend legal aid funding. However, as payments to private practitioners for legal aid work have failed to keep up with the market value of their services,[7] and private practitioners are effectively called upon to subsidise the system (Laster and Arup 2001; PricewaterhouseCoopers 2008), there is a risk that these practitioners will eventually 'withdraw this support once they feel that their contribution outweighs any potential benefit that they may be receiving' (PricewaterhouseCoopers 2008: 2).

CLC services, too, are increasingly reflecting a marketplace ideology—which has 'permeated the discourse on legal service delivery' in that sector—and concerns over competition and efficiency now drive decisions (Giddings and Robertson 2002: 438). As Giddings and Robertson (2002: 462) note, there is an 'irony that empowerment strategies pioneered and employed by [CLCs] in the 1970s to strengthen community understanding of the law have more recently been adopted as part of a much larger project to rejuvenate the legal services marketplace'. In the context of strained budgets, these strategies now serve to streamline scarce resources by encouraging consumers to take greater charge of the delivery of their legal solutions through self-help options, rather than through staff- and resource-intensive 'traditional' legal services (Giddings and Robertson 2002).

[7] Victorian criminal barristers undertaking VLA work, for example, receive about 50 per cent of the median income of their contemporaries (PricewaterhouseCoopers 2008: 17–18; see also Flynn 2010).

IV. Co-Production and Self-Help: Be Careful What You Wish For

The inadvertent confluence of progressive agendas and conservative economic thinking has underscored more general reforms that encourage, and also require, consumers to increasingly assist in the provision of their own services. The net result is that, incrementally, the obligations demanded of individual citizens have made meeting governments' needs more onerous and complex.

Each year in Australia, individual taxpayers—mostly without the assistance of a tax agent or accountant—gather expenditure receipts, income statements and pay slips, and enter their information into a government-developed computer program that automatically calculates their taxable income for the year. The program then enables individuals to electronically lodge their tax returns with the Australian Taxation Office (ATO) (Alford 2011: 148–49).

Within weeks, taxpayers receive their 'Notice of Assessment', advising them of their tax liabilities. Any tax outstanding, or which has been overpaid, is seamlessly transferred via internet banking directly into or from taxpayers' accounts. While audits are conducted on occasion, the ATO is largely reliant on the honest, accurate and timely reporting of information by the taxpayer, who does a significant amount of the work for the government.

The apparent ease of interacting with the government has obscured the reality that citizens are now doing much of the work for, or at least 'with', it. Since the mid-1980s, 'co-production' has become the preferred method of providing government services, through 'the involvement of citizens, clients, consumers, volunteers and/or community organisations in producing public services as well as consuming or otherwise benefitting from them' (Alford 1998: 128).

John Alford articulates the appeal of this mode of production to both Right- and Left-wing political values, arguing that the new obligations imposed on citizens to do things for themselves support conservative antipathy to big government, de-regulationist sentiment and a push for budgetary constraints (Alford 1998: 128). Alford also notes the attraction of the approach for the Left through co-production's emphasis on the voluntary cooperation of individuals and groups in the community and its seeming support for greater levels of citizen and client participation in community and public affairs—all demands of the protest movements of the 1960s (Alford 1998: 128; see also Giddings and Robertson 2002; Levine and Fisher 1984; Prentice 2008).

A. Self-help and the Legal Services Market Failure

As we have shown, this dual appeal is evident in the growth of self-help and co-produced services in the legal sector. But this growth has often necessitated assumptions about the capacity of consumers to engage with such services

(Giddings and Robertson 2002). For many, access to legal information and self-help guides from VLA, or one-off advice from their local CLC, is sufficient. However, as with the so-called 'digital divide' (National Telecommunications and Information Administration 1999), there is a significant gap between those who can and those who cannot adequately engage with self-help legal services.

As Giddings and Robertson (2002: 440) explain, the thinking behind the increasing role of citizens in the production of legal services

> assumes or encourages a belief in the self-directed legal services consumer, as someone willing and able to play a part in making the market work more efficiently. The legal services consumer must be a capable acquirer of information, and therefore an active learner; a person endowed with the capacity to make rational choices on the basis of that information; and, as far as possible, someone willing to take responsibility to service their own legal needs. All of this presupposes the currency of a political ideology in which individual autonomy, ability, self-interest and self-assertion are key formal characteristics.

Less socially assured clients who cannot meet such competencies fail the demands of co-production. Dealing with legal challenges is overwhelming and cripplingly stressful for many. Some simply fail to appear in court, being too disorganised or intimidated to appreciate the consequences. Others lack the relatively high baseline of education and language proficiency required for the effective comprehension of even plain language legal information (Laster and Taylor 1994), or the social competence and confidence to challenge decisions or enforce one's rights and entitlements.

For this body of legal consumers, self-help is simply not an option; according to one service provider, 'the fit isn't good unless the client is middle class' (Giddings and Robertson 2002: 452). There will always be a significant section of the population who are left bereft of essential services, and for whom self-help resources will be of little avail and only serve to create unrealistic expectations. As one CLC-based provider observed (Giddings and Robertson 2002: 452–53):

> I sometimes wonder whether for some people we do a great disservice by giving them a self-help kit. Particularly for those people who are already lacking in confidence and have felt marginalised … You give them a self-help kit and they can't do it. And then they feel like failures …

Ultimately, there are 'competing visions' of the self-directed legal consumer: one of an informed, empowered individual taking control of their legal problems; and the other of an isolated and powerless consumer for whom the law remains inaccessible (Giddings and Robertson 2002: 459). The fundamental problem is that '"the consumer" has hugely variable characteristics' (Giddings and Robertson 2002: 459).

B. Self-represented Litigants as 'the New Black'

One of the biggest challenges facing courts in many jurisdictions is the high number of self-represented litigants (see Spencer, Chapter 5, this volume). While court and tribunal data are inconsistent and not comprehensive, there does seem to be an increase in the proportion of self-represented litigants over time in Australian jurisdictions (Productivity Commission 2014: 488–89). In the Victorian Court of Appeal, for instance, the percentage of matters filed by self-represented litigants increased from 8.4 per cent in 2001 to 23 per cent in 2013 (Schade 2014). In other jurisdictions, the proportion of self-represented litigants is far greater. Sourdin and Wallace (2014: 3), reviewing some of the (albeit dated) data, detail how between approximately 80 and 90 per cent of parties are self-represented in Family Court of Australia children's matters, and a similarly substantial majority of 70 per cent of divorce matters involve self-represented litigants (see Mutha-Merennege, Chapter 14, this volume, for more updated discussions on self-represented women litigants in the Australian context, and Byrom, Chapter 12, this volume, for a discussion of self-represented litigants in the United Kingdom [UK] context).

The courts are thus increasingly dealing with inexperienced 'amateurs' in an arena that was previously the preserve of lawyers, judges and magistrates. Although some forums, such as some tribunals, encourage it, self-representation generally places a hefty (although, to date, not well-quantified) burden on already stretched court resources (Productivity Commission 2014: 499–500, 1060–62; see also Spencer, Chapter 5, this volume). Self-represented litigants are, for example, more likely to raise irrelevant issues and prepare poor submissions, and generally have difficulty complying with procedural directions (Australian Institute of Judicial Administration 2001: 3–4, 6–8; Productivity Commission 2014: 489; see also Spencer, Chapter 5, this volume). A small proportion of self-represented litigants might also be described as 'difficult' or having 'obsessive' tendencies, manifested in high-conflict behaviour and repeated meritless claims (Smith 2009; Sourdin and Wallace 2014).

In response, Victorian courts have had to dedicate ever-more resources to manage the flow of self-represented litigants, including the appointment of self-represented litigant coordinators and the development of self-help packs and other 'how to' court literature (see, for example, Supreme Court of Victoria 2014). However, none of these measures have solved the problem or stemmed the tide of self-represented litigants. If anything, the more the courts prepare themselves for self-represented litigants, the greater the expectations of such litigants that their needs will be accommodated.

The courts have attempted to stand up to the executive government, where the issue concerns the protection of fundamental rights. In a landmark 1992 High Court of Australia decision—*R v Dietrich* (1992) 177 CLR 292—for instance, it was recognised that while there is no right of an accused to be provided with a lawyer at public expense, the courts do have the power to stay criminal proceedings that would otherwise result in an unfair trial, and this power extends to cases where representation of an accused is essential to a fair trial.

More recently, in 2013, the Victorian Supreme Court effectively required VLA to alter its existing guideline that it would only provide an instructing solicitor for two half days of a trial, holding that without an instructor for the duration of the trial before it, involving serious criminal charges, the trial was likely to be unfair (*R v Chaouk* (2013) 40 VR 356). The Court adjourned the matter until counsel for the accused was granted ongoing assistance by an instructing solicitor. Initially, VLA declined to alter its policy. However, following a failed application for leave to appeal the Court's decision, the organisation felt compelled to introduce interim guidelines (which soon became permanent) to allow for 'more flexibility' in funding instructing solicitors and junior counsel in criminal trials (VLA 2013b; see also Flynn et al 2016).

Nonetheless, in summary criminal matters, and certainly within the civil and family law contexts, self-representation is now well entrenched (see Mutha-Merennege, Chapter 14, and Spencer, Chapter 5, this volume). A phenomenon that courts have regarded as an anomaly to be managed has, in fact, become part of their new incarnation. Courts are, relatively quickly, being transformed from 'wholesaler' institutions whose primary interaction hitherto has been with lawyers, into 'retail' environments that have to deal directly with the public. Judicial officers and courts are thus struggling with a shift in their self-image, mission and mode of operation (see Spencer, Chapter 5, this volume, for a discussion in the Australian context, and Byrom, Chapter 12, and Smith and Cape, Chapter 4, this volume, for a discussion in the UK context).

V. The Court as the Help Hub

> 'When sorrows come, they come not single spies. But in battalions!' (Shakespeare 1836: 859)

Legal problems, particularly those likely to be faced by people who struggle to navigate a DIY-centred system, rarely occur in isolation. Rather, they usually present as part of more complex clusters of legal and social needs (Coumarelos et al 2012: 57). Some problems act as triggers in a long sequence of wellbeing concerns such as ill health, loss of employment, family breakdown and housing problems (Citizens Advice 2010; People 2014; see also Kirwan, Chapter 10, and Organ and Sigafoos, Chapter 9, this volume). In its 2014 report into Australia's system of dispute resolution and access to justice, the Australian Productivity Commission warned that the effect of ever-scarcer allocation of legal aid funding is simply to shift the burden and costs to other areas of government and community service provision (Productivity Commission 2014: 759). But those other areas are themselves also feeling the pinch of austerity measures and the pressures of managerialism.

Confronted by shrinking budgets, service providers (both government and not-for-profit) have had to set tough priorities, and are increasingly relying on the courts to decide allocations for vulnerable people in need through judicial mandate. Courts have become what Mark Moore (1995) terms 'the authorising environment', as well as clearing houses for the assignment of social services of all kinds. In this context, some lower court hearings resemble, and effectively are, 'intake' sessions for welfare service providers.

The courts are the end-point of a downward social spiral for people who have increasingly difficult and unassisted needs. The broad church of 'therapeutic jurisprudence' has given courts a theoretical model that justifies their more activist involvement in social welfare intervention and service delivery (Wexler 1994; see also Magistrates' Court of Victoria 2014), as judges and magistrates, especially in the lower courts, explicitly coordinate 'just-in-time' treatment and other services that have been unavailable, or have not worked, previously.

The managerialist objection to the therapeutic jurisprudence approach adopted in some court lists in Victoria is that they have become 'less efficient'. Measured by crude 'throughput', this is undoubtedly true, and courts have yet to completely convince governments that what they lose in 'costs' under the new model they gain in 'effectiveness'. The legal system is hydraulic. Managerialist-inspired policies have pushed problem-solving into the pointy, and arguably most expensive, part of the system—the courts—as judges and magistrates are inevitably compelled to deal with the complex social needs of parties.

VI. Conclusion: The Undeserving Legal Client

In its 1834 report on the administration and operation of England's nineteenth-century 'Poor Laws' (Poor Law Commissioners 1834), the Poor Law Commissioners made a clear distinction between welfare assistance provided to the deserving impotent and that afforded to the less deserving able-bodied, declaring that the 'most pressing of the evils' which they described were those connected with the relief of the latter (Poor Law Commissioners 1834: 227). To remedy this 'evil', the Commissioners recommended that relief to the able-bodied be limited to that provided in the workhouse, where conditions were deliberately designed to render inmates 'less eligible' than the lowest class of independent labourers (Poor Law Commissioners 1834: 262–63).

This policy was to function as a 'self-acting test' to separate the deserving from the undeserving (Poor Law Commissioners 1834: 264):

> By the means which we propose, the line between those who do, and those who do not, need relief is drawn, and drawn perfectly. If the claimant does not comply with the terms on which relief is given to the destitute, he gets nothing; and if he does comply, the compliance proves the truth of the claim—namely, his destitution.

Like the nineteenth-century distinction between the deserving and undeserving poor, our social system draws a clear distinction between those eligible for state-funded legal services and those who should be able to fend for themselves.

This chapter has reviewed the cultural and theoretical elements that have contributed to the dilution of, and increasing pressure on, legal aid. Blaming neoliberalism for the withdrawal of funding offers a ready scapegoat, but only tells part of the story. The key question, in our view, is why the dismantling of legal aid has not been resisted more vigorously. We have argued that, perversely, the older progressive claims for greater and more direct access to law for ordinary citizens have become a victim of their own success. There are now seemingly valid alternatives to providing expensive professional help. The ready availability of legal information and other forms of self-help has gone a long way towards making law more accessible. On the face of it, these new self-help modes are not only cheaper, but also fit the cultural Zeitgeist.

In the information age, DIY problem-solving approaches abound, including for the resolution of legal issues. Unfortunately, the individuals who do not make the grade have become the marginalised. There is little public support for, and therefore no political mileage in, providing them with expensive legal services from the public purse.

At a time when 'law and order' politics prevail, protecting the rights of defendants in criminal cases is not popular (Kornhauser and Laster 2014: 447–49). Unlike the more tolerant approach to the provision of 'no fault' universal healthcare, there is an apparent contradiction in advocating tough-on-crime measures, on the one hand, and providing funded legal representation and advice, on the other. The courts have been left to cope as best they can with their new roles and responsibilities, but are then chided for not meeting new productivity standards.

The wonders of technology have seemingly turned us (or the 'capable' majority) into 'gifted amateurs'. The bar of social competence has been raised unnaturally high. Those unable to meet these standards have become the undeserving poor of the technological age. Legal aid is inadvertently a casualty of our new DIY cultural sensibilities.

References

Abbott, A (1988) *The System of Professions: An Essay on the Division of Expert Labor* (Chicago IL, University of Chicago Press).

Alford, J (1998) 'A Public Management Road Less Travelled: Clients as Co-Producers of Public Services' 57 *Australian Journal of Public Administration* 4, 128.

—— (2011) 'Public Value from Co-production by Clients' in J Benington and M Moore (eds), *Public Value: Theory and Practice* (London, Palgrave Macmillan).

Armstrong, A (1998) 'A Comparative Analysis: New Public Management—The Way Ahead' 57 *Australian Journal of Public Administration* 2, 12.

Auditor-General of Victoria (1993) *Legal Aid Commission of Victoria and Office of the Valuer-General*, Special Report No 28 (Melbourne, Auditor-General of Victoria).

Australian Institute of Judicial Administration (2001) *Litigants in Person Management Plans: Issues for Courts and Tribunals* (Melbourne, Australian Institute of Judicial Administration).

Bell, K (2008) 'The Role of VCAT in a Changing World: The President's Review of VCAT', speech delivered to the Law Institute of Victoria, 4 September 2008.

Bentham, J (1839) *The Works of Jeremy Bentham, Now First Collected* (Edinburgh, William Tait).

Citizens Advice (2010) *Towards a Business Case for Legal Aid*, available at: https://namati.org/resources/citizens-advice-towards-a-business-case-for-legal-aid/.

Cooper, D (1994) *Review of the Delivery of Legal Aid Services in Victoria* (Melbourne, Victorian Government Printer).

Coumarelos, C, Macourt, D, People, J, McDonald, H, Wei, Z, Iriana, R and Ramsey, S (2012) *Legal Australia-Wide Survey: Legal Need in Australia* (Sydney, Law and Justice Foundation of New South Wales).

Danet, B (1980) 'Language in the Legal Process' 14 *Law & Society Review* 3, 445.

Fairbrother, P, Svensen, S and Teicher, J (1997) 'The Withering Away of the Australian State: Privatisation and its Implications for Labour' 8 *Labour & Industry* 2, 1.

Figueras, I (2013) 'The LegalZoom Identity Crisis: Legal Form Provider or Lawyer in Sheep's Clothing?' 63 *Case Western Reserve Law Review* 4, 1419.

Fitzroy Legal Service (2015) 'The Law Handbook Gets Better with Age', Media release, 26 November 2015.

Flynn, A (2010) 'Victoria's Legal Aid Funding Structure: Hindering the Ideals Inherent to the Pre-Trial Process' 34 *Criminal Law Journal* 1, 48.

Flynn, A, Hodgson, J, McCulloch, J and Naylor, B (2016) 'Legal Aid and Access to Legal Representation: Re-Defining the Right to a Fair Trial' 40 *Melbourne University Law Review* 207.

Freiberg, A (2005) 'Managerialism in Australian Criminal Justice: RIP for KPIs?' 31 *Monash University Law Review* 1, 12.

Gibson, B and Stella, M (2006) 'Implementing Plain Language at Mallesons' 56 *Clarity* 22.

Giddings, J and Noone, MA (1998) 'The 1990s, a Time for Change for Legal Aid in Victoria' in J Giddings (ed), *Legal Aid in Victoria: At the Crossroads Again* (Melbourne, Fitzroy Legal Service).

Giddings, J and Robertson, M (2001) '"Informed Litigants with Nowhere To Go": Self-help Legal Aid Services in Australia' 25 *Alternative Law Journal* 4, 184.

—— (2002) '"Lay People, for God's Sake! Surely I Should Be Dealing with Lawyers?" Towards an Assessment of Self-help Legal Services in Australia' 11 *Griffith Law Review* 2, 436.

Glaser, W and Laster, K (1990) 'The Workers' Compensation System in Victoria: Who Takes the Blame?' 25 *Australian Journal of Social Issues* 2, 137.

King, M, Freiberg, A, Batagol, B and Hyams, R (2009) *Non-Adversarial Justice* (Sydney, Federation Press).

Kornhauser, R and Laster, K (2014) 'Punitiveness in Australia: Electronic Monitoring vs the Prison' 62 *Crime, Law and Social Change* 4, 445.

Kuznetsov, S and Paulos, E (2010) 'Rise of the Expert Amateur: DIY Projects, Communities, and Cultures' *NordiCHI* '10, *Proceedings of the 6th Nordic Conference on Human-Computer Interaction: Extending Boundaries* 295.

Laster, K and Arup, C (eds) (2001) *For the Public Good: Pro Bono and the Legal Profession in Australia* (Sydney, Federation Press).

Laster, K and Taylor, V (1994) *Interpreters and the Legal System* (Sydney, Federation Press).

Levine, C and Fisher, G (1984) 'Citizenship and Service Delivery: The Promise of Coproduction' 44 *Public Administration Review* 2, 178.

Magistrates' Court of Victoria (2014) *Annual Report 2013/14* (Melbourne), available at: www.magistratescourt.vic.gov.au/sites/default/files/Default/Annual%20 Report%202013-2014.pdf.

Mellinkoff, D (2004) *The Language of Law* (Eugene OR, Resources Publications).

Moore, M (1995) *Creating Public Value: Strategic Management in Government* (London, Harvard University Press).

Morris, V (2013) 'Navigating Justice: Self-help Resources, Access to Justice, and Whose Job Is It Anyway?' 82 *Mississippi Law Journal* Supra 161.

Morris, W (1908) *News from Nowhere, or an Epoch of Rest, Being Some Chapters Derived from a Utopian Romance* (London, Longmans, Green and Co).

Moukad, R (1979) 'New York's Plain English Law' 8 *Fordham Urban Law Journal* 2, 451.

National Telecommunications and Information Administration (1999) *Falling Through the Net: Defining the Digital Divide* (Washington DC, US Department of Commerce).

Noone, MA and Tomsen, S (2006) *Lawyers in Conflict: Australian Lawyers and Legal Aid* (Sydney, Federation Press).

Office of Parliamentary Counsel (2015) *Plain Language* [Online], available at: www.opc.gov.au/PLAIN/index.htm.

O'Malley, P (1996) 'Risk and Responsibility' in A Barry, T Osborne and N Rose (eds), *Foucault and Political Reason* (London, UCL Press).

People, J (2014) *Do Some Types of Legal Problems Trigger Other Legal Problems?* (Sydney, Law and Justice Foundation of New South Wales).

Plain Language Action and Information Network (2015) *Plain Writing Act of 2010: Federal Agency Requirements* [Online], available at: www.plainlanguage.gov/pllaw/law/.

Poor Law Commissioners (1834) *Report from His Majesty's Commissioners for Inquiring into the Administration and Practical Operation of the Poor Laws* (London, B Fellowes).

Prentice, S (2008) 'Childcare, Co-Production and the Third Sector in Canada' in V Prestoff and T Brandsen (eds), *Co-production: The Third Sector and the Delivery of Public Services* (New York, Routledge).

PricewaterhouseCoopers (2008) *Review of Fees Paid by Victoria Legal Aid to Barristers in Criminal Cases*, available at: www.vicbar.com.au/uploads//bar-association-documents/VLA_-_Legal_Aid_Fees_-_final_reportV1_.pdf.

Productivity Commission (2014) *Access to Justice Arrangements Inquiry*, Report No 72, 5 September 2014 (Canberra, Productivity Commission).

Raine, J and Willson, M (1995) 'New Public Management and Criminal Justice' 15 *Public Money & Management* 1, 35.

Rose, N (2000) 'Government and Control' 40 *British Journal of Criminology* 2, 321.

Schade, R (2014) *Measuring SRL Impacts: Data Collection* (Melbourne, Supreme Court of Victoria).

Schwartz, B (1978) 'The Law and Its Development: A Synoptic Survey' 3 *Southern Illinois University Law Journal* 1, 44.

Shakespeare, W (1836 [c1600]) 'Hamlet: Prince of Denmark', *The Works of Shakespeare* (London, Isaac, Tuckey, and Co).

Smith, S (2009) *Maverick Litigants: A History of Vexatious Litigants in Australia 1930-2008* (Melbourne, Maverick Publications).

Sourdin, T and Wallace, N (2014) *The Dilemmas Posed by Self-represented Litigants—The Dark Side* (Melbourne, Monash University).

Supreme Court of Victoria (2014) *2013–14 Annual Report* (Melbourne), available at: www.supremecourt.vic.gov.au/home/about+the+court/annual+reports/.

Victoria Law Foundation (2015a) *Annual Report 2014/15* (Melbourne), available at: www.victorialawfoundation.org.au/annual-reports.

—— (2015b) *Law Week* [Online], available at: www.everyday-law.org.au/law-week.

Victoria Legal Aid (2013a) *Eighteenth Statutory Annual Report 2012–13* (Melbourne), available at: www.legalaid.vic.gov.au/sites/www.legalaid.vic.gov.au/files/vla-eighteenth-statutory-annual-report-2012-13.pdf.

—— (2013b) 'Victoria Legal Aid to Introduce More Flexibility for Criminal Trial Funding', Media release, 7 May 2013, available at: www.legalaid.vic.gov.au/about-us/news/victoria-legal-aid-to-introduce-more-flexibility-for-criminal-trial-funding.

—— (2014) *Nineteenth Statutory Annual Report 2013–14* (Melbourne), available at: www.legalaid.vic.gov.au/sites/www.legalaid.vic.gov.au/files/vla-annual-report-2014.pdf.

—— (2015a) *All Publications and Resources* [Online], available at: www.legalaid.vic.gov.au/find-legal-answers/all-publications-and-resources.

—— (2015b) *Duty Lawyers at Court for Criminal Charges* [Online], available at: www.legalaid.vic.gov.au/information-for-lawyers/doing-legal-aid-work/private-practitioner-duty-lawyers/duty-lawyers-court-for-criminal-charges.

Ward, S (2011) 'The Machinations of Managerialism: New Public Management and the Diminishing Power of Professionals' 4 *Journal of Cultural Economy* 2, 205.

Wexler, D (1994) 'An Orientation to Therapeutic Jurisprudence' 20 *New England Journal of Criminal and Civil Confinement* 2, 259.

Treaties, Conventions, Principles, Directives, Rules and Legislation

Administrative Appeals Tribunal Act 1975 (Cth)
Civil Procedure Act 2010 (Vic)
Legal Aid Commission (Amendment) Act 1995 (Vic)
Plain Writing Act of 2010, 5 USC §301 note (2016)
Victoria Law Foundation Act 2009 (Vic)
Victorian Civil and Administrative Tribunal Act 1998 (Vic)

Cases

R v Chaouk (2013) 40 VR 356
R v Dietrich (1992) 177 CLR 292

8

Community Lawyers, Law Reform and Systemic Change: Is the End in Sight?

LIANA BUCHANAN

I. Community Lawyers: A Broader Vision for 'Access to Justice'

Community legal centres (CLCs) have been part of the legal assistance sector in Australia since the early 1970s, when volunteer lawyers, concerned about inequality, injustice and limited access to legal help for low-income and marginalised people, came together to set up the nation's first CLCs in Melbourne (Victoria).

The birth of CLCs coincided with, and was firmly located in, the broader transnational social change and civil rights movements of the 1960s and early 1970s (Bell 2012; McCulloch and Blair 2009: 2, 8–9). From the start of the CLC movement, community lawyers worked to improve access to justice, and this meant more than improving access to lawyers. For CLC pioneers, improving access to justice included a focus on substantive, rather than merely procedural, justice. It meant working for a fairer, more equitable justice system and society. As the first full-time lawyer at Fitzroy Legal Service,[1] Julian Gardner, has said: 'it was a time of opportunity to make the law a positive force, to make it an agent of social change' (cited in McCulloch and Blair 2009: 25).

From the outset, therefore, community lawyers identified their role as being about far more than providing legal help to individuals. The role of community lawyers was to redefine the relationship between lawyer and client and the ways in which the law, the justice system and society more broadly treated the poor and the disempowered (Chesterman 1992; McCulloch and Blair 2009: 12).

From small, activist beginnings in town hall basements and other 'shabby begged and borrowed spaces' (McCulloch and Blair 2009: 11), the community

[1] The Fitzroy Legal Service in inner Melbourne was the first non-Aboriginal CLC in Australia. It opened in December 1972 and remains open today.

legal sector has developed in size and sophistication. There are now almost 200 CLCs across Australia, assisting more than 210,000 people each year and providing a combination of legal advice and representation, community legal education and development, and law reform and policy work.

Community lawyers are recognised for their expertise in the areas of law that affect the most marginalised. Working in relatively small, independent, community-based organisations, they are also well placed to identify emerging problems and develop effective, tailored responses. Community lawyers have become known in Australia for leading the way in the development and implementation of innovative service delivery models that improve access for the most disadvantaged people. For example, CLCs such as Loddon Campaspe CLC and Inner Melbourne Community Legal have developed ground-breaking health–justice partnerships, placing community lawyers in healthcare settings so that clients' legal needs can be identified and resolved in an integrated approach (Gyorki 2013; Noble 2012a).

Increasingly, research examining the most effective ways of providing legal help to disadvantaged communities supports approaches that have been adopted and developed in CLCs over decades—approaches such as outreach services; a focus on early intervention and empowerment; and multidisciplinary, joined-up models of service delivery that address people's interconnected legal and non-legal problems (Pleasence et al 2014).

Another vital and defining feature of the work of CLCs is their capacity as independent organisations that work daily with the most marginalised and vulnerable in our communities to advocate for positive change. Yet, as a result of recent political changes in Australia, CLCs' law reform, policy and systemic advocacy work is under threat. This chapter will argue that systemic advocacy is often the most effective and efficient way to improve outcomes for CLC client groups and that it should be funded and encouraged as core CLC work, but that recent government restrictions have damaged the capacity and willingness of CLCs to engage in it. This will be achieved by an analysis of four systemic advocacy reforms, followed by an overview of the new government policy and its implications for the community legal sector and the people the sector exists to serve.

II. Systemic Advocacy by CLCs: Does It Work?

Law reform, policy and systemic advocacy are terms used to describe activities that are not focused exclusively on assisting individual clients. Rather, systemic advocacy identifies a broader or underlying problem that is likely to affect many people and seeks to address that problem. Systemic work takes many forms. It may involve running a test case, researching an issue and preparing a report to set out the case for change, writing a submission to government or a parliamentary inquiry, lobbying politicians, running community awareness and advocacy campaigns, working with regulators, organising a protest rally or raising issues through the media. Ideally, but not always, these activities are undertaken as part of a strategy to achieve a particular reform outcome.

Over the course of their long history, CLCs have driven many reforms. Some have been documented, though many have not. In 1992, Elsjie van Moorst wrote about CLCs' impact in reforming residential tenancy laws, credit laws, the conditions in women prisons and sexual assault laws (Fadden et al 1992: 290). In the 2009 history of the Victorian CLC movement, *Justice for All*, McCulloch and Blair note that the sector's list of law reform achievements is too long to adequately honour. They do, however, list several specific achievements, including mandatory third-party motor vehicle insurance; stopping a particular retailer's 'insidious debt-collecting practices'; working to raise awareness of, and support for, victims of family violence; and ending the use of chattel mortgages as security for low-income earners' debts (McCulloch and Blair 2009: 17). Yet, as Liz Curran (2007: 3) concluded in a 2007 research report, although community lawyers' client-driven systemic work has provided impetus for substantial change and improved the effectiveness and responsiveness of laws and their administration, CLCs are often not credited for the ultimate outcomes of such change. This occurs in part because of the length of time usually needed to achieve reform and the intervening involvement of other agencies, as well as a 'process of filtering that occurs at different levels of decision making' (Curran 2007: 3). In her report, Curran explored six areas of systemic reform undertaken by CLCs, to explore the impact community lawyers have had in relation to fines reform, debt collection practices, accountability for police shootings, energy regulation, violence against women and children, and prisons. Discussing the strategies used in each case and the end result of community lawyers' efforts, Curran recommended that CLCs improve the identification and ownership of reforms initiated by them.

More recent law reform and systemic advocacy also shows that this work takes many forms and has many benefits. Below, I discuss four recent examples of systemic advocacy resulting from CLCs that have fundamentally improved access to justice in both a legal and social setting for vulnerable groups.

A. Forcing Police to Recognise and Act on Police Racism

Systemic lawyering is often a means of holding government and public institutions to account for their inappropriate behaviour. When done well, systemic lawyering empowers affected community members while tackling the unjust and damaging practices that impact on often the most vulnerable groups.

One example is the Flemington and Kensington CLC's 10-year effort to tackle racial profiling and racial discrimination by police. In 2005, staff at Flemington and Kensington CLC began to receive a large number of complaints about police brutality against African and Afghan Australians in Flemington and surrounding neighbourhoods. After complaints were made to Victoria Police, the Office of Police Integrity[2] and the Australian Human Rights Commission, lawyers at Flemington and Kensington CLC were frustrated by the consistently inadequate responses they received from these organisations. Accordingly, the CLC brought a 'test' discrimination case against Victoria Police in the Australian Federal Court on behalf of 17 victims (Green 2013). Amid a significant level of media attention and public scrutiny, the matter was ultimately settled out of court, but the outcome included the CLC securing agreement from Victoria Police to commission an independent review of its training and practices. Importantly, the agreement allowed public access to the documents from the case and allowed parties to speak about the allegations and the settlement. This was crucial because the CLC used media extensively to build awareness of the issues affecting its clients, and this outcome allowed it to continue to use the media effectively after the settlement.

Following the inquiry, Victoria Police released the *Equality is Not the Same* report (Victoria Police 2013), in which it committed to a three-year action plan to address community concerns about discriminatory policing. As a result of this CLC's work, Victoria Police: introduced receipting pilots in specific areas across Victoria—a process that requires Victoria Police members to provide receipts to individuals who are stopped, as an accountability mechanism; rolled out new training for all members in relation to dealing with vulnerable groups; and established a network of 17 community reference groups, as well as a Chief Commissioner's Human Rights Advisory Committee which includes four members from different CLCs.

Throughout its work on the Police Accountability Project, Flemington and Kensington CLC made it a priority to ensure that community voices and experiences were central in the push to change the approach of Victoria Police and that the affected community was supported and empowered. The CLC worked to support those involved in the litigation, including by making sure that they were connected with health, housing, education and other services as needed, and employed a youth worker to provide ongoing support. Flemington and Kensington CLC kept the public informed of the progress of the case and the action taken afterwards by holding regular public meetings and releasing information on its website. Public meetings were also held to encourage the community to give evidence and document their experiences.

Flemington and Kensington CLC's commitment to work alongside those most affected by discriminatory practices continues to date. Since April 2014, the CLC has held regular racial profiling monitoring meetings with the community to monitor the progress of the police action plan. The meetings provide a forum for community members to discuss and document their experiences of racism by police and to discuss how the problem can be addressed.

[2] The Office of Police Integrity was the independent police oversight agency operating in Victoria between 2004 and 2013, when it was replaced by the Independent Broad-based Anti-Corruption Commission.

As the above example illustrates, it can take a long time—often decades—to transform a flawed, biased and unsafe system. The key often lies in ensuring that client experience drives advocacy, and that clients are supported throughout the advocacy effort. Systemic advocacy ensures that the experiences of CLC clients are used to shape change with positive outcomes for otherwise vulnerable, marginalised and disempowered groups in society.

B. Family Violence Reform

In the case of family violence reform, systemic advocacy can allow for the experiences of women and children who have been let down by the justice system to be channelled into reforms that—over time—build a safer, more responsive justice system for victims of family violence. In many parts of Australia, CLCs are the primary providers of legal help for people experiencing family violence. In Victoria, CLCs have a long history of supporting victims and, in the early 1990s, they started providing duty lawyer services for women seeking intervention orders at court.[3] This work was recognised in 2004, when the State government allocated specific funding for family violence duty lawyer services. Twenty CLCs now employ specialist family violence community lawyers to provide services at a total of 29 courts around the State (see also Mutha-Merennege, Chapter 14, this volume).

Family violence work provides CLCs with a unique understanding of the issues that victims of family violence face when navigating the justice system. Indeed, CLCs, including specialist centres like the Women's Legal Service Victoria (WLSV) and the Victorian Aboriginal Family Violence Prevention and Legal Service, have played a major role in informing law, policy and practice, as the legislature, police and courts work to improve responses to family violence (Mutha-Merennege, Chapter 14, this volume). For example, as part of the first Statewide Steering Committee to Reduce Family Violence in 2002, CLCs worked in partnership with government and community organisations, police and the courts to develop an integrated response to family violence. This work informed the first *Victoria Police Code of Practice for Family Violence* in 2003 and included the development of a vision for family violence systems reform. Community lawyers also advocated for a review of family violence legal responses in Victoria, leading to a 2005 Victorian Law Reform Commission review of family violence laws and, in 2008, a new, best practice Act—the *Family Violence Protection Act 2008* (Vic)—to provide for more effective, responsive intervention orders.

Since then, the body representing Victorian CLCs, the Federation of Community Legal Centres (the Federation), and the specialist WLSV have formed a

[3] Family violence intervention orders are civil orders that can be made by a magistrate to protect a person from family violence. In other jurisdictions these are called restraining orders or domestic violence protection orders. The role of a CLC family violence duty lawyer is to attend court to assist people attending court to obtain an intervention order. This assistance might include advice and representation in court on the day.

coalition with other head and State-wide family violence agencies to raise awareness of family violence and push for change. In 2014, the alliance launched the No More Deaths family violence campaign, seeking 25 policy commitments from political parties in the lead-up to the Victorian State election. The campaign included 2015 Australian of the Year and family violence survivor, Rosie Batty,[4] and other family members of women and children who had been killed as a result of family violence, all of whom had received support from CLCs and the Federation. As is often the case, the involvement and support of people with lived experience of the system increased the campaign's impact immeasurably.

In response to the alliance's strong campaign, family violence became a major election issue in the 2014 State election (and beyond), with the newly elected government initiating a Royal Commission into Family Violence and committing to: implementing the Royal Commission's recommendations, reinstating funding for the Systemic Review of Family Violence Deaths,[5] undertaking a court safety audit and provide one-off funds to meet the urgent need for duty lawyers. Like the Flemington and Kensington CLC shift in State policing policy, the work of CLCs contributed to an environment for strong legal and social change in an area of significant concern.

C. Tackling Exploitative Taxi Driver Conditions

Community lawyers sometimes see injustices and anomalies that are invisible to others. This means that CLC advocacy can be the sole reason why a problem is addressed. One example of this is the Footscray CLC's work on taxi driver conditions.

Footscray CLC established the Taxi Driver Legal Service in 2011, in recognition that many taxi drivers were being assisted by CLCs and that drivers experienced unique and complex legal problems. A high proportion of these drivers were refugees or newly arrived migrants on extremely low incomes. Casework in the Taxi Driver Legal Service identified a number of systemic issues in the taxi industry, particularly the adverse effect that employment conditions and insurance arrangements were having on drivers.

Among the issues that became apparent through Footscray CLC's casework was that taxi drivers were exposed to serious financial risk every time they drove, because most taxis were not properly insured. Taxi drivers' status as bailees, rather than employees, also meant that they were subject to a range of serious problems associated with poor pay, legal entitlements and safety at work.

[4] Rosie Batty became a high-profile campaigner against family violence after her 11-year-old son, Luke, was killed by his father in February 2014.

[5] The Systemic Review of Family Violence Deaths assists the Victorian Coroner to investigate family violence-related deaths. The process is intended to enable the Coroner to identify any systemic issues and make prevention-focused recommendations.

Footscray CLC and the Federation worked together to document the legal and financial problems affecting taxi drivers and set out recommendations for reform in a report published in August 2012 (Footscray CLC and Federation of Community Legal Centres 2012). This work coincided with the Victorian Government's initiation of a broader inquiry into the taxi industry. Although the inquiry's initial focus had little to do with driver conditions, the Federation and Footscray CLC made submissions to the inquiry. Many of the recommendations were included in the inquiry's final report and were subsequently accepted and implemented by the Victorian Government.

As a result, taxi drivers' agreements now contain a number of implied terms, including compulsory insurance for operators covering the taxi drivers against liability for third-party damage in the event of an accident. Other implied terms now require that drivers receive a greater share (55 per cent) of fares earned during a shift and that they are entitled to up to four weeks of unpaid leave where the driver has worked for 12 months or more for the same operator.

This example illustrates that, in some cases, a CLC is uniquely placed to identify systemic issues that lead to unfairness and legal need. If Footscray CLC had not noted systemic problems in the taxi industry through interactions with clients, established the clinic and worked to record and raise these issues through its joint law reform work with the Federation, these concerns simply would not have been brought to the attention of the State government.

Footscray CLC's approach to the taxi drivers' problems also highlights the clear cost benefit of systemic advocacy. Solving structural problems can prevent future legal need, ultimately saving legal assistance resources. Footscray CLC has estimated that, over time, the changes to insurance arrangements alone will protect drivers and owner-drivers in up to 1000 motor vehicle accidents per year and will remove up to 100 civil debt cases per year from the courts and the Taxi Driver Legal Service. Thus, in addition to improving the safety and conditions for taxi drivers, this change also has substantial cost savings.

D. Ending Exploitation by Door-to-door Salespeople

In 2014, the government introduced restrictions to stop CLCs from running 'campaigns'. This means that CLCs who are found to run campaigns with federal government money risk losing their funding. The ban affects all CLCs that receive federal government funds and, importantly, the term 'campaigns' is not defined—meaning that CLCs fear and anticipate a broad interpretation. Accordingly, in this final example of the value of CLC systemic advocacy, it is timely to consider how a strategic campaign can deliver significant public benefit.

Victoria's specialist consumer CLC, Consumer Action Law Centre ('Consumer Action'), launched the Do Not Knock campaign after seeing an increasing number of people who had been misled or pressured by door-to-door salespeople into signing contracts that left them worse off. Consumer Action and other CLCs saw clients, for example, who had signed documents to transfer to a new, higher cost energy provider after being falsely told by salespeople that they were receiving a discount, or that the documents were merely giving consent to check the electricity meter. Other clients had signed documents believing the salespeople to be government representatives.

As a result of these cases, Consumer Action became aware that door-to-door salespeople were selling to the elderly, people with dementia and people who speak little or no English. They were also often refusing to leave when asked, targeting refugee and remote Aboriginal communities, deliberately misleading consumers, and even forging signatures as part of fraudulent sales.

Through the Do Not Knock campaign, Consumer Action developed and distributed a 'do not knock' sticker for people's houses, provided consumer information, liaised with industry and regulatory agencies, lodged door-to-door selling complaints with regulators and contributed to law reform proposals. The CLC also established a web portal where Victorian consumers could register their desire not to be door-knocked by energy companies, which automatically registered this request with all energy providers in the State.

The campaign raised consumer awareness of the risks of door-to-door selling and resulted in the successful prosecution of two large energy companies (initiated by the regulator—the Australian Competition and Consumer Commission). It also led to three energy companies in Victoria deciding to cease selling door-to-door and a Federal Court ruling in *Australian Competition and Consumer Commission v AGL Sales Pty Ltd* [2013] that the 'Do not knock' sticker amounted to a request to leave a property, thereby giving all Australians the ability to control whether or not sales people can knock on their door.

The Federal Court ruling means that a salesperson who ignores a 'Do not knock' sticker at a person's house will be in breach of Australian consumer law and can face a substantial fine. This result has the potential to benefit all Australians.

Welcoming the decision on 11 October 2013, Gerard Brody, Chief Executive Officer of Consumer Action, said in a media release that the popularity of the sticker was a great example of what CLCs can achieve:

> Community legal centres have their ears to the ground and are often the first to know what businesses or industries are causing trouble. We saw salespeople taking advantage of vulnerable consumers, came up with a practical response, and have now distributed over 300,000 'Do Not Knock' stickers across Australia. (Consumer Action Law Centre 2013)

In the case of door-to-door selling, had Consumer Action chosen only to help each individual to resolve their dispute with the seller, they would have helped only a tiny portion of those with problems, and the numbers needing help would likely have continued to increase. Instead, as flagged above, this change has the potential to benefit all Australians.

III. Why Protect CLCs' Systemic Advocacy Role?

The examples discussed above demonstrate the significant value of systemic advocacy by CLCs. For community lawyers, advocating for improvements to the law or a change in practice is often the only way to advance towards just outcomes for certain clients. In many cases, the status quo simply cannot provide justice. This is unsurprising if we recognise, as van Moorst suggests, that 'structural inequality has been institutionalised by the legal system' (Fadden et al 1992: 290).

Indeed, early in my career as a community lawyer, it became clear that often the best role I could perform with an individual client was to minimise unfairness and to explain, in terms my client understood and with some kind of humanity, that the system simply could not deliver to them a fair or safe outcome. At best, this is an unsatisfying role; at worst, it helps to legitimise and perpetuate an unfair system.

There is also the economic argument. Besides being, at times, the only way for individuals to work towards and achieve fairer outcomes, it is clearly more efficient to tackle a systemic flaw than to provide individual legal assistance to hundreds of clients facing the same issue. Law reform and systemic work prevent future legal problems and save legal assistance resources.

Of course, removing flawed, foolish or unfair laws and policies usually creates broader cost savings and social benefits well beyond future savings to legal services. This is clear in each of the examples discussed above, whether for community members now less likely to be subject to racial profiling by police, for victims of family violence more likely to get an appropriate response from police and the courts, or for a newly arrived migrant who can avoid being trapped in an unfair contract by door-to-door salespeople.

Furthermore, we know that the vast majority of people affected by unfair laws and practices are unlikely to identify that they have a legal problem or to seek legal help (Coumarelos et al 2012). If CLCs fail to act on systemic problems, they are effectively deciding to help only those people who find their way to a legal service. In this context, an exclusive focus on providing client services to those who seek services at the expense of other constituent needs would be 'morally wrong' (Rich 2009: 15).

These arguments are not the exclusive domain of community lawyers and social justice advocates. In 2014, the Australian Productivity Commission, a Commonwealth statutory agency and the Australian Government's principal review and advisory body on microeconomic policy, reviewed access to justice arrangements in Australia. The Commission found that systemic work can be 'an efficient use of limited resources' (Productivity Commission 2014: 709), and recommended that governments should fund systemic advocacy on the basis that 'strategic advocacy and law reform that seeks to identify and remedy systemic issues, and so reduce the need for frontline services, should be a core activity of LACs and CLCs' (Productivity Commission 2014: 711).

Systemic work also allows CLCs' unique knowledge about the 'on-the-ground' impact of laws and policies, acquired through their contact with thousands of disadvantaged community members weekly, to inform public policy. As specialists in poverty law and other areas such as violence against women, community lawyers have access to information about how the laws, systems and policies impact people on a day-to-day basis. Governments often have no other access to this information and, indeed, seek CLCs' input in a myriad of ways.

Feeding this information through to government and the broader community leads to better public policy and gives voice to the experience of disadvantaged communities. In some small way, it also addresses the structural imbalance whereby the powerful in society have access to lobbyists and campaigners, and have the ear of governments.

The same can be said for any not-for-profit organisation. If it is the role of not-for-profits to serve the community, this does not mean simply providing the community with services. It also means advocating for their needs or working to change those parts of society that are negatively affecting their lives:

> The third sector plays a major role in civil society. It provides a platform of influence, enabling the voice of the disadvantaged and dispossessed to be heard. It provides a vehicle for offering services and support, and at the same time it enables collective expression of grievances and distress … At its best, the third sector provides a framework for promoting social and cultural change, and does so in a way that engages people whose voices might otherwise be silenced. (Unwin 2004: 5)

These arguments point to the benefit of CLCs' law reform and policy work from the perspective of government, disadvantaged communities and civil society more broadly. From the perspective of CLCs and those working in the sector, there are other reasons to ensure that CLC practice includes law reform and policy work. Systemic work can make the work of a community lawyer more satisfying and engaging, improving their capacity to attract and retain quality staff, despite relatively low salary levels. It can also raise a CLC's profile and reputation, increasing community awareness of the services available (Wierzbowski 2015: 11). Moreover, if a strong systemic focus is part of what makes CLC practice unique or at least gives CLCs 'an edge that is rarely found elsewhere', maintaining that focus is important (Noble 2012b: 23; see also Rich 2009: 47). Without it, CLCs risk being relegated to 'the role of providing casework on the cheap' (Fadden et al 1992: 290).

IV. A New Era of Restriction on Systemic Advocacy by Community Lawyers

Prior to 2013, CLC law reform and advocacy attracted criticism from government figures and conservative media commentators from time to time. Previous governments at both the federal and State levels had raised the threat of gag clauses and mounted public attacks against community lawyers for speaking out. Phillip Ruddock, Attorney-General in the Howard government (1996–2007), was quoted in 2006 as saying that it was 'inappropriate for Australian Government funds to be directed to the support of campaigns against legislation enacted by the Parliament of Australia' (Marr 2006).

During these periods, however, despite occasional critique and condemnation, community lawyers were not prevented from engaging in systemic work. CLC contracts, unlike others, did not attract gag clauses. The consequence of the above media statement, for example, was that former Attorney-General Ruddock refused to provide funding to support a conference for the National Association of CLCs, rather than anything more far-reaching.

Despite intermittent expressions of disapproval, therefore, law reform and systemic advocacy were established, recognised elements of CLCs' work in the lead-up to the 2013 federal election. Indeed, a 2008 review of the CLC funding programme for the federal government had noted that 'law reform and policy' were among the activities funded under that programme and that CLCs determined the 'type and mix of service delivery that best meets the needs of their client communities' (Attorney-General's Department 2008: 12).

Prior to 2014, CLCs' contracts expressly stated that funds were to be used for 'law reform and legal policy activities'. These contracts also included clause 5, an anti-gag clause clarifying that centres were free to enter public debate and criticise the Commonwealth:

> [N]o right or obligation arising under this Agreement will be read or understood by the Commonwealth as limiting the Organisation's right to enter into public debate or criticism of the Commonwealth, its agencies, employees, servants or agents.

Indeed, the biggest challenge to systemic work in CLCs at this time was how to carve out sufficient time to apply a systemic approach in the face of massive client demand. Having always exceeded capacity, demand was growing as the gap between those who could afford a private lawyer and those who could get legal aid grew wider. In some States, such as Victoria, this gap was growing with particular speed because of legal aid funding shortages that prompted guideline changes and reduced the range and number of people who could get help with summary crime and family law matters.

The accepted nature of CLCs' law reform and policy role changed in 2013. The first sign of change occurred prior to the federal election, when soon-to-be Attorney-General, Senator George Brandis, flagged his views that legal assistance funding should be used only for direct services:

> It is important that, in a resource-constrained environment, the legal aid dollar be spent where it is most needed ... The Coalition believes that casework is a more important role for legal assistance providers than advocacy, and would direct funding to community legal centres accordingly. (Boxsell 2013)

In December 2013, just three months after the election, the government announced AU$43 million (£24.4 million) worth of cuts to legal assistance services, particularly targeting CLCs and community-based Indigenous legal services. The network of specialist environment protection CLCs around Australia learned that they were to lose their funding entirely, having incurred the wrath of powerful interests such as the Minerals Council.

Attorney-General George Brandis initially explained these cuts as targeting law reform and advocacy work, although the amounts to be cut well exceeded the amounts allocated to law reform and advocacy within the sector:

> [I]ncreasingly over recent years an increasing percentage of the legal assistance dollar has been spent on what is called advocacy work or policy work, which is not directed to helping specific clients with specific needs but in participating in—as it were—society's discussion about various areas of potential law reform or identifying gaps in the legal system ... Where resources are limited, I would rather see that money spent helping individual people in need who cannot afford a lawyer rather than spent on policy development. That is where the savings will be found. (Senate Legal and Constitutional Affairs Legislation Committee February 2014: 50)

In the May 2014 budget announcements, the government announced further cuts to CLCs, meaning that by 2017–18 federal government funding for CLCs would be cut by almost 30 per cent nationally. On the same evening, the government conveyed to CLCs that their service agreements would be amended within six weeks and that the variations would prevent CLCs from undertaking law reform and policy activities using federal funds. When questioned during Senate Estimates hearings, Attorney-General Brandis again emphasised that this decision was about prioritising the needs of individuals:

> [W]here resources are finite, we need to spend them on the people who need them most, and it is my view that spending those resources on flesh and blood men and women and children, actual clients in needy circumstances, should be the first call on the resources in the access to justice budget. (Senate Legal and Constitutional Affairs Legislation Committee May 2014: 99)

In line with this decision, CLC contracts were amended in July 2014 to remove any reference to 'law reform and policy' from the definition of 'core services', meaning that federal government funds could no longer be used for these activities. The anti-gag clause was also removed. The Attorney-General said that CLC workers could engage in advocacy and systemic work 'in a voluntary way' (Senate Legal and Constitutional Affairs Legislation Committee May 2014: 100).

When asked again at Senate Estimates hearings what work CLCs were permitted to undertake, the Attorney-General replied:

> There is a very practical test I think we can apply. I am not pretending this is universal, but I think it will apply in the overwhelming majority of cases. It is whether there is a client and whether these services are actually helping a flesh and blood individual or whether they are in the nature of essentially academic work or advocacy work that is not related directly to assisting a particular client in a particular case. (Senate Legal and Constitutional Affairs Legislation Committee February 2014: 52)

The government's intention was clearly to prevent the use of funds for any work of a systemic nature. Since then, CLC contracts have been changed again. In July 2015, the federal government negotiated a new National Partnership Agreement on Legal Assistance Services (NPA) with States and Territories, which includes the following stipulation:

> Commonwealth funding should not be used to lobby governments or to engage in public campaigns. Lobbying does *not* include community legal education or where a legal assistance service provider makes a submission to a government or parliamentary body to provide factual information and/or advice with a focus on systemic issues affecting access to justice. (Council of Australian Governments 2015: B17)

No explanation was given for this change. It reflects, perhaps, the realisation by the government that it has come to rely on CLCs' advice and input. For example, in the six months after the advocacy and law reform restrictions were first imposed in July 2014, one Victorian CLC received 11 separate requests for input and advice from Commonwealth agencies that were reviewing an area of law practised by the CLC.

Under the current NPA and corresponding CLC agreements, lobbying and campaigning are not permitted, but CLCs can make submissions that provide factual information and advice on systemic issues. Community lawyers have been left to establish the distinction between gathering facts, evidence and advice, and conveying it by way of a formal submission, which is allowed, and the proscribed activities of arranging to meet with government to discuss the same content or talking to a journalist about that content to raise awareness of an issue and create pressure for change.

When explaining his position against law reform and systemic advocacy by CLCs, Attorney-General Brandis has consistently referenced the notion that systemic work is an unaffordable luxury, disconnected from the needs of real people who suffer disadvantage and experience legal need. Speaking at a national CLC conference in 2015, he said:

> I did make a decision, very early in my tenure as Attorney-General, that given that the demands and claims on the system from vulnerable Australians exceeded the available resources and was likely to do so well into the future, as a matter of priority, I wanted to see all of the money devoted to the needs of clients not causes. (Brandis 2015)

This explanation suggests that 'clients' and 'causes' are entirely disconnected, rather than interdependent. It creates a false distinction between casework for individuals and activity intended to address underlying causes highlighted by that casework. It ignores the fact that working to tackle factors that create the need for legal services will ultimately save resources. And it ignores the Productivity Commission's advice that CLCs' systemic advocacy is cost effective, beneficial to the community and should be funded.

The Attorney-General's explanation also fails to provide a rationale for why the federal government initially sought to prevent all law reform, policy and systemic advocacy but subsequently determined that certain types of systemic work are acceptable. The changing breadth of the restrictions gives insight into their true intent. Submissions to parliamentary and government inquiries are acceptable, and often sought by government, regardless of the fact that they distract CLCs from the 'flesh and blood individual' in need of help. Lobbying and campaigning—speaking out—is not acceptable. In this regard, the restrictions appear to be ideologically based, all the more so because they have been imposed amid broader government moves to stop advocacy by non-government organisations, prevent public critique of government policy and practice, and silence dissent.

Since the advocacy restrictions on CLCs were first imposed, a raft of advocacy and peak bodies have been de-funded, including the Australian Youth Affairs Council, the Alcohol and Drug Council and the National Congress of Australia's First Peoples. When one organisation, the Refugee Council, was de-funded, the relevant minister was explicit about the rationale—namely, that 'taxpayer funding should not be there to support what is essentially an advocacy group' (former Minister for Immigration, Scott Morrison, quoted in Seccombe 2014).

As well as decisions to de-fund certain advocacy organisations, the federal government has moved to review the tax-deductible status of certain not-for-profit, predominantly environmental groups. Efforts to silence not-for-profit organisations working in immigration detention facilities have been blunter. The *Australian Border Force Act 2015* (Cth) makes it a criminal offence to reveal information to the media or others outside government about conditions in offshore immigration detention centres like Nauru and Manus Island, including information about the abuse of children or adults detained there. More recently, organisations like Save the Children that work in immigration detention centres have been asked to pay large bonds that must be forfeited if staff from the organisation speak to the media (Morton 2015).

The message, overall, is clear for community lawyers and the CLCs in which they work: 'do not criticise government or government policy, other than in the polite and discrete pages of a written submission, regardless of the damage that that policy may be causing your clients or the communities with which you work'.

V. CLCs' Response and the Future of Systemic Lawyering

Given the primacy that law reform and systemic work have been given in commentary on the role of CLCs, it is surprising that these restrictions have been imposed easily and amid relatively quiet protest. But this is due in part to the fact that the government disapproval of systemic advocacy and its announcement of severe funding cuts emerged simultaneously. Imposing new restrictions on advocacy, while announcing large cuts scheduled in the near future, but not announcing which centres would be targeted by the cuts, was a well-planned and effective strategy. While CLC peak bodies have spoken out against the cuts to varying degrees, boards and managers of many CLCs have decided that it is simply too unsafe to express disagreement with government policy, as they risk additional defunding in the future. For some, the same theory applies when deciding whether to engage in law reform and policy advocacy, and on what issues. The risk of being placed high on the list of centres perceived as not using their funds appropriately is too great.

Of course, the sector's response to advocacy restrictions should be seen in the historical context of a sector that has grappled for some time with how it can retain independence and the elements that make it unique while receiving—and increasingly relying upon—government funding (Giddings and Noone 2004; Rice 2012; Schetzer 2006). It should also be seen in the context of a sector engaged in the relentless struggle to meet severe legal need with inadequate resources, as has been identified by repeated inquiries and reviews.[6] This translates into the need to make daily decisions about who should get help, what level of help they should get, and which people clearly need help but must be turned away. This context, as well as the 'rescue mission' (Rich 2009: 15) that can easily dominate community lawyers when confronted by people in need, can undermine reflective and strategic practice (Wierzbowski 2015: 14). Against this backdrop, the federal government's restrictions could sound the death knell for CLC reform activity.

In a recent study that considered 31 of Victoria's 49 CLCs, the author found that a little under half did not engage in any significant strategic or systemic legal work (Wierzbowski 2015: 14). The main reason given was 'the churn factor', defined to include 'unending legal need' as well as the funders' requirements. Another reason given was 'funding arrangements that prohibit it' (Wierzbowski 2015: 15). These findings are troubling, especially given that Victoria is often perceived as one of the States in Australia where the sector has the strongest commitment to law reform and a systemic approach. It is also a jurisdiction in which governments from both sides of politics have previously supported CLC advocacy.

There is no doubt that the federal government restrictions and the accompanying messages are having a significant and chilling effect on the amount of new

[6] Repeated inquiries have found that the legal assistance sector is under-resourced. Most recently, the Productivity Commission recommended an interim AU$200 million (£113.8 million) investment into the legal assistance sector 'given the dearth of data, and having regard to the pressing nature of service gaps' (Productivity Commission 2014: 738). See also Senate Standing Committee on Legal and Constitutional Affairs (1993), Federal Access to Justice Advisory Committee (1995), Senate Standing Committee on Legal and Constitutional Affairs (2004), Attorney-General's Department (2008), Senate Standing Committee on Legal and Constitutional Affairs (2009).

reform activity undertaken. This effect is particularly felt in centres that lack a strong culture or practice of identifying and acting on systemic problems.

The fear that may prompt centre management in some CLCs to remain quiet about the imposition of funding restrictions means that those same CLCs will be reluctant to be seen engaging in law reform, policy and systemic work. They will be particularly reluctant to take on issues perceived as politically unpopular or to engage in public advocacy that is likely to be characterised as lobbying or campaigning. Unfortunately, acting on behalf of the marginalised and the disadvantaged often involves challenging government or public institutions, and often requires public commentary and pressure—even criticism—before the need for change is acknowledged.

Despite this, however, there are also many signs that CLC activism and systemic advocacy have a sound future. Such work continues to be supported by a number of State governments and federal opposition parties. The defence of the third sector's role in speaking out on behalf of those it serves, and the importance of this role in a healthy democracy, is alive and well. Thus, while some CLCs may be shying away from law reform and policy and giving it a lower priority in the current political climate, others continue to pursue their mission undeterred. For example, early in 2015, when federal government contractual restrictions covered submissions, as well as other forms of policy and advocacy, Victorian CLCs contributed a total of 36 submissions to that State's Royal Commission into Family Violence.

The CLCs that continue to engage in advocacy rely on other funding sources to support this work—State government funding, philanthropic grants or private donations. In this regard, there are signs that philanthropy, traditionally reluctant to support advocacy due in part to the challenge of demonstrating short- or medium-term outcomes, is shifting.[7] The Victorian Environment Defenders Office, for example—one of the network of specialist environment protection CLCs that lost all its federal funding—responded boldly. Now called Environmental Justice Australia and expressly rebranded as an activist organisation, it is thriving on philanthropic and crowd funding. Other CLCs, as the Attorney-General has generously suggested they should, rely on community lawyers' volunteer contributions in their own, unpaid time.

Meanwhile, three Melbourne CLCs that have chosen to amalgamate—a process often seen as the result of a conservative, economic rationalist agenda—have done so in an explicit quest to improve capacity for systemic work (Lowe 2014: 13). The project report that informed the three CLC boards' decision to merge highlighted that, without amalgamation, those CLCs faced three risks, including 'cultural risk' or:

[7] The Flemington and Kensington CLC's Police Accountability Project, for example, has been supported in recent years by the Reichstein Foundation.

> The risk that a CLC is not able or significantly less able to operate in a manner that defines CLC practice as unique. This matters not only from the perspective of what defines a CLC as unique but also from the perspective of effectiveness of practice, and therefore funding expenditure, in achieving the outcome of addressing legal need. (Lowe 2014: 24)

Perhaps the greatest cause for optimism about the survival of CLC advocacy lies in its history. Ultimately this history shows that where those involved in the sector are committed to systemic change they will find a way to drive that change, regardless of structure, funding and the political context.

Justice Virginia Bell, who worked at Redfern CLC in Sydney for seven years, has written that 'CLCs' strength is likely to come from regular injections of the passion and commitment of young practitioners' (Bell 2012). Some of this passion is evident in a report, *Lawyering for Change*, recently released by community lawyer Agata Wierzbowski. It is evident in the Victorian CLC Adaptive Leadership Programme run each year, and in CLC discussion forums held throughout the year. It is evident in the frequency with which community lawyers are cited in media reports on significant social and legal issues, and in the regular events held to launch a law reform report or a new campaign for change. Indeed, in Victoria at present, there is a potent combination of highly experienced, long-term community lawyers and leaders with a generation of newer practitioners, committed to social justice and attracted to the unique flexibility and freedom to advocate for change offered by CLCs. This loose group has started meeting in evenings and on weekends to discuss how to achieve systemic change on the issues they see in their daily practice across CLCs.

VI. Conclusion

The current environment poses great risks for law reform and systemic advocacy. There is greater pressure than ever before for CLCs to embrace a role defined as providing 'casework on the cheap' and, in doing so, lose their defining characteristics and strength. This path would, in turn, deprive the Australian community of a force for change that has brought the experience of the disadvantaged, marginalised and vulnerable to light and improved our laws and justice system in a myriad of ways.

Fortunately, many CLCs and the community lawyers working in them remain passionate about systemic lawyering and the role of CLCs as agents of change. As Nassim Arrage, chair of the New South Wales peak body for CLCs, said at a recent forum to mark the fortieth anniversary of CLCs in that State:

> There is still a lot of social injustice, and for me CLCs are about creating the structural change or at least trying to hold government to account to make sure that the world is a better place, and sadly there are a lot of things still to fight. (Bullock 2015)

References

Attorney-General's Department (2008) *Review of the Commonwealth Community Legal Services Program* (Canberra, Attorney-General's Department).

Bell, V (2012) 'You Are Never Too Old for Community Justice' 37 *Alternative Law Journal* 2.

Boxsell, A (2013) 'Dreyfus, Brandis Set Out Key Legal Issues', *The Australian Financial Review*, 16 August 2013, available at: www.afr.com.

Brandis, G (2015) 'National Association of Community Legal Centres Conference Closing Address', Speech presented at the National Association of Community Legal Centres conference, Melbourne, 27 August 2015, available at: www.attorneygeneral.gov.au/Speeches/Pages/2015/ThirdQuarter/27-August-2015-National-Association-of-Community-Legal-Centres-Conference-closing-address.aspx.

Bullock, L (2015) 'CLC Ethos Permeates Industry', *Lawyers Weekly*, 24 November 2015, available at: www.lawyersweekly.com.au/news/17561-clc-ethos-permeates-ndustry.

Chesterman, J (1992) 'Twenty Years of Fitzroy Legal Service: A Look Back for a Look Forward' 17 *Alternative Law Journal* 257.

Consumer Action Law Centre (2013) 'Do Not Knock: Federal Court Finds Do Not Knock Sign is an Unambiguous Request to Leave the Premises', available at: donotknock.org.au.

Coumarelos, C, Macourt, D, People, J, MacDonald, HM, Wei, Z, Iriana, R and Ramsey, S (2012) *Legal Australia-Wide Survey: Legal Need in Australia* (Sydney, Law and Justice Foundation of NSW).

Council of Australian Governments (2015) *National Partnership Agreement on Legal Assistance Services 2015/16–2019/20*.

Curran, L (2007) *Making the Legal System More Responsive to Community: A Report on the Impact of Victorian Community Legal Centre (CLC) Law Reform Initiatives* (Melbourne, La Trobe University and West Heidelberg Community Legal Service).

Fadden, R, Rathus, Z, Duignan, J, Renouf, G, Nicholls, M, Whitmore, J, Harris, P, Blake, P, van Moorst, E and Butler, C (1992) 'Community Legal Centres: National Overview' 17 *Alternative Law Journal* 283.

Federal Access to Justice Advisory Committee (1995) *The Justice Statement* (Canberra, Access to Justice Advisory Committee).

Footscray Community Legal Centre and Federation of Community Legal Centres (2012) *In the Driver's Seat: Achieving Justice for Taxi Drivers in Victoria*.

Giddings, J and Noone, MA (2004) 'Australian Community Legal Centres Move into the Twenty-first Century' 11 *International Journal of the Legal Profession* 257.

Green, M (2013) 'The Long Road to Change', *Right Now*, available at: www.communitylaw.org.au/flemingtonkensington.

Gyorki, L (2013) *Breaking Down the Silos: Overcoming the Practical and Ethical Barriers of Integrating Legal Assistance into a Healthcare Setting* (Canberra, Winston Churchill Memorial Trust of Australia).

Lowe, C (2014) *Western Community Legal Centres Reform Project Summary Report*, unpublished.

Marr, D (2006) 'Ruddock Snubs Legal Centres', *Sydney Morning Herald*, 2 August 2006, available at: www.smh.com.au/news/national/ruddock-snubs-legal-centres/2006/08/01/1154198137621.html.

McCulloch, J and Blair, M (2009) *Justice for All: A History of the Victorian Community Legal Centre Movement*, available at: www.fclc.org.au/cb_pages/files/Justice%20for%20All%20History%20Booklet%202011(1).pdf.

Morton, A (2015) 'Buying Silence? Immigration Asked Charities for Multi-Million-Dollar Bond', *Sydney Morning Herald*, 30 October 2015, available at: www.smh.com.au/federal-politics/political-news/buying-silence-immigration-asked-charities-for-multimilliondollar-bond-20151030-gkmspv.html.

Noble, P (2012a) *Advocacy-health Alliances: Better Health through Medical-legal Partnerships* (Bendigo (Vic), Advocacy and Rights Centre Ltd).

—— (2012b) 'The Future of Community Legal Centres' 37 *Alternative Law Journal* 22.

Pleasence, P, Coumarelos, C, Forell, S and McDonald, HM (2014) *Reshaping Legal Assistance Services: Building on the Evidence Base—A Discussion Paper* (Sydney, Law and Justice Foundation of NSW).

Productivity Commission (2014) *Access to Justice Arrangements Inquiry*, Report No 72, 5 September 2014 (Canberra, Productivity Commission).

Rice, S (2012) 'Are CLCs Finished?' 37 *Alternative Law Journal* 17.

Rich, N (2009) *Reclaiming Community Legal Centres: Maximising Our Potential So We Can Help Our Clients Realize Theirs* (Victoria, Consumer Action Law Centre and Victoria Law Foundation).

Schetzer, L (2006) 'Community Legal Centres: Resilience and Diversity in the Face of a Changing Policy Environment' 31 *Alternative Law Journal* 159.

Seccombe, M (2014) 'Brandis Ties NGO Funding to Non-advocacy', *The Saturday Paper*, 26 July 2014, available at: www.thesaturdaypaper.com.au/news/politics/2014/07/26/brandis-ties-ngo-funding-non-advocacy/1406296800.

Senate Legal and Constitutional Affairs Legislation Committee (2014) Estimates Hearing, 24 February (Canberra, Proof Committee Hansard).

—— (2014) Estimates Hearing, 28 May 2014 (Canberra, Proof Committee Hansard).

Senate Standing Committee on Legal and Constitutional Affairs (2009) *Access to Justice* (Canberra, Senate Standing Committee on Legal and Constitutional Affairs).

—— (2004) *Inquiry into Legal Aid and Access to Justice* (Canberra, Senate Standing Committee on Legal and Constitutional Affairs).

—— (1993) *The Cost of Justice: Foundations for Reform* (Canberra, Senate Standing Committee on Legal and Constitutional Affairs).

Unwin, J (2004) *Speaking Truth to Power* (The Baring Foundation), available at: baringfoundation.org.uk/wp-content/uploads/2000/08/sttp2000.pdf.

Victoria Police (2013) *Equality Is Not the Same … Victoria Police Response to Community Consultation and Reviews on Field Contact Policy and Data Collection and Cross Cultural Training* (Victoria, Victoria Police).

Wierzbowski, A (2015) *Lawyering for Change: Seven Practice Principles of Strategic Practice for Community Legal Centres* (Victoria, Victoria Law Foundation).

Treaties, Conventions, Principles, Directives, Rules and Legislation

Australian Border Force Act 2015 (Cth)

Family Violence Protection Act 2008 (Vic)

Cases

Australian Competition and Consumer Commission v AGL Sales Pty Ltd [2013] FCA 1030 (11 October 2013).

9

What if There Is Nowhere to Get Advice?

JAMES ORGAN AND JENNIFER SIGAFOOS[1]

I. Introduction

The provision of legal advice in the third sector has undergone significant change in the past three years in the Liverpool City Region (Liverpool CR) and across the United Kingdom (UK).[2] The *Legal Aid, Sentencing and Punishment of Offenders Act 2012* (LASPO) abolished almost all civil legal aid funding for advice services in England and Wales from 2013, and significant reductions in local authority (LA) funding have led to further cuts to third-sector advice agencies. At the same time, there has been wide-reaching reform of welfare benefits, which is the largest subject-area of advice service provision by these agencies. This has led to a 'perfect storm' for the sector—greater demand for services, at the same time as drastic funding cuts. This chapter assesses the impact of both the funding cuts and recent policy changes on third-sector advice agencies in the Liverpool CR.

The Liverpool CR is an appropriate location for this study because of its high levels of deprivation and the corresponding demands that this places on the free provision of legal advice, particularly around social welfare issues. In turn, this means that changes to social welfare law and to the funding of third-sector organisations are likely to have a disproportionate impact in this geographical area. Although the study focuses on the Liverpool CR, the experience in other urban areas of high deprivation, such as Blackpool and Manchester, is likely to be similar. In the *English Indices of Deprivation*, the measure of deprivation in England, the city of Liverpool was ranked as the most deprived LA area in 2004, 2007 and 2010 (Office of the Deputy Prime Minister 2004; Department for Communities and

[1] This work was funded in part by an Early Career Fellowship from the Leverhulme Trust.

[2] The Liverpool City Region includes Merseyside (Liverpool, St Helens, Wirral, Sefton and Knowsley LAs) and the neighbouring borough of Halton.

Local Government 2007, 2010),[3] with significant issues of deprivation in neighbouring LA areas, particularly Knowsley.[4] The city of Liverpool has seen overall improvement in the 2015 indices, but still has the largest number of lower-layer super output areas (LSOAs), falling in the most deprived one per cent in England (Department for Communities and Local Government 2015). The wider Liverpool CR has also been consistently ranked as the most deprived region in England and clearly remains so in 2015, both overall, and in the individual measures of income and employment, which make the most significant contribution to the measure of multiple deprivation. It is also notable that 46 per cent of the Liverpool CR's LSOAs are in the most deprived 10 per cent in England in the domain of health and disability deprivation.[5] These levels of deprivation mean that there is a relatively high reliance on welfare benefits in the Liverpool CR, high demand for legal advice services when there are changes to the welfare benefits programme and a high impact when there are funding cuts to the third-sector agencies that provide free legal advice.

Organisations in the Liverpool CR lost legal aid contracts worth millions of pounds for housing, money advice and welfare rights following the introduction of LASPO, with the highest number of specialist advisers lost in welfare law. These drastic cuts were not unique to the Liverpool CR, with the House of Commons Justice Committee warning in 2011 of the potential for civil legal aid cuts to create 'advice deserts' in some areas of the country (House of Commons Justice Committee 2010–11: para 156). In 2014, the National Audit Office (NAO) estimated that the permitted number of 'matter starts' for legal help in 2013–14 was only 34 per cent of what it would have been without LASPO (NAO 2014: 13).[6] The quality of the government's evidence base for the reforms has been questioned, including the evidence for the continued viability of the provision of civil legal aid advice through third-sector organisations (House of Commons Justice Committee 2010–11, 2014–15; NAO 2014: 33). A 'clear majority' of the legal aid providers who responded to the NAO consultation reported that their financial position had deteriorated post-LASPO, with third-sector organisations (73 per cent) most likely to report that to be the case (NAO 2014: 33). The Low Commission on the Future of Advice and Legal Support noted in its follow-up report that:

> For the non-profit advice sector there has been a multiplier impact combined with additional cuts to local government funding, and uncertainty over the future of significant

[3] Measured according to the number of lower-layer super output areas (LSOAs) in the 10 per cent most deprived areas in England. An LSOA is a geographical unit for reporting small area statistics, with a minimum population of 1000 and a maximum of 3000 (ONS 2016).

[4] Knowsley was the fourth most deprived LA area in 2010 and in 2015 was ranked as the second most deprived according to the number of LSOAs in the 10 per cent most deprived areas in England.

[5] The second-ranked region is Tees Valley with 33 per cent.

[6] Matter starts are the number of new cases that an agency may open under its legal aid contract. Calculated from 170,545 actual matter starts, as compared to 496,549 expected without legal aid reforms.

> Big Lottery funding (i.e. the Advice Services Transition Fund). While the sector has responded positively to the changes by adapting service models and developing new partnerships, frontline agencies are increasingly 'running out of road'. (Low Commission 2015: vi)

During the same period, austerity measures have led to budget cuts across the public sector, with LA funding reductions having a significant impact on the funding of third-sector advice agencies. The largest provider of welfare rights advice in Liverpool has had its LA funding cut by 90 per cent, leaving its future very uncertain, while advice agencies across the region have typically seen cuts of more than 50 per cent, threatening the provision of their core general advice service.[7] A temporary transition fund of £100 million (AU$175.7 million) was set up to help third-sector organisations manage the move to a different funding environment post-LASPO. The applicants to the fund, who accounted for seven per cent of all state third-sector funding, reported losses of £524 million (AU$920 million) in 2011–12, £94 million (AU$165 million) of that from debt counselling and advice services alone. With further cuts since then, it is clear that the funding environment for third-sector advice agencies has deteriorated significantly.

As part of the UK Government's still incomplete austerity programme, the welfare benefits regime has undergone reform that has been described as 'the most fundamental for a generation' (Centre for Economic and Social Inclusion 2013). Part of this programme of benefits reform—the *Welfare Reform Act 2012* (WRA)—made a number of significant changes, and was described by the Secretary of State for Work and Pensions as reforming 'virtually every part of our welfare system' (DWP 2012).[8] A Local Government Association-commissioned report into the cumulative impact of the reforms found that all regions outside London face average losses per claimant of between £1500 (AU$2636) and £1650 (AU$2899) per year (Centre for Economic and Social Inclusion 2013). One example of how benefits changes affect the need for advice services is found in the transition from Disability Living Allowance (DLA) to Personal Independence Payment (PIP) for people aged between 16 and 64. Both of these programmes help disabled people with their higher care and mobility costs. The government estimated that 28 per cent of the recipients of DLA would not be eligible for any level of support under PIP (House of Commons Library 2013). In the transition period, all DLA claimants are required to re-apply for PIP, rather than being automatically transferred onto the replacement benefit. This created one of the biggest specific impacts of the WRA on the need for legal advice in Liverpool.

[7] This is reflected across England. Agencies applying for the Transition Fund reported an average 45 per cent cut.

[8] Among others, the WRA included housing benefit cuts; a benefits cap; limits on Employment Support Allowance, which replaced the Incapacity Benefit; the introduction of a new Universal Credit; and the strengthening of the sanctions regime for benefit claimants.

There is a high level of disability deprivation in Liverpool (Department for Communities and Local Government 2015), which is reflected in Employment and Support Allowance (ESA) and PIP dominating welfare benefits advice for local Citizen Advice Bureaux (CABx). Liverpool CABx reported that there were over 4200 PIP and ESA issues dealt with in the second quarter of the 2014–15 financial year alone. Benefits reforms have exacerbated the impact of the funding crisis for third-sector advice agencies because of an increased number of enquiries and increased complexity in individuals' cases. The tightening of immigration rules has also added to the quantity and complexity of cases for some individuals (see Aliverti Chapter 16, this volume, for further discussion of the impact of immigration policy change).

In May 2013, a survey was carried out to evaluate the impact in Liverpool of the cuts to civil legal aid as a result of LASPO (Sigafoos and Morris 2013). The survey was developed and piloted with the (then) Liverpool Citizen's Advice Partnership, an umbrella organisation for the CABx in Liverpool. It was distributed online in May 2013, and had a total of 81 responses, estimated to be over half of the target population. The survey included a number of qualitative open-ended questions. In addition, researchers attended a meeting of the advice services Welfare Reform Task Group, accessed past minutes and gathered data from agency heads via interviews and emailed questionnaires. This survey of advice workers was repeated in 2015 across the wider geographical area of the Liverpool CR, to assess the impact—two years on—of the legal aid and other funding cuts on the delivery of advice services. The questionnaire was updated and redistributed online in August to October 2015. Fifty-one responses were collected, and again this was estimated to be over half of the now-reduced population.

The analysis comparing the two surveys was performed using SPSS. In addition, eight interviews with agency heads or other key employees identified by agency heads were also carried out in June to September 2015 to add an organisational perspective to the survey data. The data from the interviews, along with qualitative responses to the surveys, were coded and analysed for themes. Themes were identified around the impact on services, agencies' responses and the barriers thereto. Preliminary research results were presented at a focus group of 11 participants, primarily local advice agency managers, in December 2015. A guided discussion provided clarification and confirmation of the preliminary research results.

It is clear from the study that advice agencies have lost large numbers of highly skilled staff and have been forced to remodel their service delivery, and that the greatest impact is in the area of welfare rights advice. Client cases have increased in complexity, but the availability of services has reduced and, despite their flexibility, agencies are unable to meet demand. The study has thus highlighted significant pressures on service delivery, which will be discussed in more detail below. Agencies have had to be flexible in their response to the challenges, to greater and lesser degrees of success, but have been hampered by some significant barriers, such as a lack of skills and resources. The result is growing levels of uncertainty about how services are to be funded, what services third-sector advice agencies can continue to provide and whether these agencies can survive at all.

II. Impact on Services

A. Reduced Service Provision

Both the qualitative survey and interview data indicated that, as a result of the funding cuts, there has been a dramatic reduction in the number of employees, especially specialist advisers, and a reduction in the hours that some services or sites are open. These findings accord with the Low Commission's second report (2015: v), which highlighted 'the decline in the number of people who are able to access specialist advice through CABx and other non-profit providers' as a major concern.

One agency head reported a reduction in staff from 29 to only nine over a three-year period, and further redundancies are anticipated in April 2016 (Interview 5). Another reported that staff numbers had dropped by almost half, from 40 to 22, over the past three years (Interview 8). Survey respondents, as well as agency heads, identified loss of staff—especially specialist advisers—as a key challenge: 'the CAB has to rely on volunteers when it comes to clients with benefit issues as there are no specialists' (22/9/15 Survey Response). The staffing cuts have been felt particularly intensely in the area of welfare benefits advice, after what one agency head described as the 'swingeing cuts to legal aid, with barely anything left for social welfare law' (Interview 1). One agency reported stripping its welfare benefits services 'back to basics', with 18 welfare benefits advisers reduced to three (Interview 5); another had two welfare rights workers previously funded through legal aid replaced by one part-time adviser funded through a National Health Service (NHS) contract (Interview 8); and another previously had three specialist welfare rights workers, but now has only one (Interview 2).

Some agencies have managed to replace a small part of the specialist provision through other funding sources, but, even where they have done so, these sources are temporary and under threat. For example, the only housing legal aid contract still held in Liverpool is having its funded matter starts reduced again and is now facing a 20 per cent staff cut (Interview 6), and the APP Project, funded by the NHS, which provides advice services in GP surgeries, is out for re-tender. This reduction in specialist advice is in line with the national picture, with Gillian Guy, the Chief Executive of Citizens Advice,[9] estimating that CABx have lost 350 specialist advisers since the civil legal aid cuts came into play (House of Commons Justice Committee 2014–15: para 78).

[9] Citizens Advice is an operating name of the National Association of Citizens Advice Bureaux.

One survey respondent in 2013 summed up the situation as: 'no funding, no specialist advice. The equation is simple' (Survey response 21/5/13). In 2015, another stated that 'legal aid cuts reduced the level of funding which meant we had fewer specialists in housing and welfare rights and the type of cases they could advise on was limited' (Survey response 15/10/15). Others noted that they had previously provided support at tribunals and now were unable to do so. One agency, however, was considering a strategy of re-focusing on specialist advice and reducing the provision of a generalist advice service (Interview 5). Although unusual in the Liverpool CR, this strategy has been pursued by a number of agencies in other parts of the country, particularly those that previously had a high percentage of legal aid funding, which is the case for this particular agency in Liverpool (House of Commons Justice Committee 2014–15: para 78).

All agency heads and a number of individual survey responses highlighted the fact that, despite these reductions, the demand for welfare rights advice and the complexity of cases have increased. As one agency head explained, 'We are responding to a whole raft of new benefits and legislative changes at the same time that legal aid went. We are at the saturation point now' (Interview 2). Yet there has been a lack of targeted support for areas of high deprivation or for specific areas of law, which might have been expected given the extent of the welfare reforms, the reduction in legal aid and the further funding cuts since then (see Byrom, Chapter 12, this volume, for an overview of the civil legal aid cuts).

The number of locations across which advice services are provided has also been reduced. One agency closed shortly after the legal aid cuts went into effect. Others have closed locations, or are contemplating closing locations, even in very deprived areas. Even where locations remain open, sometimes the range of advice that is offered has been reduced; for example, in Liverpool, as of April 2016, only one agency is able to provide specialist housing advice across the entire city (Focus group 17/12/15) and opening times have been shortened. This creates issues with client trust, as clients must now seek advice other than at the trusted locations where they have previously received advice, and alternatives provided by the local authority are viewed with suspicion (Interview 4). Clients are also faced with longer journeys of several miles on foot, or a bus ride.

B. What Have Agencies Done to Help Clients?

Within the constraints of the current financial situation, agencies have implemented a number of service changes to enable them to help more clients and to mitigate some of the impact of losing the specialist services that were funded through legal aid. These include the provision of evening advice surgeries, an increase in client self-help, an increase in telephone advice services and improvements in information available online.

A major change has been the increased use of volunteers to provide services at both a general and a specialist level. One manager commented that this reversed what had been to some extent the 'de-skilling' of volunteers during the period of legal aid, when agencies could rely on paid specialists and use their volunteers predominantly for generalist advice, thereby requiring fewer training resources and less commitment from volunteers (Interview 7). However, volunteers are not a free alternative to paid staff, and significant extra training and supervision is needed to support an increased volunteer workforce, particularly if they are to take up some of the specialist advice work that was previously carried out under legal aid contracts. This training and supervision also requires flexibility in the workforce so that the remaining specialist caseworkers and other staff can provide this extra training and supervision (see Kirwan Chapter 10, this volume, for a discussion on volunteers post-LASPO).

There are limits on the numbers of volunteers that can be recruited and supported in an agency, and there are limits on the resources that are available for training volunteers. One of the authors has been trying to place law students as volunteers with CABx and, in doing so, has been informed by several agency heads that their organisations have no capacity to train and supervise more volunteers. Furthermore, the recruitment and retention of volunteers are uncertain. Once trained, there is always the possibility that volunteers will leave, particularly to get paid employment. One agency said that they were lucky to have had several volunteers who had the time and capability to be trained up to a more specialist level, but two of the first four volunteers who were trained left soon after completing their training—one to take a paid job and the other to go onto higher education. A manager commented that this training functions as if it were a back-to-work service, which is remunerated for private firms contracted under the Department for Work and Pensions' Work Programme, but CABx are not participants.

The largely volunteer-run general advice services are an important source of flexibility for clients because anyone is able to seek advice on any issue of their choosing, not only as defined by the funder of a specific project or the service provider. For example, as discussed above, local CABx have recently been addressing a spike in PIP and ESA advice issues. This highlights the benefit of a grant-funded general advice service that is able to respond flexibly to the most pressing needs of clients, as well as the impact that government policy has on the demands for advice. The training and supervision needed to support these general services, however, are under threat because of the reduction in LA funding. One CAB manager noted that the resources for supervision of the general advice service had been pared down and could be hit by further cuts next year, and that 'if there is no supervision, there is no service' (Interview 7). This threat to the core service is also a threat to management time, making a highly flexible approach to management necessary. For example, another manager said that the funding cuts have meant that she does everything from funding bids to changing light bulbs (Interview 5).

In turn, this puts pressure on the resources available to respond strategically to changes in the funding environment and to service provision.

C. Quality

In discussing the quality of the services provided, large majorities in both surveys reported that they were providing a worse or somewhat worse service than they had before the funding cuts (91 per cent in 2013, and 73 per cent in 2015). However, things had improved somewhat over the 2013–15 period. In 2015, survey respondents were more likely to report that the quality of the service was about the same as it had been prior to the funding cuts (27 per cent versus 9 per cent of respondents in 2013). Additionally, although 51 per cent of respondents felt in 2013 that they were now providing a much worse service, only 31 per cent felt that way in 2015. At the focus group, however, agency heads overwhelmingly thought there had been a clear lowering of expectations as a result of two years of a dire funding situation, which could explain this improved perception of service quality by survey respondents (Focus group 17/12/15). Respondents said that alternative pots of money and approaches had allowed some services to fill gaps, but that the effect was frequently a lower overall service for clients.

Some respondents also felt that the service that they were still able to provide was good, but limited in terms of the number of clients they could assist:

> I don't believe that the quality of the service that I provide has become worse. In fact, with the experience that I have gained, I think that the quality has improved. There are just fewer advisers providing the service and overall there is unmet need. (Survey response 29/9/15)

More survey respondents reported feeling squeezed themselves, noting that they were 'unable to spend the time with clients like we used to. It's now much more about referring clients out and self-help' (Survey response 22/9/15); and there was 'less time available to investigate all of a person's case' (Survey response 23/9/15). This was further demonstrated by the comments of one manager who noted that they had decided to focus more on self-help to free up resources for the more complex cases (Interview 8).

D. Unmet Need

The survey revealed that services are struggling to meet local need. In 2013, 86 per cent of respondents did not believe that all of the people in their area who needed advice were able to get it. By 2015, that number had risen to 94 per cent. Despite this, respondents perceived that they were meeting more of the demand in 2015. In 2013, 77 per cent believed that there were 'many more' people with an unmet need for advice than there had been six months prior, whereas in 2015 only

54 per cent held that view. One interviewee provided a potential reason for this change: 'People are just accepting sanctions. It's like they have lost hope. It is such an effort to just survive, they've lost the energy to challenge decisions, even when they might have grounds' (Interview 2). Focus group respondents agreed with this explanation:

> 'Things are so bad, they don't feel there is anything they can do.'
>
> 'Before, clients would have a choice between food and fuel, but now they don't have either.'
>
> 'Clients are accepting that they will spend a couple of days without electricity or gas before each pay day.' (Focus group 17/12/15)

In 2013, 95 per cent of respondents reported unmet need in their area for advice on welfare benefits, 50 per cent reported unmet need for both debt and housing advice, while employment advice was identified by 45 per cent of respondents. By 2015, that picture had changed somewhat. Welfare benefits were still the primary subject area for unmet need, identified by 73 per cent of respondents, followed by advice on employment, housing and family, children and domestic abuse, with 65 per cent of respondents identifying each of these subject areas. Debt had fallen out of the top seven areas, being identified by only 23 per cent of respondents. In the interviews, managers stated that there were a number of money advice and financial capability projects that may account for this drop, such as a major, nationally funded money advice project called the Greater Merseyside Money Advice Project,[10] which covers the Liverpool CR, and the NHS-funded Income Maximisation Project across the city of Liverpool.[11] There has also been a privately funded initiative, the PALs Project, which has allowed three CABx in Merseyside to fund a specialist adviser in welfare benefits for three years. This may account for the reduced identification of welfare benefits advice as an area of unmet need. Despite this funding success, managers reported significant threats to the welfare benefits work: 'it is a real struggle at present to fund welfare rights advice. It is the stuff of nightmares. It is unthinkable not to have welfare rights services' (Interview 6).

Survey respondents' perceptions of where need is unmet is perhaps influenced by clients not seeking advice as a result of a mistaken belief that advice is not available in particular issue areas. After hearing the presentation of the initial research results, an agency head expressed surprise that employment law was not perceived as an area of large unmet need, as there is only one specialist agency in the Liverpool

[10] The Greater Merseyside Money Advice Project (GMMAP) is funded by the Money Advice Service, an independent body with statutory functions under the *Financial Services Act 2012* to assist the public with managing debt, and works with other organisations to provide quality debt advice services. GMMAP is a collection of agencies providing free debt advice under these terms in the Greater Merseyside area.

[11] The Income Maximisation Project is a referral service providing advice, information and representation to clients with mental health problems around welfare benefits and debt issues.

CR and they have suffered significant funding cuts, forcing them to merge with another agency (Personal communication 14 January 2016). As is implicit in the agency head's response, the limited *provision* of third-sector specialist advice in employment law over many years may perhaps have led to a reduction in clients *seeking* advice and therefore the perception from respondents that there is little unmet need in this area. In addition, the large increases in the costs of taking a case to an employment tribunal have reduced the number of people interested in pursuing tribunal cases (Busby and McDermont 2014).

E. Loss of Funding for Disbursements/Medical Evidence

Participants also identified the lack of funding available to help clients obtain medical evidence to support their applications or appeals for welfare benefits as compounding the problems of accessing specialist advice. Under legal aid, this advice could be paid for, although this encouraged general practitioners (GPs) to charge for reports—sometimes £50 (AU$87.8) or £100 (AU$175). However, now GPs are charging less, but many have stopped providing medical reports at all, because they have been inundated with requests. As one manager explained:

> Tribunals love medical evidence to back decisions up, unless the client's condition is very obvious. The burden is now on clients to fund this evidence, and many clients do not have the resources. They may not have received any support for weeks or months while on mandatory reconsideration of ESA. (Interview 2)

This lack of disbursement funding for medical evidence is felt very keenly in the region due to the high level of disability deprivation.

F. Loss of Referrals

Another challenge has been the lack of available places to which agencies can refer those whom they cannot help. A referral is an appointment made at another agency on behalf of a client—as opposed to signposting, where a client might be provided with a list of agencies that might be able to help. Survey respondents reported an improvement in referral opportunities for welfare benefits from 2013 to 2015. This may reflect the opportunities afforded by the PALs Project's specialist welfare benefits advisers. The APP Project in GP surgeries is also able to take welfare benefit referrals; however, focus group participants reported that 75 per cent of the clients handled by the APP Project were not referred from elsewhere, so this is a limited source of referral support (Focus group 17/12/15). Survey respondents also reported improvements in referral opportunities for debt and mental health advice, which could be related to alternative funding gains identified in the interviews. However, some managers questioned the efficacy of these referrals. Participants noted that clients for whom a proper referral could not be made were often signposted from agency to agency, and it is difficult to track whether the client's needs in such cases were in fact being successfully addressed. As one manager explained:

> Clients started off in the benefits agency, who pushed them off to an advice agency. All have said 'come to us'. People have been messed around and have gone around the system, which is completely overstretched. (Interview 7)

This circular set of signposting and referrals is more likely to contribute to referral fatigue, whereby clients become so demoralised by constant referrals that they fail to resolve otherwise resolvable problems (Pleasence et al 2004: 78).

III. Flexibility

It is clear that agencies have been, and have had to be, flexible in their response to the funding cuts. The reduction in funding and the corresponding reduction in staff numbers have meant inevitable change to services in terms of availability, level and location. Agencies have responded to these internal changes by altering the manner of service delivery and increasing the use of volunteers. They have also needed to be flexible in responding to external changes, such as in welfare and immigration law, in respect of which the number of clients seeking advice and the complexity of cases have increased, and to be open to the possibility of seeking funding outside their usual areas of service delivery. As charities, these organisations' purpose is to provide a service to clients, not to make a profit, so perhaps it should be expected that they will adapt as best they can to survive in order to enable clients to still receive the service. One manager said, 'clients have turned up because they need us … the needs of the clients keep the doors open' (Interview 7).

The decision about how and where to continue to provide services is not always in the hands of an organisation's management. Funders are also important stakeholders and their decisions about what they will fund have a strong influence on the types of services delivered. Scarce funding has meant that third-sector agencies have been forced to deliver services according to the funding that is available, rather than to seek funding that supports their core services and organisational aims. This is reflected in the increase in financial capability projects and the shift towards NHS-funded projects, such as the APP Project and Income Maximisation Project. One frustration expressed by agency heads was that 'all the funders want you to produce something else. Nobody wants to pay you to carry on doing what you're doing now' (Interview 5). This is a challenge for CABx, previously reliant on LA funding to support the supervision and training of their largely volunteer-run general advice service, which resolves a high proportion of client issues and acts as the gateway for many of their other services.

Agency heads also talked about increased competition for funding and the uncertainty surrounding the funding environment. Inevitably, as a result of the drastic funding cuts, agencies will need to find funding from different sources. Unusually, one agency has been successful in obtaining funding from the police service.[12] There is also evidence that agencies continue to have some success with other, usually smaller, sources of funds for more narrowly targeted projects or those outside the core advice work—such as a service for the lesbian, gay, bisexual and trans (LGBT) community, democratic engagement, back-to-work funding, wellbeing, and financial capability and budgeting projects. There are, however, limitations on how far agencies can stray from their charitable aims and operating constraints—for example, CABx are constrained by the Citizens Advice membership agreement, and specific staffing skills need to be available for particular projects—and how much funding there is to bid for. Most new funding streams are still specifically focused on the delivery of legal advice, and it seems unlikely that there would be significant funding available to agencies with a more flexible funding strategy. Funding approaches at present appear to be mostly reactive and the focus for agency heads is on how to manage and cope in a more competitive environment, where funding is scarcer and agencies need to spend more time writing bids and tenders.

Changing organisational structures is another path that has been taken by some organisations in response to the reduction in funding and especially difficulties in funding back office and managerial roles. Liverpool CABx are part way through a project to unify as one legal entity, rather than five. Two other agencies have merged and become a Law Centre. The CABx in the neighbouring boroughs of Knowsley, Halton and Sefton are already a single entity covering an LA area. Organisational changes may have many causes, but it seems unlikely that an agency in a robust financial position would seek to change its overarching legal structure unless compelled to do so. Agencies may hope that there are efficiencies from streamlining administrative costs as merged entities, or that they will be more competitive in funding bids as larger providers. This demonstrates flexibility even in the governance of these organisations.

IV. Hampered Response

A number of factors have hampered the response of advice agencies to the funding cuts and legislative and policy changes. Participants identified the lack of skills and resources, the increased complexity in the welfare regime, the policies themselves that have led to the increase in demand and the public's perception of the charities that provide legal advice, as barriers to a flexible response.

[12] The agency in question is funded to provide advice as part of a pilot project to provide support for victims of crime in Cheshire.

As indicated above, one of the responses has been, where possible, to use the skills of redundant staff in alternative projects. This response, however, is sometimes hampered by the extent of the change in the type of service being delivered and the limited opportunities to shift staff who have specialised in a particular area of law into a different project delivering advice in the same area. There has often been a need, to some degree at least, to stretch the skills of staff and provide them with retraining so that experience is not lost.

Managers need more time to spend on funding bids, and on planning service delivery and the strategic use of resources. However, as funding and staff numbers are cut, they get dragged into day-to-day operational issues to plug gaps, with the result that the time they can spend on organisational change is limited. Agency heads did not talk about strategic changes to funding, but instead about the need to chase any available funding in the shrinking pot. A manager bemoaned the fact that there was no time to consider a strategic response: 'You never have time to come up with a strategy. You just have to chase everything' (Interview 5). One manager said that she 'felt sick from January to March' while waiting for funding decisions to come in (Interview 7); another said that 'searching for funding is all I do' (Interview 5). Even if there is time to plan a funding strategy, it cannot create new funds where none exist.

Resources continue to be a major limitation at all levels in agencies. As commented above, volunteer-led services need training resources and supervision to directly provide services to clients. Available funds, such as the legal aid transition fund, fall considerably short of previous funding levels. Financial pressures are felt across the public sector and there is no guarantee that new projects will be sustained as cuts continue. For example, one agency's funding from the police service may be under threat as police budgets also are cut further (Interview 8). The NHS funding is also insecure, as the shift of services to the LA public health budget could threaten funding for preventative services such as legal advice (Interview 8). On this point, agency heads cited a lack of awareness of the cost-savings of preventative services, and a lack of appreciation of the success of legal advice in improving people's lives.

Prior to the introduction of LASPO, the two biggest funders for all agencies were the Legal Aid Agency, which funded specialist services, and the LA, which was used by many agencies to fund staff and running costs, and enabled agencies to be flexible in supporting specific projects. For example, one agency used LA funding to pay for a small amount of childcare to enable single parents to volunteer and gain employment skills that often led to them returning to work; it can no longer provide this opportunity. Flexibility has been restricted by the withdrawal of the LA grant funding that facilitated this approach. On the other hand, there has been some limited increase in flexibility where specialist services, such as the PALs Project and the NHS Advice Project, have replaced legal aid, which had become increasingly structured and restrictive. The increased flexibility in terms of who can be referred to these projects also may account for the improved perceptions of referral possibilities in the 2015 survey. Referrals are limited by the available capacity, but also by who can be referred under a programme's rules; and because the projects that have replaced legal aid have more generous rules in this regard, it may be that respondents feel there are more referral options, even if the number of people who actually get seen post-referral is reduced. In this sense, agencies have somewhere they can send the clients whom they cannot serve directly, but there appears to be little awareness of what happens after a referral has been made.

Policy changes have also increased the difficulty of recruiting volunteers in a number of ways. For example, reductions in childcare funding and changes to the benefits regime have made it harder for single parents to volunteer. Increases in benefits' conditionality and sanctions also have had an impact on volunteer opportunities, which might previously have provided experience and skills to help transition people into work. The stronger obligations on benefits claimants in terms of attendance and applications have reduced the time available to them for volunteering. The ability to recruit and support volunteers is therefore hampered by policy changes, as well as by funding cuts that limit the resources available to supervise and train those volunteers.

V. Concluding Remarks

Sudden change and uncertainty in their financial situation has become the norm for Liverpool CR advice agencies. There is a continual hunt for new funding, as projects rarely last more than three years and grant funding from LAs has been dramatically reduced. Long-term planning of services tailored to fit the needs of the client base and/or the most vulnerable is difficult, as funding dictates how and what services clients can access. Agency heads emphasised that their responses have been stop-gap measures in many cases, and have not created organisational stability. Many agencies are under threat. Increasing competition from the private sector for profitable contracts also puts agencies at risk. For-profit agencies, which have the resources to advertise and are not restricted by charitable aims and objectives, are able to 'cherry pick' the clients who can be served under more lucrative contracts, putting third-sector agencies at a disadvantage when tendering, and also leaving them to pick up the clients who cannot be funded under these contracts.

Agency heads described scrambling for funding to keep programmes running and adjusting their service provision to align with the funding sources available. Alternative funding has been particularly difficult to find for welfare benefits advice, which one agency head described as being like a 'dirty word' for funders (Interview 5). Agencies are competing for dwindling resources, which has placed them in opposition to one another at a time when collaborative solutions are needed. This need to chase any funding in order to keep their doors open may create 'mission drift' for these charities, if they diversify too far from their core charitable objects. Charity Commission (2007) research has indicated that charities providing public services are less likely to agree that their service provision is directed by organisational priorities, rather than funding. The 'contract culture', whereby charities tender for the provision of services that were previously provided by the public sector, has certainly penetrated the charitable advice sector. Mission drift may be more of a risk for local, rather than national, charities, as the more leverage a charity is able to exert on its potential funders, the lower will be the risk (Morris 1999). Although it is possible that all of the available pots of money will align with their charitable purpose or mission, these circumstances do not appear favourable for advice charities, as many are local and none in a position to exert leverage.

Membership of Citizens Advice may reduce the risk of mission drift, but at the same time it limits the flexibility of service provision, as their funding is distributed to the network. Agency heads did not mention mission drift as a current concern, but it might be that the exigency of their circumstances makes worry about mission drift a 'luxury' they simply cannot afford (Bennett 2008: 289).

One response to the precariousness faced by organisations has been to look towards forming larger ones through merger, in order to increase their financial robustness, make administrative savings and improve their ability to cope with sudden changes in funding. This brings with it uncertainties for staff and clients of these agencies, but might bring savings in terms of operational costs. However, we have seen in this study that larger agencies, which cover a whole LA area, are not immune to the cuts. On its own, without, for example, a change in attitude to the third sector and preventative services, merging is unlikely to be a solution that provides substantially improved services for clients or stability for agencies.

The fourth objective of LASPO was to 'deliver better value for money for the taxpayer'. At the national level, the Ministry of Justice (MoJ) is incurring increased court costs because of a lack of funding for mediation and increasing numbers of litigants in person. Government policy is also pushing the costs of legal aid onto other agencies (House of Commons Justice Committee 2014–15). In the Liverpool CR, the NHS and, in one example, police budgets are backfilling some of the gap left by the cuts to legal aid and LA budgets, which results in short-term savings. However, in the longer term, the lack of preventative services, such as legal advice, could lead to greater costs that exceed any short-term savings. There is evidence that legal problems frequently lead to health problems, from stress-related illness to mental health issues (Legal Services Commission 2010: 37). There is also evidence that advice services help to relieve or prevent some of this potential burden of ill health (CAB 2012, 2014; Legal Action Group 2014; see also Kirwan, Chapter 10, this volume). Citizens Advice estimates that the overall savings to the public purse from its advice provision is over £1 billion (AU$1.76 billion) from an expenditure of £200 million (AU$351 million), equalling a five to one benefit, and that four-fifths of people who receive CABx advice experience improved mental health (Public Accounts Committee 2014–15). This strong effect perhaps is why the NHS has attempted to fill some of the gaps left in advice provision in recent years, and the expansion of the duty related to advice and information imposed by the *Care Act 2014* may strengthen this connection between advice and health further.[13] However, celebration of this potential good news for the sector should be tempered by the continued financial constraints on all parts of the public sector.

The Local Government Association-commissioned report on the impact of the welfare reforms found that, although the cuts were broadly the same across all areas of the country, there was a disparate impact in areas of greater deprivation (Centre for Economic and Social Inclusion 2013). There has been no targeting of the transition response towards more deprived areas. A large part of the responsibility for transitioning the welfare reform programme and for mitigating its impact on the most vulnerable in society is being passed to the third sector without adequate funding, and there is no sign of a let-up in the programme of reforms, with the continued rollout of universal credit and the cuts to tax credits.

If the budgets of third-sector advice agencies are to be cut, then it would seem logical for the remaining budget to be carefully targeted towards, for example, the most deprived geographical areas, the most vulnerable in society or the aspects of law that are the subject of government reform. The evidence from this study of the Liverpool CR is that none of these approaches is currently being taken to public-sector funding for the third-sector agencies that provide advice services. The government strategy has failed to support the transitioning necessary for its welfare reform agenda, and has demonstrated a lack of evidence-based decision-making when making funding cuts (House of Commons Justice Committee 2010–11, 2014–15; NAO 2014: 33). Instead of the government's promise to 'target legal aid to those who need it most',[14] there has simply been an across-the-board cut to all areas of civil law, all parts of the country and all agencies.[15]

Despite the flexibility of the third-sector agencies in responding to the dramatic funding cuts, the threat to their sustainability brings us back to the question posed in the title of this chapter: 'What if there is nowhere left to go?' There remain places to which citizens in need of legal advice and assistance can turn in the Liverpool CR, but the increasing precariousness of third-sector legal advice agencies means that we may need to answer this question sooner rather than later.[16]

[13] Apart from the education and research aspects of the legislation, the *Care Act 2014* generally extends to England and Wales but applies to LAs in England only, as social care is a devolved matter for Wales, Scotland and Northern Ireland.

[14] The second stated objective of LASPO.

[15] This criticism was also made by the House of Commons Justice Committee: 'We were not impressed by the Minister's response to our concerns about the impact of the legal aid reforms on providers of publicly-funded legal services. We share the concerns of the National Audit Office, concerns we raised in our report in 2011, that the legal aid reforms were carried out without adequate evidence of the likely impact on the sufficiency and sustainability of the legal aid market' (House of Commons Justice Committee 2014–15: para 87).

[16] The MoJ's recent report, *Survey of Not for Profit Legal Advice Providers in England and Wales*, was released too late to be included in the analysis of this chapter. A majority of respondent organisations to this survey of advice providers agreed that changes to legal aid had required them to make major

References

Bennett, R (2008) 'Marketing of Voluntary Organizations as Contract Providers of National and Local Government Welfare Services in the UK' 19 *Voluntas* 268.

Busby, N and McDermont, M (2014) 'Employment Tribunal Fees Deny Workers Access to Justice' *Policy Bristol Policy Briefing 6/2014*, available at: www.bristol.ac.uk/media-library/sites/policybristol/migrated/documents/employmenttribunalfees.pdf.

Centre for Economic and Social Inclusion (2013) *The Local Impacts of Welfare Reforms*, available at: cesi.org.uk/sites/default/files/publications/The%20local%20impacts%20of%20welfare%20reform%20version%207.pdf.

Charity Commission (2007) *Stand and Deliver: The Future for Charities Delivering Public Services* (London, Charity Commission).

Citizen's Advice Bureau [CAB] (2012) *An Overview of Possible Links between Advice and Health*, available at: www.healthyadvice.org.uk/reports/Links%20to%20Innequalities%20of%20health%20reports.pdf.

—— (2014) *The Cost of a Second Opinion: The Impact of Mandatory Reconsideration in Employment Support Allowance (ESA) on CAB Clients*, available at: www.citizensadvice.org.uk/global/migrated_documents/corporate/the-cost-of-a-second-opinion-report-july-2014final2.pdf.

Department for Communities and Local Government (2007) *The English Indices of Deprivation 2007* (London, Department of Communities and Local Government).

—— (2010) *The English Indices of Deprivation 2010: Statistical Release* (London, Department of Communities and Local Government).

—— (2015) *The English Indices of Deprivation 2015: Statistical Release* (London, Department of Communities and Local Government).

Department for Work and Pensions (DWP) (2012) *Iain Duncan Smith: Welfare Reforms Realised*, Press Release (London, Department for Work and Pensions).

House of Justice Committee (2010–11) *Government's Proposed Reform of Legal Aid* (London, Justice Committee).

—— (2014–15) *Impact of Changes to Civil Legal Aid under Part 1 of the Legal Aid, Sentencing and Punishment of Offenders Act 2012* (London, Justice Committee).

operational changes. However, the national picture seems to be much more positive than we found in this study of the Liverpool CR. The median organisational income across the sector was stable, but this was because the 23 per cent of organisations that had experienced a 20 per cent or more decrease in revenue was balanced out by 24 per cent of organisations that had experienced a 20 per cent or more increase. Overall, 39 per cent of organisations had about the same number of employees since April 2013, 32 per cent had more, and 29 per cent had fewer employees. The results were not all encouraging, as 10 per cent of responding agencies reported that they were likely to have to close, and 13 per cent that they were likely to merge. The differences may be accounted for in the differing methodological approaches to identifying advice organisations, or it may indicate that the Liverpool CR is disproportionately impacted. We intend to pursue this in future research.

House of Commons Library, *Draft Social Security (Personal Independence Payment) Regulations 2013*, HC Briefing Papers SN06538 2013 (London, House of Commons Library).

Legal Action Group (2014) *Healthy Legal Advice: Findings from an Opinion Poll of GPs* (London, Legal Action Group).

Legal Services Commission (2010) *Civil Justice in England and Wales 2009* (London, Legal Services Commission).

Low Commission on the future of advice and legal support (2015) *Getting it Right in Social Welfare Law*, available at: www.lowcommission.org.uk/dyn/1435772523695/Getting_it_Right_Report_web.pdf.

Ministry of Justice (2015) *Survey of Not for Profit Legal Advice Providers in England and Wales*, available at: www.gov.uk/government/uploads/system/uploads/attachment_data/file/485636/not-for-profit-la-providers-survey.pdf.

Morris, D (1999) *Charities and the Contract Culture: Partners or Contractors? Law and Practice in Conflict* (Liverpool, Charity Law Unit).

National Audit Office (2014) *Implementing Reforms to Civil Legal Aid* (London, National Audit Unit).

Office for National Statistics (2016) *Super Output Area*, available at: www.ons.gov.uk/ons/guide-method/geography/beginner-s-guide/census/super-output-areas--soas-/index.html.

Office of the Deputy Prime Minister (2004) *The English Indices of Deprivation 2004: Summary* (London, Office of Deputy Prime Minister).

Personal communication from James Nolan to author (14 January 2016).

Pleasence, P, Buck, A, Balmer, N, O'Grady, A, Genn, H and Smith, L (2004) *Causes of Action: Civil Law and Social Justice* (London, The Stationery Office).

Public Accounts Committee (2014–15) *Implementing Reforms to Civil Legal Aid* (London, Public Accounts Committee).

Sigafoos, J and Morris, D (2013) *The Impact of Legal Aid Cuts on Advice-Giving Charities in Liverpool: First Results*, available at: www.liv.ac.uk/media/livacuk/law/cplu/Impact,of,Legal,Aid,Cuts,on,Advice,Charities,in,Liverpool.pdf.

Treaties, Conventions, Principles, Directives, Rules and Legislation

Care Act 2014
Financial Services Act 2012
Legal Aid, Sentencing and Punishment of Offenders Act 2012
Welfare Reform Act 2012

10

The End of 'Tea and Sympathy'? The Changing Role of Voluntary Advice Services in Enabling 'Access to Justice'

SAMUEL KIRWAN

I. Introduction

In the 2010 Ministry of Justice (MoJ) consultation paper proposing the cuts to civil legal aid that would be implemented in the *Legal Aid, Sentencing and Punishment of Offenders Act 2012* (LASPO), it was noted that 'very significant sums are currently spent on providing legal advice for issues where individuals are in fact looking for practical advice rather than the specific professional expertise offered by a lawyer' (MoJ 2010: 35). When considering 'how high a priority should be accorded to the provision of publicly funded legal advice', the paper stated that particular importance should be accorded to the fact that 'several voluntary sector organisations' already provide legal advice in certain areas included in the civil legal aid budget. Thus, underpinning the cuts introduced in LASPO was an assumption that voluntary advice providers outside the formal legal system could fill in for the services previously provided by lawyers (see also Byrom, Chapter 12, Organ and Sigafoos, Chapter 9, and Smith and Cape, Chapter 4, this volume, for more detailed discussions of the effects of LASPO).

Foremost among the 'voluntary sector organisations' envisaged in this paper by the MoJ is the largest and most well-known advice provider in the United Kingdom (UK): the Citizens Advice Bureau (CAB).[1] Across separate organisations in England and Wales, Scotland, and Northern Ireland, the CAB Service comprises central offices (based in the respective capital cities) and 316 member 'Bureaux' (CABx) (Citizens Advice 2015a), together referred to hereafter as 'the

[1] As part of a service rebrand in 2015 the term 'Bureau' was dropped from the title (Ricketts 2015). We have retained the term in this chapter as it remains in use within the service.

CAB Service', providing advice on a range of problem areas, notably welfare, debt, housing, employment, immigration and family matters (Citizens Advice 2015a). This chapter draws upon material collected in the New Sites of Legal Consciousness research programme (2012) based at the University of Bristol.[2] This research commenced in 2012 in response to concerns regarding the many challenges facing advice work, and has in the intervening period been examining the legal dimensions of the work of advisers, managers and trainers within the CAB Service. This chapter addresses how changing conditions for advice have affected the organisation and provision of advice, and considers what these changes imply for the future of the CAB Service and the advice sector.

The chapter begins by setting out the project methodology, before turning to examine the distinctive role, both historically and in the present, played by the CAB Service. Drawing from interviews with Bureaux managers, it discusses how changes to legal aid and 'welfare reform' have affected the funding, organisation and everyday work of Bureaux. Informed by the experiences of advisers, the chapter then presents two areas of concern regarding the changing nature of advice. The first is the *voluntary* nature of the service and the fact that the vast majority of its advisers are not contractually obliged to continue their work—an aspect of the CAB Service often overlooked by referring agencies, government ministers and clients alike. The chapter highlights in this respect the importance of the emotional connection with advice as a practice, and how increasing pressures upon time and responsibility place this connection under threat. The second concern relates to the lack of understanding of the complex dimensions of advice work: 'doing' advice is not simply passing on information, but encompasses practices that enable information to be fully understood and acted upon by clients of the CAB Service.

In the context of expectations that advice services can fill the gaps left by cuts to legal aid, this chapter highlights how ongoing changes to the funding of advice coupled with rising (and more complex) demand have affected the work of advisers. I argue that the impact which advice is able to make in the face of rising household debt burdens and precarious living conditions is placed at serious risk in these circumstances; 'access to justice', as access to the legal frameworks that shape and determine everyday lives, becomes an increasingly distant ideal.

II. Methodology

This chapter draws upon material gathered through the New Sites of Legal Consciousness research programme. Encompassing three intertwined projects,[3] the

[2] Funded by the European Research Council (Award No 284152).

[3] For more information on the programme see bris.ac.uk/adviceagencyresearch.

programme was launched in 2012 with the aim of understanding the legal dimensions of advice work amid changing political, legal and financial conditions. The concept of 'legal consciousness', describing everyday understandings of law and the ways in which individuals approach, interact with and discuss (or do not discuss) law (Ewick and Silbey 1998), framed the project. In this chapter, I use the term to describe the situated and applied knowledge of law held by advice clients, recognising the increasingly important role played by advice services in intervening and shaping these understandings.

The chapter draws upon the interviews, focus groups, audio and written diaries, and participant observation carried out as part of the Ideas of Legality and Citizenship strand of the research programme. Between March and November 2014, the project carried out 34 interviews and three focus groups with advisers and trainers at four partner Bureaux, and eight interviews and three focus groups with Bureaux managers at these and other Bureaux.[4] In addition to these methods, I carried out participant observation of the adviser training programme and collected written and audio diaries from three trainees on the programme which documented their transition to becoming advisers.[5]

Three main findings from the research are presented in this chapter: (i) the funding and organisation of Bureaux and the changing challenges they face; (ii) how participants came to undertake advice work and where they drew most satisfaction from it; and (iii) how advisers approach and carry out their work, emphasising the modalities and complexities of advice work beyond the mere passing on of information. Before presenting these findings, the chapter presents an overview of the unique and distinctive role played by the CAB Service within the advice and broader social context.

III. The CAB Service

The first CABx opened in 1939 as a response both to the burgeoning need for information linked to the expansion of the welfare state in the inter-war years, and the anticipated dislocations of wartime (Citron 1989: 1). The CAB Service was founded on the principles of being free and unbiased, and being both delivered by, and serving, local communities (Citron 1989: 2). By January 1940, it had grown to 1040 Bureaux operating across the UK (Hynes 2013: 15). Today, the CAB Service involves 20,700 volunteers across 316 member Bureaux (Citizens Advice 2015a).

[4] Interviews were of approximately an hour, while focus groups were approximately two hours.

[5] Of these methods, the participant observation raised the most significant ethical challenges with regard to how other participants were kept informed of, and were able to consent to, my participation in the research, and how one enabled a critical relationship with practice given the development of a relationship with an institution (a question raised also by the role played by Citizens Advice as gatekeeper to the project team's building relationships with partner Bureaux).

It remains, by some distance, the largest advisory service in the country and one of the largest voluntary organisations, in terms of the number of volunteers. The public identity of the service is closely tied to this image of a 'peer-to-peer' service and to its distinct organisational structure (Jones 2010). This structure comprises individual Bureaux, rooted in and responsive to local communities, operating semi-independently of the national organisations,[6] which provide technical and administrative support, case management and information systems, and national-level social policy interventions.

Following significant professionalisation of the training in the 1970s (Citron 1989: 3), one key difference between the CAB Service and other large voluntary services is the considerable length of the adviser training programme (around nine months) and the ongoing commitment that advice work involves. In the Bureau in which I trained as a participant observer, it is expected that advisers contribute at least one day a week in order to keep their skills up to date.

IV. Changing Times for Advice

As part of the interviews, participants were asked to consider how the work they do had changed in the previous few years. Turning first to the changes described by Bureaux managers, these focused upon the diversification of advice 'channels'—'channel' in this context refers to the format through which clients access and receive advice—and the significant changes to how Bureau funding is secured and organised.

The primary channels at the time of the research involved 'face-to-face', 'phone' and 'online self-help' (Citizens Advice 2015a). Several managers of Bureaux with significant rural populations noted having invested heavily in maintaining efficient and reliable phone services, with one noting the significant hurdles in getting volunteers with a history of face-to-face work to accept this. He explained:

> We still have quite a few volunteers who want to put that tea and sympathy in, and that often is easier when you're sat down with somebody, whereas on the phone you can run a much more robust gateway and if I had my way, personally I wouldn't have open door [sessions]. It would all be: 'you want to access us, come through the phones. We will decide then which track you come along'. And it would take all that pressure out of those open door sessions. (Gordon: Manager in a rural Bureau)[7]

At the national level, the foregrounding of online self-help advice can be seen in the transformation of the Citizens Advice website as part of the service re-brand in 2015 (Ricketts 2015).[8] The expansion of Advice Guide (the previous online information system) had already significantly altered the *scale* on which the service

[6] Citizens Advice, which serves England and Wales, and Citizens Advice Scotland, serving Scotland.
[7] All names used in the chapter are pseudonyms.
[8] The Citizens Advice website is available at: citizensadvice.org.uk.

operates (Jones 2010); no longer would Citizens Advice solely be considered a 'local' service defined by a physical bureau. While a visitor to the website in 2014 would have seen a link to 'Advice Guide—self-help from Citizens Advice' (Citizens Advice 2014), alongside links to explore volunteering and recent social policy work, 'Advice Guide' has now been abandoned as a separate online space, with the website instead organised around a search bar that asks: 'How can we help?' (Citizens Advice 2016). The 'new approach to digital advice' represented in this shift is explained in the following terms:

> Citizens Advice currently hosts myriad topics that give advice on what something is and tries to cover every angle—despite there being little or no evidence that we need to do so. As a charity competing in a saturated marketplace, we now need to be ruthless in focusing on the core proposition of the organisation: we help people to solve a problem. We don't need to tell people what something is—they wouldn't be coming to us if they didn't know it affects them—we need to tell them what they can do with their current circumstance. (Burks 2015)

Turning to Bureau funding, managers who had been in the service for five or more years described overseeing significant changes both in the levels of funding and the ways it is structured and secured. As one manager described:

> When I first joined the CAB 10 years ago the funding was mainly in the forms of grants not contracts. We didn't really have to even ask for it, it was very much here you are, you're doing a great job, get on with it, particularly with the Local Authority … Now it's sort of turned on its head completely with a lot more competition coming in and really having to commission … you know, bid for the services and prove our worth and even as a Bureau here, we've lost out on contracts that we thought were in the bag. So it's changed a lot. (Jill: Manager of a semi-urban Bureau)

The most frequently raised specific change to Bureaux funding was that generated by the end of Legal Services Commission (LSC) contracts, as LASPO made provision for the abolition of the LSC. For the above Bureau, which had pulled out of legal aid contracts shortly before these changes, 'it was the best thing we ever did because we weren't involved in this awful round that just happened—of losing the majority of income—that a lot of the CABx's have just gone through' (Jill: Manager of a semi-urban Bureau). As implicit in Jill's comments, other Bureaux had been forced to make significant alterations to how they fund and organise their paid caseworkers:

> I know in the benefits team—they don't have any money now to do any specialist level benefits … So, you know, who can we send them to? There's no one. So in some cases we might have to say, 'We don't have the resources, there's no one to send you to'. They've cut legal aid and it's very difficult and people are suffering from that. They had good outcomes with the benefits appeals and we just don't have it, and people have to do it themselves and probably struggle. (Rebecca: Specialist adviser in an urban Bureau)

As flagged in the previous chapter (Organ and Sigafoos, Chapter 9, this volume), these changes in funding arrangements can be broadly summarised as a shift from a service funded by large grants directed through local and national government and LSC contracts, to one in which Bureaux construct, out of necessity, complex mosaics of different funding arrangements on different temporal scales. Above, Jill described the different sums provided by the Local Authority, the Money Advice Service, the Primary Care Trust, Sure Start Children's Services and the RAF Benevolent Fund. Further to these sources, Jill explained that 'the rest of the money comes through donations from parish councils, town council, our own fundraising efforts and then mainly applying for small grants and that is the bulk of it really, that is it [*laughs*]'.

These mosaics are constructed in an increasingly competitive funding environment in which advice services are forced to compete with each other and other services. Bureau managers all described the need to devote increased amounts of time and resources to securing and maintaining diverse funding streams. Following several high-profile closures of Bureaux after losing LA contracts (*Gloucestershire Echo* 2012), several managers raised the imperative to *survive* as a Bureau. As Ryan (Manager of an urban Bureau) explained, 'it's a diverse funding base and we have a principle of trying to retain as diverse a funding base as we can. Survival seems to depend on that these days'.

One area of concern relates to how this diversification of funding arrangements will affect advice delivery. Questions over the impact of funding upon advice are, of course, not new. As Francis (2000: 62), writing following the introduction of 'Franchise' agreements in 1999, noted: 'the CAB and its staff have consistently complained about the difficulties of working in an environment of financial instability'. Yet the reliance upon *restricted* funds, whether tied to a particular project or group, has been seen to compromise the 'independence' and 'impartiality' of the advice provided,[9] while the different targets set by varied funders create new pressures for advisers. Discussion in one focus group turned to how the need to serve different funders affects the practice of advice provision. As one adviser began:

> Grace: I've been with the CAB Service a long time and because of the funding, I think, a lot of the work that we're doing, the nature of the way we're supposed to see clients has changed dramatically. When I was a money adviser, we were funded by the Local Authority. There wasn't any Legal Service funding. We were just given the grant to have money advice and there were no targets, there were no times set, there were no … we were just completely client driven … And it's a very, very different way that you're working now. (Focus Group in an urban Bureau)

The conversation then turned to the impact of the targets set by funders:

> Abi: Having these targets increases the problems that, you know, the question should be asked: can we give our client each the service that they require, that they need? Because we are so target driven, you know, there are problems there.
>
> Fred: Exactly, that's the thought that I had. Quality versus quantity.

[9] These are two of the four key pillars of the service—the others are that advice be free and confidential.

> Abi: And will it go back to being a 'tick box' exercise or a quick fix, where the more investigative work that caseworkers have been trained to do is harder to achieve, isn't it, or harder to do, because the work … the caseload is so heavy. (Focus Group in an urban Bureau)

A further effect of the legal aid cuts, that deepened as the fieldwork continued, concerned the 'list' of solicitors to whom Bureaux could refer clients in relation to certain problem areas (notably, family and immigration issues), where advisers were only able to provide limited advice. Of concern was that, with fewer solicitors being prepared to give free advice, the lists were becoming shorter and less reliable. This resulted not only in reducing the ability of advisers to assist those in need, but also in increased demand upon Bureaux in areas not necessarily within their remit or expertise.

In the accounts of advisers, the most significant changes noted were those introduced under the term 'welfare reform', principally through the *Welfare Reform Act 2012*. As flagged in the previous chapter (Organ and Sigafoos, Chapter 9, this volume), the most potentially wide-reaching change in relation to advice provision was the introduction of Universal Credit (UC). Drawing together several existing means-tested benefits, UC was to introduce new rules governing the conditionality of payments and would significantly cut the total amount to which households would be entitled. Due to ongoing implementation problems, UC had not yet been introduced in any of the localities in which this research fieldwork took place. Nonetheless, several changes implemented in the first years of the coalition government being in power had significantly affected welfare entitlements, principally: the 'under-occupancy penalty' (otherwise known as the 'Bedroom Tax'), which reduced entitlements to Housing Benefit for social housing tenants judged to have a surplus of bedrooms; a tougher regime of sanctions for Job Seeker's Allowance (JSA) claimants, leading to clients who had missed an appointment being left with no money at all; and more stringent regulations and assessments, and a lengthy waiting period, for the two principal disability benefits in the UK (Employment Support Allowance and Personal Independence Payments), leading to many individuals with no capacity to work being forced to claim JSA. Additionally, towards the end of the fieldwork period, highly restrictive changes were introduced to the delimitation of Worker Status affecting European nationals and the Right to Reside for benefits purposes (Department for Work and Pensions 2014; see also Aliverti, Chapter 16, this volume). These changes were widely agreed to have created a system that is both more punitive and unfairly weighted against the most vulnerable in society.

In addition to their frustrations with a system that was seen to be failing clients, advisers noted that these problems typically created many-stranded household debt burdens, and that cases were, on average, becoming far more complex. From the perspective of Bureaux managers, it was these changes to benefits entitlements that were seen to have taken the heaviest toll upon adviser morale. Benefit sanctions in particular were seen to have limited the successful resolutions advisers could achieve beyond certain emergency payments and food bank vouchers. Despite knowing that options were limited, several advisers described feeling like they had failed their clients. As Julian (Generalist adviser in a semi-urban Bureau) observed, 'when I can't give them options I suppose then that's the ones that I feel I've failed'.

Considering the practice of face-to-face advice, the changes outlined above can be separated into three areas of effects. The first concerns the effects upon the types of cases seen by advisers. Cases are increasingly complex with many-stranded and multidimensional issues; and clients are finding themselves in increasingly desperate positions, with advisers able to bring about little meaningful change. Secondly, the changes have affected the desired *outcomes* of advice—these being increasingly no longer dictated only by advice itself, but also, whether implicitly or explicitly, by the objectives of the funder. The third concerns the time advisers can give to those cases. As client numbers increase, and with diminishing support from specialist units and external agencies, there is increasing pressure to fit the advice interview to strict temporal limits.

Each of these areas of change raises significant concerns for the ongoing capacity of the CAB Service to carry out its work. Moving now to a more in-depth account of how advice is provided, the next sections focus upon the less visible effects of these changes. They describe, with reference to advice provision, how these changes might affect both the capacity of the service to retain its volunteers and the effectiveness of the advice as a 'translation' of law that endures in the everyday life of the client.

V. Maintaining Volunteers' Attachments to Advice

Central both to the image and functioning of the CAB Service is the pivotal role it gives to volunteers. Yet, despite the 'voluntary nature' of these positions, the role requires significant levels of dedication and training, and many of the volunteers I observed were startled at the breadth of information covered in their training. Likewise, several advisers reported the widespread assumption among clients, particularly those from outside the UK, that the volunteers must be in paid roles, given their breadth of knowledge and experience. With this level of commitment in mind, the research sought to understand and shed light on why individuals had become involved with the CAB Service, and what maintained their attachment to it, to then examine how the changing conditions of advice provision (described above) might affect these attachments.

Echoing the findings of other surveys, our research found that many participants cited the capacity to help and assist people in difficult times and having spare time on one's hands as major motivating factors in volunteering (Low et al 2007: 33). Alongside these reasons, certain situations specific to advice were also influences—most notably, having experienced a problem themselves and, in some cases, having been a client of the Bureau in question. As Andre explained, 'because it made a huge impact on my life when I needed it and I got [help from] the Service and ordinary people helping other ordinary people to move forward—that's what it was for me' (Focus Group of Bureaux Managers).

When asked to identify the area that provided the most satisfaction in their work, advisers again cited the ability to help, describing particular situations in which a client had left with 'a weight off their shoulders' (Annette: Specialist adviser in a semi-urban Bureau) or stating that they would be able to 'sleep tonight' (Kayley: Specialist adviser in an urban Bureau). A number of advisers placed particular emphasis on moments in which a client had expressed generosity and gratitude in the moments, days or months following their interaction. In the quote below, the adviser highlights both the emotional risks taken by advisers, given the potentially highly fragile state of clients, and the effect and importance of those moments in which care is reciprocated:

> I would have to say that, over the years … there has been many occasions where you've had clients where they've either committed suicide or where you've really got … you really think that the client is so on the edge. They might not have said it, but you think that may … the thoughts are there, definitely, and they could potentially be going down that route … A few times I've received [thank-you] letters after I've given advice … When I was in welfare benefits, I used to get like, chocolates every week. Well, my debt clients can't afford that, so now I get the occasional scribbled note, but it's worth just as much, you know. If you've got a note and it says on it, 'Thank you so much for the advice—it's really helped. I understand things much better and you have saved my life' … meaning that, you know, 'I had suicidal thoughts many, many times and you have genuinely saved my life'. That's [sic] the days where it's all worthwhile really. (Naomi: Specialist adviser in a semi-urban Bureau)

James and Killick (2010) argue that the success of the process of advice provision relies upon this emotional connection between adviser and client, and it is this connection that compels advisers to work beyond their contractual duties in assisting those in need. What the descriptions of these moments between advisers and clients reveal is the way in which this emotional connection exists through a certain play between the interaction itself, which is temporally punctual and in which one's emotional state must be tightly managed, and the longer-term experience of the adviser, as that particular client remains in their thoughts and experiences in a way that is affectionate, caring and *unmanaged*.

What also emerged as a theme in the responses was the importance given to the practice of advising. As Ben (Generalist Adviser in an urban Bureau) observed:

> A situation they perceived as hopeless when they came in, and then we were the last resort and they walk out the door thinking, okay it's not hopeless, there is a way forward here … if that happens through advice, not through counselling, I just want to be totally clear about that, because that's not what we're here for; if that happens through advice then clearly that is some source of satisfaction.

This emphasis upon the practice of advice provision recurred in numerous participant responses. At various points in the fieldwork, an adviser or manager expressed a simple or straightforward description of 'what advice is': namely, the administering of options, procedures and consequences. Yet, on reflection, many of the same advisers would then recognise the significant relational skills and emotional labour that are necessary to carry out this work, and therefore the more complex composition of the practice of advice provision. In particular, they recognised that advice provision requires a practical expertise enacted in subtle but important variations in how information is communicated, an expertise particularly important for clients with anger and mental health problems or for those for whom English is not a first language. In this context, it becomes clear that the task of advice provision is not simply to know information, but to be able to communicate it in particular situations—a skill that advisers learn and refine in the course of their work.

What also became clear when advisers described the satisfaction they derive from their work is the experience of a certain *ownership* over this work and its successes, either individually or as a local Bureau. As one adviser responded:

> When you can close a case [*laughter*]; knowing you've done everything you can for that client, they're happy with the outcome, you've had a good outcome, you know, and you've done a really satisfying piece of work because the client's said, 'Thank you very much', and it's made a difference to them, you can see the difference it's made to them and you probably know it wouldn't have happened without our intervention. (Ruth: Specialist adviser in a semi-urban Bureau)

In some cases, this ownership was expressed in terms of the specialist knowledge accumulated through extended work in a particular problem area, and in others, in terms of more prosaic, administrative and local knowledge that a website or online resource cannot offer. Thus, one adviser noted how:

> The longer you're here, hopefully the more you can learn about different ways to help people; you know like I'm the—I'm the Homeless Adviser—you could—you would initially know about how to help people from like looking up AdviserNet[10] and things like that, but the longer you're here and the more that you—you find new ways to help people. You get to understand the ways things are locally so that—that's one of the things I quite like about it. (Alice: Specialist adviser in an urban Bureau)

Another respondent framed this in more combative terms, in relation to external institutions and agencies:

> Maude: Personally I like taking on authority and winning. I like the phone calls to the CSA [Child Support Agency] or the DWP [Department for Work and Pensions] when you go, 'Do you know what? You have another look at that record because you're not right'. You know, and knowing more about it than they do and yet they're paid to know. (Focus Group in a semi-urban Bureau)

[10] AdviserNet is the Citizens Advice internal information system used by advisers. It is more detailed and less user-friendly than the publicly accessible system.

In sum, the different ways in which advisers find satisfaction in their work and their attachment to volunteering with the CAB Service is maintained stem as much from a commitment to assisting those in need as from one's *embodied* and *particular* experience of enabling this transformation. Thus, in contrast to certain imaginings of a uniform advice service, central to the success of the CAB Service is the *diverse* individual and local–collective experiences of advising.

Returning to the three areas of effect described in the previous section, it is the changing nature of cases and limitations on the outcomes of advice that have clear implications for the ability of advisers to maintain these attachments, and thus for the CAB Service and other voluntary advice services to maintain their volunteer work forces.

For some advisers, the increasing complexity of cases offered greater challenges, and gave them a determination to seek good outcomes amid these difficulties. Yet the interviews were also peppered by expressions of exasperation with governmental changes and a fatalism with regard to the large number of cases in which there were no foreseeable solutions. Indicative of this situation were those clients awaiting a 'Mandatory Reconsideration' of a refusal for ESA, or who had received JSA Sanctions (whether or not these had been appealed)—meaning that individuals were left with no income, and there were no avenues for advisers to help them aside from signing a food voucher on their behalf. The effect upon adviser morale was reflected in the account of one manager, who had assisted volunteers in setting up a food bank service as a way of mitigating adviser disengagement. He noted that this was the only response available to him when faced with clients whose benefits had been cut: 'that's right, that is what the new system allows' (Stefan: Manager in an urban Bureau).

Similarly, the moments of satisfaction described above relied upon the lack of a fixed advice agenda and outcome; the smile, a good night's sleep or a scribbled thank-you note was affecting in part *because it was not the stated goal of the advice process*. Advice that is driven, whether implicitly or explicitly, by the demands of the funder places at risk the connection between the adviser and their work. As one adviser explained with regard to a project funded by the LA:

> Fred: I feel that sometimes I'm being put in a position of some sort of proxy rent collector for the Local Authority and it's very, very difficult sometimes not to get into that mindset, particularly if the follow-up from the initial appointment is the Housing Officer badgering me by email or telephone: 'oh, they've not paid their rent this week'. And I'm thinking, that is not my job, that's your job. I've advised them about what they can do. I'm implementing the strategy that we've agreed. If the tenant is still not choosing to pay their rent, then that is their choice and they know the consequences. So it is sometimes quite difficult. And, as I say, I've been with the service for 10 years. The way that the funding now works has changed radically with the loss of legal aid and all this sort of thing. There's a lot of little pots of money and the requirements of the funders—it does push the barriers of, how independent are we? How impartial are we? (Focus Group in an urban Bureau)

VI. Legal Understandings

While the ways in which the broader dimensions of the practice of advice provision are tied to certain forms of satisfaction experienced by advisers are relevant in this discussion, it is also important to consider clients' understandings of their problems and the legal frameworks that shape and define them. Advisers deployed their own form of 'legal consciousness', defining the different levels at which clients are able to understand the information being discussed. Enabling a legal consciousness through which clients can engage with such frameworks, as one adviser recognised, is not an easy part of their role:

> And that's the other difference—it's knowing that the other person's understood. Just because you've told them doesn't mean they've understood it and you need to be confident as an adviser that the client's actually taken on board what you said and actually understood everything you said before you move forward with a strategy that is effectively going to change their life to quite a big thing … You're talking about clearing up to £15,000[11] worth of debt … it's a big decision, it's insolvency at the end of the day, it's a legal tool and it's not to be taken lightly. And I think just because we do it here doesn't mean that we can be quite blasé about it; we can't. (Kayley: Specialist adviser in an urban Bureau)

The most frequent barriers to understanding raised by advisers were language, mental health issues and the particular emotional states, tied to particular forms of problems, in which clients arrived at the CAB Service. Advisers described the varying forms of explanation and degrees of patience required for certain clients, whether the adviser was limiting the amount of information given or making sure that the client was in the right state to absorb advice:

> And she was so upset, and you've got to actually try and think … well, first of all, to give her a bit of reassurance, to try and calm her down a bit and so on. And you get people like that who have had a shock or whose, maybe, husband has died unexpectedly and they don't know where to turn, etc. etc. So you've got these vulnerable people … people with mental health issues. And then you get the people who are very angry or aggressive. Somebody, for example, who has been made redundant or, in fact, who has been dismissed from employment, and they're very angry and wonder what they can do about that. So, again, you've got to somehow or other get a rapport with them and try and get that anger subsided a bit. (Rosalyn: Generalist adviser in an urban Bureau)

Another area in which advisers described the tailoring and management of information concerned clients with a particular emotional attachment to one course of action. In the following case, the adviser described trying to shift this attachment and ensure that the client understood the rights held by other parties in their situation:

> You know we have clients come in 'I know my rights, they said that, I know they can't do it' and you have to sometimes say, 'You're absolutely right, you are absolutely right, you

[11] Equates to AU$28,232.

are well within your rights to do that, but this is the other side, this is what they can do so you have to now go away and think very carefully of what level you want to throw this back at them'. (Annette: Specialist adviser in a semi-urban Bureau)

This task was particularly important in employment and housing work, where the 'rights' of employees or private tenants are significantly offset by the precarity of these positions as they are defined by employment and housing law.

In sum, enabling the client to 'understand' the law goes beyond simply describing certain rules, concepts and implications; it relies upon particular forms of engagement with the client. While most advisers agreed that they lacked the 'professional expertise' of lawyers, notably in the form of specialised knowledge, this work reveals a legal expertise of a different kind, one geared towards enabling understanding across a variety of situations and through different forms of labour—a labour that is no less reliant upon certain conditions. But such capacities to undertake such detailed, intensive work are likely to be affected by the changing conditions for advice provision discussed above, in particular, the diversification of advice channels and the restrictions upon the time available to advisers in their face-to-face work.

In the interviews, advisers disagreed on whether this work can be carried out as effectively over the phone as it can be face-to-face. While some stressed the importance of being able to pick up on physical and emotional signals in the interview room, others noted the advantage for the client of being in a known space, and for the adviser of being able to suspend the call to allow the client time to compose themselves. Yet these further dimensions of advice do raise important questions when considering the concerted push, at the national level, towards online self-help and web chat advice channels (Burks 2015), in which there is no (or very minimal) connection between adviser and client. That there is no tailoring of the advice in this context to the client's inclination to act, say, upon their 'rights' as a tenant raises questions as to whether the relationship established via these channelsis a proper one in which to give 'advice' in the form established through the face-to-face work of Bureaux.

As described above, the lack of time available to advisers frames the outputs. Funding relies upon the number of clients the CAB Service is able to see and, in debt terms, the figures the CAB Service is able to deal with and 'write off'. Far more difficult to quantify, and as such to enter into these evaluative frameworks, are the different levels and textures of understanding that clients take away with them. Time to carry out an interview in an engaged (meaning there is time to enable the client's understanding and ownership through effective translation) and holistic (meaning all possible problems and implications are explored) manner is essential to successful resolutions, as is the time needed to develop as an adviser. When one adviser, describing their work, defined 'advice' as needing 'as long as it takes', they were responding to the (misguided) assumption with which this chapter began—namely, that voluntary services can pick up the slack left by retreating state support, because advice is simply giving information, and can be done quicker and more efficiently.

VII. Conclusion

A broader understanding of 'justice' that encapsulates the ability to engage with and relate to the legal processes and frameworks that affect and shape our lives is a key component of 'access to justice', as is access to the spaces in which the law is translated and negotiated (Hynes 2013; McDermont 2013). While such spaces are typically addressed as physical and temporal spaces, and, as such, considered to be at risk inasmuch as these spaces are limited, it is important also to recognise how changing conditions for advice provision affect the practices of advice provision and the ability of voluntary services to retain their volunteers. This chapter has argued that such outcomes are placed at significant risk as cases become more complex and desperate, advice outcomes are tied to funding restrictions, and there is increasingly inadequate time to carry out advice. This changing context for advice provision stems from 'practical advice' being seen as a service provided by a non-legal resource who is merely passing on legal information, and from whom increasing productivity can be found as funding continues to be cut. What is at stake in these changes goes beyond individual applications of and encounters with legal frameworks; it is the extent to which these frameworks are rooted in and answerable to the communities they serve.

References

Brodbeck, S (2015) *Citizens Advice Investigates Rogue Pension Wise Branch Money Marketing*, available at: www.moneymarketing.co.uk/citizens-advice-investigates-rogue-pension-wise-branch/.

Burks, BK (2015) 'New and Improved Digital Advice Goes Live', *Citizens Advice*, available at: alphablog.citizensadvice.org.uk/2015/07/new-and-improved-digital-advice-goes-live/.

Citizens Advice (2014) 'Citizens Advice: The Charity for Your Community', *Citizens Advice*, available at: web.archive.org/web/20140122130734/http://www.citizensadvice.org.uk/.

—— (2015a) *Advice Trends: Quarterly Client Statistics of the Citizens Advice Service in England and Wales* [2015–16 Quarter 1, April–June 2015], available at: www.citizensadvice.org.uk/about-us/difference-we-make/advice-trends/advice-trends/advice-trends-201516/.

—— (2015b) 'Citizens Advice to Deliver Pension Wise from More than 500 Locations', available at: www.citizensadvice.org.uk/about-us/how-citizens-advice-works/media/press-releases/citizens-advice-to-deliver-pension-wise-from-more-than-500-locations/.

—— (2016) 'Welcome to Citizens Advice', available at: www.citizensadvice.org.uk/.

Citron, J (1989) *Citizens Advice Bureaux: For the Community, by the Community* (London, Pluto).

Department for Work and Pensions (2014) *Minimum Earnings Threshold for EEA migrants introduced*, Press Release, available at: www.gov.uk/government/news/minimum-earnings-threshold-for-eea-migrants-introduced.

Ewick, P and Silbey, S (1998) *The Common Place of Law* (Chicago IL, University of Chicago).

Francis, A (2000) 'Lawyers, CABx and the Community Legal Service: A New Dawn for Social Welfare Law Provision?' 22 *Journal of Social Welfare and Family Law* 59.

Gloucestershire Echo (2012) 'Travesty to Let CAB Close', *Gloucestershire Echo*, available at: ilegal.org.uk/thread/4315/cheltenham-cab-threat

Hynes, S (2013) *Austerity Justice* (London, Legal Action Group).

ilegal (2015) 'Just What Is Happening to Citizens Advice?', *ilegal*, available at: ilegal.org.uk/thread/8976/happening-citizens-advice?.

James, D and Killick, E (2012) 'Empathy and Expertise: Case Workers and Immigration/Asylum Applicants in London' 37 *Law and Social Inquiry* 430.

Jones, R (2010) 'Learning beyond the State: The Pedagogical Spaces of the CAB Service' 14 *Citizenship Studies* 725.

Low, N, Butt, S, Ellis Paine, A and Davis Smith, J (2007) *Helping Out: A National Survey of Volunteering and Charitable Giving*, report prepared for the Office of the Third Sector in the Cabinet Office, available at: www.ivr.org.uk/images/stories/Institute-of-Volunteering-Research/Migrated-Resources/Documents/H/OTS_Helping_Out.pdf.

McDermont, M (2013) 'Acts of Translation: UK Advice Agencies and the Creation of Matters-of-Public-Concern' 33 *Critical Social Policy* 218.

Ministry of Justice [MoJ] (2010), *Proposals for the Reform of Legal Aid in England and Wales*, Ministry of Justice Consultation Paper CP 12/10 (Cm 7967), available at: webarchive.nationalarchives.gov.uk/20111121205348/http://www.justice.gov.uk/downloads/consultations/legal-aid-reform-consultation.pdf.

New Sites of Legal Consciousness (2012) *Programme Overview*, available at: bris.ac.uk/adviceagencyresearch

Ricketts, A (2015) 'Citizens Advice Begins £1m Rebrand and Drops 'Bureau' from Names of Local Branches', *Third Sector*, available at: www.thirdsector.co.uk/citizens-advice-begins-1m-rebrand-drops-bureau-names-local-branches/communications/article/1345312.

Treaties, Conventions, Principles, Directives, Rules and Legislation

Legal Aid, Sentencing and Punishment of Offenders Act 2012
Welfare Reform Act 2012

11

Reasoning a Human Right to Legal Aid

SIMON RICE

I. Introduction

Legal aid and human rights have more in common than is usually appreciated: both are concerned with guaranteeing equality and justice, and both are underpinned by respect for human dignity (Fleming 2007: 26; Luban 2005: 817–18, 839–40). But these shared characteristics are not usually the basis on which the relationship between legal aid and human rights has been explored; rather, the exercise in the literature is often to propose that one—legal aid—ought to be brought within the scope of the other—human rights (see, for example, Jüriloo 2015; *Kyiv Declaration* 2007). Legal aid advocates look to achieving human rights status as a way of entrenching legal aid, thereby guaranteeing its availability. Legal aid advocates want legal aid to be admitted into the international human rights regime, and they make their case not on the basis that legal aid and human rights are conceptual cousins, but in a rhetorical manner, on the basis that there is something essentially important about legal aid that means it should be accepted as a human right.

In this chapter I examine the nature of the relationship between human rights and legal aid, informed by a prior consideration of what are 'human rights' and 'legal aid'. I define their nature and scope because the positivist nature of one and a contextual understanding of the other are important to understanding how they interact. I then give a brief account of the well-recognised right to legal aid in criminal matters, before analysing the jurisprudence that is emerging for a right to legal aid in non-criminal matters. I give this account because advocates for 'legal aid as a human right' tend to start with their particular idea of what legal aid is and then look for space within the human rights regime into which they can fit that idea. Instead, the exercise needs to start with being clear about what human rights are, and working backwards from that, asking whether, when and how the enjoyment of human rights requires something that is recognisable as legal aid.

It is apparent from the human rights jurisprudence that legal aid and human rights, through their shared aspirations of achieving equality, justice and respect for human dignity, have a relationship that, in some circumstances, renders what I call the 'standard conception' of legal aid—the state's provision to poor people of conventional legal services related to court proceedings—integral to the enjoyment of some human rights. The reasoning behind the recognition of legal aid as a human right is that, in some circumstances, legal aid is necessary for the enjoyment of substantive human rights. I question whether legal aid can or needs to be established as a substantive right itself. Instead, I suggest that the process of identifying legal aid as an aspect of established substantive human rights carries the possibility that a right to legal aid can be found in other rights, and that broader ideas of legal aid could emerge in this way.

II. The Intersection of Human Rights and Legal Aid

A. Human Rights

Human rights are often first, and sometimes only, thought of as legal rights that are posited in international human rights law. But '[h]uman rights are moral rights' (Raz 2010: 335); that is, 'they are rights that exist irrespective of whether they are underwritten, or apparently over-ridden, by positive law' (Skorupski 2010: 358). The fact that these moral rights are underwritten by positive law tends to separate discussion of human rights into two corresponding streams: the philosophical and the political.

Philosophical discussions of human rights explore the many contestable rationales for, and pervasive disagreements about, the idea of 'human rights' (Evans and Evans 2006, citing Waldron 1999: 11). But political discussions of human rights tend towards a consideration of *Realpolitik*—that is, defining human rights by the context in which they manifest and operate. Raz (2010: 336), for example, argues that a moral right is a human right only when it is formally posited such that it can operate to limit state sovereignty. In this lies the very attraction that human rights language has for policy advocates: when trying to influence states' practice, a moral claim is more readily enforceable when it is a legal right. Precisely because of their political origins in the aftermath of the Second World War (Glendon 2001), the posited rights 'are terse about their derivations or foundations in moral or political thought' (Alston and Goodman 2013: 3), but what matters to practitioners is that the moral claim they make has been 'transformed into normative structures' (Arnold 2013: 3).

These state-limiting human rights are formally posited in the 1948 *Universal Declaration of Human Rights* (UDHR). Their detail and context are elaborated on in related United Nations (UN) treaties,[1] and human rights law is generated through norm interpretation and application; instruments such as judgments, reports, general comments and observations; and the processes of courts, commissions, committees, expert bodies and special rapporteurs (Tams and Sloan 2013: 394). Much the same rights that are set out in the UDHR are set out in various regional treaties,[2] and the related human rights law develops similarly.

To have legal aid recognised as one of these human rights is an understandable aspiration. Rights talk is powerful. As Sax (1970, cited in Vlavianos 2012: 2) put it:

> The citizen who comes to an administrative agency comes essentially as a supplicant, requesting that somehow the public interest be interpreted to protect the … values from which he[/she] benefits. The citizen who comes to court has quite a different status—he[/she] stands as a claimant of rights to which he/she is entitled.

Advocates for a right to legal aid are attracted by 'the perceived usefulness of attaching the label "human right" to a given goal or value' (Alston 1984: 614). Human rights are valued because they invariably present as a 'trump' (Dworkin 1977)—a position that the state must accept and comply with, and against which state conduct is evaluated. In the context of environmental advocacy, for example, a human rights claim is pursued precisely because of its 'legal force in the decision-making process' (Vlavianos 2012: 2). It is understood that, '[b]y framing perceived environmental entitlements as human rights, rights-holders … can assert maximum claims on society, juridically more elevated than commonplace standards, laws, or other policy choices' (Weston and Bollier 2013: 122).

Advocates for a right to legal aid tend to make the case from outside the human rights system, wanting to see a moral claim for legal aid transformed into the normative structure of a human right. For example, 'legal aid must be translated into a human right' (Jüriloo 2015: 218; see also *Kyiv Declaration* 2007). But 'legal aid' can take many forms, and so far it is only the standard conception that has been recognised as a human right.

B. Legal Aid

In domestic legal systems (Productivity Commission 2014: 24–25; Smith 2007: 261, 277; UN Special Rapporteur on the Independence of Judges and Lawyers 2013: 20), the term 'legal aid' most commonly means legal advice, legal assistance and legal representation—sometimes and confusingly called collectively

[1] *International Covenant on Civil and Political Rights; International Covenant on Economic Social and Cultural Rights; Convention against Torture and Other Cruel, Inhuman or Degrading Treatment; Convention on the Elimination of All Forms of Racial Discrimination; Convention on the Elimination of All Forms of Discrimination against Women; Convention on the Rights of the Child; Convention on the Rights of Persons with Disabilities; Convention on the Protection of the Rights of All Migrant Workers and Members of Their Families; Convention for the Protection of All Persons from Enforced Disappearance.*

[2] *European Convention on Human Rights; African Charter on Human and Peoples' Rights; American Convention on Human Rights.*

'legal assistance'—provided to criminal suspects and defendants and to parties in non-criminal proceedings, funded by the state, and limited to people who cannot afford to purchase legal assistance in the market.

These last considerations—'provided to poor people, by the state'—are a constant in all discussions of legal aid, but other elements of legal aid differ from state to state. States assess indigence differently, and whether legal aid is provided in all types of criminal matters, at all stages of criminal proceedings, or for parties in non-criminal matters at all, differs among states (Cape et al 2010; Smith 2002: 33). States provide legal aid in different ways, such as funding their own 'legal aid' lawyers, contracting private practitioners, or providing grants to non-government organisations (Ontario Legal Aid Review 1997; Smith 2002: 17–24). Subject to these variations, the standard conception of legal aid is, effectively, the state's provision to poor people of conventional legal services related to court proceedings.

There are, however, conceptions of legal aid that depart from this standard. Legal aid can, for example, extend to the provision of 'legal education, access to legal information ... alternative dispute resolution mechanisms and restorative justice processes' (UN Special Rapporteur on the Independence of Judges and Lawyers 2013: 26; see also *Kyiv Declaration* 2007). Legal aid can extend, too, to advocacy for law reform (Legal Action Group 1996: 78–79) and can have more ambitious social justice goals such as 'changing unequal structures in society', addressing 'social exclusion from participation as a result of physical or economic deprivation' or empowering vulnerable groups to increase rights enforcement (Jüriloo 2015: 208). This expansive conception of legal aid is at the least controversial, and even paradoxical (Abel 1996), because of its potential to challenge institutions of the very state that funds it; in a discussion about legal aid as a human right, it is improbable that states confronting this paradox would universally accept an obligation to provide legal aid of this type.

The fact that legal aid takes various forms illustrates that the term 'legal aid' has a meaning that is dependent on its context; precisely what is meant by the term will differ according to where the term is used, by whom and for what purpose. Smith's account (2007: 277) of European negotiations around the meanings of 'legal advice' and 'legal assistance' illustrates this variable understanding for that region alone. But, as I describe below in the context of human rights, the term 'legal aid' has so far been understood in its standard conception, and other forms that legal aid might take are yet to be recognised as a human right.

The standard conception of legal aid has arisen in the human rights jurisprudence that explores the full extent of substantive human rights. Although a common framework for discussions of legal aid is 'access to justice', this has not so far informed the development of a right to legal aid in human rights law. Jüriloo (2015: 203–4) collects a number of human rights under the 'umbrella term' of 'access to justice', but this only adds to the many meanings that the term 'access to justice' has in international law (Franciomi 2007: 1), and reflects an aspiration for how a right to legal aid *might* be seen, rather than the reality of how *it is* seen in human rights law.

As the following sections show, the more developed human rights jurisprudence on legal aid exists in relation to criminal matters, where the standard conception of legal aid is well established as an integral part of the right to a fair hearing (Flynn et al 2016). The jurisprudence in relation to non-criminal matters is less developed.

III. A Human Right to Legal Aid in Criminal Matters

It is now well established in international human rights law that there are circumstances when the right to a fair hearing in criminal proceedings will not be realised without legal aid, in its standard conception. Legal aid has been identified as an aspect of existing substantive rights; the Report of the UN Special Rapporteur on the Independence of Judges and Lawyers (2013: 86) makes this clear, saying that legal aid is:

> A foundation for the enjoyment of other rights, including the right to a fair trial and the right to an effective remedy, a precondition to exercising such rights and an important safeguard that ensures fundamental fairness and public trust in the administration of justice.

Article 14(3)(d) of the *International Covenant on Civil and Political Rights* (ICCPR) guarantees a person's right,

> [i]n the determination of any criminal charge against him[/her] … to have legal assistance assigned to him[/her], in any case where the interests of justice so require, and without payment by him[/her] in any such case if he[/she] does not have sufficient means to pay for it.

The right is 'axiomatic' in capital punishment cases (UN Human Rights Committee 2007: 38). In similar terms to the ICCPR, Article 6(3)(c) of the *European Convention on Human Rights* (ECHR) guarantees a person's right, when 'charged with a criminal offence', to be given free legal assistance 'when the interests of justice so require', if the person does not have sufficient means to pay for it. I discuss below the conditions that attach to the right: insufficient means and the interests of justice.

In the Americas, under Article 45(i) of the *Charter of the Organization of American States*,[3] Member States 'agree to dedicate every effort to … [a]dequate provision for all persons to have due legal aid in order to secure their rights'. Giving effect to this, Article 8(2)(e) of the *American Convention on Human Rights* recognises

[3] (A-41) 119 UNTS 3,48 (E).

> the inalienable right to be assisted by counsel provided by the state, paid or not as the domestic law provides, if the accused does not defend himself[/herself] personally or engage his[/her] own counsel within the time period established by law.

The *African Charter on Human and Peoples' Rights* has a broad guarantee in Article 7 that a person has 'the right to have his[/her] cause heard', and Part H(a) of the *African Commission* on *Human and Peoples' Rights' Principles and Guidelines on the Right to a Fair Trial and Legal Assistance in Africa* guarantees an accused's right 'to have legal assistance assigned to him or her in any case where the interest[s] of justice so require, and without payment … if he or she does not have sufficient means to pay for it' (and see *Dakar Declaration* 1999 and *Lilongwe Declaration* 2006).

This recognition of the right to legal aid in criminal proceedings in the ICCPR and regional arrangements underpins wider recognition of the right by a range of UN mechanisms (UN Special Rapporteur on the Independence of Judges and Lawyers 2013: 26–34), although the scope of the right is not completely settled. One issue is whether the right is 'too trial centred' (Skinnider 1999; see also *Salduz v Turkey* (2008), citing *Imbrioscia v Switzerland* (1993)), and another is the competence of the state-provided legal representation (Joseph and Castan 2013: 498). Further jurisprudence will explore and define these aspects of the right.

IV. A Human Right to Legal Aid in Non-criminal Matters

A. A Note on Terminology

In the following discussion I want to avoid a risk that reference to 'civil' matters, cases or law could be construed narrowly, limited to private rights such as those related to torts and contracts, and not including public rights such as those that arise in administrative law and regulatory enforcement, and in proceedings between private parties under statutory regimes such as family law and labour law. To avoid this risk, I use the more cumbersome but broader term 'non-criminal', although quotes from other sources below usually use the term 'civil'.

B. Comparing Criminal and Non-criminal Proceedings

As I describe above, the benchmark for recognition of a human right to legal aid has been set in the context of criminal proceedings, led by the jurisprudence under Article 14(3)(d) of the ICCPR and Article 6(3)(c) of the ECHR. Before looking at the direction that the jurisprudence has taken for non-criminal proceedings, I consider the conceptual differences and similarities that will bear on an argument that a right to legal aid in criminal proceedings arises equally in non-criminal proceedings.

The fair hearing rights in ICCPR Article 14 could have been guaranteed for all hearings. Weissbrodt and Hallendorff (1999: 1071) report that the scope of the draft article initially covered 'the determination of … rights and obligations' generally, but was amended when 'Mr. Hodgson (Australia) proposed the inclusion of the words "… of any criminal charge against him …"'. Weissbrodt and Hallendorff (1999) do not record what Hodgson had in mind, and they offer no comment on this dramatic narrowing of the fair hearing guarantees from all matters to criminal matters. But had the original draft remained intact, guaranteeing a fair hearing generally, it is not obvious that the same right to legal aid would have been identified in both criminal and non-criminal matters. Even if the growing 'interdependence and permeability' of human rights norms does mean that 'the grounds for making a distinction between criminal and civil proceedings when affording legal aid are becoming less tenable' (Durbach 2008: 63, citing Scott 1989: 778), criminal and non-criminal matters do have essential differences, in ways that complicate a simple argument that a right to legal aid that attaches to one necessarily attaches to the other.

One difference is the status of the parties. A defendant is an involuntary participant in criminal proceedings, whose presence in court is mandatory and, if necessary, forced. Parties in non-criminal matters have a different relationship with the proceedings: a moving party (a plaintiff or applicant) needs to choose (even if reluctantly) to approach a court for a remedy, and an opposing party (a defendant or respondent) needs to attend the court (usually reluctantly) to engage in the contest. A criminal defendant is necessarily involved in proceedings, and is concerned that those proceedings will be fair, while a party in non-criminal proceedings must first have access to proceedings before any question about the fairness of those proceedings can arise. Thus while both a criminal defendant and a non-criminal party will be concerned with their right to a fair hearing, a non-criminal party could be concerned as well with their right of access to court, illustrated in the *Airey* decision I discuss below (see also Hunter et al, Chapter 13, this volume, for a discussion of access to mediation becoming the primary 'mode' of justice, as opposed to accessing a court in the family law context).

Another relevant difference between criminal and non-criminal matters is in the nature of the hearing: serious criminal matters are usually dealt with by a court, judge and possibly jury, while non-criminal matters are usually dealt with by a court, a specialist tribunal or, increasingly, alternative processes such as arbitration, mediation, conciliation and negotiation. The 'fair hearing' concerns for an accused that are implicit in the formality and complexity of an adversarial criminal trial are different from those of parties in non-criminal proceedings, where there are many commonly used measures to mitigate the risk of an unfair hearing, such as waiving procedural requirements and dispensing with rules of evidence. That is not to say that fair hearing concerns are absent in non-criminal matters. Although Kunc says (2013: 10) that it is 'arguably less obvious that the just resolution of a [non-criminal] dispute would be threatened without the presence of a state funded legal representative', experience and empirical studies show that inequality of arms in a non-criminal matter is often as significant as it is between the state and the accused in a criminal matter. The disparity between parties was classically illustrated by Marc Galanter's (1974) 'typology of parties' as one-shotters and repeat-players (describing those who are involved in litigation only once and those who are involved in litigation as a matter of course), and the David-and-Goliath contest is a persistent theme in popular representations of the law.[4] So while procedural concessions and judicial interventions can promote a fair hearing in non-criminal matters, their availability does not necessarily obviate a need for legal assistance. There is only so far that procedural measures and the judicial management of litigation (Sackville 2002) can go in mitigating the difficulties that a self-represented litigant faces (Richardson, Sourdin and Wallace 2012; Trinder and Hunter 2015). Nevertheless, procedural differences between the nature of the hearing in criminal and non-criminal matters do influence the reasoning that gives rise to a right to legal aid (illustrated in the *Airey* decision discussed below).

A commonly identified difference between criminal and non-criminal matters is that the former can carry the threat of incarceration, with an implication that this threat of incarceration makes legal representation more important in criminal than in non-criminal matters. My own experience in practising poverty law leads me to agree with Kelley (2013: 98; and see Durbach 2008: 66) when he says that,

> [w]hile it may be true that a defendant risks losing his physical freedom in a criminal context, it is not true, nor would it be logical to assert, that a defendant in that instance has more to lose than in a civil action.

It is simply not possible to say, as a general rule, that a person who loses their liberty loses 'more' or 'less' than a person who loses their home, their livelihood, their children, their reputation, their earning capacity, their freedom of expression, their right to vote, and so on. Nevertheless, the 'incarceration is more serious' argument persists and is commonly treated as a relevant factor in deciding whether a right to legal aid arises (even in the context of only criminal matters).[5] As I discuss below in Part G, the perceived seriousness of outcome is a defensible basis on which states, under cover of 'the interests of justice', can allocate limited resources to making legal aid available.

[4] See, for example, the films, *Silkwood* (1983), a dramatisation of *Silkwood v Kerr-McGee Corp* 464 U.S. 238 (1984); *Class Action* (1991), based on *Grimshaw v Ford Motor Company* 119 Cal App 3d 757 (1981); *Erin Brokovitch* (2000), a dramatisation of *Anderson et al v Pacific Gas and Electric* (Superior Ct for County of San Bernardino, Barstow Division, file BCV 00300); and *North Country* (2005), a dramatisation of *Jenson v Eveleth Taconite Co*, 824 F Supp 847 (D Minn 1993).

[5] In Victoria (Australia), for example, legal aid grants are only provided to defendants in summary offence cases where there is a risk of imprisonment upon conviction (Flynn et al 2015).

C. The Emerging Human Rights Jurisprudence

Although there is discussion in domestic legal systems regarding a right to legal assistance, I limit my analysis to the international human rights regime because there is no real interaction between it and domestic legal systems on this issue. A right to legal aid in the international human rights regime is not necessarily the same, or arrived at in the same way, as a right to legal aid in a state's own law, which is usually referable to constitutional guarantees and common law traditions (Budlender 2004; Durbach 2008: 59; Kelley 2013; Rice 2010).

In the international human rights regime, the different paths that have been taken in developing a right to representation in non-criminal matters are illustrated by the interpretation of similar provisions of the ICCPR and the ECHR: in Article 14(1) of the ICCPR for 'rights and obligations in a suit at law', and in Article 6(1) of the ECHR for 'civil rights and obligations'. I start with the ECHR and the jurisprudence of the European Court of Human Rights (ECtHR), because it sets a standard against which the approach of the UN Human Rights Committee to the ICCPR can be measured. I then note similar developments in the Americas and Africa.

D. A Right to Non-criminal Legal Aid under the ECHR

Article 6(1) of the ECHR states that '[i]n the determination of his[/her] civil rights and obligations … everyone is entitled to a fair and public hearing'. Although the Council of Europe Committee of Ministers declared in 1978 that 'all persons should have a right to necessary legal aid in court proceedings' (Council of Europe Committee of Ministers 1978: 1), it was not until the ECtHR's decision in *Airey v Ireland* (1979) that this declaration, and Article 6 of the ECHR, were given real meaning.

In *Airey*, as has been well documented (Mowbray 2005: 73), Josie Airey sought provision by the state of legal representation in family law proceedings, saying that without legal representation 'her right of access to a court was effectively denied' (*Airey* 1979: 24). The ECtHR agreed that there is an implicit guarantee in Article 6(1) of a 'right of access to the courts' (*Airey* 1979: 24), and that the Convention 'is intended to guarantee not rights that are theoretical or illusory but rights that are practical and effective'. What mattered was 'whether Mrs. Airey's appearance before [court] without the assistance of a lawyer would be effective, in the sense of whether she would be able to present her case properly and satisfactorily' (*Airey* 1979: 24).

The ECtHR concluded that it was 'most improbable that a person in Mrs. Airey's position … can effectively present his or her own case' (*Airey* 1979: 24) and, therefore, that Article 6.1 'may sometimes compel the State to provide for the assistance of a lawyer when such assistance proves indispensable for an effective access to court' (*Airey* 1979: 26). But the Court was at pains to warn against generalising from its conclusion, saying that it 'does not hold good for all cases concerning "civil rights and obligations" or for everyone involved therein', and that 'much must depend on the particular circumstances' (*Airey* 1979: 26; see also *Steel and Morris* 2005: 61). The ECtHR's jurisprudence since *Airey* has kept a tight rein on the right to legal aid, allowing non-arbitrary limitations on the right due to a state's constrained resources or the want of a claim's merit (*Steel and Morris* 2005: 62), and accepting that effective access to courts is possible through sound processes rather than, necessarily, by being legally represented (Reid 2011: 183–84).

Airey and the subsequent jurisprudence illustrate the distinctive features of non-criminal matters that I noted above. First, in non-criminal matters, the substantive procedural right of access to the courts comes into play, and it is from that right that a right to legal aid has been derived. Secondly, non-criminal matters are amenable to procedural interventions that may mean that a right to legal aid is not engaged. The point is made, for example, in the terms of Article 47 of the European Union (EU) *Charter of Fundamental Rights*, which guarantees legal aid to 'those who lack sufficient resources *in so far as such aid is necessary to ensure effective access to justice*' (emphasis added). This is reinforced by the EU's comment on Article 47: 'in accordance with the case-law of the European Court of Human Rights [specifically *Airey*], provision should be made for legal aid *where the absence of such aid would make it impossible to ensure an effective remedy*' (EU 2007, emphasis added). I note that the extensive literature in the United States (US) on a constitutional right to counsel in non-criminal matters takes the same approach, proposing that procedural measures and reforms ought to precede reliance on legal representation (Barton 2010: 1269; Engler 2006: 200–202, cited in Lucas 2014: 4; Rhode 2004).

Even if, after procedural measures are exhausted, it is apparent that a right of access to court is possible only with legal assistance, it does not follow that the state must provide lawyers on every occasion that a person is unable to retain a lawyer in the private market. It is not necessarily cost, or cost alone, that prevents a person from retaining a lawyer, but also socio-economic factors such as language, location, social disadvantage (Jüriloo 2015: 206; Schetzer, Mullins and Buonamano 2002) and ethical issues, such as conflict of interest (Kyle, Coverdale and Powers 2014). In these circumstances, a state could address the right of access to court by measures other than providing a lawyer, such as intervening in the market and enabling people to overcome barriers to retaining a lawyer.

Despite these reservations about defaulting too quickly to the need for the state to provide legal assistance, Article 47 of the EU *Charter* seems to have given strong momentum towards wide acceptance in Europe of a right to the standard conception of legal aid. Under the 'Copenhagen criteria' for accession to the EU, the internal legal aid arrangements of aspiring Member States have been subject to scrutiny, thereby providing 'a strong motivational force for the growth and protection of legal aid schemes' among newer Member States (Smith 2007: 278). The

EU's power to issue binding directives[6] can give added impetus to Member States' obligations, but the EU is making very slow progress (see, for example, Heard and Schaeffer 2011: 278–80; *Perinaud* 2015) towards a proposed directive 'on provisional legal aid for suspects or accused persons deprived of liberty and legal aid in European arrest warrant proceedings'. The proposed directive is accompanied by a Recommendation (European Commission 2013) to foster convergence among Member States on legal aid eligibility (Hodgson 2016: 180). The proposed directive would complement the three directives (on rights to interpretation and translation,[7] information,[8] and access to a lawyer[9]) that make up the EU's *Roadmap for Strengthening Procedural Rights of Suspects and Accused Persons in Criminal Proceedings*.[10]

E. A Right to Non-criminal Legal Aid under the ICCPR

The jurisprudence under Article 14(1) of the ICCPR has not developed in the same way that the jurisprudence has developed under Article 6(1) of the ECHR. Although the coverage of the two provisions is much the same—with a broad meaning given to 'suit at law' in Article 14(1) (Joseph and Castan 2013: 434–39)—the UN Human Rights Committee has not been as insistent as the ECtHR on the 'effectiveness principle' and has been less inclined 'to look beyond appearances and formalities, and to focus on the realities of the position of the individual' (Ringelheim 2013: 205, citing van Dijk and van Hoof 1998: 74).[11]

Even though the ECtHR's jurisprudence under Article 6(1) is a clear invitation to the UN Human Rights Committee to recognise a right to legal aid, none of the Committee's views on individual communications has gone down this path; nor did its General Comment 32 (UN Human Rights Committee 2007), published well after *Airey*. The Committee (2007: 10) does acknowledge that '[t]he availability or absence of legal assistance often determines whether or not a person can access the relevant proceedings' but it is not definitive in saying that a state has an obligation to provide legal aid, saying instead that '[s]tates are encouraged to provide free legal aid in [non-criminal] cases, for individuals who do not have sufficient means to pay for it'. The Committee notes that, '[i]n some cases, [states] may even be obliged to do so', but cites as an example only the rare and compelling case where 'a person sentenced to death seeks available constitutional review of irregularities in a criminal trial' (Joseph and Castan 2013: 444).

[6] Article 288, Treaty on the Functioning of the European Union, [2012] OJ C326/1–390, 26/10/2012.
[7] [2010] OJ L280/1, 26.10.2010; Directive 2010/64/EU.
[8] [2012] OJ L142/1, 1.6.2012; Directive 2012/13/EU.
[9] [2013] OJ L294/1, 6.11.2013; Directive 2013/48/EU.
[10] Council of the European Union Brussels, [2009] OJ C295/1, 4/12/2009.
[11] On the effectiveness principle, see also Mowbray (2005: 72–73) and Hollis (2012: 540–46).

F. A Right to Non-criminal Legal Aid under Other Treaties

Although the ICCPR has not yet given rise to a definitive right to legal aid in non-criminal matters, it is arguable that such a right to legal aid, in both criminal and non-criminal matters, exists under the *Convention on the Rights of Persons with Disabilities* (CRPD). The uniquely worded Article 13 of the CRPD guarantees 'effective access to justice for persons with disabilities on an equal basis with others ... in order to facilitate their effective role as direct and indirect participants ... in all legal proceedings'. It would be surprising, but it is clearly arguable, that because of Article 13 'people with disabilities have a general right to legal aid' (Gibson 2010: 312), while people without a disability do not. The question now is whether jurisprudence under Article 13 of the CRPD will develop in that direction.

It is arguable, too, that there is a right to legal aid for persons belonging to racial, ethnic and national minorities in both criminal and non-criminal matters, under the *Convention on the Elimination of All Forms of Racial Discrimination* (CERD). In its concluding observations on the United States' periodic reports under CERD, the UN Committee on the Elimination of All Forms of Racial Discrimination (2000: 22) considered the guarantee in Article 5(1) of '[t]he right to equal treatment before the tribunals and all other organs administering justice'. It recommended that, for criminal matters, the US 'improve the quality of legal representation provided to indigent defendants and ensur[e] that public legal aid systems are adequately funded and supervised'. For non-criminal matters, it recommended that the US 'allocate sufficient resources to ensure legal representation of indigent persons belonging to racial, ethnic and national minorities in civil proceedings'. It is in comments such as this that the seeds are sown for the development of a right to legal aid—in this case, as an aspect of the right to equal treatment.

It has also been argued that under all human rights treaties a right to legal aid arises as an aspect of the right to a remedy for a human rights violation (Curran and Noone 2008; Durbach 2008). States are obliged to ensure that an effective remedy is available for a human rights violation,[12] and the effectiveness of that

[12] Article 8 of the UDHR; Article 2(3)(b) of the ICCPR, and Human Rights Committee, General Comment No 31 The Nature of the General Legal Obligation Imposed on States Parties to the Covenant CCPR/C/21/Rev.1/Add.13, 26 May 2004; *Convention against Torture and Other Cruel, Inhuman or Degrading Treatment or Punishment* Article 14, and UN Committee Against Torture, General Comment No 3 (2012) Implementation of Article 14 by States parties, CAT/C/GC/3; *Convention on the Elimination of All Forms of Discrimination against Women* Article 2, and UN Committee on the Elimination of Discrimination against Women, General Recommendation No 28 on the core obligations of States parties under Article 2 of the *Convention on the Elimination of All Forms of Discrimination against Women*, CEDAW/C/GC/28, 16 December 2010; CERD Article 6 and UN Committee on the Elimination of All Forms of Racial Discrimination General Recommendation XXVI, 24 March 2000; CRPD Article 13, and UN Committee on the Rights of Persons with Disabilities, General Comment No 1 (2014) Article 12: Equal recognition before the law, CRPD/C/GC/1, 19 May 2014, [38]; *UN Committee on Economic, Social and Cultural Rights*, General Comment No 9, The domestic application of the Covenant 03/12/98. E/C.12/1998/24, [3].

remedy may depend on legal aid. However, the point has been made that it is not in every case that the effectiveness of that remedy *will* depend on legal aid. Similarly to the point above that legal aid may not be necessary to ensure a right of access to courts, access to courts may not be necessary to ensure a right to a remedy for a human rights violation: '[t]he right to an effective remedy need not be interpreted as always requiring a judicial remedy. Administrative remedies will, in many cases, be adequate' (UN Committee on Economic, Social and Cultural Rights 1998: 9; see also UN Committee Against Torture 2012: 38; UN Committee on the Elimination of Discrimination against Women 2010: 34; UN Committee on the Rights of Persons with Disabilities 2014: 38).

Turning to regional human rights regimes outside Europe, there is no explicit reference to a right to legal aid in non-criminal matters in the *American Convention on Human Rights*, but as the ECtHR in *Airey* saw that the right of access to court could depend on a right to legal aid, so the Inter-American Court of Human Rights (IACHR) identifies a right to legal aid in Article 25 of the Convention, which guarantees to everyone 'the right to simple and prompt recourse, or any other effective recourse, to a competent court or tribunal for protection against acts that violate his[/her] fundamental rights'. In the *Case of Hilaire, Constantine and Benjamin et al v Trinidad and Tobago*, the petitioners were unable to pursue a constitutional motion relating to their death penalties. Informed by the same 'effectiveness principle' that has motivated the ECtHR, the IACHR reiterated 'that it is not enough that legal recourse exist in theory, if such recourses do not prove effective in preventing violations of the rights protected in the Convention', and stated that 'there exists a positive duty … to take all necessary measures to remove any impediments which might exist that would prevent individuals from enjoying the rights the Convention guarantees' (*Case of Hilaire* 2002: 150–51; see also IACHR 2003: 126; Organization of American States Inter-American Commission on Human Rights 2007: 56).

Article 7 of the *African Charter on Human and Peoples' Rights* guarantees that a person has 'the right to have his[/her] cause heard'. Accordingly, the *Principles and Guidelines on the Right to a Fair Trial and Legal Assistance* in Africa state, at H(a), that 'a party to a civil case has a right to have legal assistance assigned to him or her in any case where the interest of justice so require, and without payment … if he or she does not have sufficient means to pay for it'; and Article 8 of the Protocol to the *African Charter on Human and People's Rights on the Rights of Women 2003* obliges states to ensure 'effective access by women to judicial and legal services, including legal aid'. Despite acknowledgement by the African Commission on Human and Peoples' Rights that 'it cannot be said that the remedies available in terms of the Constitution are realistic remedies for [poor people] in the absence of legal aid services' (*Purohit and Moore*: 37), it is the case that 'many [African states] specifically disclaim the right to legal aid at public expense, and such assistance generally is not widely available' (Kahn-Fogel 2012: 731).

The overall picture is that a right to legal aid in non-criminal matters is taking shape, in international human rights law, led by the decision of the ECtHR in *Airey* and being developed, under the ICCPR and the *American Convention on Human Rights*. It is being seen as a part of the substantive procedural right of access to courts, and there is potential for it to emerge as part of a right to remedy for human rights violations, and as a right under other treaties such as CERD and the CRPD.

G. Conditions under which a Right to Legal Aid is Engaged

The obligation on the state to provide legal aid is consistently said to be conditional on two criteria: that the person has insufficient means to secure legal assistance themselves, and that legal aid is required in the 'interests of justice'.

The effect of the criterion of insufficient means in non-criminal matters is that a right to legal aid is unlikely to be engaged in commercial disputes or by litigants who are creditors, landlords and employers, while it may be engaged by litigants who are debtors, residential tenants and workers. But this is only to predict what is likely to be the case; eligibility cannot be predetermined. A right to legal aid is engaged by the particular circumstances of proceedings, and the sufficiency of a person's means must be determined by their ability to enjoy effective access to court in that context. This has implications for the conditions a state imposes in providing legal aid.

Guidelines for providing legal aid in non-criminal matters usually exclude certain types of matters based on an assumption that they involve parties who have financial means,[13] and guidelines for the provision of legal aid in all matters usually use financial eligibility criteria that are set at fixed levels,[14] dictated by the state's budgetary considerations, although in England and Wales the state funds legal advice for a person under arrest in police custody, regardless of the person's means.[15] This prescriptive approach to financial eligibility is at odds with the idea of legal aid as it has developed as a human right. The UN Human Rights Committee (2011a: 6), for example, has expressed concern when application of a means test for legal aid 'fails to take account of the actual circumstances of the applicants and is assessed without regard to the actual cost of the legal service being sought'. A state's denial of legal aid according to an arbitrary means test could, therefore, be a violation of a substantive procedural human right such as rights to a fair hearing or access to court.

The 'interests of justice' criterion is imprecise. It seems to operate as a type of 'get-out' provision, giving room to both the state and a court to draw a line as to

[13] See, for example, Schedule 1, Part 1, *Legal Aid, Sentencing and Punishment of Offenders Act 2012* (England & Wales) (LASPO); Victoria Legal Aid, *Grants guidelines: State civil law guidelines*, available at: handbook.vla.vic.gov.au/handbook/7-state-civil-law-guidelines.

[14] See, for example, s 21 LASPO; Regulation 7(4), The Civil Legal Aid (Financial Resources and Payment for Services) Regulations 2013 (SI 2013/480); Victoria Legal Aid, *Grants guidelines: means test*, available at: handbook.vla.vic.gov.au/handbook/12-means-test.

[15] Section 58, *Police and Criminal Evidence Act 1984* (England & Wales); Revised Code of Practice for the Detention, Treatment and Questioning of Persons by Police Officers—Code C May 2014, Part 6.

when legal aid ought be available. Drawing on a distinction Galowitz (2006: 48) makes, there is a tension between an 'access-based' approach which sees legal aid as necessary to ensure a right of access to court, and an 'interest-based' approach which sees legal aid as necessary depending on the interests that are at stake. The latter is something about which both the state and a court can exercise discretion, declaring when a matter is, and is not, in the interests of justice. In criminal matters, the interests of justice are commonly assessed with regard to the gravity of the offence or, on appeal, the existence of some objective chance of success (UN Human Rights Committee 2007: 38). But the breadth of the discretion is illustrated in England and Wales by the collection of different considerations, given equal weight, that are relevant to 'the interests of justice'[16]—ranging from loss of liberty, loss of livelihood and damage to reputation, to whether a substantial question of law arises, whether the person may be unable to understand the proceedings and whether an expert must be cross-examined (Durbach 2008: 70).

The effect of the criterion of the interests of justice in non-criminal matters is that a right to legal aid is unlikely to be engaged for a claim or defence that is vexatious, frivolous or misconceived, or by a person with the resources to represent themselves or for whom other means of legal assistance are available, such as through a pro bono retainer or fee recovery arrangement (*Steel and Morris* 2005: 62). If not for the size and complexity of Steel and Morris's case against McDonalds, they may not have needed legal aid because they were 'articulate and resourceful' and 'received some help on the legal and procedural aspects of the case from barristers and solicitors acting pro bono' (*Steel and Morris* 2005: 68).

Consideration of sufficiency of means and the interests of justice serves to limit the circumstances where the right to legal aid is engaged in non-criminal matters, and that seems appropriate for a right that has resource implications for the state. It is to address 'concerns about public policy and budgetary implications' that Durbach (2008: 70) proposes additional criteria 'to guide the judicial process in the determination of the right to legal aid'. An approach such as this is familiar when dealing with rights that have resource implications (Saul, Kinley and Mowbray 2014: 169–72), but does seem to resolve Galowitz's tension in favour of interests over access.

V. Reasoning a Right to Legal Aid

The analysis above leads to some important observations on the development of a right to legal aid. The first is that legal aid is a human right only if the human rights system—internationally and regionally, in its treaties and jurisprudence—accepts it as such; it is the human rights system that generates its own need for legal aid. A second observation follows from this: while legal aid can and does take many forms outside a human rights context, it has so far taken on quite a specific meaning as

[16] Section 17 *Legal Aid, Sentencing and Punishment of Offenders Act 2012*.

an aspect of a substantive procedural human right; it is the provision by the state of the legal assistance that is necessary to realise the right. I discuss below the prospects for recognition in human rights law of other forms that legal aid might take.

A third observation is that legal aid is unlikely to be recognised as a right on its own, and there does not seem to be a need for it; the real work that legal aid has to do is ensuring the realisation of substantive rights. It is, for example, the right to a fair hearing that has generated recognition of a right to legal aid in criminal matters and, so far, it is the right of access to courts that has been the basis for a growing recognition of a right to legal aid in non-criminal matters. There is potential for a right to legal aid to be recognised in jurisprudence relating to the right to a remedy for human rights violations, particularly violation of rights to non-discrimination and the equal protection of the law. A right to legal aid may arise as a part of the right to access to justice for persons with disabilities under the CRPD, and it has been suggested as a part of the right to equal treatment in CERD. Looking for a right to legal aid in this way is a fundamentally different approach from promoting a preconceived idea of legal aid into the human rights system. If a right to legal aid is an aspect of substantive rights, then whether it arises and what form it takes cannot be predetermined: 'legal aid as a human right' is what the human rights system needs and defines it to be.

A fourth observation is that a right to legal aid arises only when procedural measures and reforms fail to achieve realisation of the substantive right. This is the approach taken in the jurisprudence of the ECtHR and in the literature in the United States on a constitutional right to counsel, and is likely to characterise the continuing articulation of a human right to legal aid in non-criminal matters. A related observation is that a state does not necessarily have to provide a free lawyer to meet its obligation to ensure that a person has the required legal assistance to enjoy a substantive procedural right. There may be barriers to obtaining a lawyer that the state can address, thereby facilitating a person's access to a lawyer in the private market.

Returning to the observation that the process of human rights jurisprudence has led to legal aid having the quite specific meaning of provision by the state of legal assistance, there is the prospect of acceptance of broader ideas of legal aid as a human right. By dint of the same reasoning that has led to the standard conception of legal aid being an aspect of certain substantive rights, it is arguable, for example, that provision by the state of plain language information about the law (*Kyiv Declaration* 2007; Rice 2010) is an aspect of both the right to information in Article 19(2) of the ICCPR and the right to take part in the conduct of public affairs in Article 25(a) of the ICCPR. There is already some basis for this in the UN Human Rights Committee's (2011b: 19) comments that 'States parties should make every effort to ensure easy, prompt, effective and practical access to [government information of public interest]', particularly if such an obligation is animated by the effectiveness principle. It is even possible, though perhaps unlikely, that human rights jurisprudence under the *International Covenant on Economic, Social and Cultural Rights* (ICESCR) could develop a right to the expansive—if paradoxical—conception of legal aid where a person is entitled to legal assistance in pursuing systemic change. There is a right to a remedy under the ICESCR (UN Committee on Economic Social and Cultural Rights 1998b: 3; UN Committee on Economic Social and Cultural Rights 1998a: 51; UN Independent Expert 2011: 10), and an effective remedy for, say, violation of rights to social security in Article 9, and an adequate standard of living in Article 11, would of its nature, challenge existing state processes and seek systemic change in proceedings supported by legal aid.

VI. A Substantive Right to Legal Aid?

Progress is being made towards recognising the standard conception of legal aid as an integral part of existing substantive procedural rights, and there is the possibility of recognition of broader ideas of legal aid through a similar approach. Nevertheless, there is a persistent aspiration to see legal aid recognised as a substantive right in itself (Knaul 2013). In light of the way that the human rights jurisprudence is developing, this aspiration is unnecessary and misconceived. The nature of legal aid is such that it is not obviously amenable to being a new, substantive human right.

A 'new' human right is a product of the normative processes of the human rights system itself; the UN General Assembly is the definitive arbiter of what a human right is, or, as Alston states (1984: 607), quoting Richard Bilder (1969: 173), 'in practice, a claim is an international human right if the United Nations General Assembly says it is'. Alston (1984: 613) explains how the process of adopting a new right is necessarily a 'painstaking and time-consuming' one. Progress, for example, towards a treaty that recognises enforceable rights of indigenous peoples has indeed been painstaking and time-consuming (Davis 2012), and steps towards formal UN recognition of sexual orientation rights have been in development since the 1990s (Alston and Goodman 2013: 220–38; Otto 2015).

Perhaps because of the tortuous and highly politicised process of articulating a new human right, some advocates identify a 'new' right as implicit in existing posited rights, waiting for its explication in human rights law (Creta 2012; Kessler 2013; McCombs and González 2007; Shaver 2015; Winkler 2013). It has been said for a 'right to identity', for example, that 'the right has existed implicitly in treaties and constitutions', and that the task is therefore 'not to create a right, but rather to interpret an existing right that … still lacks clear and complete definition' (McCombs and González 2007: 4). The right to develop and discuss new human rights ideas[17] is itself 'an elaboration of the right to freedom of opin-

[17] Article 7, *Declaration on the Right and Responsibility of Individuals, Groups and Organs of Society to Promote and Protect Universally Recognized Human Rights and Fundamental Freedoms* A/RES/53/144, 8 March 1999.

ion and expression, the right to freedom of assembly and the right to freedom of association' (UN Special Rapporteur on the Situation of Human Rights Defenders 2011: 83). This process—inferring a right from an existing right—happens when a substantive right is examined and applied in a particular context, in the views, comments and recommendations of human rights treaty bodies and the reports of UN Special Mechanisms.

If a case were to be made for legal aid as a new, substantive right among the posited human rights, it would have to meet the five criteria set out by the UN (UN General Assembly 1986: 4), such that it is consistent with international human rights law: its fundamental character derives from the inherent dignity and worth of the human person; it is sufficiently precise to give rise to identifiable and practicable rights and obligations; it provides appropriate, realistic and effective implementation machinery; and it attracts broad international support. A right to legal aid might have difficulty meeting at least two of these criteria. Legal aid in its more expansive sense may not attract broad international support, and it is not clear that its fundamental character derives from the inherent dignity and worth of the human person.

When Luban (2005: 819) argues for a connection between legal aid and dignity, he invokes Donagan's principle (1984: 130) that 'one fails to respect [a person's] dignity as a human being if on any serious matter one refuses even provisionally to treat his or her testimony about it as being in good faith', and argues that a corollary to this is that litigants must be able to 'tell their stories and argue their understandings of the law'. Tying human dignity to a right to legal representation, Luban (2015: 821–22) argues that '[t]o deny my subjectivity is to deny my human dignity … [so] to honor a litigant's dignity as a person requires us to hear the story she has to tell'. This, he says, leads to a litigant's right to have a lawyer in their role as a courtroom advocate. But Luban is too quick to identify the lawyer as a solution, at least in non-criminal matters. If accepting that human dignity requires that a person be able to tell their story and be heard, it does not necessarily follow that a person who is not able to tell their story needs a lawyer. Telling a story and being heard are dependent on a number of considerations, many of which can be addressed procedurally (waiving rules of evidence), with resources (a support person or interpreter) or with innovative practice (reconfiguring or relocating courtrooms). The right that Luban argues for is the right to be heard—to really be heard—and his dignity-based argument does not arrive at a right to representation that is different from its being an aspect of a right to fair hearing.

It is difficult to conceive of legal aid as a substantive human right on its own terms, and it seems unnecessary to promote it along that 'painstaking and time-consuming' path. The Special Rapporteur's claim (Knaul 2013) that '[l]egal aid is … a right in itself' is not supported by human rights law to date. Her further claim that legal aid is 'an essential precondition for the exercise and enjoyment of a number of human rights' much more closely reflects the human rights jurisprudence that sees a right to legal aid as an aspect of existing human rights.

VII. Conclusion

There is still work to be done in establishing a human right to legal aid. In criminal matters, aspects of the right—such as the stages of criminal proceedings where it arises and the competence of the assigned lawyer—need to be clarified. More significantly, in non-criminal matters, the right has not been established as definitively in the international human rights regime as it has been in the European system. As well, the extent to which legal aid is an aspect of a range of other substantive rights, under all the human right treaties, is still to be explored.

Establishing and clarifying a right to legal aid requires jurisprudence on the substantive procedural rights. In the international human rights system, this jurisprudence will be developed through, for example, treaty bodies' views on individual communications, and concluding observations on states' periodic reports, reports in the Universal Periodic Review process and observations made in special mandate procedures.

However far a right to legal aid develops, it is apparent that its genesis and explication are functions of the way that human rights systems, internationally and regionally, explore the full dimensions of substantive human rights. To date, a right to legal aid has been shown, to different degrees, to be a part of the right to a fair hearing in criminal matters and of the right of access to the courts in non-criminal matters. Vigorous and imaginative use of human rights mechanisms, and adoption by human rights bodies of the effectiveness principle, can continue to develop a clear articulation and deeper understanding of a human right to legal aid.

References

Abel, R (1996) 'The Paradoxes of Legal Aid' in A Paterson and T Goriely (eds), *A Reader on Resourcing Civil Justice* (Oxford, Oxford University Press).

Alston, P (1984) 'Conjuring Up New Human Rights: A Proposal For Quality Control' 78 *American Journal of International Law* 607.

Alston, P and Goodman, R (2013) *International Human Rights* (Oxford, Oxford University Press).

Arnold, R (2013) 'Reflections on the Universality of Human Rights' in R Arnold (ed), *The Universalism of Human Rights* (New York, Springer).

Barton, BH (2010) 'Against Civil *Gideon* (And For Pro Se Court Reform)' 62 *Florida Law Review* 1227.

Bilder, R (1969) 'Rethinking International Human Rights: Some Basic Questions' *Wisconsin Law Review* 171.

Budlender, G (2004) 'Access to Courts' 121 *South African Law Journal* 339.

Cape, E, Namoradze, Z, Smith, R and Spronken, T (2010) *Effective Criminal Defence in Europe* (Antwerpen/Oxford, Intersentia).

Council of Europe Committee of Ministers (1978) *Resolution (78) 8 on Legal Aid and Advice*, Adopted by the Committee of Ministers on 2 March 1978 at the 284th meeting of the Ministers' Deputies, Appendix, Part I: Legal aid in court proceedings.

Creta, A (2012) 'A (Human) Right to Humanitarian Assistance in Disaster Situations? Surveying Public International Law' in A de Guttry, M Gestri and G Venturini (eds), *International Disaster Response Law* (The Hague, Asser Press).

Curran, L and Noone, M (2008) 'Access to justice: a new approach using human rights standards' 15 *International Journal of the Legal Profession* 195.

Dakar Declaration and Recommendations on the Right to a Fair Trial in Africa adopted by the African Commission on Human and Peoples' Rights at its 26th Ordinary Session, November 1999.

Davis, M (2012) 'To Bind or Not to Bind: The United Nations Declaration on the Rights of Indigenous Peoples Five Years On' 19 *Australian International Law Journal* 17.

Donagan, A (1984) 'Justifying Legal Practice in the Adversary System' in D Luban (ed), *The Good Lawyer: Lawyers' Roles And Lawyers' Ethics* (Totowa, Rowman & Allanheld).

Durbach, A (2008) 'The Right to Legal Aid in Social Rights Litigation' in M Langford (ed), *Social Rights Jurisprudence—Emerging Trends in International and Comparative Law* (Cambridge, Cambridge University Press).

Dworkin, D (1977) *Taking Rights Seriously* (Cambridge MA, Harvard University Press).

Economic and Social Council, Concluding Observations on Canada, E/C.12/1/Add.31 (10 December 1998).

European Union 'Title VI, Justice', [2007] OJ C303/17, 14.12.2007.

Engler, R (2006) 'Towards a Context-Based Civil Right to Counsel Through "Access to Justice" Initiatives' 40 *Clearinghouse Review* 196.

European Commission (2013) 'Recommendation of 27 November 2013 on the right to legal aid for suspects or accused persons in criminal proceedings', 2013/C 378/03, [2013] OJ C378/11, 24.12.2013.

Evans, C and Evans, S (2006) 'Evaluating the Human Rights Performance of Legislatures' 6 *Human Rights Law Review* 545.

Fleming, D (2007) *Legal aid and human rights*, Paper presented to the International Legal Aid Group Conference, Antwerp, 6–8 June 2007.

Flynn, A, Freiberg, A, McCulloch, J and Naylor, B (2015) *Access to Justice: A Comparative Analysis of Cuts to Legal Aid* (Melbourne, Monash University).

Flynn, A, Hodgson, J, McCulloch, J and Naylor, B (2016) 'Legal Aid and Access to Legal Representation: Re-Defining the Right to a Fair Trial' 40 *Melbourne University Law Review* 207.

Franciomi, D (2007) 'The Rights of Access to Justice under Customary International Law' in F Franciomi (ed), *Access to Justice as a Human Right* (Oxford, Oxford University Press).

Galanter, M (1974) 'Why the "Haves" Come out Ahead: Speculations on the Limits of Legal Change' 9 *Law & Society Review* 95.

Galowitz, P (2006) 'Right to legal aid and economic, social and cultural rights litigation', in M Langford and A Nolan (eds), *Legal Practitioners Dossier* (Switzerland, Centre on Housing Rights and Evictions).

Gibson, F (2010) 'Article 13 of the CRPD: A Right to Legal Aid?' 15 *Australian Journal of Human Rights* 123.

Glendon, M (2001) *World Made New: Eleanor Roosevelt and the Universal Declaration of Human Rights* (New York, Random House).

Heard, C and Schaeffer, R (2011) 'Making Defence Rights Practical and Effective: Towards an EU Directive on the Right to Legal Advice' 2 *New Journal of European Criminal Law* 270.

Hodgson, J (2016) 'Criminal Procedure in Europe's Area of Freedom, Security and Justice: The rights of the suspect' in Valsamis Mitsilegas, Maria Bergström, Theodore Konstadinides (eds), *Research Handbook on EU Criminal Law* (Cheltenham, Edward Elgar Publishing).

Hollis, D (2012) *The Oxford Guide to Treaties* (Oxford, Oxford University Press).

Inter-American Court of Human Rights (2003) *Juridical Condition and Rights of the Undocumented Migrants*, Advisory Opinion OC-18/03, 17 September 2003, (Series A) No 18 (2003).

Joseph, S and Castan, M (2013) *The International Covenant on Civil and Political Rights: Cases Materials and Commentary*, 3rd edn (Oxford, Oxford University Press).

Jüriloo, K (2015) 'Free Legal Aid—a Human Right' 33 *Nordic Journal of Human Rights* 203.

Kahn-Fogel, NA (2012) 'The Troubling Shortage of African Lawyers: Examination of a Continental Crisis Using Zambia as a Case Study' 33 *Journal of International Law* 719.

Kelley, JD (2013) 'Gideon's Bullhorn: Sounding a Louder, Clearer Call for a Civil Right to Counsel' 4 *Sanford Journal of Public Policy* 87.

Kessler, JK (2013) 'The Invention of a Human Right: Conscientious Objection at the United Nations, 1947–2011' 44 *Columbia Human Rights Law Review* 753.

Knaul, G (2013) *Legal aid, a right in itself*, Media release of the UN Special Rapporteur on the independence of judges and lawyers, Geneva, 30 May, available at: www.ohchr.org/EN/NewsEvents/Pages/DisplayNews.aspx?NewsID=13382&.

Kunc, F (2013) 'Shall ye be heard? Legal representation in civil claims', [2013] *NSW Judicial Scholarship* 43, available at: www.austlii.edu.au/au/journals/NSWJSchol/2013/43.html.

Kyiv Declaration on the Right to Legal Aid (2007) Conference on the Protection and Promotion of Human Rights through Provision of Legal Services Best Practices from Africa, Asia and Eastern Europe Kyiv, Ukraine 27–30 March, available at: www.irf.ua/en/knowledgebase/news/the_kyiv_declaration_on_the_right_to_legal_aid.

Kyle, L, Coverdale, R and Powers, T (2014) *Conflict of interest in Victorian rural and regional legal practice* (Melbourne, Centre for Rural Regional Law and Justice, Deakin University), available at: hdl.handle.net/10536/DRO/DU:30064938.

Legal Action Group (1996) 'The Scope of Legal Services' in A Paterson and T Goriely (eds), *A Reader on Resourcing Civil Justice* (Oxford, Oxford University Press).

Lilongwe Declaration on Assessing Legal Aid in Criminal Justice System in Africa adopted by the African Commission on Human and Peoples' Rights at its 40th Ordinary Session, November 2006 (Resolution 100(XXX) 06).

Luban, D (2005) 'Lawyers as Upholders of Human Dignity (When They Aren't Busy Assaulting It)' [2005] *University of Illinois Law Review* 815.

Lucas, LS (2014) 'Deconstructing the Right to Counsel', *The American Constitution Society Issues Brief*, July 2014, available at: dro.deakin.edu.au/eserv/DU:30064938/coverdale-conflictof-2014.pdf.

McCombs, T and González, JS (2007) *Right to Identity* (California, University of California, Berkeley School of Law).

Mowbray, A (2005) 'The Creativity of the European Court of Human Rights' 5 *Human Rights Law Review* 57.

Ontario Legal Aid Review (1997) *A Blueprint for Publicly Funded Legal Services* (Canada, Ontario Government).

Organization of American States Inter-American Commission on Human Rights (2007) *Access to Justice as a Guarantee of Economic, Social, and Cultural Rights. A Review of the Standards Adopted by the Inter-American System of Human Rights* OEA/Ser.L/V/II.129 Doc 4, 7 September.

Otto, D (2015) 'Queering Gender [Identity] in International Law', 33 *Nordic Journal of Human Rights* 299.

Perinaud, C (2015) *Legal aid in criminal proceedings: Will the European Parliament improve the Council's 'general approach'?*, 16 March 2015, available at: free-group.eu/2015/03/16/legal-aid-in-criminal-proceedings-will-the-european-parliament-improve-the-councils-general-approach/.

Productivity Commission (2014) *Access to Justice Arrangements Inquiry*, Report No 72, 5 September (Canberra, Productivity Commission).

Raz, J (2010) 'Human Rights Without Foundations' in S Besson and J Tasioulas (eds), *The Philosophy of International Law* (Oxford, Oxford University Press).

Reid, K (2011) *A Practitioner's Guide to the European Convention on Human Rights* (London, Sweet & Maxwell).

Rhode, DL (2004) *Access to Justice* (Oxford, Oxford University Press).

Rice, S (2010) 'A Human Right to Legal Aid' in P Dalton and H Thelle (eds), *Legal Aid: International experiences and promising practices for legal aid providers (Denmark*, Danish Institute for Human Rights).

Richardson, E, Sourdin, T and Wallace, N (2012) *Self-Represented Litigants: Literature Review* (Melbourne, Australian Centre for Court and Justice System Innovation).

Ringelheim, J (2013) 'Integrating Cultural Concerns in the Interpretation of Traditional Individual Rights: Lessons from the International Human Rights Jurisprudence' in Merle J (ed), *Spheres of Global Justice: Volume 1 Global Challenges to Liberal Democracy: Political Participation, Minorities and Migrations* (Dordrecht, Springer Science & Business Media).

Sackville, R (2002) 'From access to justice to managing justice: the transformation of the judicial role' [2002] *Federal Judicial Scholarship* 9.

Scott, C (1989) 'The Interdependence and Permeability of Human Rights Norms: Towards a Partial Fusion of the International Covenants on Human Rights' 27 *Osgoode Law Journal* 769.

Saul, B, Kinley, D and Mowbray, J (2014) *The International Covenant on Economic Social and Cultural rights: Commentary, Cases and Materials* (Oxford, Oxford University Press).

Sax, JP (1970) *Defending the Environment: A Strategy for Citizen Action* (New York, A Knopf).

Schetzer, L, Mullins, J and Buonamano, R (2002) *Access to justice & legal needs, a project to identify legal needs, pathways and barriers for disadvantaged people in NSW: Background paper* (Sydney, Law and Justice Foundation of New South Wales), available at: www.lawfoundation.net.au/ljf/site/articleIDs/012E910236879BAECA257060007D13E0/$file/bkgr1.pdf.

Shaver, L (2015) 'The Right to Read' 54 *Columbia Journal of Transnational Law* 1.

Skinnider E (1999) *The Responsibility of States to Provide Legal Aid* (China, The International Centre for Criminal Law Reform and Criminal Justice Policy).

Skorupski, J (2010) 'Human Rights' in S Besson and J Tasioulas (eds), *The Philosophy of International Law* (Oxford, Oxford University Press).

Smith, R (2002) 'Legal Aid: Models of Organisation', Paper to European Forum on Access to Justice, Budapest, 5–7 December, available at: www.legalaid-reform.org/resources/civil-legal-aid-resources/item/100-legal-aid-models-of-organisation.

____ (2007) 'Human rights and access to justice', 14 *International Journal of the Legal Profession* 261.

Tams, C and Sloan, J (2013) *The Development of International Law by the International Court of Justice* (Oxford, Oxford University Press).

Trinder, L and Hunter, R (2015) 'Access to justice? Litigants in person before and after LASPO' *Family Law* 535.

UN Committee Against Torture, General Comment No 3 (2012) *Implementation of Article 14 by States parties*, CAT/C/GC/3.

UN Committee on Economic, Social and Cultural Rights (1998a) General Comment 9, *The domestic application of the Covenant*, 3 December 1998. E/C.12/1998/24.

UN Committee on Economic, Social and Cultural Rights (1998b) *Concluding Observations on Canada*, E/C.12/1/Add.31 (10 December 1998).

UN Committee on the Elimination of Discrimination against Women (2010) *General Recommendation No 28 on the core obligations of States parties under*

Article 2 of the Convention on the Elimination of All Forms of Discrimination against Women, CEDAW/C/GC/28, 16 December 2010.

UN Committee on the Elimination of All Forms of Racial Discrimination (2000) *General Recommendation XXVI*, 24 March 2000.

—— (2008) *Concluding observations on US' fourth, fifth and sixth periodic reports* CERD/C/USA/CO/6, 8 May 2008.

UN Committee on the Rights of Persons with Disabilities (2014) General Comment No 1, *Article 12: Equal recognition before the law*, CRPD/C/GC/1, 19 May 2014.

UN General Assembly (1986) *Setting International Standards in the Field of Human Rights*, GA Res 41/120, UN GA, 41st session, 97th plenary meeting, UN Doc A/Res/41/120 (1986).

UN Human Rights Committee (2004) General Comment No 31, *The Nature of the General Legal Obligation Imposed on States Parties to the Covenant* CCPR/C/21/Rev.1/Add.13 26 May 2004.

—— (2007) General Comment No 32, *Article 14: Right to equality before courts and tribunals and to a fair trial* CCPR/C/GC/32 23 August 2007.

UN Human Rights Committee (2011a) *Concluding Observations on Norway*, CCPR/C/NOR/CO/6 (18 November 2011).

—— (2011b) General Comment No 34, *Article 19: Freedoms of opinion and expression* CCPR/C/GC/34 (12 September 2011).

UN Independent Expert on the Question of Human Rights and Extreme Poverty (2011) *Mission to Ireland*, 17 May 2011, A/HRC/17/34/Add.2.

UN Special Rapporteur on the Independence of Judges and Lawyers (2013) *Report of the Special Rapporteur on the independence of judges and lawyers—Legal aid* (21 May 2013), UN Doc A/HRC/23 /43.

UN Special Rapporteur on the Situation of Human Rights Defenders (2011) *Commentary to the Declaration on the Right and Responsibility of Individuals, Groups and Organs of Society to Promote and Protect Universally Recognized Human Rights and Fundamental Freedoms*, 2011.

van Dijk, P and van Hoof, GJH (1998) *Theory and Practice of the European Convention on Human Rights* (The Hague, Kluwer).

Vlavianos, N (2012) 'The Intersection of Human Rights Law and Environmental Law', paper presented at the *Symposium on Environment in the Courtroom: Key Environmental Concepts and the Unique Nature of Environmental Damage*, 23–24 March 2012, University of Calgary.

Waldron, J (1999) *Law and Disagreement* (Oxford, Oxford University Press).

Weissbrodt, D and Hallendorff, M (1999) '*Travaux Preparatoires* of the Fair Trial Provisions—Articles 8 to 11—of the Universal Declaration of Human Rights' 21 *Human Rights Quarterly* 1061.

Weston, BH and Bollier, D (2013) 'Toward a recalibrated human right to a clean and healthy environment: making the conceptual transition' 4 *Journal of Human Rights and the Environment* 116.

Winkler, IT (2013) *The Human Right to Water* (Oxford, Hart Publishing).

Treaties, Conventions, Principles, Directives, Rules and Legislation

African Charter on Human and Peoples' Rights
American Convention on Human Rights
Charter of the Organization of American States (A-41) 119 UNTS 3, 48 (E)
Convention against Torture and Other Cruel, Inhuman or Degrading Treatment
Convention on the Elimination of All Forms of Discrimination against Women
Convention on the Elimination of All Forms of Racial Discrimination
Convention for the Protection of All Persons from Enforced Disappearance
Convention on the Protection of the Rights of All Migrant Workers and Members of Their Families
Convention on the Rights of the Child
Convention on the Rights of Persons with Disabilities
Directive 2010/64/EU.
Directive 2012/13/EU.
Directive 2013/48/EU.
European Convention on the Protection of Human Rights and Fundamental Freedoms
European Union *Charter of Fundamental Rights*
International Covenant on Civil and Political Rights
International Covenant on Economic, Social and Cultural Rights
Kyiv Declaration 2007
Universal Declaration of Human Rights

Cases

Airey v Ireland (1979–80) 2 EHRR 305, [1979] ECHR 3.
Case of Hilaire, Constantine and Benjamin et al v Trinidad and Tobago, Judgment of 21 June 2002; 17 September 2003, Inter-Am Ct HR (Series A) No 18 (2003).
Imbrioscia v Switzerland, 24 November 1993, Series A no 275, §36.
Purohit and Moore v The Gambia, African Commission on Human and Peoples' Rights, Comm No 241/2001 (2003).
Salduz v Turkey (Application no 36391/02), [Grand Chamber] 27 November 2008, §50.
Steel and Morris v United Kingdom (2005) 41 EHRR 22, [2005] ECHR 103.

12

Cuts to Civil Legal Aid and the Identity Crisis in Lawyering: Lessons from the Experience of England and Wales

NATALIE BYROM

I. Introduction

In 2015, the United Kingdom (UK) entered its fifth year of a government-mandated programme of austerity, and following the election of a majority Conservative government in May 2015, plans were put in place to extend this programme until 2019. The measures introduced have focused on reducing public spending by making significant changes to the welfare state. By 2019–20, public service spending is forecast to be at its lowest share of national income since at least 1948 (Emmerson, Johnson and Joyce 2015: 151). These cuts have not been distributed equally across government departments—with public spending on official development assistance, health and some aspects of education being protected in the current period of austerity (Emmerson et al 2015: 160). In contrast, the civil legal aid scheme has been a primary casualty of cuts to public spending. In April 2013, the *Legal Aid, Sentencing and Punishment of Offenders Act 2012* (LASPO) came into force, ushering in spending cuts that were predicted to reduce government spending on civil legal aid by £300 million (AU$527 million) per year in the long term (Comptroller and Auditor-General 2014). This £300 million (AU$527 million) represents cuts of a third from 2009–10, when the total spend on the civil legal aid scheme stood at £900 million (AU$1.58 billion).

This chapter is divided into three sections. The first section briefly outlines the cuts that were made to the civil legal aid scheme in 2013 and their impact on the provision of legal services in England and Wales. The second section discusses the contextual factors that made such drastic cuts possible, with the aim of providing lessons for other jurisdictions. The third and final section argues that the new funding landscape requires a fundamental reconsideration of the role of lawyers in society, and the ways in which the importance of civil justice is communicated to outside audiences. Providing a compelling answer to the question 'What are lawyers for?' is essential if the profession is to mount an effective, principled defence for the protection of what remains of public funding for civil legal aid.

II. LASPO and Cuts to Civil Legal Aid

On 1 April 2013 the cuts imposed by LASPO came into effect with the aim of cutting the legal aid budget. Despite widespread opposition from many in the legal profession and parliament, including the Law Society and the House of Lords, the cuts focused mainly on the areas of family law, immigration, welfare benefits, employment and clinical negligence. The reductions in spending were created through a combination of limiting the scope of the legal aid scheme by reducing the areas of law for which legal aid is available, and implementing a more stringent means test—to qualify for legal aid, a person's income and capital must be within specified and strictly enforced limits (Higgins 2014: 15). Prior to the introduction of LASPO, all areas of civil law were within the scope of the legal aid scheme, unless specifically excluded under Schedule 2 of the *Access to Justice Act 1999*.[1] Since the cuts were implemented, the only areas that remain in scope are family law cases involving child protection and domestic violence, cases involving an application for asylum, cases relating to the treatment of patients with mental health problems, discrimination cases, and some cases relating to debt, welfare benefits and housing (Comptroller and Auditor-General 2014: 10).[2] In addition to these measures, some people who receive legal aid are required to make increased contributions to the cost of their case. In an attempt to reduce costs further, the Ministry of Justice (MoJ) implemented a telephone gateway for accessing advice and representation in some areas of law, thereby changing the way in which individuals with civil law problems access advice and representation (Comptroller and Auditor-General 2014: 10; see also McKay, Chapter 6, and Laster and Kornhauser, Chapter 7, this volume, for a discussion of new technologies and greater requirements on individuals to manage their own problems in the Australian context).

[1] Schedule 2 of the *Access to Justice Act 1999* excluded certain types of cases including personal injury (apart from in respect of clinical negligence), conveyancing, and boundary disputes, among others, from the scope of the legal aid scheme.

[2] For example, under LASPO, it is possible to get legal help and representation for housing issues such as unlawful eviction and rent possessions. Advice is available both face-to-face and via a telephone line and through a Housing Duty Solicitor scheme. However, this advice is only accessible when the situation has reached crisis point ie a notice for possession has been issued. Importantly, no funding is available to provide legal advice in resolving issues with welfare benefits or employment that are often implicated in eviction proceedings.

Compounding the measures introduced by LASPO were changes introduced in July 2013 that restricted access to judicial review and introduced fees of between £160 (AU$281) and £950 (AU$1669) for bringing a claim before an employment tribunal. Shortly after the introduction of LASPO, further reforms to the sector were announced by the Justice Secretary. In January 2014, the government altered the merits test to restrict legal aid for those cases where the prospects of success are 'borderline'—this was met with objections from the legal profession, who claimed that cases with the potential to change existing law will likely be denied funding. From April 2014, legal aid in respect of judicial review cases was reformed, with lawyers being denied payment for work carried out on cases where courts decided not to grant permission for the case to proceed to a full hearing. Concerns have been raised that this decision will substantially reduce the capacity and willingness of lawyers to proceed with even low-risk cases. These measures compounded reductions in the level of fees paid to civil legal aid lawyers that had been implemented in October 2011 and February 2012.

The cuts to legal aid have changed the manner in which services are provided to the public in a number of important ways. The reforms have reduced the absolute number of providers available; they have affected the geographical distribution of legal aid funded civil law advice across England and Wales, creating 'advice deserts'; and they have altered the nature of the service provided by moving the focus away from early intervention and complex casework, onto one-off pieces of advice provided once a situation has already escalated.

The cuts have led to an overall reduction in the number of providers of legal advice that are funded by legal aid, by nearly 50 per cent since 2007–08. They have also altered the ways in which these services are delivered, by forcing many not-for-profit organisations that previously provided legal advice—particularly in relation to social welfare law—out of the sector entirely. Those that remain, do so with vastly reduced capacity; the charity Citizens Advice has reported that the number of people it is able to help per year since the introduction of the cuts has fallen by 120,000, from 136,000 to just 16,000 (Guy 2014; see also Kirwan, Chapter 10, and Organ and Sigafoos, Chapter 9, this volume).

This reduction in the number of agencies and firms available to provide legal aid-funded civil law advice has created problems for frontline generalist advice agencies, who are finding it increasingly difficult to refer clients who are in need of legal advice and representation to appropriate providers. In evidence given to the Justice Select Committee in July 2014, the Chief Executive of Citizens Advice reported on a survey of all Bureaux across England and Wales, which identified that 92 per cent of Bureaux report difficulties accessing legal aid-funded representation for individuals who are eligible for legal aid-funded civil law advice. Figures presented by the National Audit Office (NAO) demonstrate that, in 2013–14, the Legal Aid Agency's spending on representation in civil law matters was £9.7 million (AU$17 million) *less* than predicted, which may indicate problems in the ability of individuals to access civil legal representation. The Justice Select Committee heard evidence from the Civil Justice Council, which reported that solicitors with legal aid contracts are reluctant or unable to take on eligible work, due to the cost involved in establishing whether an individual is eligible for legal aid. Several not-for-profit agencies reported to the Committee that finding a solicitor who is willing to take on legal aid cases is becoming increasingly challenging. The areas of law particularly implicated in this crisis of availability are specialist social welfare advice, specialist immigration advice and legal assistance for domestic violence victims in family law proceedings (Justice Select Committee 2014–15: 33; see also Mutha-Merennege, Chapter 14, this volume).

There is increasing evidence that the cuts have fundamentally altered the geographic distribution of legal aid-funded civil law advice across the UK. A survey conducted in conjunction with the UK's largest online forum for civil legal aid providers, published in April 2013, indicated that the South West of England was likely to be disproportionately affected by the reduction in the availability of specialist advice, and that agencies in the Midlands were over-represented among those who stated that their service was under threat of closure (Byrom 2013). It was reported that individuals living in rural areas were particularly likely to be affected by the reduction in the number of providers of legal advice (Byrom 2013). The NAO found that 14 local authority areas saw no face-to-face civil legal aid work *at all* in 2013–14, and very small numbers of cases were started in a further 39 local authority areas, leading the Justice Select Committee to remark that it was deeply concerned that these figures indicated the existence of a substantial number of 'advice deserts' (Justice Select Committee 2014–15: 34).

The removal of legal aid for all but the most complex cases has altered the nature of the work that legal aid-funded civil law practitioners can undertake on behalf of their clients. Successive witnesses who appeared before the Justice Select Committee emphasised that the effect of the changes was to prevent legal advisers from intervening early, with the result that problems often escalated before clients received any assistance (Justice Select Committee 2014–15: 60). In addition, it was reported that the lack of funding for complex, holistic casework reduces the likelihood of finding enduring solutions to civil law issues. The final report of the Low Commission on the Future of Advice and Legal Support (2014), an independent commission established to develop a strategy for improving access to advice and support on social welfare law matters in the new funding context, concluded that the focus on only providing legal aid to those claimants who are in the most serious position 'creates a perverse incentive to wait until things reach a crisis point' (Low Commission 2014: 17). The Commission further argued that:

> If individuals are only able to access support on crisis issues, and advisers are not funded to address clusters of associated problems or the fundamental cause of the problem (such as unemployment, not receiving the correct benefit, or resolving underlying financial problems), then the individual will keep returning to crisis point as the problem will only be temporarily masked, not solved. (Low Commission 2014: 17)

A. LASPO and the Legal Profession

While the immediate impact of cuts to legal aid on civil law practitioners has been stark, many in the sector emphasise that the full impact of the measures introduced by LASPO on the profession are unlikely to be understood for some time yet. Preliminary evidence suggests that the changes will impact on the profession in three key areas: (i) diversity and social mobility, (ii) the existence of not-for-profit agencies as providers of legal advice, and (iii) the retention and generation of legal expertise in the areas of law formerly funded through legal aid (see also Smith and Cape, Chapter 4, this volume).

A report published in 2012 indicated that British black, Asian and minority ethnic (BAME) majority partner firms are more likely than others to work for a majority of legally aided individuals (Pleasence, Balmer and Moorhead 2013: 20). Lawyers from BAME backgrounds are disproportionately represented among those who practise in the areas of law that were funded through legal aid prior to the introduction of LASPO. The same report noted that women are also more likely to practise in these areas of law. A report by Jon Robins published in October 2015 stated that the crisis in legal aid has had a disproportionate impact on diversity in the legal profession (Robins 2015). Robins interviewed Cordella Bart-Stewart, one of the founders of the Black Solicitors Network, which was established in 1995. Bart-Stewart stated: 'Legal Aid is what gave most of us a start ... it gave us our opportunity ... that is going to go' (Robins 2015). If the concerns around the implications of the legal aid cuts for diversity within the profession are justified, this could compound existing problems with judicial diversity, as judges are recruited from the ranks of the legal profession. Statistics published in 2010 by the Advisory Panel on Judicial Diversity indicate that only 19 per cent of judicial post-holders were women, rising to 25.3 per cent by 2014 (Judicial Diversity Statistics 2014), and only 4.5 per cent (Advisory Panel on Judicial Diversity 2011) of judges came from ethnic minority backgrounds, rising to 5.8 per cent by 2014 (Judicial Diversity Statistics 2014). This lack of diversity was cited by the chair of the advisory panel as a significant risk to the court system as a whole.

The reductions to legal aid have also impacted on the types of providers that deliver civil law advice and representation. A statistical release published by the Legal Aid Agency revealed that not-for-profit agencies have been the worst affected by the cuts, with few remaining in the sector. Numbers of not-for-profit providers within the sector fell from nearly 450 in 2012 to fewer than 250 in the first quarter of 2015 (Legal Aid Agency 2015). This represents a significant change in the composition of the sector, and may foreshadow the departure of not-for-profit agencies from the sector in the near to medium term.

In addition, the recent cuts to civil legal aid threaten to erode expertise in areas of civil law, from both the top and bottom ends of the profession. The withdrawal of legal aid—a sustainable, relatively reliable source of income—has had a detrimental impact on the ability of organisations to plan for the future and commit to training new solicitors and barristers interested in working in the areas of civil law that were previously funded by legal aid. In addition, the lack of job security in these areas of law may act as a deterrent for graduates (already leaving university facing significant debt) from considering entering the profession in the first place. A study published by the Young Legal Aid Lawyers concluded that high levels of debt, low salaries and diminishing numbers of training contracts and pupillages act as a barrier to the pursuit of a career in the areas of law previously funded by legal aid (Young Legal Aid Lawyers 2013). In addition to the implications for expertise development at the junior end of the profession, research has revealed that the cuts introduced by LASPO may disproportionately affect the most experienced and qualified practitioners in the civil law sector. A survey of legal aid practitioners published in April 2013 (Byrom 2013) reported that it is the most experienced and qualified advisers whose jobs are most at risk as a result of the cuts: those who have worked in the sector for over 10 years are the worst affected by redundancy. As the routes to qualification as both a solicitor and barrister depend on the professional mentorship provided by senior colleagues, attrition at senior levels of the profession threatens to permanently erode expertise—this drain of knowledge and skills from the sector may prove to be the lasting legacy of the LASPO cuts.

III. Cutting Civil Legal Aid: What did we Learn about the Factors Facilitating the Cuts?

The previous section outlined the drastic cuts to public spending on civil legal aid and provided an overview of some of the ways in which the impact of these cuts has manifested itself. While the election of the Conservative-led Coalition government in 2010 ushered in a period of austerity-based policy-making,[3] predicated on the notion that restricting public spending was the only way to reduce the deficit created by the global financial crisis of 2008, these cuts were not evenly distributed across government departments. In addition to cutting spending, the Coalition government has attempted to institute a widespread programme of public sector reform, the unifying feature of which appears to involve 'significant transfers of responsibility from the state to the private sector and the citizen' (Taylor-Gooby and Stoker 2011: 4), and the net effect of which has been to reduce the level of state intervention to below that found in the United States (US) (Taylor-Gooby and Stoker 2011: 14). As such, the reforms instituted may be best understood as 'systematic' rather than 'programmatic' (Pierson 1994: 13). Programmatic reforms

[3] The Liberal Democrats entered a coalition with the Conservative Party in order to avoid a minority government after the general election of 2010.

target immediate cost savings, while systematic reform 'moves beyond immediate cost-saving and seeks to modify the context in which future struggles over welfare provision take place, so that pressures for future spending are stifled' (Taylor-Gooby 2012: 63). The systematic reforms introduced by the Coalition government have been instituted, it has been argued, in an attempt to permanently 'embed … cutbacks in future patterns of provision' (Taylor-Gooby 2013: 14) by breaking up national services and devolving responsibility for delivery from national to local government or non-state, mainly private sector providers. The approach taken to cutting the amount of money spent on civil legal aid may be considered to be emblematic of this type of systematic reform.

The following section argues that the civil legal aid scheme was vulnerable to government spending cuts for three principal reasons. First, civil legal aid was and is very far from a universal benefit, as it is only available to those on the lowest incomes. Secondly, public perceptions of lawyers are often less than positive, and government rhetoric capitalised on these perceptions in ushering in the cuts. Thirdly, low levels of public understanding of law and the legal process, and the role the law can play in securing rights and fair treatment, have meant that arguments for the retention of the civil legal aid scheme did not resonate with the general public.

A. Austerity, Civil Legal Aid and Universal versus Non-universal Benefits

Many of the arguments raised against the state provision of funding for individualised legal advice and representation relate to the high absolute cost of funding the scheme that is currently in place. This, in itself, does not tell us a great deal about why the state should not continue to fund it—after all, the National Health Service (NHS), which was established in the same period, is also costly. While multiple reports have noted the increase in government spending on legal aid since the inception of the scheme—established in 1950 as a result of the recommendations of the 1949 *Rushcliffe Report*[4]—the same might be said of the amount spent on healthcare, which has increased on average as a percentage of gross domestic product since 1950.[5] Comparing the development of the two schemes is instructive as it enables us to compare the contrasting destinies of two schemes born out of the post-war settlement.

While the NHS has expanded in terms of coverage and is now firmly established as a central feature of modern British society, the coverage of the civil legal aid

[4] *Report of the Committee on Legal Aid and Legal Advice in England and Wales* (Cmd 6641) (London, HMSO, 1945).

[5] Data obtained from: www.ukpublicspending.co.uk/spending_chart_1950_2014UKp_12c1li011mbn_10t.

scheme has fallen since its inception. When the legal aid scheme was first established, it was estimated to cover almost 80 per cent of the population of England and Wales (Paterson and Goriely 1996). By 2007, figures compiled by the MoJ using a model based on the Family Resources Survey estimated that only 29 per cent of the population of England and Wales were eligible for civil legal aid-funded advice and representation (Griffith 2012). In contrast, the NHS was established on the basis of universal access at the point of need, regardless of means—a principle that has not yet been eroded.

The contrast between the treatment of universal and non-universal services in successive budgets since 2010 has been marked. Those services that might be categorised as universal or 'mass services', such as health and social care, education and pensions emerge from the cuts relatively unscathed (Taylor-Gooby 2013: 3), in spite of the fact that the costs of these services represent the bulk of government spending on the welfare state (Taylor-Gooby 2013: 7). In contrast, those benefits and services that redistribute wealth and other benefits to the poor, such as the welfare benefits system and civil legal aid scheme, have seen their budgets dramatically reduced. Government rhetoric has reflected this division. In the June 2013 Spending Review, the Chancellor of the Exchequer George Osborne, discussing the funding of the NHS, stated that:

> Even in these tough times, the decisions we make mean we keep to our commitments, and that includes our commitments to the National Health Service, the institution that is the very embodiment of fairness in our society. The NHS is much more than the government's priority; it is the people's priority and when we came to office the health budget was £96bn, in 2015/16 it will be £110bn and capital spending will rise to £4.7bn. (HC Debate, 26 June 2013: Column 312)[6]

In contrast, in relation to proposed further changes to legal aid—a need-based benefit—Osborne remarked:

> [T]he cost of legal aid per head is double the European average. My Rt. Hon. Friend the Lord Chancellor is reforming all of these things and by doing that he will make savings of ten per cent in his departmental budget … Mr Speaker, it's an example of the reform we are bringing across government and every step of the way, every penny saved, every programme reformed, every entitlement reduced, every difficult choice taken, has been opposed by vested interests. (HC Debate 26 June 2013: Column 309)

Cuts to spending are frequently prefaced with statements such as, 'we are all in this together', and repeated reference is made to ideals such as 'fairness' in relation to the goals of the programme of restructuring. George Osborne, in announcing the 2013 Spending Review, stated that the goal of his latest reforms was to produce a budget that was grounded in 'fairness, making sure we are all in it together, by making sure that those with the broadest shoulders bear the largest burden

[6] These figures equate to AU$180 billion (£102 billion), AU$207 billion (£117 billion), and AU$8.8 billion (£5 billion).

and making sure the unfairness in our "something for nothing" welfare culture is changed' (HC Debate 26 June 2013: Column 303). This repositioning of non-universal services that allocate resources on a 'need' basis as agents of 'unfairness' is key to understanding the ideological appeal of the reforms made by the Coalition government to the legal aid scheme.[7] Unlike many other European welfare states, the British welfare state is financed 'mainly through taxation, rather than social insurance payments from employers, workers and government' (Taylor-Gooby 2013: 3). It has been argued that a system based on tax-finance, encouraging as it does the drawing of comparisons between those who pay into the system and those who receive benefits from the system, immediately raises questions of stigma and desert, particularly in the context of non-universal services. The diminishing coverage of the civil legal aid scheme, facilitated through the institution of an increasingly stringent means test, meant that civil legal aid was implicated in this characterisation. And this characterisation matters because it posited civil legal aid as a scheme that instantiated unfairness and redistributed scarce resources from the taxpayer to the undeserving poor and vexatious, frivolous litigants.

B. Public Perceptions of Legal Aid Lawyers, the Civil Justice System and Cuts to Civil Legal Aid

The debates that took place prior to the introduction of LASPO are instructive in highlighting the ways in which the cuts were framed. Arguments for cutting government spending on civil legal aid were premised on three grounds: (i) that the current scheme was too expensive, both in absolute terms and when compared with schemes in other countries; (ii) that the legal aid system was encouraging people to litigate where they otherwise would not, and that lawyers with vested interests were encouraging these claims; and (iii) that it was unfair to require the taxpayer to pay for individuals to litigate where the 'ordinary citizen' would not, because they could not afford to do so. Additionally, it was claimed that legal or court-based solutions were being sought in relation to problems that were non-legal in character, as the following quote from the then Justice Secretary Kenneth Clarke demonstrates:

> I accept that access to justice for the protection of fundamental rights is vital for a democratic society—something on which I will not compromise. However, our current legal system can encourage people to bring their problems before the courts when the basic problem is not a legal one and would be better dealt with in other ways. The scope of legal aid has been expanded too far. (HC Hansard, 29 June 2011: Column 986).

The root of the issues implicated in statements of this kind lies in the construction of the civil legal aid scheme that emerged from the post-war consensus.

[7] For example, welfare benefits for the unemployed.

The legal aid scheme established following the *Rushcliffe Report* created a system of taxpayer-funded legal services that were administered by lawyers in private practice. Unlike the NHS, which saw hospitals nationalised and doctors directly employed by the state, the civil legal aid scheme was managed by the Law Society of England and Wales—the representative body for the solicitors' profession. The Rushcliffe Committee, which heard evidence regarding the benefits and drawbacks of different models of service provision, concluded that a system of taxpayer-funded legal advice that placed administration of the scheme in the hands of the private profession was essential to the maintenance of the rule of law, as complaints against the state could not and should not be conducted by state-employed lawyers (Webley 2015: 2352). However, the decision to allow the scheme to remain one through which lawyers in private practice claimed for remuneration from the government in a similar manner to the way in which they would bill a private client (Higgins 2014: 15) meant that those who provided legal aid-funded advice and representation were open to accusations of pursuing their own self-interest at the expense of the taxpayer. As early as 1999, academics and commentators were questioning whether the civil legal aid scheme created perverse incentives for litigation, regardless of whether pursuing this course of action was in the best interest of the client (Zuckerman 1999: 30).

These arguments were alluded to by Kenneth Clarke in his comments on the introduction of LASPO when he argued that legal aid had created a 'litigious society' where cases were pursued through the court system unnecessarily, regardless of the merits of pursuing litigation. He further contended that '[o]rdinary citizens find the law … expensive, daunting, nightmare, not a public service' (HC Hansard, 29 June 2011: Column 985). This argument seems to be supported by research published by the MoJ in December 2013, which identified that only three per cent of individuals surveyed through the Opinions and Lifestyle Survey run by the Office of National Statistics strongly agreed that civil courts should be free to use, and fully funded by the taxpayer through general taxes (Franlin 2013).

Attempts by the legal profession to mobilise against the cuts to civil legal aid were undermined by a media narrative that the objections to LASPO were motivated by lawyers seeking to defend their own livelihoods. Legal Action Group, an independent charity that exists to promote access to justice, and a vocal opponent of cuts to both civil and criminal legal aid, published research that identified three distinct narratives in the press coverage of cuts to legal aid. These included that lawyers who provide the service are overpaid, that legal aid funding is awarded to the 'undeserving', and that the legal aid system in England and Wales is the most expensive in the world (Hynes 2014). Reporting of high-cost cases funded by legal aid, including recent coverage of the Al-Sweady inquiry, where prominent legal aid lawyers acted on behalf of Iraqi citizens who were eventually determined to have falsely alleged that British forces had murdered and tortured Iraqi civilians in the aftermath of a fierce battle in 2004, may have further undermined public perceptions of legal aid lawyers. Commenting on the findings of the inquiry in

December 2014, the then Secretary of State for Defence, Michael Fallon, stated that:

> The Iraqi detainees, their accomplices and their lawyers must bear the brunt of the criticism for the protracted nature and £31 million cost of this unnecessary public inquiry. The falsity of the overwhelming majority of their allegations, the extraordinarily late disclosure of a document showing the nine detainees to have been insurgents and the delay by their lawyers in withdrawing the allegations of torture and murder have prompted the Solicitors Regulation Authority to investigate possible breaches of professional standards. (HC Hansard, 17 December 2014: Column 1048)[8]

Particularly damning were the accusations that counsel for the Iraqi detainees were late to concede evidence that pointed overwhelmingly to the fact that the bodies of Iraqis alleged to have been civilians murdered by British forces were actually killed in the course of battle, and were therefore combatants, not civilians. The Secretary of State for Defence went on to conclude that:

> Had the concession been made (at the time the lawyers were aware of this information), it would not have been necessary for so many soldiers to give evidence, Sir Thayne (the chair of the Inquiry) could have concluded his hearings more quickly, and there would have been a significantly smaller bill to the taxpayer … The delay in making this concession is both inexplicable and shameful. (HC Hansard, 17 December 2014: Column 1407–8)

Qualitative research commissioned by the Legal Services Board found that negative media portrayals of lawyers were more likely to impact on trust in the profession than positive ones, and that high-profile cases had damaged trust in the profession through exposing instances of lawyers exploiting legal loopholes to win morally dubious cases (Spicer et al 2013). The Legal Services Consumer Panel commissioned a tracker survey to be administered by YouGov, a leading polling company that measures (among other things) levels of public trust in lawyers. In 2012, when the cuts introduced by LASPO were being debated in parliament, public trust in lawyers stood at 43 per cent, with lawyers less trusted to tell the truth than doctors or teachers (Legal Services Consumer 2014). All of these factors, taken together, mitigated against the ability of civil legal aid lawyers to argue effectively and successfully for the importance of retaining public funding for civil legal aid.

C. Public Knowledge and Understanding of Civil Law in England and Wales

Low levels of public knowledge of civil law and the civil justice system impede attempts to communicate the importance of retaining public funding for civil legal

[8] £31 million equates to AU$54.5 million.

aid. Empirical research has demonstrated that public understanding of the law as it relates to civil legal problems is low. Analysis of the findings of a large-scale study of legal need in England and Wales (the Civil and Social Justice Panel Survey 2010 and 2012), published in 2015, demonstrates a substantial legal knowledge deficit among the general public (Pleasence, Balmer and Denvir 2015: iii), with the oldest and youngest respondents displaying the lowest levels of understanding when faced with questions designed to test their knowledge of legal rights relating to employment, housing and consumer law. Low levels of public knowledge around legal rights may result in individuals failing to recognise instances where their legal rights are being infringed.

The lack of public awareness and understanding of the civil law, as it applies to individuals in their everyday lives, also makes it more difficult to communicate the importance of retaining free legal advice and representation in relation to civil law problems. Successive legal needs surveys in England and Wales have identified that problems that are justiciable[9] are most likely to be characterised as 'bad luck', with 47 per cent of problems reported by respondents as part of the Civil and Social Justice Panel surveys of 2010 and 2012 being characterised in this way. This has an impact on the strategies adopted by individuals to resolve these problems—if issues are not characterised as 'legal' those experiencing these problems are more likely to attempt to handle them alone and less likely to seek the advice of a lawyer (Pleasence et al 2015: vi). Failure to recognise the role that legal services can play in resolving everyday problems can lead individuals to see the law and legal services as irrelevant to their everyday lives, despite the important role that these services can play in securing rights, protection and fair treatment. Evidence suggests that where people have previously experienced problems that they recognise to be 'legal' in nature, their faith in their own ability to resolve future problems of a legal nature declines (Pleasence et al 2015: x), suggesting that individuals may not realise the importance of accessing legal advice in relation to civil law problems until they have already experienced a problem they recognise as legal. As evidence indicates that the majority of individuals do not recognise when they are experiencing civil law problems, arguments for the importance of retaining the provision of state-funded legal advice and representation fail to resonate.

The case for funding for criminal legal aid may be easier to make, as individuals facing criminal legal issues do not face the same difficulties in identifying that the problem they are experiencing is of a legal nature (see Rice, Chapter 11, this volume). The lack of parity of esteem between civil and criminal legal aid is not restricted to England and Wales, but affects the discourse around legal aid provision in other jurisdictions globally, including Australia (see Buchanan Chapter 8, and Rice, Chapter 11, this volume).

[9] Problems that may be resolved through recourse to the civil justice system.

IV. Cuts to Civil Legal Aid in England and Wales: What Now?

The preceding section outlined the factors that facilitated the drastic cuts to civil legal aid provision enacted by LASPO. The concluding part of this chapter seeks to advance some suggestions for the ways in which what remains of public funding for civil legal aid can be protected, and outlines steps that could form the basis of a principled argument for increasing funding in the future.

A. How Do We 'Do' Lawyering? Thinking Creatively about the Provision of Legal Services

While public funding for civil legal advice and representation has been drastically reduced, there is little evidence to suggest that the need for legal assistance among the most vulnerable has decreased. See, for example, Organ and Sigafoos (Chapter 9, this volume), who suggest that the need for legal assistance among the most vulnerable has increased, given the increasing complexity of recent welfare reforms and legislation. Organisations that deliver legal services to marginalised groups must think creatively about how to direct what remains of public funding for civil legal advice and representation to those who have the greatest need of it. Partnerships between social workers and lawyers that deliver embedded models of legal service provision to individuals already identified as marginalised or at risk—such as an initiative pioneered by Coventry Law Centre whereby a legal advice worker was embedded within the Children's Services Team at Coventry City Council[10]—enable the targeting of limited funds to the most vulnerable.

In order to ensure that the needs of the vulnerable are met, it is critical that the legal profession as a whole meets the challenge of ensuring that the pipeline of talented lawyers entering the field of community lawyering does not dry up. As discussed above, one barrier to the development of the next generation of talented and committed community lawyers is the lack of training contracts available to enable individuals to qualify. The Legal Education Foundation is leading a coalition of charitable foundations who are attempting to address this issue through funding training contracts at leading community law organisations, including Child Poverty Action Group, Shelter and the Public Law Project. It has been argued that commercial firms, who benefit financially from the UK justice system and its international standing as a bastion of the rule of law, have a moral obligation to

[10] For more information see: www.lawcentres.org.uk/policy/news/news/coventry-law-centre-up-for-social-justice-gong-for-troubled-families-work.

increase their contribution to enhancing access to justice. In June 2015, the newly appointed Justice Secretary Michael Gove argued that commercial firms could and should do more to support the parts of the legal sector previously funded by legal aid, through increasing their pro-bono work. In October 2015, Gove floated plans for a one per cent levy on the turnover of the top 100 commercial firms, which was predicted to raise between £190 (AU$334) and £200 million (AU$351 million): this has been strongly opposed by the Law Society (Downey 2015).

B. Getting the Message Across: Changing Communication around Civil Law and Civil Justice

Low levels of public understanding of civil law and the civil justice system make it more difficult to communicate why it is important that individuals be able to access advice and representation in respect of their civil law problems. Arguments made against the cuts to civil legal advice and representation have often framed the withdrawal of civil legal aid in terms of its impact on the legal system and abstract legal concepts (such as the rule of law—see Lord Neuberger 2013) and terminology, which fails to resonate outside rarefied circles of lawyers and legal academics. Philanthropic funders of civil legal assistance in the US have recognised that using legal language to frame debates on civil legal assistance impacts detrimentally on their ability to argue for funding for the provision of civil legal advice. In an attempt to address this issue, in 2013, the US Public Welfare Foundation, a major funder of civil legal assistance, established 'Voices for Civil Justice'—a communications hub that is attempting to publicise the role of civil legal advice in advancing social, economic and health goals, particularly among impoverished and marginalised communities. Voices for Civil Justice aims to deliver increased visibility for civil legal aid in the national media, increased capacity for media advocacy across the civil legal aid sector, and a new and strengthened 'brand' of civil legal aid, in order to address low levels of public recognition. Research conducted on behalf of Voices for Civil Justice in 2013 found that more than one-third of Americans have either never heard of or have no opinion on civil legal aid (Lake Research Partners, Terrace Group and Voices for Civil Justice 2013). By commissioning polling research to identify those messages that resonate with the public in relation to civil legal assistance, Voices for Civil Justice hopes to raise public consciousness of the role and importance of civil legal aid in achieving positive outcomes for people in respect of the problems they experience in their everyday lives.

Similar initiatives should be adopted in other jurisdictions, in order to bolster public support for legal advice and assistance in relation to civil legal problems. Universities also have a role to play in educating their law students about the crisis in public funding for civil legal aid, and in presenting a vision of lawyering that encompasses ideals of social justice and public service.

C. Answering the Question: What Are Lawyers For?

The crisis in civil legal aid funding requires lawyers to address the question of the distinctive value they contribute to society. What is the law for, and why is it important? In particular, those with an interest in protecting and restoring public funding for civil legal aid must be able to mount a compelling argument for its importance in the face of competing demands from other services with universal coverage, such as the NHS. It may be, however, that for the reasons outlined above, lawyers themselves are not best placed to advocate for their own importance.

Research demonstrates that civil legal advice and representation has an important role in addressing problems before they escalate; for example, civil legal advice to assist an individual in securing the correct level of welfare benefits can prevent the same individual from falling into rent arrears and being made homeless, thus preventing costs accruing to the local council tasked with securing housing for homeless individuals. Evidence from Switzerland indicates that delays in access to naturalisation procedures adversely impact the ability of individuals to integrate and participate democratically once their immigration status has been resolved (Hainmueller, Hangartner and Pietrantuono 2015). As such, access to high-quality immigration and asylum advice may contribute to social cohesion. Increasing attention is being paid to the link between the experience of civil law problems and adverse health outcomes (Pleasence, Balmer and Buck 2008).

Siloed government budgets make it difficult for lawyers to demonstrate the impact of their work in terms of reducing state spending overall. Likewise, allegations of self-interest restrict the ability of lawyers to advocate for the preservation and expansion of public funding for civil legal aid. Lawyers engaged in the provision of civil legal advice and representation need to form alliances with representatives of those agencies whose clients benefit from the provision of legal advice and assistance. These include public health professionals, and representatives of local councils and central government agencies, who can benefit from the role played by civil lawyers in ensuring government policies are effectively and consistently applied. However counterintuitive it might seem, lawyers may need to argue directly for their own existence less, and instead work with others to ensure that the genuine contribution their work makes to society advocates for itself.

References

Advisory Panel on Judicial Diversity (2011) *Improving Judicial Diversity: Progress toward delivery of the 'Report of the Advisory Panel on Judicial Diversity 2010'* (London, Ministry of Justice).

Byrom, N (2013) 'The State of the Sector: The Impact of Cuts to Civil Legal Aid on Practitioners and Their Clients', available at: www2.warwick.ac.uk/fac/soc/law/research/centres/chrp/spendingcuts/153064_statesector_report-final.pdf.

Comptroller and Auditor-General (2014) *Implementing reforms to civil legal aid*, Session 2014–2015, HC 784 National Audit Office, 20 November 2014.

Downey, S (2015) 'So much for the Global Law Summit—Gove floats £60m-plus tax on City law firms to fund criminal courts', *Legal Business*, 22 October 2015, available at: www.legalbusiness.co.uk/index.php/lb-blog-view/4837-so-much-for-the-global-law-summit-gove-floats-60m-plus-tax-on-city-law-firms-to-fund-criminal-courts.

Emmerson, C, Johnson, P and Joyce, R (2015) *IFS Green Budget* (London, The Institute for Fiscal Studies).

Franlin, R (2013) 'Ministry of Justice Analytical Summary: Public Attitudes to Civil and Family Court Fees', available at: www.gov.uk/government/uploads/system/uploads/attachment_data/file/262917/public-attitudes-civil-family-court-fees.pdf.

Griffith, A (2012) 'The Rise and Fall of Civil Legal Aid', *Legal Action Magazine*, October, available at: asauk.org.uk/wp-content/uploads/2013/08/The-Rise-and-Fall-of-Civil-Legal-Aid.pdf.

Guy, G (2014) *Justice Committee, Oral evidence (8 July 2014): Impact of changes to civil legal aid under the Legal Aid, Sentencing and Punishment of Offences Act 2012*, HC 311 data.parliament.uk/writtenevidence/committeeevidence.svc/evidencedocument/justice-committee/impact-of-changes-to-civil-legal-aid-under-laspo/oral/11320.html.

Hainmueller, J, Hangartner, D and Pietrantuono, G (2015) 'Naturalisation Fosters the Long-Term Political Integration of Immigrants', *Proceedings of the National Academy of Sciences*, available at: www.pnas.org/content/112/41/12651.full.pdf.

Higgins, A (2014) 'Legal Aid and Access to Justice in England and India' 26 *National Law School of India Review* 13.

HC Hansard (2014) *House of Commons Hansard*, 17 December (Col 1407–8).

HC Hansard (2011) *House of Commons Hansard*, 29 June (Col 985–86).

HC Debate (2013) *House of Commons Debate*, 26 June (Col 303, 309, 312).

Hynes, S (2014) 'Legal Aid at 65: Is the Government Losing the Argument over Cuts?', available at: www.lag.org.uk/media/175004/legal_aid_at_65.pdf.

Judicial Diversity Statistics 2014 (2014), available at: www.judiciary.gov.uk/publications/judicial-diversity-statistics-2014/ (Courts diversity statistics 2013–14).

Justice Select Committee (2014–15), *Impact of changes to civil legal aid under Part 1 of the Legal Aid, Sentencing and Punishment of Offenders Act 2012* (London, Justice Select Committee).

Lake Research Partners, Terrace Group and Voices for Civil Justice (2013) 'Expanding Civil Legal Aid: Strategies for Branding and Communications', available at: voicesforciviljustice.org/?p=4664.

Legal Aid Agency (2015) 'Legal Aid Statistics: January to March 2015', available at: www.gov.uk/government/statistics/legal-aid-statistics-january-to-march-2015.

Legal Services Consumer (2014) 'Tracker Survey 2014: Briefing note—Confidence and Satisfaction', available at: www.legalservicesconsumerpanel.org.uk/ourwork/CWI/documents/2014%20Tracker%20Briefing%202_Trust_Sat.pdf.

Lord Neuberger (2013) *Justice in an Age of Austerity*, Tom Sargant Memorial Lecture (Justice), p 15 (October 15), available at: www.supremecourt.uk/docs/speech-131015.pdf.

Low Commission on the Future of Advice and Legal Support (2014) *Tackling the Advice Deficit: A strategy for access to advice and legal support on social welfare law in England and Wales* (Final Report), available at: www.lowcommission.org.uk/dyn/1389221772932/Low-Commission-Report-FINAL-VERSION.pdf.

Paterson, A and Goriely, T (1996) *A Reader on Resourcing Civil Justice* (Oxford, Oxford University Press).

Pierson, P (1994) *Dismantling the Welfare State? Reagan, Thatcher and the politics of retrenchment* (Cambridge, Cambridge University Press).

Pleasence, P, Balmer, NJ and Buck, A (2008) 'The Health Cost of Civil-Law Problems: Further Evidence of Links Between Civil-Law Problems and Morbidity, and the Consequential Use of Health Services' 5 *Journal of Empirical Legal Studies* 351.

Pleasence, P, Balmer, N and Denvir, C (2015) 'Understanding, capability and the experience of civil legal problems' (Cambridge, April 2015), available at: www.thelegaleducationfoundation.org/wp-content/uploads/2015/12/HPUIL_report.pdf.

Pleasence, P and Balmer, N J and Moorhead, R (2013) 'A Time of Change: Solicitors' Firms in England and Wales', 16 January 2013, available at: www.ssrn.com/abstract=2202126.

Report of the Committee on Legal Aid and Legal Advice in England and Wales (Cmd 6641) (London, HMSO, 1945).

Robins, J (2015) 'Opening Up or Shutting Out? Social Mobility in the Legal Profession', Byefield Consultancy, available at: www.byfieldconsultancy.com/wp content/uploads/Opening-up-or-shutting-out_Social-mobility-in-the-legal-profession.pdf.

Spicer, N et al (2013) 'Consumer Use of Legal Services Understanding Consumers Who Don't Use, Don't Choose or Don't Trust Legal Services Providers' available at: research.legalservicesboard.org.uk/wp-content/media/Understanding-Consumers-Final-Report.pdf.

Taylor-Gooby, P (2012) 'Root and Branch Restructuring to Achieve Major Cuts: The Social Policy Programme of the 2010 UK Coalition Government' 46 *Social Policy & Administration* 61.

—— (2013) *The Double Crisis of the Welfare State and What We Can Do About It* (London, Palgrave Macmillan).

Taylor-Gooby, P and Stoker, G (2011) 'The Coalition Programme: A New Vision for Britain or Politics as Usual?' 82 *The Political Quarterly* 4.

Webley, L (2015) 'Legal Professional De(Re)Regulation, Equality and Inclusion and the Contested Space of professionalism within the Legal Market in England and Wales 83 *Fordham Law Review* 2349.

Young Legal Aid Lawyers (2013) 'Social Mobility and Diversity in the Legal Aid Sector: One Step Forward, Two Steps Back', available at: www.younglegalaidlawyers.org/sites/default/files/One%20step%20forward%20two%20steps%20back.pdf.

Zuckerman, A (ed) (1999) *Civil Justice in Crisis: Comparative Perspectives of Procedure* (Oxford, Oxford University Press).

Treaties, Conventions, Principles, Directives, Rules and Legislation

Access to Justice Act 1999

Legal Aid, Sentencing and Punishment of Offenders Act 2012

13

Access to What? LASPO and Mediation

ROSEMARY HUNTER, ANNE BARLOW,
JANET SMITHSON AND JAN EWING

I. Introduction

As noted in previous chapters, the *Legal Aid, Sentencing and Punishment of Offenders Act 2012* (LASPO) was one of the austerity measures introduced by the 2010–15 Coalition government in the United Kingdom (UK) to cut public sector spending. Its target for cuts was the civil legal aid fund, and since family law constituted a significant proportion of civil legal aid spending, it was particularly hard hit. All private family law disputes—that is, disputes between divorcing or separating couples over arrangements for their children, and disputes between divorcing couples over financial arrangements—were removed from the scope of legal aid for legal advice and representation. A very narrow exception remains for parties who are able to prove by means of specified evidence that they have been a victim of recent domestic violence or that they are attempting to protect a child who has been a victim of sexual abuse (LASPO Schedule 1, paragraphs 12–13; see also, *Civil Legal Aid (Procedure) Regulations 2012* regulations 33–4). In all other private family law cases, legal aid remains available only for mediation.

The policy preference for mediation rather than solicitor negotiations or court proceedings, as manifested in LASPO, was motivated by moral as well as economic considerations. Clearly, it is cheaper for the legal aid fund to pay one mediator rather than two solicitors (or possibly even one solicitor if only one party is legally aided) to resolve a family dispute; it is certainly cheaper to pay a mediator than to incur the public costs of a case going to court. But mediation is also promoted as part of a neoliberal ideology of 'responsibilisation'—of encouraging parties to take responsibility for sorting out their own 'private' disputes with minimal impact on public resources (see Laster and Kornhauser, Chapter 7, this volume). The constitution of family disputes as essentially 'private' matters that the parties themselves should resolve in a sensible, cooperative fashion, without relying on the crutch of state intervention, could be seen even prior to LASPO—for example, in the *Pre-Application Protocol for Mediation Information and Assessment* (2011). This was a Practice Direction that required all applicants and 'expected' all respondents to attend a Mediation Information and Assessment Meeting (MIAM) prior to commencing court proceedings, to learn how mediation could help them to resolve their dispute without needing to go to court.[1] And, subsequent to the introduction of LASPO, the *Children and Families Act 2014* repealed the former requirement that, in order for a divorce petition to be approved, the court must be satisfied that satisfactory arrangements have been made for the welfare of the parties' children, including their residence, education and financial support.[2] As a consequence, the state no longer takes an interest in the welfare of children following divorce, seeing this as purely a matter for the parents to determine.[3]

The privatisation of family disputes revives an old question about access to justice. This was a question raised initially in response to the rise of the alternative dispute resolution (ADR) movement: if dispute resolution is relocated into private, confidential fora, how do we know whether justice is being delivered, particularly for the less powerful (see, for example, Bottomley 1985; Fiss 1984; Grillo 1991)? Such concerns around ADR had been dissipated to a considerable extent in family law in England and Wales by the fact that, in practice, mediation remained very much an *alternative* to other forms of dispute resolution, and lawyers remained an integral part of family law processes.[4] Since the passing of LASPO, however, this is no longer the case for parties who fall under the legal aid means threshold. Unless they can provide evidence that their case falls within the domestic violence/child abuse exception noted above, their only legally aided option is mediation. Further, since the legal aid threshold is low,[5] and was further reduced by LASPO, there will be many people of limited means who are unable to afford legal representation and for whom mediation may again be the only realistic option. In this context, the question might be rephrased as: does access to mediation constitute access to justice?

Answering this question requires consideration of different possible meanings of 'access to justice'. The phrase may be understood in procedural or substantive terms. At its most minimal, it could simply mean access to an appropriate process

[1] See now *Children and Families Act 2014*, s 10 and *Family Procedure Rules, Practice Direction 3A*.

[2] *Matrimonial Causes Act 1973*, s 41, repealed by the *Children and Families Act 2014*, s 17.

[3] cf s 11 of the *Children and Families Act 2014*, which introduced the presumption that a child's welfare will be furthered by the ongoing involvement in the child's life of both parents. However, this provision functions more as a normative message than as a direct regulatory mechanism, and is thus, we would argue, consistent with the neoliberal governance of behaviour through 'nudging' and encouragement to citizens to make the 'right' choices.

[4] This is perhaps less true in Australia after the introduction of the *Family Law Amendment (Shared Parental Responsibility) Act 2006* (Cth), although the initial exclusion of lawyers from Family Relationship Centre processes was subsequently reversed. It is also less true in the United States where mediation prior to court proceedings is mandatory in many States.

[5] See, for example, Trinder et al (2014) for observations of people appearing in family courts as litigants in person whose income put them above the legal aid threshold but who were unable to afford to pay for legal representation.

for resolving disputes. Or it could have a 'thicker', procedural meaning in terms of access to a particular kind of process, such as access to adjudication by a court. It could also be taken to have a substantive content in terms of access to law or legal entitlements. In the following discussion, we consider the current situation in England and Wales by reference to each of these conceptions of access to justice in reverse order, beginning with substance and moving to consider the 'thicker' and 'thinner' versions of procedure. We conclude, supporting many other authors in this volume, that what many people of limited means now have access to does not constitute justice in any sense.

In the course of the discussion, we draw particularly on evidence from the Mapping Paths to Family Justice project, a three-year, Economic and Social Research Council-funded study of out-of-court family dispute resolution processes, which investigated and compared awareness, experiences and outcomes of three different forms of out-of-court family dispute resolution: solicitor negotiations, mediation and collaborative law.[6] The study commenced with a large, nationally representative survey of public awareness of the three forms of family dispute resolution and of the experiences of dispute resolution of people who had divorced or separated from a cohabiting relationship between 1996 and 2011. Phase 2 involved in-depth interviews with 95 parties who had experienced one or more forms of family dispute resolution since 1996 (although in most cases their experience had been relatively recent), and with 40 professionals trained and practising in one or more of the relevant processes. Phase 3 involved the recording and analysis of the transcripts of five solicitor–client first interviews, five mediation processes and three collaborative law processes, in order to gain a deeper understanding of process dynamics, triangulate with the interview data and identify good practices. While the majority of the data was gathered prior to the introduction of LASPO, the proposed cuts to legal aid were well within the consciousness of the practitioners interviewed, and the parties' pre-LASPO experiences also provide a baseline against which the changes brought about by LASPO can be assessed. All names of interviewees given below are pseudonyms.

II. Access to Law

Access to law might be provided in two different ways in the mediation process: by means of legal advice received prior to, during and/or after mediation; and by means of mediation itself taking place in the 'shadow of the law'. In relation to legal advice, mediation research has consistently emphasised the important role played by solicitors as a supplement to mediation, as reported by both mediators

[6] Economic and Social Research Council Grant No ES/I031812/1 (2011–14). For a summary of findings see Barlow et al (2014).

and parties. In research conducted in the UK on all-issues mediation in the early 1990s, Janet Walker et al found that mediators strongly encouraged parties to seek legal advice before and/or after mediation, and the majority of mediating couples both received legal advice and consulted with independent lawyers as to whether the settlements reached in mediation were 'sensible'. Mediation clients sought reassurance and protection from lawyers to ensure that they were not selling themselves short and that their agreements would be acceptable to the court (Walker 1996). For some clients, lawyers provided comfort and security: 'a safety check on private ordering' (Walker 1996: 72). Subsequent research on information and mediation pilots set up under the *Family Law Act 1996* found that 90 per cent of those who went to mediation also consulted a solicitor (Walker et al 2004: 123, 131–32). Along similar lines, Parkinson (2011: 90) maintains that 'legal advisors provide a system of checks and balances' and that clients are encouraged to seek advice between mediation sessions and at the conclusion of mediation.

In the Australian context, Becky Batagol and Thea Brown found lawyers to be the 'most effective mechanism' for making the law relevant to mediated agreements (Batagol and Brown 2011: 260). In post-mediation consultations, lawyers tried to offer their clients the protection of the law while balancing this with the client's wishes, resulting, in particular, in modifications to unfair or unjust agreements (Batagol and Brown 2011: 241–42, 245, 260). Clear themes that emerged in our party interviews were that those who had received legal advice prior to the mediation process found it very helpful, while others expressed frustration at their inability to obtain clear legal advice as a basis for mediation or at the mediator's inability to give legal advice. For example, Esther said that her solicitor told her straight out what a reasonable financial settlement would be, and she was then happy to mediate armed with that knowledge. By contrast, Jayne felt that in mediation she was negotiating in a legal vacuum. She had wanted her solicitor to give her advice about a reasonable percentage split of the assets but they failed to do so, and she was forced to do her own research via the internet. Mediators interviewed referred to strategies of encouraging parties to obtain legal advice in situations of power imbalance between the parties, and in our recorded sessions we observed mediators referring parties for legal advice as a way of managing expectations, and of ensuring that each party's financial interests were protected.

Prior to the introduction of LASPO, legally aided parties typically consulted a solicitor first, who would then refer them to mediation. So parties would generally enter mediation armed with some initial legal advice. There was little scope for ongoing consultations during the mediation process, but legal aid was available to review agreements reached in mediation and to convert financial agreements into consent orders which, once approved by the court, would make them legally binding. Since the passing of LASPO, however, in Parkinson's (2013: 467) words, legal help to accompany mediation has been 'pared to the bone'. There is no longer any option of pre-mediation legal advice. And while legally aided parties are still eligible for a small amount of funding to pay for a lawyer to draw up consent orders, the minimal payment provided does not allow for comprehensive review and potential fine-tuning of the agreement.

Access to law in the form of explicit, tailored legal advice provided by a solicitor has thus been cut off for legally aided parties under LASPO, and this is likely to have a deleterious effect on the mediation process, with parties forced to negotiate 'in the dark', rather than with knowledge of their legal position. Further, if an agreement is reached that is unfair to one party, post-mediation legal assistance is unlikely to provide an effective back-up, since it is not designed to cover further negotiations, and, as discussed below, there is no legal aid funding to enable a party to take their case to court as a last resort. The alternative, though, is that parties may have implicit access to law, through the mediation process taking place 'in the shadow of the law'.

The concept of bargaining in the shadow of the law was developed by United States (US) socio-legal scholars Robert Mnookin and Lewis Kornhauser (1979), who posited that legal entitlements operate not only in court proceedings, but also in out-of-court negotiation processes, in which they function as bargaining chips for the parties. Batagol and Brown (2011) tested this theory in the context of family mediation in an Australian study in which they observed that the shadow of the law did not fall in a straightforward fashion. They found that, rather than their legal position conferring power on mediating parties, 'the power of the law was often eclipsed by other forms of power in mediation' (Batagol and Brown 2011: 258). One issue identified was the uncertainty of the law, in a context in which parties had no access to specialist legal advice and mediators were unable to fill the gap, or in which the parties had received conflicting legal advice (Batagol and Brown 2011: 200–11, 257–58). More generally, a party's legal position was often mitigated by moral issues of blame and fault (Batagol and Brown 2011: 212–16, 257), and in any event was only as good as their willingness to go to court to enforce it. If they were averse to doing so, for whatever reason, the other party could exploit the situation to bargain them down (Batagol and Brown 2011: 183–200, 257). Since aversion to litigation is a gendered phenomenon, Batagol and Brown concluded that the shadow of the law was weaker for women than for men (2011: 267, 196–99). Overall, they found that the law played a fairly minimal role in mediation, and did not operate in a simple, top-down manner, but was actively constructed or marginalised in the mediation process (Batagol and Brown 2011: 259, 264, 270). The (gendered) power relationship between the parties, rather than the law, was the central factor driving the process and determining outcomes (Batagol and Brown 2011: 184–92, 265).

In the Mapping Paths to Family Justice study, we attempted to determine the extent to which the shadow of the law fell on mediation by reference to two features of mediators' practices: first, giving parties information (as opposed to advice) about the law as a means of educating them about appropriate norms; and secondly, measuring proposed agreements against what a court might order and (explicitly or tacitly) steering parties towards an agreement that fell within the parameters of legal acceptability. There was considerable variation among mediators in both of these practices, but some general patterns emerged. The first was that mediators were more likely to give information about the law in financial cases than in children's cases. The driver for this appears to be the ultimate aim of obtaining a consent order in financial cases, so the negotiations must be legally focused and the outcome must be something a court will endorse. By contrast, it is not expected that agreements reached in children's cases will be submitted to a court; indeed, section 1(5) of the *Children Act 1989* positively discourages the making of court orders in children's cases unless clearly required. Secondly, the majority of mediators said they would be concerned in both children's and financial cases that proposed agreements fell within the 'band of reasonableness' or the 'ambit of discretion' within which a court might decide, or within legally defined notions of fairness to each party. If a proposed agreement fell outside this ambit, mediators would provide information about what courts have laid down as fair and appropriate in similar circumstances, explore other options, reality test and discuss the practical implications, recommend legal advice and/or flag their concerns to the parties' solicitors in the Memorandum of Understanding produced at the end of the mediation process.

We concluded that, in England and Wales, the law casts a light but discernible shadow over mediation, perhaps more so in financial than in children's cases. This was also evident in the fact that the non-legal norms that parties brought into mediation, such as arguments for fathers' rights or a desire to punish the other party for their behaviour in causing the breakdown of the relationship, were clearly filtered out of the agreements reached. Agreements broadly followed legal norms, indicating at least some level of access to law in mediation, and an apparently greater level of access than was found by Batagol and Brown in the Australian context. However, to the extent that this was achieved by means of legal advice as a supplement to mediation, this option is now effectively unavailable for legally aided clients in England and Wales. Thus, it may be expected that access to law has been diminished, if not entirely negated, under LASPO, since both mediators and parties have been deprived of a key tool for ensuring that mediation outcomes are informed by legal norms.

III. Access to Court

Access to a family court is precisely the commodity that LASPO was designed to restrict. Within the small neoliberal state, separating couples are encouraged to take responsibility for sorting out their personal disputes privately, rather than resorting to the courts and thereby consuming scarce public resources. In fact, it has long been maintained in many jurisdictions that the courts should be considered a 'last resort' in family law; that parties are better off reaching their own agreements; and that their children are much better off if their parents do so themselves. The need for court intervention—and, worst of all, a judicial decision—is thus perceived as an index of failure. Nevertheless, it has been conceded that courts have a legitimate role to play in protecting vulnerable parties (who would not be well served by private agreements), in resolving disputes about people's legal rights, and in making decisions in situations in which the parties, for whatever reason, simply cannot agree (see, for example, Eekelaar and Maclean 2013: 4–5).

LASPO, however, denies the last two rationales for court proceedings and reduces the first (the protection of the vulnerable) to a tiny category of cases in which the requisite evidence of domestic violence can be obtained. The Ministry of Justice's (MoJ) Consultation Paper on proposed legal aid reforms, for example, stated:

> [T]he Government's proposed reforms to legal aid are intended to encourage people, rather than going to court too readily at the taxpayer's expense, to seek alternative methods of dispute resolution, reserving the courts as a last resort for legal issues where there is a public interest in providing access to public funding. (MoJ 2010: paragraph 1.8)

In relation to private law children's matters, the paper stated:

> We do not consider that it will generally be in the best interest of the children involved for these essentially personal matters to be resolved in the adversarial forum of a court. The Government's view is that people should take responsibility for resolving such issues themselves, and that this is best for both the parents and the children involved … Legal aid funding can be used to support lengthy and intractable family cases which may be resolved out of court if funding were not available. In such cases, we would like to move to a position where parties are encouraged to settle using mediation, rather than protracting disputes unnecessarily by having a lawyer paid for by legal aid. (MoJ 2010: paragraphs 4.210–4.211)

Not only is the notion of going to court constructed as both moral failure and social irresponsibility on the part of litigants, but the courts are also demonised, with court proceedings portrayed as inevitably adversarial, conflict-inflaming, bitter, drawn-out, expensive and destructive. For example, the government's information leaflet on family mediation, designed to promote mediation in the wake of the introduction of LASPO, persistently contrasts mediation with 'long drawn-out court battles', as if these were the only available alternatives.[7] This ignores the fact that court may be the only appropriate option to protect a vulnerable party, enforce their rights or overcome one party's domination or abuse of power; or that the initiation of court proceedings may be necessary to bring a reluctant party to the negotiating table, to move stalled discussions forward or where attempted mediation has been unsuccessful. These points are discussed further below.

It must be noted, however, that LASPO does not actually prohibit access to a family court; it simply makes legal aid unavailable for court proceedings. So a

[7] Available at: www.gov.uk/government/uploads/system/uploads/attachment_data/file/389896/family-mediation-leaflet.pdf.

party who, for whatever reason, declines the offer of mediation and insists on going to court may still do so, but they either have to pay for representation themselves or go to court as a litigant in person. The absence of legal aid thus operates as a disincentive but not an absolute bar to accessing the court. In fact, what has transpired post LASPO casts doubt on its disincentive effect. While the number of private law court applications fell by around 15 per cent between April 2012 and June 2015,[8] the number of mediation starts fell by around one-third in the same period (MoJ 2015a: 24). And among private law cases proceeding to court, the proportion in which both parties were unrepresented rose from 13 per cent to 31 per cent, with a further 47 per cent of cases in which only one party was represented. Thus, cases with at least one unrepresented party now constitute the great majority of private law cases (MoJ 2015b: 14), suggesting that going to court as a litigant in person has in fact proved more popular—or at least more possible—than engaging in mediation.

We cannot assume from this, however, that people who represent themselves in court are gaining access to justice (see also, Spencer, Chapter 5, this volume, for a discussion of self-representation issues in the criminal law context). A study of litigants in person in private family law cases carried out just prior to the introduction of LASPO pointed out the multiple difficulties experienced by litigants in person in effectively representing themselves in family law proceedings, particularly in more complex matters and at the stage when forensic tasks are required, such as arranging for testing to be conducted, obtaining evidence from third parties and the preparation of bundles and cross-examination (Trinder et al 2014; see also Trinder and Hunter 2015). That study found that, even prior to the passing of LASPO, around half of all litigants in person in private family law cases—most of whom were in person because they were unable to afford legal representation—had some form of vulnerability, such as being a victim of domestic violence, or suffering from mental ill-health, learning difficulties, a physical disability, drug or alcohol dependency or language difficulties, which made self-representation even more challenging and, in some instances, completely defeated their efforts to put their case forward (Trinder et al 2014: 12–21, 26–28). The study also noted that the 'new' litigants in person, disenfranchised from legal aid after LASPO came into force, would likely be even more disadvantaged and vulnerable as a group (Trinder et al 2014: 102–5), and thus have even less capacity to represent themselves effectively in the Family Courts.

The fact that the proportion of litigants in person in private family law proceedings has increased, therefore, is not a cause for celebration or even complacency. Rather, it is a cause for profound unease about what is happening to those litigants (and their children) and the ability of overstretched judges and court welfare

[8] Family Court tables April–June 2015, available at: www.gov.uk/government/statistics/family-court-statistics-quarterly-april-to-june-2015.

officers to provide them with any semblance of a fair process which they are able to understand and in which they are effectively able to participate.[9]

IV. Access to an Appropriate Dispute Resolution Process

As noted above, it is argued that mediation, as a process, is vastly superior to court proceedings or (where these are acknowledged as a process at all) solicitor negotiations. The supposed advantages of mediation are that it is quicker, less traumatic, less inclined to inflame conflict, less damaging to children and less damaging of parental relationships. Indeed, mediation can support and bolster the ongoing co-parental relationship between separating parties, help to improve communication in the future and provide strategies for avoiding or dealing with future conflicts. Most importantly, mediation is said to promote and support parties' autonomy and self-determination. The parties set the agenda rather than having their issues 'translated' into legal terms that may not reflect or deal adequately with their actual concerns. The mediator facilitates discussion between the parties, but does not impose a decision upon them. The parties are free to reach whatever agreement they like, whereas lawyers and courts take decisions out of their hands; and agreements reached between the parties are more likely to prove durable than decisions imposed by a judicial stranger who knows little about their family. The promotion of mediation, therefore, is represented as being in the best interests of parties and their children. More than being *an* appropriate dispute resolution process, it is seen as *the most* appropriate dispute resolution process.

This argument hinges, however, on two key conditions. First, entry into mediation, and the agreements reached, must be voluntary. Autonomy and self-determination are not promoted by coercing people into mediation. This is implicitly recognised by the MIAM process: people may be compelled to receive information about the benefits of mediation, but must retain a free choice as to whether to proceed with it. However, voluntariness of entry is compromised by the lack of realistic alternatives. If the alternatives are undesirable (such as doing nothing), unaffordable (hiring a solicitor, for example) or unimaginable (such as self-representation in court), then mediation ceases to be a voluntary process and its benefits are unlikely to be realised. Just as importantly, as Batagol and Brown's

[9] The Children and Family Court Advisory and Support Service (Cafcass) provides expert social work input to Family Court cases involving children. Among other things, Cafcass officers undertake initial safeguarding checks to identify any safety issues when cases are filed, and thereafter may meet with parties at court to assist them to reach agreement; meet with children to obtain their views, wishes and feelings; write reports and make recommendations to the court on child arrangements as requested.

(2011) research demonstrated, there need to be realistic alternatives to a mediated agreement. If it proves impossible for one party to reach an agreement that reflects their interests and does not simply perpetuate the power differentials in the relationship, that party must have somewhere else to go. An agreement reached because there is nowhere else to go likewise cannot be described as voluntary. Such an agreement is effectively imposed by the other party, and hence is not autonomy enhancing, not in the party's best interests and not likely to prove durable. Paradoxically, by promoting mediation to the exclusion of other options, LASPO is likely to have reduced the appropriateness of mediation for publicly funded clients.

The second condition is that, while mediation may be the most appropriate form of dispute resolution in many cases, it is widely acknowledged *not* to be appropriate for some kinds of parties and cases, by no means confined to those who fall within the very narrow domestic violence/child abuse exceptions under LASPO. To begin with, (alleged) *perpetrators* of domestic violence and child abuse are not eligible for litigation legal aid, but LASPO itself acknowledges that their cases are not suitable for mediation. Secondly, mediation is not appropriate in many cases of domestic violence where the victim is unable to produce the evidence necessary to obtain legally aided representation, or where she may have evidence but is unable to find a legal aid solicitor to represent her. A recent study conducted by Rights of Women found that around half of all women who had experienced or were experiencing domestic violence did not have any of the prescribed forms of evidence to access litigation legal aid. This might be because they had experienced primarily emotional abuse and controlling behaviour which is less likely to generate the kinds of evidence required. Or they did not know how to obtain relevant evidence, or they sought evidence but it was either not provided or they were charged a prohibitive amount for it to be provided. Finally, it might be because of the fact that evidence 'expires' after two years, whereas the ongoing effects of abuse do not.[10] The study also found that almost one-third of 141 respondents to an online survey in England and Wales found it very difficult to locate a legal aid solicitor who deals with family law in their area or within affordable travelling distance (Rights of Women, Women's Aid and Welsh Women's Aid 2013).

Thirdly, parties and cases may be unsuitable for mediation for a range of reasons other than domestic violence. In the Mapping Paths to Family Justice study, we concluded that one size does not fit all when it comes to family dispute resolution, and we sought to 'map' the kinds of parties and cases best suited to different forms of dispute resolution (see Hunter et al 2014). We found that a party-interactive process such as mediation is appropriate where both parties: are willing to engage in the process; share a degree of mutual trust and respect; are relatively amicable; have little conflict and/or share a mutual desire to maintain

[10] Following the Court of Appeal's decision in R *(Rights of Women) v The Secretary of State for Justice and the Lord Chancellor* [2016] EWCA Civ 91, the time limit for certain types of evidence of domestic violence was extended in April 2016 from two years to five years.

cordial relations; want to achieve the best outcomes for their children; are committed to financial transparency and willing to make full financial disclosure; are on a relatively equal footing in terms of resources, information and power; either communicate well or wish to improve communication; are willing and able to listen and appreciate the other's point of view; are not starting from widely divergent positions; and are open-minded and willing to compromise. On the other hand, some parties need the support, advice and guidance of a lawyer through the process because they are at a significant psychological disadvantage (for example, having difficulty coming to terms with the end of the relationship); have significantly less power in the relationship (for example, due to intellectual capacity, bullying or domination); or are vulnerable in some other way (for example, guilty about the breakup, unable to make decisions or find it difficult to grasp the details of their financial position). Among our party interviewees, for example, Tracy felt too emotionally raw to contemplate mediation: 'That's why I said I didn't want to go for mediation at that point because I just didn't feel that I could do it … I didn't really feel strong enough'. Similarly, Marcus felt he needed legal representation:

> Because I was emotionally still in quite a weak space, I didn't feel in a strong enough position to negotiate on my own behalf with just a mediator, say. I needed someone as I was distraught and struggling with digesting all the information, as my head was spinning with what was going on emotionally, and so yes, I felt that I needed someone with me to guide me through it.

Kim, on the other hand, could see that she would be pressurised in mediation: 'his personality can be of a bullying tendency and I just felt that I could be in that room just being kind of talked at … and feeling bullied into backing down. So I was resistant'.

An arm's-length process rather than face-to-face negotiations is needed where one or both parties are: unwilling to listen to the other party or understand their position, very controlling, entrenched in their position and not prepared to compromise, seeking vindication or vengeance, prepared to 'fight to the bitter end' on principle, intent on securing the best deal for themselves in negotiations or unwilling to make financial disclosure. And in some cases, only court proceedings will be appropriate: for example, where a party refuses to make full financial disclosure, refuses to accept that the relationship is over when the other party has an urgent need to finalise post-separation arrangements, is not prepared to take responsibility for decision-making or is entrenched in a strategic position (for example, in possession of the house or children) with nothing to gain by compromise.

Other kinds of cases in which mediation is unlikely to be appropriate include: factual disputes over matters such as paternity or drug or alcohol abuse, where the relevant party will not agree to voluntary testing; relocation disputes where the scope for compromise is severely limited; urgent matters such as cases of child abduction; and where a party has a mental illness that affects their own or the other party's ability to participate in the process safely and effectively, potentially affects the safety of a child, or where the severity and consequences of their condition are in dispute.

Fourthly, while one party may be willing to attend mediation, the other party may refuse to do so. This may particularly be the case where one party is eligible for legal aid but the other is not, and would therefore have to pay for mediation. In order to encourage non-legally-aided parties to attend MIAMs, the Legal Aid Agency will fund both MIAMs so long as one of the parties is legally aided. But this still leaves the self-funded party paying for mediation. Following a recommendation by the Family Mediation Task Force (2014), the free MIAM for self-funded parties where the other party is legally aided has been extended to a free first mediation session as well. But this simply displaces the problem: the self-funded party may be unwilling to continue with mediation after the first session if agreement is not reached, or there may be undue pressure to reach agreement in the first session (Parkinson 2015). Regardless of incentives, however, our research indicated that some parties simply resisted or refused to engage with whatever process their ex-partner wanted to pursue. This is a particular example of a lack of trust and respect rendering mediation inappropriate. Indeed, prior to the introduction of LASPO, the major reason for mediators certifying cases as inappropriate for mediation under the Legal Aid Funding Code or the Pre-Application Protocol was the unwillingness of the other party to engage in the process (Bloch, McLeod and Toombs 2014: 35).

Finally, mediation is by definition no longer appropriate when it fails to resolve the dispute. Resolution rates for publicly funded mediation have remained stable at around 65 per cent (MoJ 2015a: 24–25). That leaves 35 per cent of publicly funded cases attempting mediation unable to reach a resolution. In the past, the failure of mediation would have resulted in either continuation of dispute resolution by means of solicitor negotiations, or the issuing of court proceedings. As a result of the introduction of LASPO, however, clients in around one-third of publicly funded mediation cases will not be offered an alternative appropriate process after mediation breaks down.

The space between the ability to reach a successful (and we should also emphasise voluntary) resolution of a dispute in mediation and eligibility for litigation legal aid has been labelled 'the LASPO gap' (Hunter 2014). It is clear that this space is occupied by a wide variety (and significant number) of people with family law disputes. While these people technically have access to mediation under LASPO, they do not have access to justice, even within its most minimal meaning.

V. Conclusion

Combining the three conceptions of access to justice discussed above, Hazel Genn has argued that a just process is one that is 'readily accessible and effective', and provides reasonable access to legal advice and representation, to appropriate form(s) of dispute resolution, and to the courts, without undue delay or cost and not dependent on personal resources (Genn 2010: 18, 115; see also Cornford 2016: 28–29). Clearly, what LASPO provides to people with family disputes who are unable to afford their own legal representation falls far short of these prescriptions. Mediation may be readily accessible, and it may also be effective in the majority of cases in which it is attempted, but it is not effective in producing agreement in a substantial minority of cases, or for the significant group of people for whom it is not an appropriate process at all. Reasonable access to legal advice and representation, to other appropriate forms of dispute resolution (such as solicitor negotiations) and to the courts is no longer available. And while mediation is accessible, independently of personal resources, and without undue delay or cost, this is not true of any other form of dispute resolution or of court proceedings, as alternatives, if mediation is unsuccessful or inappropriate. On any measure, therefore, a regime that provides only for access to mediation does not provide access to justice.

It must be acknowledged, though, that this does not represent a failure of legislative objectives. For all the claims made for mediation, providing access to justice is not one of them. Rather, providing access to justice for people with private family law disputes is no longer taken to be a relevant goal of the legal aid system, or of the neoliberal state more generally. According to the government's response to the consultation on legal aid reform, 'it is not the case that everyone is entitled to legal representation, funded by the taxpayer, for any dispute or to a particular outcome in litigation' (MoJ 2011: paragraph 140). Instead, the policy focus on mediation is justified on the basis that mediation is the best and most cost-effective means to assist people to take personal responsibility for resolving disagreements resulting from their private choices. As the Mapping Paths to Family Justice project and the post-LASPO experience to date demonstrate, however, even this objective may not be achieved, as divorcing and separating parties may have good grounds for not embracing mediation, and in fact have largely failed to do so. Conversely, the growing ranks of litigants in person suggest that aspirations towards access to justice remain strong.

References

Barlow, A, Hunter, R, Smithson, J and Ewing, J (2014) *Mapping Paths to Family Justice: Briefing Paper and Report on Key Findings* (Exeter, University of Exeter).

Batagol, B and Brown, T (2011) *Bargaining in the Shadow of the Law: The Case of Family Mediation* (Sydney, Themis Press).

Bloch, A, McLeod, R and Toombs, B (2014) *Mediation Information and Assessment Meetings (MIAMs) and Mediation in Private Family Law Disputes: Qualitative Research Findings* (London, Ministry of Justice).

Bottomley, A (1985) 'What is Happening to Family Law? A Feminist Critique of Conciliation' in J Brophy and C Smart (eds), *Women in Law: Explorations in Law, Family and Sexuality* (London, Routledge).

Cornford, T (2016) 'The Meaning of Access to Justice' in E Palmer, T Cornford, A Guinchard and Y Marique (eds), *Access to Justice: Beyond the Policies and Politics of Austerity* (Oxford, Hart Publishing).

Eekelaar, J and Maclean, M (2013) *Family Justice: The Work of Family Judges in Uncertain Times* (Oxford, Hart Publishing).

Family Mediation Task Force (2014) *Report of the Family Mediation Task Force* (London, Ministry of Justice).

Fiss, O (1984) 'Against Settlement' 93 *Yale Law Journal* 1073.

Grillo, T (1991) 'The Mediation Alternative: Process Dangers for Women' 100 *Yale Law Journal* 1545.

Hunter, R (2014) 'Exploring the LASPO Gap' 44 *Family Law* 660.

Hunter, R, Barlow, A, Smithson, J and Ewing, J (2014) 'Mapping Paths to Family Justice: Matching Parties, Cases and Processes' 44 *Family Law* 1404.

Ministry of Justice [MoJ] (2010) *Proposals for the Reform of Legal Aid in England and Wales* (Cm 7967) (London, Ministry of Justice).

—— (2011) *Reform of Legal Aid in England and Wales: The Government Response* (Cm 8072, 2011) (London, MoJ).

—— (2015a) *Legal Aid Statistics in England and Wales: April to June 2015* (London, MoJ).

—— (2015b) *Family Law Statistics Quarterly: April to June 2015* (London, MoJ).

Mnookin, RH and Kornhauser, L (1979) 'Bargaining in the Shadow of the Law: The Case of Divorce' 88 *Yale Law Journal* 950.

Parkinson, L (2011) 'Family Mediation: Ideology or New Discipline? Part I' 41 *Family Law* 88.

—— (2013) 'Co-mediation on Family Matters: Cost-Effective or Unaffordable?' 43 *Family Law* 467.

—— (2015) 'Mediation and the Government Response to LASPO' 45 *Family Law* 1131.

Rights of Women, Women's Aid and Welsh Women's Aid (2013) *Evidencing Domestic Violence: A Barrier to Family Law Legal Aid* (London, Rights of Women).

Trinder, EJ and Hunter, R (2015) 'Access to Justice? Litigants in Person before and after LASPO' 45 *Family Law* 535.

Trinder, L, Hunter, R, Hitchings, E, Miles, J, Moorhead, R, Smith, L, Sefton, M, Hinchly, V, Bader, K and Pearce, J (2014) *Litigants in Person in Private Family Law Cases* (London, Ministry of Justice).

Walker, J (1996) 'Is There a Future for Lawyers in Divorce?' 10 *International Journal of Law, Policy and the Family* 52.

Walker, J, McCarthy, P, Stark, C and Laing, K (2004) *Picking Up the Pieces: Marriage and Divorce Two Years after Information Provision* (London, Department of Constitutional Affairs).

Treaties, Conventions, Principles, Directives, Rules and Legislation

Children Act 1989
Children and Families Act 2014
Civil Legal Aid (Procedure) Regulations 2012
Family Law Act 1996
Family Law Amendment (Shared Parental Responsibility) Act 2006 (Cth)
Family Procedure Rules, Practice Direction 3A—Family Mediation, Information and Assessment Meetings (MIAMS)
Legal Aid, Sentencing and Punishment of Offenders Act 2012
Matrimonial Causes Act 1973

14

Insights into Inequality: Women's Access to Legal Aid in Victoria

PASANNA MUTHA-MERENNEGE[1]

I. Introduction

There is a widely held belief in Australia that legal aid is a cornerstone of our justice system, and it provides the most marginalised and disadvantaged in our society with real and meaningful access to justice. In 2013, the United Nations Special Rapporteur on the independence of judges and lawyers, Gabriela Knaul, declared legal aid to be a human right in itself:

> Legal aid is both a right in itself and an essential precondition for the exercise and enjoyment of a number of human rights, including the rights to a fair trial and to an effective remedy … It represents an important safeguard that contributes to ensuring the fairness and public trust in the administration of justice. (Office of the High Commissioner for Human Rights 2013)

Despite the importance of legal aid for those most marginalised, Australia struggles to meet the lofty ideals of universal access and equality in the justice system. Nationally, funding for the legal assistance sector is comprised of a patchwork of contributions from federal, State and Territory governments, spread across legal aid commissions (LACs), community legal centres (CLCs) and Aboriginal and Torres Strait Islander legal services. In 2014, the Productivity Commission of Australia, in a review of access to justice arrangements, noted that Australia's funding for legal assistance services was, per capita, lower than that of other nations with similar legal systems (Productivity Commission 2014: 734). The Commission's report also found that funding had failed to keep up with demand for free legal services. In some instances, funding had been cut, leaving providers with difficult decisions regarding the availability of their services.

In recent years in Australia, the legal problems arising from family violence and separation have emerged as two areas of growing unmet legal need. The legal

[1] The author wishes to acknowledge and thank Helen Matthews, Principal Solicitor of WLSV, for her assistance in the writing of this chapter.

issues for which assistance is commonly sought include family law property disputes; family violence intervention orders—a civil order that restricts an abuser from, for example, approaching or contacting their victim; and family law parenting matters, such as whether a child spends time with an abusive parent and whether that time is supervised.

In 2014, in Victoria alone, there were 68,134 family violence incidents recorded by Victoria Police—an increase of 82.2 per cent since 2010 (Crime Statistics Agency Victoria 2014). Similarly, information related to separation and divorce was the most requested legal information from Victoria Legal Aid (VLA) in the 2013–14 financial year (VLA 2014: p 18, see Table 1 below).

Table 1: Top five legal information service matters (VLA 2014)

Matter type	Number of matters
Spending time with children	8827
Family violence intervention orders	8086
Property settlement	6539
Infringements	6038
Who children live with	4550

In addition, VLA's statistics highlight that in this single financial year (2013–14), over 13,000 matters related to children in family law disputes.

It is widely accepted that women experience family violence at higher rates than men. Furthermore, leaving an abusive relationship may give rise to legal issues involving separation, children and divorce. As a result, women are more likely to seek legal assistance in the areas of family law and family violence law than, for example, summary or indictable crime. Yet despite this level of legal need in family law, access to legal aid for family law matters has become increasingly limited—often vulnerable to budget deficits in LACs, Commonwealth government funding cuts and the failure of Commonwealth funding to keep up with demand.

This chapter provides an insight into the real experiences of women who lost their entitlement to family law legal aid in Victoria in 2013, after VLA introduced changes to its eligibility guidelines. These changes included ceasing to fund final contested family law hearings ('the trial') in certain circumstances, which resulted in parties (in some instances) losing their legal representation only weeks before their trial date. The chapter illustrates the precariousness of legal aid and, more importantly, how limiting access can have broader social, economic and health-related consequences for women who struggle to secure good outcomes in their family law cases. The chapter also considers the ways in which CLCs were impacted as demand for their services increased, and the response of private practitioners who increasingly withdrew from legally aided family law work due to the restrictive nature of the funding. Finally, it examines more recent developments including roll-back measures by VLA and the future of funding for LACs.

In exploring these issues in this chapter, I draw from my experiences while working at the Women's Legal Service Victoria (WLSV). The WLSV assists some of the most marginalised women to access justice in family law. The service has a unique, on-the-ground perspective of the consequences for women of being unable to access legal aid—not only in relation to their immediate legal matter, but also in terms of their long-term social, economic and personal wellbeing.

II. The Crisis in Victoria's Legal Aid Funding in 2013

In December 2012, VLA announced significant changes to how it would fund criminal and family law cases in Victoria. Citing a budget deficit, Managing Director of VLA, Bevan Warner, stated:

> The changes we are making in family law reflect the fact that we cannot meet the need for legal help without additional investment, especially from the Commonwealth whose share of legal aid funding has dropped from half to a third since 1997. (VLA 2012)

Of particular relevance to women experiencing family violence were changes to the eligibility guidelines in family law proceedings. Until 2013, parties who met VLA's general eligibility criteria and were deemed 'priority clients' could access grants of legal aid for representation in their family law trials in parenting disputes. Priority clients included persons experiencing or at risk of family violence; persons with an intellectual disability, serious physical disability or acquired brain injury; and persons at risk of homelessness. The grants of legal aid available included funding for both an instructing solicitor and a barrister to appear for the duration of the trial. These grants of legal aid could be accessed by private lawyers representing legally aided clients, CLCs and in-house VLA lawyers.

The changes that came into effect on 7 January 2013, however, restricted access to funding in family law trials. VLA's new eligibility guidelines provided that, if one party were unrepresented at a trial in parenting disputes, the other party would not be eligible for legal aid. Should one party have existing private or pro bono (not legally aided) representation, this guideline did not apply—in other words, the opposing party was able to access legally aided representation should they meet the other stringent eligibility and means-tested criteria. At a practical level, this guideline change impacted parties most at need, who were considered priority clients—where one or other party could not afford or chose not to have legal representation. Perversely, it also meant that if both parties in a case had legal aid leading up to the trial, both would lose their legal aid (and thereby their legal representation) at the actual *trial*. Restrictions were also placed on eligibility criteria in a range of other areas of law, including summary crime and child protection. The changes were met with surprise and dismay by the legal profession, the judiciary and individuals affected by the change. The very real consequences of the changes for women victims of family violence are explored in more detail below.

III. What Happens when Women cannot Access Legal Aid?

Often family law matters that proceed to trial are complex cases that frequently include a long history of serious family violence, drug and alcohol abuse, physical and mental health issues, and issues of child safety (particularly in relation to child sexual abuse). Such issues may be related to one or both parties to the dispute.

The cohort most impacted by the legal aid restrictions imposed on family law guidelines in 2013 included women who had experienced family violence (who were deemed to be VLA's priority clients) and who were in entrenched legal disputes with their ex-partner regarding the care of their children. On the ground, the outcomes included legally aided clients being advised that they would not be eligible for legal aid to fund their trial, while private practitioners were withdrawing from family law proceedings on the basis that they would not be paid by VLA to represent their clients at trial.

Without legally aided representation at trial, women who had experienced family violence were faced with the options of representing themselves at trial, or negotiating a settlement with the other party. In high-conflict cases, where women are dealing with issues such as post-traumatic stress disorder (PTSD), drug and alcohol abuse, and often recovering from long histories of family violence, self-representation could not offer a good (or just, or fair) legal outcome. Frequently added to this mix are the significant barriers that exist in the family law system for women from Aboriginal and Torres Strait Islander communities, women who are newly arrived in Australia and have limited English skills, and women with intellectual or physical disability. For these women, engaging in the family law system without legal representation is close to impossible.

A further disincentive for women wishing to represent themselves in court was the fact that they risked being directly cross-examined by their abusive ex-partner, who was likely to be unrepresented either due to having also lost their legal aid for trial or because they were unable to access other forms of legal representation. Unlike the legislative protections that exist for 'vulnerable witnesses' in sexual offence trials and intervention order final hearings, no such protections exist for vulnerable witnesses under the *Family Law Act 1975* (Cth). This means that not only may women find themselves subject to cross-examination by abusive ex-partners, but they also face the burden of having to cross-examine their abusive ex-partner in order to test the evidence being presented in court.

Family law is governed by complex legislation, processes and procedures, which make it particularly difficult for unrepresented parties to manage and run their own cases. In particular, there is a requirement that episodes of family violence and risk be set out in supporting affidavit material. Articulating the incidents of family violence in a manner that is relevant to the court proceeding is difficult without the assistance of a lawyer. For women forced to represent themselves following the 2013 changes, drafting detailed affidavit material setting out the history of family violence was near impossible. It meant that important, legally relevant information regarding risk to children and the history of abuse was not available to the judge hearing the case.

For some WLSV clients, they lost their legal representation only weeks or even days before their final trial date, leaving the women involved particularly vulnerable. While WLSV lawyers spent a great deal of time and effort securing barristers to act pro bono in trials, unfortunately, family law is an area where there is limited availability of pro bono legal assistance, which made it particularly difficult after the VLA changes to secure legal representation for women. Additionally, in cases where pro bono legal representation was secured, a perverse benefit to the other party emerged, as they then became eligible for legal aid according to the guidelines (as the funding restriction did not apply where one party had private or pro bono legal representation at trial).

In the context of the above considerations, achieving access to justice for women became near impossible. Specifically, women who were forced to negotiate a settlement or proceed to trial unrepresented were: at risk of being directly cross-examined by their abusive ex-partner and subjected to emotional stress, trauma and exacerbation of physical and psychological issues; unable to articulate their case and their fears for their children at trial, resulting in poor legal outcomes (with the risk of losing the care of their child); and pressured into settling and agreeing to children's care arrangements that were inappropriate in order to avoid having to go to trial.

To address some of these limitations, the WLSV's staff, located at the Melbourne Federal Circuit Court and Family Court, assisted women who came to court on the day of their trial without any legal representation. The case study below reflects the experience of one woman assisted by WLSV on the day of her trial. Identifying details of the case have been removed.

> *Jenny is a single mother with three children under the age of 18. Her ex-partner, David, has spent time in prison and has drug and alcohol issues. During the relationship, there were serious incidents of family violence and a longstanding intervention order exists. Jenny suffers from PTSD as a result of a serious assault against her by David. David was convicted of this assault. Jenny's children have not seen their father in several years. Jenny applied to the Federal Circuit Court in 2012 for an order that her children live solely with her.*
>
> *Jenny was granted legal aid and had private lawyers (funded by legal aid) to assist her in preparing her case. After the VLA guidelines changed, her private lawyer wrote to VLA requesting that legal aid funding continue for trial representation. Her lawyer argued that she was extremely vulnerable as a victim of family violence and as someone who suffered mental health issues. VLA responded by saying that the guideline changes provided no flexibility for special circumstances and that she would not be eligible for trial representation if her ex-partner was also unrepresented. Unfortunately, her ex-partner also lost his legal representation for trial, as he too had a grant of legal aid. Both Jenny and David came unrepresented to court on the day of the trial.*

Jenny was terrified of facing David in court. She asked to sit in the safe room while she spoke to the WLSV court duty lawyer. The court duty lawyer then spoke to David to try to negotiate a settlement. Every time it was mentioned to Jenny that if negotiations broke down she would have to go into court by herself, she fell apart. She started shaking and crying. The thought of David not only being in the same room as her, but also being able to directly cross-examine her, was too much for Jenny to handle.

It took five hours for the duty lawyer to negotiate a settlement between David and Jenny. During that time, Jenny sat in the safe room contemplating the real possibility that she would have to run a trial by herself, against the man who had seriously assaulted her.

At the time Jenny's case was listed, there were no exceptions provided by VLA in relation to eligibility for trial funding. In late 2013, however, VLA introduced some narrow exceptions regarding certain categories of people—namely, people diagnosed with a mental illness, those with an acquired brain injury and, in limited circumstances, family violence victims. However, the exceptions had limited applicability, due to the very specific nature of the criteria listed. For example, a person with a diagnosed mental illness had to be receiving services under the *Mental Health Act 1986* (Vic)[2] in order to satisfy the exception, and in the case of a victim of family violence, the perpetrator had to have a criminal conviction for breaching an intervention order or a conviction for a related family violence offence. Thus, similar problems to those identified by Organ and Sigafoos (Chapter 9, this volume) existed for vulnerable women in having to 'prove' a history of family violence to be eligible for an exemption from the no-funding rule.

A. The Broader Social and Economic Consequences for Women and Their Children

There is limited empirical research on the broader social and economic impacts of the 2013 legal aid cuts for women who were unable to access legal aid in their family law proceedings. However, as part of my experience working with disadvantaged women at the WLSV, I observed first-hand the long-term social and economic consequences for those who were unable to access legally aided representation, and discuss these outcomes below.

Access to legally aided representation in family law cases not only assists women to secure more just legal outcomes, but it also promotes safety, housing security, economic security and overall wellbeing. For example, an equal and just family law property settlement may enable a woman to remain in her family home, or provide sufficient funds to ensure that she and her children can obtain long-term, secure housing. Access to legal representation may also assist a woman to secure sole parental responsibility where an ex-partner's behaviour places a child or children at risk of harm.

[2] Note: this act has now changed to the *Mental Health Act 2014* (Vic).

The inverse is true where women are *unable* to access legally aided representation in family law cases (see, for example, Figure 1 below). The long-term consequences may include a heightened risk of violence and/or death; financial hardship and poverty; homelessness; and diminished emotional, mental and physical wellbeing. These negative consequences are far worse for women who experience intersecting forms of disadvantage, such as disability or being newly arrived in Australia, because of the entrenched discrimination and systemic barriers.

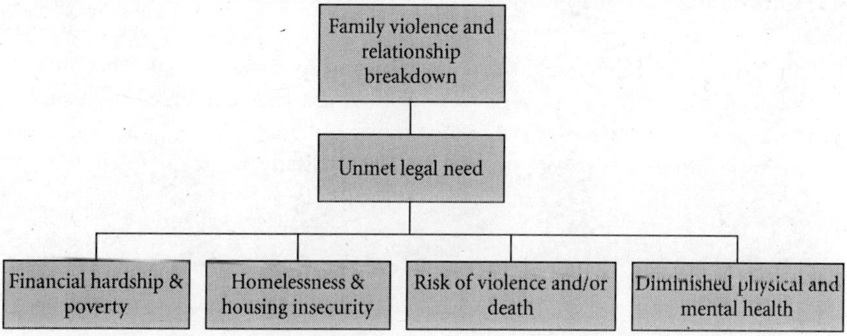

Figure 1: Nexus between 'unmet legal need' and social/economic problems

B. Risk of Future Family Violence and/or Death

The most significant consequence of being unable to access legal aid for women who experience family violence and relationship breakdown is the future risk to their safety and that of their children. The following case study provides an illustration of how free legal information, advice and representation can be critical to the decisions that women make with respect to leaving a violent relationship and negotiating safe arrangements for their children in spending properly supervised time with a violent parent.

> *Adriana has a four-year-old son, James, and lives with her husband, Simon. She has a part-time job, yet spends most of her time caring for James. Simon has a long history of being violent and abusive towards Adriana. He has assaulted her and verbally abused her on many occasions, including in front of James. He has also been intimidating towards James, and James is evidently frightened of him. James has now developed his own behavioural problems as a result of the violence, including bed wetting.*
>
> *Whenever Adriana tells Simon that she wants them to separate, he threatens to violently come after her and to make sure she never sees James again. He says that he'll drag her through the courts if he has to, to get full custody of James. He has also said that he'll make sure she doesn't get a cent of his money.*
>
> *Adriana is terrified of Simon and the consequences of leaving him. She fears losing James and the thought of leaving her son in his care is too much for her to handle. She also can't imagine how she would support herself and her son if she had to leave their home and survive on her small, part-time wage.*

For Adriana, effective legal advice and representation could allay some of her fears with respect to the care of James were she and Simon to separate. It could also address her fears in relation to her financial and housing security. Securing access to good legal advice and representation during negotiations may also avoid any pressure Adriana might feel to agree to unsafe parenting arrangements, where James might be placed with an abusive parent.

C. Financial Hardship and Poverty

Family violence and the breakdown of a relationship are key social determinants of financial hardship and poverty for women and their children in Australia. Figure 2 below illustrates how women who are unable to access good legal outcomes in the family law system may be financially disadvantaged.

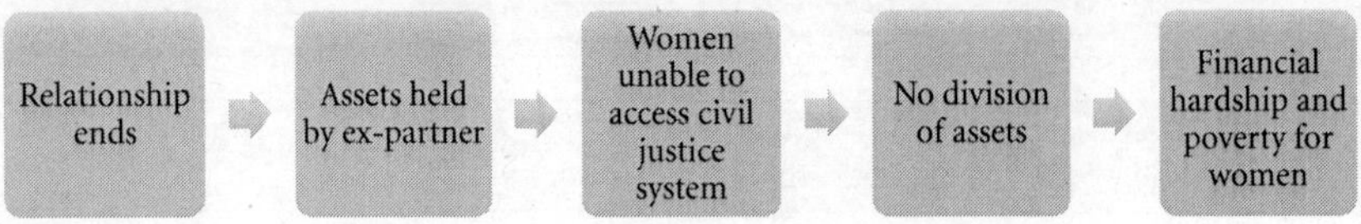

Figure 2: Poor outcomes for women unable to access the justice system

When women are able to access legal aid in family law cases, they are more likely to secure equitable outcomes in relation to property settlements, allocation of debt, access to spousal maintenance and appropriate child support payments. Although the financial benefit for women may be small, it can have a significant impact on their economic and social wellbeing well into the future. For example, a small settlement in relation to the division of property can provide a woman with the money needed to pay a bond for a rental property, a car (if it is transferred into her name) so that she can drop her children off at school and drive to work, and/or a share of superannuation to provide some financial security for her retirement.

Securing effective family law remedies is particularly important given the disproportionate impact of relationship breakdown and family violence on women. A 2009 study by the Australian Institute of Family Studies found that at least 60 per cent of separated women experience some form of financial hardship, such as going without food or being unable to pay bills, in the first year after divorce. Four years after divorce, in financial terms, women were still found to be significantly worse off than divorced men, and compared with single women who had never divorced (De Vaus et al 2009).

According to the Australian Bureau of Statistics (ABS), women continue to be the primary carer in most single-parent families, accounting for 83 per cent of such families. It is these women who are most vulnerable to financial hardship and poverty (ABS 2011). The ABS also found that women who reported violence by an intimate partner were more likely than women who reported no violence to have received a minority share of assets at the end of a relationship, highlighting again the importance of representation in these separation contexts.

Economic abuse is a key element in the dynamics and nature of family violence. A 2007 Australian study into family violence found that 80 per cent of victims surveyed had experienced financial abuse (Evans 2007). Economic abuse limits women's ability to 'acquire, use and maintain' economic resources and can lead to women and their children experiencing financial hardship and poverty (Adams et al 2008: 564). Additionally, women's economic recovery from relationship breakdown and family violence is constrained by a range of factors, including debt incurred during a marriage (such as mortgages and credit cards); reduced earning capacity due to having a greater role in caring for children after separation; lack of adequate child support; and increased household expenses (such as transport, food, school fees) which must be covered by a sole income or Centrelink benefit.[3] Effective legal remedies in family law can assist women to become financially stable and avoid homelessness. However, where women are unaware of such interventions or cannot access them due to the lack of legal advice and representation, then the fear of financial hardship and related factors like homelessness (discussed below) can compel them to remain with a violent partner.

D. Homelessness

Poor legal outcomes in family law cases for women experiencing family violence and relationship breakdown can also lead to housing insecurity and homelessness. The reasons for this occurring include women who leave the family home after a family violence incident being unable to return, and women being unable to negotiate positive outcomes in property settlements, leading to financial insecurity and loss of their home. If women are unable to access timely and specialist legal advice and representation, they will likely be unaware of their options in terms of securing an outcome in their family law case that enables them to remain in their home safely.

Marginalisation, disability and unemployment can further compound women's exposure to housing insecurity and homelessness. The 2008 White Paper on homelessness, *The Road Home: A National Approach to Reducing Homelessness*, identified family violence as a major driver of homelessness and the single biggest reason for people seeking homelessness assistance. The White Paper also identified relationship breakdown as the second most common reason for people seeking assistance from specialist homelessness services.

Women and their children experience homelessness in different ways from men. For example, women may be more likely to flee a violent home and stay with

[3] Centrelink was established in 1997 as a statutory agency responsible for the delivery of human services under the provisions of the *Commonwealth Service Delivery Agency Act 1997* (Cth).

a friend, sleeping on their floor, or with a family member, which is still a form of homelessness. While research suggests that over 40 per cent of people experiencing homelessness are women (Colak 2008), women's experiences of homelessness and strategies to meet their specific housing needs are not always part of the mainstream policy debate. Additionally, women experiencing family violence and relationship breakdown may struggle to keep or access safe, secure and appropriate housing. Without access to temporary housing, women are left with few options other than to return to an abusive and dangerous relationship.

IV. Broader Consequences of Legal Aid Cuts for the Justice System

Recent cuts to legal aid also provide a useful example of how narrowing access to legal aid can have an impact on the broader legal system. The 2013 cuts impacted on the operation of the Federal Circuit Court and Family Court, the number of private practitioners engaged in legally aided family law work and other legal assistance providers such as CLCs. Each of these impacts is discussed in the sections below.

A. Impact on the Courts

The changes to legal aid funding directly correlate with a rise in the number of unrepresented parties in the Family Court. According to the Family Court of Australia's 2014–15 Annual Report, almost 30 per cent of cases before the Court involved at least one party with no legal representation (Family Court of Australia 2015: 8). There was also a sharp increase in the number of cases where both parties were unrepresented before the Court: in 2011–12, five per cent of all cases had both parties unrepresented. In 2012–13, this figure rose to nine per cent, and has remained at this level since that time (Family Court of Australia 2015: 66). At the time of the cuts, the Chief Justice of the Family Court, Diana Bryant, expressed her concerns regarding their potential impact: 'Courts can only make decisions on the evidence, and the failure to provide representation to both parties severely compromises that … and makes it harder to make the optimum decisions for children' (cited in Lee 2013).

As flagged above, the complex legislative requirements in family law and the complex procedural steps place a significant burden on unrepresented parties attempting to navigate the legal system. Accordingly, courts are now required to spend extra resources and time assisting unrepresented parties, which itself has budgetary and efficiency consequences, including adjournments and unworkable parental agreements.

At the time of the cuts, the WLSV's lawyers observed an increase in the number of adjournments of trial dates being sought, in circumstances where parties were desperately attempting to secure alternative legal representation. This in turn contributed to court delays, long court lists and the prolonging of already lengthy family court proceedings. The WLSV's lawyers also observed that in some cases where parties made parenting arrangements without legal assistance these arrangements proved to be unworkable and unrealistic, giving rise to parties returning to court to have the arrangements changed.

B. Impact on CLCs

For legal assistance providers such as CLCs, the changes resulted in an increase in demand for services. Greater numbers of women were contacting the WLSV, seeking assistance for family law trials that were only weeks away. Lawyers scrambled to secure pro bono barristers for their own clients that were no longer legally aided. For a sector that was already stretched and battling to meet existing demand, the changes placed further pressure on their services and resources.

C. Impact on the Private Legal Profession

The 2013 changes also had an impact on private family law practitioners undertaking legally aided cases. In existing cases, practitioners were unable to access grants of legal aid to continue to act at trial, forcing many of them to file notices of discontinuance. These changes also acted as a disincentive to taking on new legally aided cases, as practitioners were not prepared to take on a case knowing that they might be unable (and unpaid) to act for the client at trial.

V. The Response From VLA

In September 2014, VLA commenced a broad review of its family law legal services, including its family law eligibility guidelines. In discussing the review, VLA acknowledged that the 2013 cuts had been 'difficult for many people' and highlighted the need for a comprehensive review of its family law services (VLA 2015). An options paper was released in January 2015 and written submissions were sought from stakeholders. In June 2015, VLA released a final report responding to the concerns raised, which included 35 actions to improve VLA's family law services. Among the proposed actions were changes to the family law eligibility guidelines (VLA 2015). The proposed changes included removing the restriction on funding for representation at trial for clients who would otherwise be eligible for legal aid. The effect of this change when implemented was to reinstate legal aid funding for family law trials—the position before the 2013 changes. VLA also proposed reintroducing grants of legal aid for property disputes in family law where a parent was seeking to retain the family home or where the case involved a superannuation split or pool of equity valued at less than AU$50,000 (£28,400). These changes came into effect on 30 October 2015.

At the time of writing, it is not known how these changes will impact on women experiencing family violence in the family law system. It is hoped that they will broaden access to justice for women in family law and provide women with improved outcomes in relation to housing and economic security as well as promoting safety and wellbeing, but only time will tell.

VI. The Future of Legal Aid in Family Law

For disadvantaged Victorians relying on legal aid in family law cases, the last two and a half years have been a period of uncertainty and change. Unfortunately, we have no reliable data on how many disadvantaged Victorians fell through the gaps and were unable to access legal aid to resolve their family law disputes during this time; nor can we quantify the number of women who remained in violent relationships or negotiated unsafe parenting arrangements because they were unable to access legally aided representation.

This chapter has sought to highlight the consequences of the decisions made by VLA to 'chop and change' its eligibility criteria with little notice to, or consultation with, those affected by the changes. The test for LACs into the future will be around how best to adopt practices that provide a level of consistency and certainty in access to legal aid. This challenge will require LACs to be transparent in identifying the necessary changes and to consult with those affected by the changes. It is an ongoing responsibility of LACs to implement such changes in a way that minimises the impact on the most disadvantaged.

At a national level, it is clear that the level of funding contribution by the Commonwealth Government to LACs impacts significantly on the availability of legal aid in family law cases. Funding from State and Territory governments is allocated primarily for State or Territory specific areas of law, such as crime. According to the 2014 Australian Productivity Commission report, 94 per cent of the 30,000 Commonwealth-funded legal aid grants approved were for family law matters in 2012–13 (Productivity Commission 2014: 677). This indicates a substantial reliance on Commonwealth funding to promote access to legal aid in family law cases.

In 2012–13, the total income of LACs across Australia was AU$625 million (£355 million), with State and Territory governments the primary contributors of funding (46 per cent). Commonwealth Government funding represented just over one-third of LAC funding (Productivity Commission 2014: 677). Accordingly, the Productivity Commission report recommended that an additional AU$200 million (£113.8 million) be committed annually to LACs.

VII. Conclusion

As with many issues, legal assistance sector funding is a political football. Without a secure and ongoing funding commitment, legal aid services are vulnerable to the political agenda of the government of the day. Like the experiences being faced in England and Wales (see Aliverti, Chapter 16, Byrom, Chapter 12, and Hunter et al, Chapter 13, this volume), sadly, the people most impacted by the slow erosion of legal aid in Australia are those in our community who are most in need of legal advice and representation (see also Schwartz, Chapter 15, this volume). Without sufficient legal aid funding and services, the lives of the most vulnerable are impacted in profound ways. For women experiencing family violence, it could well mean losing their children, their homes, or even their lives.

References

Adams, AE, Sullivan, CM, Bybee, D and Greeson, MR (2008) 'Development of the Scale of Economic Abuse' 14 *Violence Against Women* 563.

Australian Bureau of Statistics (2011) *Labour Force Status and Other Characteristics of Families* (Canberra, Australian Bureau of Statistics).

Colak, S (2004) 'Homelessness: New Understanding, New Responses—Snapshot 2004' (Mission Australia), available at: www.sapo.org.au/pub/pub283.html.

Commonwealth of Australia (2008) *The Road Home, A National Approach to Reducing Homelessness* (Canberra, Commonwealth Government).

Evans, I (2007) *Battle-scars: long-term effects of prior domestic violence* (Victoria, Centre for Women's Studies and Gender Research, Monash University).

Family Court of Australia (2015) *Annual Report 2014–2015*, available at: www.familycourt.gov.au/wps/wcm/connect/15bcbde4-460f-4498-8c10-aee4f64ddff1/2181-FCoA_AR_2014%E2%80%9315_WEB.pdf?MOD=AJPERES.

De Vaus, G, Gray, M, Qu, L and Stanton, D (2009) *The effect of relationship breakdown on income and social exclusion* (Canberra, Australian Family Studies), available at: aifs.gov.au/cfca/bibliography/financial-issues-related-separationdivorce.

Lee, J (2013) 'Cuts Will Strip Most Vulnerable of Help in Court, Judges Say', *The Age*, 21 April 2013.

Office of the High Commissioner for Human Rights (2013) Media Release: 'Legal Aid a right in itself—UN Special Rapporteur', Geneva, 30 May 2013.

Productivity Commission (2014) *Access to Justice Arrangements Inquiry Report*, Vol 2, No 72, 5 September 2014.

Victoria Legal Aid [VLA] (2014) *Nineteenth Statutory Annual Report 2013–14* (August), available at: www.legalaid.vic.gov.au/sites/www.legalaid.vic.gov.au/files/vla-annual-report-2014-section-1.doc.

—— (2012), Media Release: *Increased demand forces changes to legal aid eligibility guidelines in 2013* (11 December 2012), available at: www.legalaid.vic.gov.au/about-us/news/increased-demand-forces-changes-to-legal-aid-eligibility-guidelines-in-2013.

—— (2015) *Information for Lawyers—Family Law Legal Aid Services Review*, available at: www.legalaid.vic.gov.au/information-for-lawyers/doing-legal-aid-work/family-law-legal-aid-services-review.

—— (2015) *Family Law Legal Aid Services Review—Final Report*, June 2015, available at: www.legalaid.vic.gov.au/information-for-lawyers/doing-legal-aid-work/family-law-legal-aid-services-review.

Victorian Crime Statistics Agency (2014) *Key movements in the number and rate of family incidents table (March) Victoria*, available at: www.crimestatistics.vic.gov.au/crime-statistics/historical-crime-data/year-ending-31-december-2014/family-incidents.

Treaties, Conventions, Principles, Directives, Rules and Legislation

Commonwealth Service Delivery Agency Act 1997 (Cth)
Family Law Act 1975 (Cth)
Mental Health Act 1986 (Vic)
Mental Health Act 2014 (Vic)

15

Indigenous People and Access to Justice in Civil and Family Law

MELANIE SCHWARTZ[1]

I. An Old and Urgent Story

Justice Robert Sackville recently noted that, 'at almost any given time in Australia, there is an inquiry under way into access to justice or consideration is being given to the latest report on the subject'. The terms of reference of a 2011 inquiry were, he observed, 'dispiritingly familiar' (Sackville 2011: 231). In the case of Indigenous Australians, government inquiries into access to justice repeatedly acknowledge a range of specific obstacles, and the serious consequences that ensue. As one report recently concluded, 'there is no shortage of reports, analysis and recommendations on how to improve the legal system. There is a shortage of the type of government action required to address this crisis' (Community Law Australia 2012: 12).

Much has been written about Indigenous people and access to justice in the criminal justice system, and the rationale for focusing on this site of glaring dysfunction and trauma is obvious. What has been perhaps less obvious is the significance of the obstacles to accessing justice in relation to non-criminal legal issues. It is important to understand that criminal justice system interventions usually represent the *end* of a story that often involves a range of unaddressed civil or family law issues. This is because ongoing experiences of disadvantage, disruption or discrimination in areas like housing, education, consumer matters, credit/debt, social security and child protection can escalate to become criminal law concerns (or snowball into other areas of civil law). Unaddressed civil or family law need also further entrenches the complex needs of Indigenous people, increases social exclusion, and compounds the load of legal service providers.

[1] The author acknowledges with thanks the excellent research assistance provided by Alisa Wicks and Leah Hecht. She is also indebted to her colleagues Chris Cunneen and Fiona Allison for their input.

Until recently, there has not been a solid evidence base for understanding the range and nature of Indigenous legal need in civil and family law, and the obstructions to accessing justice in these areas. However, various studies have now investigated the legal needs of Indigenous people (Allison et al 2012; Allison, Schwartz and Cunneen 2014; Coumarelos et al 2012; Cunneen, Allison and Schwartz 2014a; Cunneen and Schwartz 2008a; Schwartz, Allison and Cunneen 2013), and this research is critical to understanding the experiences and barriers that Indigenous people face with respect to the legal system.

This chapter draws on the work of the Indigenous Legal Needs Project (ILNP), the most in-depth study of Indigenous legal need and access to justice in non-criminal areas of law ever conducted in Australia.[2] The ILNP commenced with a pilot in New South Wales (NSW) in 2008,[3] and was extended from 2011–15 with the support of the Australian Research Council and in partnership with Aboriginal and Torres Strait Islander Legal Services (ATSILS), legal aid commissions (LACs) and, in the Northern Territory (NT), Indigenous Family Violence Prevention and Legal Services (IFVPLS). In total, the ILNP travelled to 40 remote, regional and urban Indigenous communities across five jurisdictions (NSW, NT, Victoria, Queensland [QLD] and Western Australia [WA]). Data was collected from around 800 Indigenous focus group participants across these sites, with participants completing a questionnaire on recent legal events that they had experienced and taking part in a discussion on legal needs and access to justice issues. In addition, close to 3500 interviews were conducted with organisations that provide services to ILNP focus communities, including with legal services, welfare agencies and Indigenous community organisations.

The ILNP fieldwork covers the five jurisdictions in which 85 per cent of Indigenous people reside in Australia, and provides the most comprehensive picture to date of both legal need and matters relating to Indigenous access to justice in non-criminal law matters. This chapter explores some of the most common and pressing obstacles to access to justice for Indigenous people in civil and family law. The discussion is couched in terms of the findings of a range of relevant government inquiries over the past decade or so, and is then situated alongside the research findings of the ILNP.

The obstacles to effective service delivery in civil and family law are varied and often complex. Some obstacles are exacerbated by geographic isolation, given the severe dearth of legal services available to large geographic regions. The ILNP research shows that, even in smaller States like Victoria, remoteness presents a challenge for access to justice because of a 'Melbourne-centric' (Victoria's capital city) focus in legal service delivery.

[2] The author is one of three Chief Investigators to the ILNP, an Australian Research Council Linkage Grant (LP100200455). The others are Professor Chris Cunneen (UNSW) and Professor Larissa Behrendt (UTS). The Senior Research Associate to the project is Fiona Allison (James Cook University).

[3] This research was funded by Legal Aid NSW.

While the issues discussed below are not focused on the problems caused by geographic remoteness, it must be noted that access to justice in these areas is 'so inadequate that remote Indigenous people cannot be said to have full civil rights' (Senate Legal and Constitutional References Committee ['Senate Committee'] 2004: paragraph 5.120). Further, geographic isolation and socioeconomic disadvantage are often linked (Productivity Commission 2014: 764) and, as explored below, disadvantage engenders a range of obstacles to accessing justice. A significant proportion of Aboriginal and Torres Strait Islander people live in remote areas (eight per cent in remote areas and 14 per cent in very remote areas), compared with less than two per cent of non-Indigenous Australians living in remote, plus very remote areas (Productivity Commission 2014: 9).

This chapter highlights only a small number of the difficulties faced by Aboriginal and Torres Strait Islander people in accessing justice in civil and family law, occurring in both remote and urban communities (although their shape may change from locality to locality). It goes without saying that there are a myriad of other matters that hinder access to justice for Indigenous people in these areas of law. The issues discussed here are: a lack of knowledge of what civil law encompasses among Aboriginal and Torres Strait Islander people; the complex needs of Indigenous clients and the issues that these needs raise for effective communication and for providing culturally secure services; particular concerns around access to justice for Indigenous women; and the impact of inadequate resourcing of ATSILS.

II. Lack of Knowledge or Understanding of Civil Law

ATSILS have repeatedly submitted to major government inquiries that for Indigenous people 'civil matters such as family law work, debt recovery, credit, consumer, and tort related law matters are sidelined by criminal law matters' (Senate Committee 2004: paragraph 5.118). This concern has been reiterated in all major inquiries into access to justice. The serious gap in service provision was highlighted by National Legal Aid's submission to the 2009 inquiry into Access to Justice:

> Indigenous legal services have never been sufficiently funded to establish a family or civil law practice, meaning that these needs must either be met by mainstream legal assistance services, are otherwise neglected; or result in self-representation in the court system. (Senate Committee 2009: para 8.45)

In addition to inadequate service provision in civil and family law, there is a low level of knowledge about these areas within Aboriginal and Torres Strait Islander communities. Indigenous people participating in the ILNP tended to associate the law and legal service provision with a criminal law context. What is significant about this is that the way in which an individual comes to engage with the criminal justice system is very different from one's interaction with the civil law (and some aspects of the family law) system. Where criminal charges are laid, an individual is forced into contact with the legal system, which is invariably experienced as coercive and punitive. The legal resolution of civil and family law issues, on the other hand, requires proactivity from the party initiating a matter. For many Indigenous people, contact with or knowledge of the legal system involves predominantly negative experiences with the criminal justice system, so the idea of engaging voluntarily with the law is unappealing.

To make informed decisions about how to respond to civil and family law problems, knowledge about rights and obligations is required. A lack of understanding about what civil law is may prevent people from recognising that a problem has a legal dimension or that a remedy is available. In this respect, knowledge of one's rights and being able to identify when a legal issue arises are essential precursors to effective access to justice.

Where people do not recognise a problem as a legal issue, this can lead to an underestimation among service providers of the level of need in the client base. For example, the ILNP identified wills and estates as an area of *unrecognised need* due to a lack of knowledge of the potential benefits of legal solutions in these areas. It is not uncommon for Aboriginal and Torres Strait Islander people to experience a dispute after a death—about the site of burial, for example—yet these were not directly identified as *legal* issues by focus groups because so few Indigenous participants had wills (between 5.7 per cent and 13.1 per cent of participants across the five focus jurisdictions). Indigenous people generally associate wills with property ownership and therefore do not see making a will as a priority. This view was put forward by focus group participants in communities across the country, and is well summarised by one participant in Narrogin, WA, who commented: 'None of us done that, we've got nothing to give'.

Some participants, however, spoke of the utility of a will in decreasing the likelihood of disputes about burial or children and assisting with accessing a deceased person's superannuation, for example. In Charleville, QLD, women focus group participants put it this way:

> I said to mum, when you die, you better write down where you want to be buried because I'm not fighting with anyone about it. A lot of Murris don't realise how important wills are.[4] ... I know Murris, they've worked in a lot of places and they've got super[annuation][5] everywhere ... you'd be surprised how much people fight over little things.

What is important to note in the context of access to justice is that, when the subject of having a will in place was raised, the majority of focus group participants

[4] The Murri are the Indigenous people of QLD, Australia.

[5] Retirement provision.

said that they would like help to create one: thus, lack of knowledge about the usefulness of having a will masked the degree of need for assistance in this area. A woman in the Laverton, WA, focus group noted: 'Nobody been come talk about this, nobody. You're the first to come and talk about this'.

On average, across all focus sites, about 60 per cent of focus group participants who did not have a will expressed a desire to receive legal assistance to create one. This illustrates the potential correlation between knowledge of the benefits of the civil law system and a desire to engage with it.

If they are unaddressed, civil law issues such as unpaid debts, housing problems and social security disputes can escalate to become full-blown legal matters. Better knowledge of the law can help to avoid disputes in the first place and enable Indigenous people to make informed decisions about dealing with matters appropriately as they come up, at as early a stage as possible. Delaying dealing with a legal issue can make it more unwieldy to address down the track, as explained by an Aboriginal staff member in a NSW legal service provider interviewed for the ILNP:

> 'Civil'—you might as well be talking in Chinese! I think a lot of the time, people find themselves in situations that, if they had known what to do about it in the first instance, they wouldn't have found themselves in X, Y, Z situation.

Unaddressed legal issues not related to the criminal law can also escalate to become criminal matters (see Schwartz and Cunneen 2009b). In relation to family law issues, it was identified that, in the absence of a legal resolution, 'the only way they know how to deal with it is to go out and have a big punch-up' (Legal support worker, Wagga, NSW). These examples illustrate how important it is for Indigenous people to have a sound understanding of how the civil and family law systems may help to resolve disputes or assert rights.

III. The Complex Needs of Indigenous People as Clients

Indigenous people are more likely to have complex needs that demand a great deal from legal practitioners, legal services and, indeed, the legal system as a whole, to maximise the chances for a just outcome. These complexities arise from a range of matters, including language barriers and cross-cultural issues, and the interplay with non-legal issues such as disadvantage, poor literacy, disability and substance addiction.

A. Language and Communication

Difficulties with communication, whether related to language, culture, literacy or socioeconomic disadvantage, are ongoing and serious impediments to

Indigenous people accessing legal assistance (Senate Committee 2004: paragraph 5.100). The 2004 Senate Committee inquiry (at paragraph 5.101) into Legal Aid and Access to Justice heard that English is a second, third or even fourth language for most of the clients of the Top End Women's Legal Service.[6] In 2009, the Committee heard similar submissions, with the Australian Human Rights Commission adding that, 'in addition to English not being the first language in some Indigenous communities, the nuances of Aboriginal English can also lead to misunderstandings between clients and their lawyers (and the justice system)' (Senate Committee 2009: paragraph 8.52). A survey conducted by the Office of Evaluation and Audit (2003: 3.6.4.1; see also Productivity Commission 2014: 763) further reported that 13 per cent of ATSILS practitioners experience difficulty in understanding what their clients are saying 'very often/often', and a further 50 per cent 'sometimes' experience such difficulties. Practitioners also reported that their clients often struggle to understand what they are trying to convey, because of the client's shyness or discomfort (65 per cent), an inability to communicate adequately in English (40 per cent) or because clients do not understand the legal process (77 per cent).

Given the prevalence of communication issues and impact of this on basic access to justice, the pressing need for effective interpreter services is clear. Even where funding exists for interpreters, however, it can be difficult to find suitably qualified personnel, as explained by one ILNP interviewee from an Indigenous legal service in the NT:

> When something comes up urgently [the legal service] may not be able to find anyone ... they might have something better to do or they might be out bush, so there are problems getting particular languages from time to time, and what those languages are, shift ... That's a daily issue.

Stakeholders have consistently recommended that governments provide increased funding to interpreter services (see, for example, Senate Committee 2009, recommendation 28). While the Australian Federal Government has made a substantial funding contribution to Indigenous interpreting services since 2000—including over AU$6 million (£3.41 million) in 2014–15 to improve the supply of Indigenous interpreters in areas with high numbers of Indigenous people where traditional languages are spoken in the NT, South Australia, WA and QLD—the development of a national framework for the provision of Aboriginal and Torres Strait Islander interpreters has posed ongoing challenges (Productivity Commission 2014: 780, 792). Additionally, interpreter services are only one part of the solution. As recognised by the Productivity Commission (2014: 763):

> [T]he use of interpreters may not overcome communication barriers since not all communication is verbal. The use of body language, such as hand gestures and movement

[6] The Top End Women's Legal Service provides free legal advice, community legal education and advocacy on issues of importance to women in Darwin and surrounding areas, in the NT, Australia.

> of the head and eyes, is an integral part of communication for many Aboriginal people. The presence of elders can also influence the effectiveness of communication with Indigenous people and the justice system.

Socioeconomic disadvantage can also increase the likelihood of individuals experiencing legal problems and make it harder to resolve such matters when they do arise. An ILNP interviewee from a community legal service in NSW explained it in the following way:

> In addition to being Aboriginal and what marginalisation might occur from that, they also happen to have substance abuse, mental illness from post-traumatic stress and whatever else might be going on. They are poor, and very often have a range of things like un-picked-up learning disabilities, there might be levels of then self-fulfilling prophesies of foetal distress syndrome, all the sexual violence and family violence that has gone on. Because of that soup of additional problems that go on that happen to be in the community that is Aboriginal, but which are not necessarily Aboriginal per se ... we always feel like we have to work miracles to undo all the barrage of other issues that have gone unattended to, to even get to the legal issue they have come in with.

The factors arising from disadvantage impact on communication. Poor literacy is a good example of this relationship, with Indigenous people being less likely to have literacy and numeracy skills equal to that of the non-Indigenous population (Australian Government 2015: 22). Legal problems can flow from situations where literacy is low—for example, in cases where Centrelink uses formal written letters to advise clients of mandatory appointments.[7] Failure to attend such a meeting results in benefits being cut off, yet the formal letter is an entirely inappropriate mode of communication for many Indigenous people. A legal service provider interviewee in the ILNP described it in the following way:

> One [Centrelink] letter read, 'Dear Sir, you have been identified as a disengaged youth'. And I thought, 'Well, you've lost him already!' So communication is a difficulty given that people don't speak English all the time and don't necessarily read it even if they speak it well.

Finally, it is important to highlight that communication problems are by no means always attributable to issues that arise on the client side. The variable abilities of legal practitioners to communicate effectively with clients were raised repeatedly in the ILNP fieldwork, exemplified in the following comment by a participant in the women's focus group in Dubbo, NSW:

> They go to school and get their big education, their big law degrees and stuff, but a lot of them aren't educated in how to communicate with non-educated people, and they'll sit there and they'll talk to you in words that you've never heard of and you'll say to them, 'What does that mean?' and they'll look at you like you don't belong there. You can tell

[7] Centrelink was established in 1997 as a statutory agency responsible for the delivery of human services under the provisions of the *Commonwealth Service Delivery Agency Act 1997* (Cth). It is responsible for allocating and managing social security payments.

> that they're standing there thinking, 'Gee this is a dopey little thing here sitting' ... We're not all solicitors! We don't know the law jargon.

B. Providing Cultural Security

Related to the communication skills required by practitioners to ensure equity in access to justice for Indigenous people, is the need for cultural sensitivity in legal service delivery. Cultural differences can have a profound impact on Indigenous people's interaction with the legal system. As a starting point, traditional law is a real and influential factor in the lives of many Aboriginal and Torres Strait Islander people. In contrast, the Australian legal system is:

> Relatively recent and ... has been externally imposed on Indigenous Australians ... Mistrust of the justice system, and the 'government' in general, affects all aspects of the interaction between Indigenous Australians and access to justice. (Productivity Commission 2014: 765)

The Productivity Commission (2014: 765) heard that 'some Indigenous Australians tend not to distinguish between the criminal and civil arms of the justice system. The legal system as a whole is associated with incarceration, deaths in custody and the removal of children'. It is therefore essential that those working with Indigenous clients in civil and family law contexts understand the impact of these lived experiences of the legal system, including the impact on people's willingness to engage with the law, and the ramifications for how legal services ought to be delivered. The Access to Justice Taskforce of the Federal Attorney-General's Department (Attorney-General's Department 2009: 143; see also Cunneen and Schwartz 2008b) reiterated that:

> [T]he availability of culturally appropriate legal assistance services for Indigenous people with family and civil law problems is limited and this compromises the ability of Indigenous Australians to realise their full legal entitlements. It also introduces a danger that civil or family law issues can escalate to criminal acts resulting in charges and a perpetuation of the cycle of over-representation in the criminal justice system.

Ideally, legal services for Indigenous clients should be provided by ATSILS (see discussion below), however, Indigenous clients may be 'conflicted' out of accessing such a service or may choose to seek assistance at a mainstream provider for other reasons. Non-Indigenous legal services must be equipped to serve the needs of their Indigenous clients in ways that create a culturally safe environment, to avoid the scenario recounted by an Aboriginal staff member at a non-Indigenous legal service in NSW, who said that 'You'll actually get clients who call up and say, "Do I have to come into white man's world?"'

Through the ILNP fieldwork, a wide range of strategies were suggested to create more culturally secure environments for the delivery of legal services, including cultural awareness training, greater flexibility in service delivery such as 'drop-in' appointments and the provision of outreach services in community locations. In order to get proper instructions from clients, a departure from the often-transactional nature of legal service delivery may be necessary. This was highlighted by an Indigenous staff member from a mainstream legal aid provider:

> One of the big things about Aboriginal people, we like to yarn. The talking, that's a big thing. And we're not particularly blunt people, in that we don't just come out with 'My other half stole the kids and I want them back'; there's going to be a story and it's going to be round about, and so the build-up of the trust and rapport, that's so important.

The value of having Aboriginal and Torres Strait Islander staff members as a point of contact was one of the most frequently reiterated ILNP recommendations for improving access to justice. A women's focus group participant in Dubbo spoke of the importance of 'knowing that there were Aboriginal people on the front desk; talking to Aboriginal people before you got to see your lawyer. When I went to the Legal Aid office they all just sort of ... *look*. I got real nervous'.

Legal Aid QLD has employed Indigenous Liaison Officers since 2008, based in Cairns, Townsville, Mount Isa and Rockhampton, who also visit the Cape, Gulf and western areas of North QLD. The Commission reported that in the first two years of operation, the number of advices in civil and family law increased by almost 200 per cent (Legal Aid Queensland 2009: 2). Some CLCs also employ Indigenous field officers; a non-Indigenous lawyer working in a community legal service in Dubbo reflected on the value of their field officers as follows:

> They are worth their weight in gold. There are issues here in trying to find clients—to have the field officer assist with that and with cultural appropriateness—that is how you should do things in that community. It is important ... Some Aboriginal people can't read or write and they are very reluctant to tell you that they can't read or write, very reluctant. You've got to ask them other questions like whether they went to school, how long they went to school, and get an idea that way. Sometimes they will say, 'I haven't got my glasses, can't you read that?' They don't want to appear downgraded in front of a white person. Having the field officer with me meant that I was able to learn a lot. Without a field officer you've got no way of knowing.

In 2010, Legal Aid NSW began a pilot programme employing field officers in Campbelltown, Coffs Harbour and Walgett, with the specific mandate of increasing access to justice for Indigenous clients in civil and family law. A 2014 evaluation of the pilot found that the initiative increased the trust between Legal Aid staff and Indigenous communities, increased the usage of the service by Indigenous clients, and helped to create stronger and more sustainable partnerships between the community, community organisations and legal aid (Cunneen and Schwartz 2014).

In the ILNP research, community focus group participants and stakeholders alike were clear on the imperative of having Indigenous staff as a way of accessing Aboriginal and Torres Strait Islander clients and providing a culturally secure service. For example, in Redfern, NSW, a women's focus group member commented on the need to:

> Employ an Aboriginal person and go to community … get involved in our community and our culture and the things that we do … come into the community centre and talk about what you do … get an understanding of who we are and what kind of people we are … show us a bit of initiative and a bit of oomph mate, and show us that you *do* give a damn, rather than just sitting behind the office and answering the phone. Get out there, get amongst it.

Having an Indigenous person act as a bridge between the legal system and the community has direct flow-on effects to access to justice. An Indigenous person holding such a role in an Indigenous legal service in WA illustrated this point:

> If they see an Aboriginal person come out or an Aboriginal field officer come out with the lawyer, I think it gives the community comfort. At the end of the day, lawyers are still western-trained professionals … I'm there to support them in engaging with institutions that make no sense in their day-to-day life. The driving example's the perfect example. If I can drive perfectly well and the only reason I don't have an official licence is either because I don't have my birth registered, I don't have my birth certificate or because I don't understand the driving instruction booklet because either it talks about traffic lights and I haven't seen a traffic light in my life, even though I've been driving all my life, or the actual driving instruction booklet's too complicated … [or] the driving instruction centre's maybe so far. None of these make sense for me because it doesn't relate to me driving in my day-to-day life. So me, as the lawyer, even if I'm on their side, I'm still representing a system that's really ridiculous for anyone who lives in a remote area, you see. So for that reason, it's so key for there to be a field officer or an Aboriginal liaison person, because that person, I believe, is ultimately creating that bridge of trust. Where the system has failed them for 240 years, there's someone that's saying well, look … this is part of the system that you're part of, whether you like it or not. Let's try and engage you with the system so that system actually meets your needs rather than fails you again.

The importance of the field officer role was further highlighted in the ILNP research by the finding that some mainstream legal service providers call upon ATSILS field officers to carry out field officer duties for their clients. While this level of cooperation between legal services increases the prospect of access to justice exponentially, the obvious problem with this is that ATSILS resources are already stretched beyond capacity. Calling on ATSILS field officers to assist other legal services simply adds to an often-unsustainable work environment at ATSILS (see discussion on resourcing of ATSILS below).

C. The Particular Needs of Indigenous Women

Inquiries into access to justice have identified the urgent need for increased services for Indigenous women, 'who remain chronically disadvantaged in terms of advice as to their legal rights, access to legal services and the high levels of violence which many of them experience within their communities' (Senate Committee 2004: xvii). The Joint Committee of Public Accounts and Audit ('Joint Committee 2005': paragraph 3.42) reported that 'the close knit social connections that operate in Indigenous communities can operate in particularly forceful ways in restricting access to legal services and the justice system by victims of family violence'. Other barriers to accessing legal services include the view that representation will be refused by 'under-resourced ATSILS' (Senate Committee 2004: paragraph 5.88) and the risk that a child might be removed if a woman raises difficulties that she is facing (Joint Committee 2005: paragraph 3.46).

Conflict of interest has been identified as a significant barrier preventing Aboriginal and Torres Strait Islander women from accessing legal services (see Ludlam and Lawrey 2010). This is especially problematic in family law and family violence matters, where a lot of women 'feel that if there is a conflict of interest, [ATSILS] will not represent them' (Senate Committee 2004: paragraph 5.83). The Joint Committee (2005: xxiv) indicated that 'ATSILSs are often restricted in providing family or civil law services (beyond referrals) to persons in danger of harm because they are already representing the alleged offender and thus find themselves in a conflict situation'. This highlights the importance of IFVPLS in ensuring access to legal services for Indigenous women, particularly when they are in danger of harm.

The need for a nationwide legal service specifically for Indigenous women has been discussed repeatedly in government inquiries (see, for example, Senate Committee 2004: paragraph 5.63; Senate Committee 2009: paragraphs 8.120, 8.126). The National Indigenous Law and Justice Strategy released by the Commonwealth in 2007 commented that, despite the creation of several legal services for Indigenous women, significant disadvantages still exist and services for Indigenous women 'need to be targeted, culturally sensitive and more work needs to be done on assessing unmet needs' (cited in Senate Committee 2009: paragraph 8.120). IFVPLS Victoria (cited in Senate Committee 2009: para 8.126) has also emphasised that it is 'critical that Aboriginal women have ownership of and drive future initiatives to advance law and justice outcomes'.

Another obstacle to Indigenous women's access to justice has been the lack of an evidence base about their specific legal needs. The 2009 Senate Committee (para 8.129) commented that it received limited evidence regarding Indigenous women's legal needs, which reflected that 'Indigenous women are not getting adequate legal assistance to afford them access to justice'. In this regard, the work of the ILNP has made significant progress in identifying gendered differences in Indigenous legal needs. For example, the NT fieldwork found that 'there were pronounced gender differences both in the identification of issues and in the likelihood of seeking legal advice or assistance' (Cunneen, Allison and Schwartz 2014b: 223). Indigenous women were more likely than men to identify legal issues in relation to housing, neighbourhood disputes and Centrelink, but less likely to seek assistance. The need for in-depth research in this area remains high, in order to promote Indigenous women's access to the law.

IV. Resourcing of ATSILS

Inadequate funding of ATSILS has been said to lie 'at the heart of equitable access to legal services by Indigenous Australians, particularly the access of women and children and people living in regional and remote areas' (Joint Committee 2005: paragraph 2.1). The Senate Legal and Constitutional References Committee (2004: paragraph 5.138) stressed that the provision of adequate legal services to Indigenous people is only achievable if proper funding is provided on the basis of assessed need. Again in 2009, a Senate Committee (2009: xix) heard significant criticisms of core funding levels of ATSILS, particularly as compared to other legal aid service providers and notwithstanding the additional expenses associated with the provision of Indigenous legal services.

In 2014, the Australian Productivity Commission conducted an inquiry into access to justice arrangements and made recommendations with respect to funding Indigenous legal services. The key findings included that the nature and unpredictability of funding arrangements constrain the capacity of legal assistance providers to direct assistance to the areas of greatest benefit (Productivity Commission 2014: 2); that funding allocation models currently used to determine LAC and ATSILS funding should be updated to reflect more contemporary measures of legal need (Productivity Commission 2014: 64); that the Australian Government should undertake a cost–benefit analysis to inform the development of culturally tailored alternative dispute resolution services (including family dispute resolution services) for Aboriginal and Torres Strait Islander people, particularly in high-need areas (Productivity Commission 2014: 66); and that State and Territory governments should contribute to the funding of ATSILS and IFVPLS services as part of any future legal assistance funding agreement with the Australian Government (Productivity Commission 2014: 66).

The Commission strongly criticised cuts to ATSILS funding planned at the time, calling for reductions to be reversed and for additional funding of AU$200 million (£113.8 million) for civil legal assistance services (Productivity Commission 2014: 741). Following huge public outcry, in May 2015, the Australian Government reversed the proposed cuts and agreed to five years of further funding (Cleary 2015). The IFVPLS had faced similar uncertainty and, 'following a gruelling open tender process, in March 2015 the IFVPLS were told they will receive funding at 2013–14 levels for the next 2–3 years' (Cleary 2015). The NSW Custody Notification Service (CNS), an ATSILS 24-hour phone service for Indigenous people who have been arrested, was also due to lose all of its federal funding, as the federal government insisted that the Aboriginal Legal Service (NSW/Australian Capital Territory [ACT]) should pay for the service. At the 11th hour, the Attorney-General's Department committed to funding the programme.

The CNS was originally established following a recommendation of the Royal Commission into Aboriginal Deaths in Custody (Davidson 2015).[8]

The community legal sector has faced similar funding uncertainty, with planned cuts of AU$20 million (£11.3million) also reversed in March 2015. Shulman notes that not all of the funding cuts in relation to CLCs were reversed and that 'the latest government backdown can be understood as not so much a final victory for CLCs, but more as an historical exception in the trend towards defunding CLCs' (Shulman 2015; see also Buchanan, Chapter 8, this volume).

Chronic underfunding of ATSILS (along with other legal aid and community legal service providers) is a central issue impacting all other barriers to justice. Despite an overwhelming and well-documented need for increased resources, there have been threats of, and actual cuts to, available funding, and no significant progress in reaching a sustainable funding model. Reports over the past decade highlight an ever-increasing need and urgency, as ATSILS and CLCs report being unable to meet expenses and demand for services. In 2004, the Aboriginal and Torres Strait Islander Commission highlighted for the Senate Committee the shortfalls of funding provided to ATSILS compared with that provided for LACs (Senate Committee 2004, paragraph 5.9). A 2008 study (Cunneen and Schwartz 2008b: 51) noted that 'in real terms, the total funding for Legal Aid for 2007–08 was AU$163.8 million, while the figure for ATSILS funding in the same period was AU$50.25 million'.[9] In its submission to the Senate Committee in 2009 (Senate Committee 2009: paragraph 8.14), the Aboriginal Legal Service of Western Australia (ALSWA) stated that:

> [T]he main issue, being lack of funding, has not changed. In our view the funding provided is now even more inadequate due to the increase in the demand for Indigenous legal services. The funding has not increased to meet ALSWA's additional operational expenses of running existing services or to meet the increase in demand for services. The need for additional funding for ATSILS is critical and should be one of the highest priorities for the Australian Government.

The Aboriginal Legal Service (NSW/ACT) also questioned 'whether Indigenous people are being provided with a second-rate service due to inadequate funding of the ATSILS' (Senate Committee 2009: paragraph 8.23). The Senate Committee (2009: paragraph 8.25) recorded its concern over the decline in funding, 'particularly in view of the increased Indigenous population, the average age of the Indigenous population, and the increasing rates of incarceration for Indigenous people', and noted that all governments should be financially contributing to the

[8] The Royal Commission was established in 1987 to investigate Aboriginal deaths in custody over a 10-year period. Its report contained more than 330 recommendations for structural changes to reduce the hugely disproportionate levels of incarceration of Indigenous people.

[9] AU$163.8 million equates to £93.2 million and AU$50.25 million equates to approximately £28.5 million.

provision of Indigenous legal services (Senate Committee 2009: paragraph 8.26). In light of this repeated acknowledgement of funding disparities and the failure to remedy the problem of inadequate core funding levels, the Principal Legal Officer of the North Australian Aboriginal Justice Agency (Hunyor 2012: 28) recently stated that

> the gap between ATSILS' funding and the legal needs of our clients is therefore becoming more acute. A fair estimate is that a funding increase of at least 50 per cent for the ATSILS is required for there to be parity with mainstream legal aid funding.

The uncertain funding environment means that ATSILSs are 'unable to appropriately plan ahead and provide staff with employment certainty' (Productivity Commission 2014: 752). Between 2000 and 2005, solicitors at the ALSWA reported the average period of employment to be 17 months, largely attributable to heavy workloads, difficulties in retaining staff in regional and remote areas, and uncompetitive salaries compared to those paid by LACs (Schwartz and Cunneen 2009a: 20):

> Clients report frustration that their matters are not managed continuously by one legal practitioner, and that time is inefficiently used due to duplication and re-briefing. High workloads mean that practitioners often have insufficient time to prepare cases adequately. Further, low salaries mean that ATSILS practitioners are likely to be nearer the beginning of their careers; practitioner inexperience is a key concern for clients and magistrates alike. Taken together, these factors lead to a situation where ATSILS have effectively become 'a training ground for either the Legal Aid Commission or private firms'. (Schwartz and Cunneen 2009b: 20, footnotes omitted)

Increased and sustained funding is a prerequisite for the provision of quality and appropriate Indigenous legal services. As stated by an NT Registrar interviewed for the ILNP:

> It keeps coming back to a well-resourced Aboriginal legal aid service that can do civil work … we've got to improve access to the civil law system by Aboriginal people by having a well-funded Aboriginal legal aid service that provides civil assistance … because without that, the walls are just too thick and too high … There is no doubt that Aboriginal people are well and truly overrepresented in the criminal law system … and I would say well and truly *unrepresented* in the civil law system.

With increased funding, ATSILSs would be able to do more than simply try to keep up with their overwhelming workload; they would be better able to empower Aboriginal and Torres Strait Islander people and advance their interests and aspirations.

V. Conclusion

Access to justice for Indigenous people extends well beyond questions of good legal service delivery. To truly deal with Indigenous obstacles to justice, matters such as social inclusion, colonial legacies, cultural strength and structural discrimination must be addressed. It has long been recognised that reform of the legal system runs the risk of striking only 'at the symptoms of the problems experienced by Aboriginals rather than at the causes' (Sackville 1975: 288). To make meaningful inroads into the issues that underpin Indigenous disadvantage in relation to the legal system, political and economic reform is necessary. Even reform confined to the legal system must do more than tinker around the edges. As the Senate Committee (2009: xx) recognised: '[T]he Australian legal system is beset with various weaknesses, some endemic, some deeply rooted and some based in non-legal causes, all of which are interconnected, thus requiring large scale rather than microeconomic reforms'.

However, there is a role to be played by the legal system in addressing entrenched disadvantage, especially in the civil and family law areas. The ILNP identified seven areas of law as national priority areas of legal need for Indigenous people: housing (tenancy); discrimination; credit and debt, and associated consumer law; social security; child protection; and wills and estates.

Where problems in these areas go unaddressed, they *increase* disadvantage and social exclusion, and can lead to criminal offending, thereby contributing to Indigenous over-representation in the criminal justice system. Where people have access to secure housing, for example, or where financial stress is reduced, more building blocks for stable families and communities are in place. Civil and family law does have a function in bolstering stability in these areas, where legal services are offered that are effective avenues to just outcomes. Increased knowledge of the civil law system, better understanding of and catering to the complex needs of Indigenous clients, and proper resourcing of ATSILS are but some of the prerequisites for ensuring adequate Indigenous access to justice in civil and family law.

References

Allison, F, Cunneen, C, Schwartz, M, and Behrendt, L (2012) *Indigenous Legal Needs Project: NT Report* (Cairns, James Cook University).

Allison, F, Schwartz, M and Cunneen, C (2014) *The Civil and Family Law Needs of Indigenous people in WA* (Cairns, James Cook University).

Attorney-General's Department (2009) *Strategic Framework for Access to Justice in the Federal Civil Justice System*, September (Canberra, Commonwealth of Australia).

Australian Government (2015) *Closing the Gap: Prime Minister's Report 2015* (Canberra, Commonwealth of Australia).

Cleary, J (2015) 'Why Are Indigenous Legal Services So Important?', *Amnesty International*, 15 May, available at: www.amnesty.org.au/indigenous-rights/comments/37194/.

Community Law Australia (2012) *Unaffordable and Out of Reach: The Problem of Access to the Australian Legal System*, available at: www.communitylawaustralia.org.au/wp-content/uploads/2012/07/CLA_Report_Final.pdf.

Coumarelos, C, Macourt, D, People, J, Mcdonald, M, Wei, Z, Iriana, R and Ramsey, S (2012) *Legal Australia-Wide Survey: Legal Need in Australia*, vol 7 (Sydney, Law and Justice Foundation of New South Wales).

Cunneen, C, Allison, F and Schwartz, M (2014a) *The Civil and Family Law Needs of Indigenous People in Queensland* (Cairns, James Cook University).

—— (2014b) 'Access to Justice for Aboriginal People in the Northern Territory' 49 *Australian Journal of Social Issues* 219.

Cunneen, C and Schwartz, M (2008a) *The Family and Civil Law Needs of Aboriginal People in New South Wales: Final Report* (Sydney, University of New South Wales).

—— (2008b) 'Funding Aboriginal and Torres Strait Islander Legal Services: Issues of Equity and Access' 32 *Criminal Law Journal* 38.

—— (2014) *Review of the Legal Aid NSW Aboriginal Field Officer pilot program in civil and family law*, May 2014, unpublished.

Davidson, H (2015) 'NSW Indigenous Custody Notification Service Gets Federal Funding Lifeline', *The Guardian*, 1 July 2015, available at: www.theguardian.com/australia-news/2015/jul/01/nsw-indigenous-custody-notification-service-gets-federal-funding-lifeline.

Hunyor, J (2012) 'Aboriginal and Torres Strait Islander Legal Services and Access to Justice' 2 *Balance* 26.

Joint Committee of Public Accounts and Audit (2005) *Access of Indigenous Australians to Law and Justice Services*, June 2005, Report 403 (Canberra, Commonwealth of Australia).

Legal Aid Queensland (2009) *Submission to the Commonwealth Attorney-General's Department on the National Indigenous Justice Framework* (Queensland, Legal Aid Queensland).

Ludlam, S and Lawrey, C (2010) 'Closing the Justice Gap for Indigenous Australians' 7 *Indigenous Law Bulletin* 17, 12.

Office of Evaluation and Audit (2003) *Evaluation of the Legal and Preventative Services Program* (Canberra, Office of Evaluation and Audit).

Productivity Commission (2014) *Access to Justice Arrangements Inquiry*, Report No. 72, 5 September (Canberra, Productivity Commission).

Sackville, R (1975) *Law and Poverty in Australia* (Canberra, AGPS).

—— (2011) 'Access to Justice: Towards an Integrated Approach' 10 *The Judicial Review* 221.

Schwartz, M, Allison, F and Cunneen, C (2013) *The Civil and Family Law Needs of Indigenous People in Victoria* (Cairns, James Cook University).

Schwartz, M and Cunneen, C (2009a) 'Working Cheaper, Working Harder: Inequity in Funding for Aboriginal and Torres Strait Islander Legal Services' 7 *Indigenous Law Bulletin* 10, 19.

—— (2009b) 'From Crisis to Crime: The Escalation of Civil and Family Law Issues to Criminal Matters in Aboriginal Communities in NSW' 17 *Indigenous Law Bulletin* 5, 18.

Senate Legal and Constitutional References Committee (2004) *Legal Aid and Access to Justice* June (Canberra, Parliament of Australia).

—— (2009) *Access to Justice* December (Canberra, Parliament of Australia).

Shulman, J (2015) 'Access to Justice under Threat' 2 *Law Society Journal* 4, 24.

Treaties, Conventions, Principles, Directives, Rules and Legislation

Commonwealth Service Delivery Agency Act 1997 (Cth).

16

Austerity and Justice in the Age of Migration

ANA ALIVERTI

I. Introduction

The recent reforms to legal aid funding in Britain should be considered within the broader context of welfare reform—one of the flagship policies of the Coalition government that took office in May 2010. The strict austerity programme announced then was aimed at halting a culture of welfare dependency, rewarding work and making the resort to public funds conditional on the applicant performing back-to-work activities (HM Government 2010; Patrick 2012: 6). In the 'welfare-to-work' programme, work is cast not just as a right but as a duty; in fact, the crucial duty of being a good and responsible citizen (Anderson 2013: 27; Patrick 2012). The reform of the welfare system thus has not been marketed merely as a cost-cutting programme, but also as a cultural revolution that should yield fruits to taxpayers and benefit dependants alike. This cultural revolution is premised on ideas of 'active citizenship' and 'civic conservatism' or 'neocommunitarianism' (Ramsay 2012: 105; Schierup, Hansen and Castles 2006: 61). In this context, citizenship has been mobilised along punitive lines to impart a sense of civic duty on 'failed citizens' to 'get on their bikes' and find work (Aliverti 2015: 215; Anderson 2013: 27), and as a marker of deservingness to exclude the 'globalised proletariat' from welfare benefits reserved for citizens (De Giorgi 2010: 151; Wacquant 2014: 277).

In this context, immigration reform was quickly wedded to the broader welfare benefit reform agenda. In his first speech on immigration, Prime Minister David Cameron made that abundantly clear:

> Migrants are filling gaps in the labour market left wide open by a welfare system that for years has paid British people not to work. That's where the blame lies—at the door of our woeful welfare system, and the last government who comprehensively failed to reform it. So immigration and welfare reform are two sides of the same coin. Put simply, we will never control immigration properly unless we tackle welfare dependency.

> That's another powerful reason why this government is undertaking the biggest shake-up of the welfare system for generations … making sure that work will always pay … and ending the option of living a life on the dole when a life in work is possible. (Cameron 2011)

Immigration controls, in other words, are presented as a key piece of the broader overhaul of the national social security system—a system designed and meant for citizens (Anderson 2010). Both sets of policies complement each other and are geared by a 'post-national workfare regime' that prioritises market requirements, including labour flexibility, employability and individual responsibility, as an end in themselves, and as a means to attain social cohesion (Schierup et al 2006: 79). Immigration controls pursue a further function, that of drawing the boundary of 'civic deservingness' (Chauvin and Garcés-Mascareñas 2012: 243). In the context of stringent austerity measures, migration status and citizenship gain importance for determining hierarchies of civic deservingness, fixing who is worthy of protection and who should be forthrightly excluded.

This chapter examines recent policies designed to restrict access to legal aid based on residence. Amid stringent reductions to public spending, the British Government sought to make substantial savings in the legal aid budget by restricting the matters covered under the scheme and introducing further eligibility requirements. One of the last attempts at squeezing publicly funded legal representation was the proposed introduction of the 'residence test'. The proposed new qualification requirement sought to restrict access to civil legal aid to those with a strong connection to the United Kingdom (UK), thus barring access to people who have not been legal UK residents for a continuous period of 12 months prior to the request for funding (Ministry of Justice [MoJ] 2013c: 13). Symptomatic of broader social policy trends, the residence test illustrates the novel ways in which migration control is deeply implicated in the reconstitution of social citizenship. Through the proposed qualification requirement, the government sought to exclude from legal aid certain non-residents, while clearly stating which claims deserve to be publicly funded.

This chapter explores the rationale behind this proposal and the adverse decision by the High Court which ruled the test unlawful, virtually halting its implementation. It considers the arguments for and against the proposed restrictions against the background of broader cuts to criminal and civil legal aid, particularly immigration law litigation, and their impact on non-British nationals. The High Court's Public Law Project (PLP) judgment should no doubt be praised for challenging direct legal discrimination on grounds of nationality and migration status,[1] thus contributing to an emerging constitutional jurisprudence that is seeking to limit state sovereign powers over non-citizens. Yet, it fails to ask serious questions about the fairness and legality of unequal treatment in the immigration

[1] *Public Law Project v Secretary of State for Justice* [2014] EWHC 2365 (Admin) ('the *PLP* case' or '*Public Law Project* judgment').

sphere, and assumes that 'the immigration context' is fairly circumscribed and clearly bounded. In doing so, the judgment also fails to tackle less overt sources of discrimination that impinge on the ability of lower-income foreign nationals to access justice.

II. Legal Aid in Britain

The right to legal advice is often cast as a precondition to the right to access justice and a fair trial. The more severe the potential consequence of a judicial proceeding, the more pressing will be the need for expert legal counsel and representation. Hence, in various jurisdictions criminal defence is guaranteed free of charge. A qualified right to free legal advice in criminal proceedings is enshrined in Article 6(3)(c) of the *European Convention for the Protection of Human Rights and Fundamental Freedoms*, which states that criminal defendants have a right 'to defend [themselves] in person or through legal assistance of [their] own choosing or, if [they have] not sufficient means to pay for legal assistance, to be given it free when the interests of justice so require'.[2]

Although nineteenth-century legislation introduced a limited right to free legal advice, in Britain, a significant expansion of legal aid in both civil and criminal proceedings took place during the post-war period, hand in hand with the development of the welfare state (McConville et al 1994: 2). Considered as one of the pillars of the welfare state, the *Legal Aid and Advice Act 1949* in England and Wales guaranteed a generous provision of legal aid for the purpose of litigation in virtually every court of law to those who are entitled to it[3]—namely, 'poor litigants', or those with limited financial means, provided that they demonstrate a *probabilis causa litigandi*.[4] Further, criminal advice at the first stages was warranted to all accused persons (Thomson 1950: 35).

While the extent to which those generous provisions were fully realised in practice is contested, from the outset the institution of legal aid was underpinned by the ideology of the welfare state and social citizenship (Goriely 1999: 93). In TH Marshall's tripartite model of citizenship, social citizenship encompasses 'the right to defend and assert all one's rights on terms of equality with others and by due process of law' (Marshall 1950: 10). For citizens to be able to voice their concerns and enforce their rights through legitimate avenues, they should have

[2] The *Charter of Fundamental Rights of the European Union* extends the provision to non-criminal litigation 'for those who lack sufficient resources in so far as such aid is necessary to ensure effective access to justice' (Article 47). The Legal Aid Directive recognises and regulates the right to legal aid in cross-border disputes involving two or more Member States (Council Directive 2002/8/EC of 27 January 2003 to improve access to justice in cross-border disputes by establishing minimum common rules relating to legal aid for such disputes [2003] OJ L26).

[3] In Scotland, the *Legal Aid and Solicitors (Scotland) Act 1949* established similar provisions.

[4] In English, 'substantial grounds for commencing a legal action'.

at their disposal the adequate means to do so—including resorting to the justice system. In this vein, the state should remedy existing social inequalities through positive measures that guarantee equal and universal access to justice, and concomitantly advance social inclusion. Yet, the existence of a legal aid scheme is at odds with one of the main premises of the ideology underpinning the welfare state: namely, that the state is the benefactor of those less well-off in society and is the main conduit for achieving social justice. From this perspective, lawyers and judicial solutions to progress the goal of social justice are at best redundant and at worst counterproductive. Given this ideological backdrop, Tamara Goriely (1994: 561) has argued that it is no coincidence that legal aid was originally envisaged by the founders of the British welfare state as limited in scope, aimed at covering matters that could not be resolved administratively.

The foundational stages and the changing fortunes of legal aid in Britain are strongly wedded and can be traced back to the reconfiguration of the modern welfare state in the past 65 years. Their vicissitudes are also linked to notions of social solidarity, citizenship and civic deservingness. Although, as several authors have documented since its inception, legal aid has suffered from chronic underfunding and a demand–supply mismatch (McConville et al 1994: 28), the scheme had its heyday during the period just after its institution and until the early 1970s, evidenced by a substantial expansion of legal aid spending and an increased demand for legal services (Newman 2013: 15). The 1980s marked the beginning of a period in which cuts to social welfare spending, increased social inequalities and mounting criminal and civil litigation contributed to further overburdening an already strained public service. In what one politician recently characterised as 'salami slicing' legal aid (Khan 2014), successive governments have introduced a myriad of changes aimed at reducing the legal aid budget.

III. Foreign to Justice? The Residence Test and its Judicial Challenge

Amid a range of austerity measures introduced by the Coalition government to reduce public spending and the welfare bill, in September 2013, then Minister of Justice, Chris Grayling, announced that a 'residence test' would be introduced by way of secondary legislation so that only people with a strong connection to the UK would be able to receive civil legal aid. In its consultation paper, *Transforming Legal Aid*, the government considered that such a test was necessary to avoid 'unfairness to the UK taxpayer' given that people who had never 'set foot' in the country or paid UK taxes, and whose connection to the country was tenuous, were eligible for legal aid (MoJ 2013b: 27). This proposed test for eligibility would restrict access to public funds for civil litigation for those who have not lawfully resided in the country for a continuous period of at least 12 months at the time of the application, save for members of the armed forces and their families, and asylum seekers.[5] The proposed residence test resembles the 'habitual residence' test introduced by the Conservative government in 1994. Originally established to tackle 'benefit tourism' through rules in welfare law, the test restricts access to welfare benefits—like income, housing and tax benefits—for those without a 'right to reside' in the UK, who have not been residents for an 'appreciable period of time' (usually a minimum of two years), and have no 'settled intention' to reside (Kennedy 2011).

Although the residence test was in principle equally applicable to non-resident British and foreign nationals, it was primarily aimed at excluding the latter, given the emphasis in related policy papers on non-UK citizens. The consultation paper indicated that in the current system, nationality and residence were irrelevant for accessing legal aid, and foreign nationals residing in or outside England or Wales were eligible for civil legal aid—a situation characterised as 'anomalous' (MoJ 2013b: 27). Moreover, while its impact was impossible to measure since the residency of litigants is not routinely recorded in court statistics, in its equality analysis the government acknowledged that the new measure would 'have the potential to put non-British nationals at a particular disadvantage compared with British nationals' (MoJ 2013a: 4). Arguably, introducing an explicit distinction between British and foreign nationals would have made the measure less defensible under domestic and European non-discrimination law.

An example of what Anderson (2013: 52) refers to as the disjuncture between the migrant in law and the migrant in politics, the decision to draw the line on residence rather than migration status or nationality relates to domestic and international legal obligations. And yet, it does not fit neatly within the political aim of excluding from access to legal aid those who, in the words of the Parliamentary Under-Secretary of State for Justice, are not 'our people'.[6] Glossing over the line between nationals and non-nationals in the law made the exclusionary measure more legally palatable, while ensuring that in practice it would disproportionately apply to the targeted group—foreigners. Indeed, some of the claimants in the *PLP* case sought to exploit the 'unintended' potential consequences of the new test which, in being aimed at excluding foreigners, would leave out people who are not able to prove their residence, 'even if someone looked and sounded British'.[7] A vivid illustration of how determining who counts as a

[5] Following the consultation, the exemptions were extended to children under 12 months' old—who, however, were still required to satisfy the first criterion of lawful residency—and to civil litigation in certain matters, including detention cases and victims of domestic violence, trafficking and forced marriage.

[6] In the parliamentary debate before the House of Commons, the Parliamentary Under-Secretary of State for Justice, Mr Shailesh Vara, explained: 'We have made it absolutely clear that for the residence test it is important that they are our people—that they have some link to this country' (HC Hansard, 18 March 2014: Col 623).

[7] For example, the deposition by Lucy Scott-Moncrieff. A similar argument was made by some organisations against the introduction of a civil penalty regime for landlords who fail to abide by their

'citizen' is tangled up with race and ethnicity (Aliverti 2016; Bosworth 2012), this line of argument strategically exploits the disjunction referred to above, thus warning of the potential slippages that can ensue—the exclusion of vulnerable British nationals—from the implementation of the proposed test.

The majority of respondents to the public consultation objected to the introduction of the test. Some of them, including the Public Law Project and other non-government organisations (NGOs), challenged it before the courts by way of judicial review. In the first place, they argued that the introduction of the test through secondary legislation by the government was ultra vires—beyond its legal power or authority—because it was not authorised by primary legislation. Secondly, it was claimed that the test amounted to unlawful discrimination against foreigners since it 'is plainly more likely to apply to non-UK nationals' and will place them at a disadvantage on grounds of national or social origin, which is prohibited by domestic and European law (Fordham, Jaffey and Mehta 2013: 3).[8]

In its ruling, the High Court agreed with the claimants on both grounds. On the ultra vires ground, the Court considered that by introducing a new criterion for eligibility to civil legal aid—residence—the government was acting outside the delegated powers granted by Parliament and hence was acting unlawfully. Indeed, the only criterion established in the primary legislation (the *Legal Aid, Sentencing and Punishment of Offenders Act 2012* [LASPO]) for determining eligibility is 'need'. 'Residence' was thus an entirely different condition not contemplated by the Act. In his vote, Moses LJ bluntly asserted: 'This test has nothing to do with need or an order of priority of need. It is, entirely, focussed on reducing the cost of legal aid' (*PLP*: [43]), and it does so by 'depriv[ing] non-residents of the opportunity to take advantage of that service' (*PLP*: [49]).

In relation to the second ground, the Court first assessed whether the residence test amounted to discrimination. It concluded that it did: 'The test is more likely to be satisfied by a United Kingdom national than a national of another member state' (*PLP*: [60]). It went on to examine whether that distinction was lawful—that is, non-arbitrary and proportionate. In trying to persuade the High Court that it was, the Secretary of State likened legal aid to social welfare benefits. He argued that since 'residence' is a legal criterion for eligibility to social benefits, it can be equally imposed to restrict the pool of people entitled to legal aid. In both fields there is no obligation on the state to provide assistance and therefore the state has discretion to introduce restrictions for granting that benefit.[9] One such

duties to check identity documents of tenants during the parliamentary debates on the Immigration Bill 2014. See the evidence by Katharine Sacks-Jones (HC Hansard, 29 October 2013: Col 60).

[8] Similar arguments were made by a group of NGOs to exhort the Parliament to vote against the test: '10 Reasons to vote against the Legal Aid Residence Test', available at: www.liberty-human-rights.org.uk/sites/default/files/10%20Reasons%20to%20vote%20against%20the%20residence%20test.pdf.

[9] Following the jurisprudence of the European Court of Human Rights (ECtHR) *Stec and Others v UK* (Application 65731/01), Judgment of 12 April 2006 (related to gender discrimination in access to the state pension scheme); and *Carson and Others v UK* (Application 42184/05), Judgment of 16 March 2010 (related to the right to uprated pension payments for non-residents).

restriction is the applicant's type and length of residence. Excluding non-residents, the government argued, is underpinned by legitimate policy reasons: cost savings and public confidence in the legal aid system.

In response to the government's argument and drawing on domestic and European jurisprudence, the Court conceded that residence might be an appropriate criterion for determining qualification to welfare benefits, since residents are 'more likely to have made an economic contribution and are more closely connected socially' to the country (*PLP*: [67]). According to the Court, restricting welfare benefits based on residence can be justified since 'residence' usually reflects the applicant's capacity as a taxpayer and the length of that financial contribution. Instead, in the context of legal aid, 'residence' has no bearing on the considerations that the Parliament had established to prioritise cases deserving subsidy ('high priority need' cases). The Court went further to explain that, provided the other criteria are fulfilled (namely, the means test and the more than 50 per cent chance of success requirement), non-residents should stand on equal grounds with residents: 'What a non-resident claimant seeks, just as much as a resident, is judicial protection … his[/her] underlying legal rights and underlying need for help are the same whether he[/she] is resident or not' (*PLP*: [76]). Indeed, the Court recognised that the plight of non-residents seeking legal aid might be even more acute and justified given linguistic barriers and the lack of familiarity with the vernacular of the legal system.[10]

Ultimately, the Court drew a fundamental distinction between entitlement to legal advice and welfare assistance based on state sovereignty. Since non-residents are subject to the jurisdiction of the state and obliged to obey its laws, they are concomitantly entitled to its protection on the same footing as nationals. Interestingly, while the exclusion of non-citizens from the protections afforded to citizens—particularly in the sphere of migration controls—has been often justified by the principle of territorial sovereignty bestowed by the nation-state (Cornelisse 2011; Dembour 2012), in the *PLP* case, the High Court appealed to that very principle as a source of protection for non-members. In reaching that conclusion, it relied on the opinion of Lord Scarman in *Ex parte Khawaja and Khera* (1984).[11] One of the central questions in the latter case was around whether the status of the applicants as 'non-partials', hence subject to migration controls, deprived them of the right to resort to the courts to attack the Home Secretary's decision to detain them. Lord Scarman, in his vote, made it blatantly clear that it did not: 'Every person

[10] In this regard, the British court distanced itself from the stance taken by the ECtHR. In *Yula*, the ECtHR ruled that, although the right of access to court is not absolute and could be restricted, Belgium had violated the applicant's right by depriving the applicant of their right to claim legal aid. Given the seriousness of the case (contestation of paternity) and the applicant's efforts to regularise her status in the country, the ECtHR found that Belgium had breached Art 6. However, the ECtHR did not directly attack the domestic law that restricted legal aid to irregular migrants (*Anakomba Yula v Belgium* (Application 45413/07), Judgment of 10 March 2009).

[11] *R v Secretary of State for the Home Department, ex parte Khawaja; R v Secretary of State for the Home Department, ex parte Khera* [1984] AC 74 (HL).

within the jurisdiction enjoys the equal protection of our laws. There is no distinction between British nationals and others. He[/She] who is subject to English law is entitled to its protection' (*Ex parte Khawaja* 1984: 111).

The government sought to rely on two justifications for restricting access to legal aid for non-residents: cost savings and public confidence in the legal aid system. Neither of these arguments holds sway. In relation to the former, the Court raised doubts about the net cost-saving benefits ensuing from the exclusionary provision and the possibility of estimating ex ante those benefits. Even if that evidence was forthcoming, the Court concluded that it is still not sufficient justification for impairing the ability to vindicate one's rights, for the reason outlined above.

In relation to the second argument, Moses LJ was far more candid:

> Feelings of hostility to the alien or foreigner are common, particularly in relation to the distribution of welfare benefits. But they surely form no part of any justification for discrimination amongst those who, apart from the fact that they are 'foreign', would be entitled to legal assistance … In the context of a discriminatory provision relating to legal assistance, invoking public confidence amounts to little more than reliance on public prejudice. (*PLP*: [84])

It could be added that the exclusion of non-citizens from free legal assistance is not just discriminatory. The claim that it purports to increase *public* confidence and legitimacy is misleading. It portrays the 'public' as a homogenous entity—thus glossing over important differences within society—while claiming to voice those demands by virtue of the democratic mandate (Pratt 2006: 32). Such exclusion is also deeply problematic because it panders to fears and anxieties among sectors of the population about incoming migrants. In taking stock of social hostility and resentment towards certain foreigners, instead of seeking to challenge and placate them, through its policies, the state bolsters prejudices and social fragmentation (Aliverti 2015: 218). As criminologists have long argued, populism operates within a simplistic idea of democracy 'that delivered flawed criminal justice policies simply because there was an apparent public demand for them' while overlooking the fact that politicians, in forging public policies, lead, and not just follow, the 'public' (Roberts et al 2003: 161).

The High Court's decision was rightly celebrated by practitioners and NGOs[12] for halting one of the most controversial aspects of the Coalition government's austerity programme and for advancing progressive jurisprudence.[13] Indeed,

[12] See the extensive coverage of the judgment in the following blogs and websites: ukhumanrightsblog.com/2014/07/15/plan-to-stop-non-residents-getting-legal-aid-is-unlawful-rules-high-court-angela-patrick/; familylawweek.co.uk/site.aspx?i=ed131045; righttoremain.org.uk/blog/residence-test-found-to-be-unlawful-by-high-court/; lag.org.uk/magazine/2014/07/court-rules-legal-aid-residence-test-%27unlawful%27.aspx; freemovement.org.uk/legal-aid-residence-test-found-unlawful-big-time/; lawsociety.org.uk/news/stories/high-court-government-s-residence-test-for-legal-aid-unlawful/; refuge.org.uk/2014/07/15/1008557/; ohrh.law.ox.ac.uk/the-irrelevance-of-residence-the-unlawful-residence-test-for-legal-aid/.

[13] The Public Law Project was defeated before the Court of Appeal in November 2015 when it ruled that the 'residence test' was lawful (*Public Law Project v Lord Chancellor* [2015] EWCA Civ 1193).

having garnered the support of the House of Commons, the government put forward the measure in the form of an Order before the Lords. After the High Court delivered its judgment, the government decided to withdraw the Order from the second chamber and announced that it would appeal the Court's decision. Yet, questions can be raised about the significance of the ruling for ensuring equal access to justice for non-citizens in criminal and civil matters.

IV. A *Pyrrhic* Victory? Immigration Exceptionalism, Legal Aid and Justice

The non-discrimination principle recalled by Moses LJ in the *PLP* judgment has become part of an emerging constitutional jurisprudence that seeks to limit state sovereign powers over non-citizens. In his judgment in *A and others v Secretary of State for the Home Department* (*Belmarsh*) (2004),[14] Lord Bingham resorted to the same principle to reach the conclusion that the indefinite detention of foreign nationals suspected of terrorism is discriminatory. He admitted that, in the immigration context, discrimination between nationals and non-nationals can be lawfully justified, particularly the open-ended regime of immigration detention and the deportation of foreign nationals convicted for crimes. Yet, in the context of national security, he observed, a severe deprivation of the right to individual freedom, such as indefinite detention, could not be lawfully circumscribed to non-deportable foreigners since the threat of terrorism stems from both nationals and non-nationals. Outside immigration law, unequal treatment based on alienage is not legally acceptable.

While this embryonic jurisprudence should no doubt be praised for challenging direct legal discrimination on grounds of nationality and migration status, and for advancing progressive standards of treatment, it fails to ask serious questions about the fairness and legality of unequal treatment in the immigration sphere.[15] It also problematically assumes that 'the immigration context' is fairly circumscribed and clearly bounded. I shall explain below why this is not entirely accurate. In relation

The Court judged the test as within the powers granted to the Lord Chancellor by LASPO, since the ultimate aim of saving public money is well within those reflected in the primary legislation and is not incompatible with the exclusion of certain classes based on priority of needs. It also rejected the argument that the test amounts to prohibited discrimination. Given that the discriminatory measure is not based on a specially protected category—such as gender and race, the criteria to exclude non-UK residents from eligibility to legal funds, cost saving, is justifiable unless 'manifestly without reasonable foundation'. At the time of writing, this decision was being challenged before the Supreme Court.

[14] *A and others v Secretary of State for the Home Department* [2004] UKHL 56 (HL).

[15] In the *Khawaja* case, the House of Lords allowed the appeal for one of the appellants (Mr Khera) but denied it to Mr Khawaja, adding that the decision 'should not be construed as a charter to alleged illegal entrants who challenge their detention and proposed removal'.

to the first critique, immigration controls and the concomitant coercive powers attached to them have been recognised by the European Court of Human Rights (ECtHR) as an 'undeniable sovereign right' of Member States.[16] Forging an 'immigration exceptionalism' (Aliverti 2014; Cornelisse 2011; Dembour 2003, 2012), the ECtHR has ruled that in the sphere of immigration control Member States have wide prerogatives, including the power to detain non-nationals so long as it is reasonably required for preventing unauthorised entry or enforcing a deportation order.[17] As Marie Bénédicte Dembour (2012: 698) has noted, the 'immigration exception' in international human rights reflects the tension between universalism and particularism at the heart of human rights norms. While human rights should be recognised for everyone by dint of their humanity, in certain circumstances human rights norms allow unequal treatment based on nationality.

The blind spot noted above in relation to the domestic and international jurisprudence reflects developments in legal aid reform in Britain. Although the High Court declared the proposal to restrict access to legal aid for non-residents unlawful, more drastic and wider restrictions to legal aid funding have been implemented without much fanfare. Legal aid in immigration matters has been slashed to the bear minimum by LASPO, restricting its use to specific cases (namely, asylum casework, where the applicant claims that she has been the victim of domestic violence or human trafficking or that she is being detained unlawfully under immigration law powers, and for limited non-asylum judicial review).[18]

One of the reasons for introducing these changes was the simplicity and informality of immigration proceedings. As the government argued, 'individuals in immigration cases should be capable of dealing with their immigration application, and it is not essential for a lawyer to assist' (MoJ 2011: 83). Much in the same way that the alleged triviality and legal irrelevance of the matters discussed in lower criminal courts trump the rights of defendants through the relaxation of formal proceedings—including the lack of access to legal aid—this 'summary justice' ideology (Feeley 1979: 192; McBarnet 1981a: 124; McBarnet 1981b; McConville et al 1994: 158) underpins the latest reforms to immigration legal aid funding. However, the seeming straightforwardness of immigration matters is contested by practitioners and academics. Sheona York has explained that, given the increased complexity and rapidity of change in immigration law, '[w]ithout specialist advice virtually no migrants would be aware of any of these changes, or be able to state in written representations or orally in a tribunal why any particular one of [the] landmark decisions [in immigration law] supported their application' (2013: 116).

[16] See *Amuur v France* (Application 19776/92), Judgment of 25 June 1996, ECtHR, at 41; *Chahal v UK* (Application 22414/93), Judgment of 15 November 1996, ECtHR, at 73; *Abdulaziz, Cabales and Balkandali v the United Kingdom* (Applications 9214/80; 9473/81; 9474/81), Judgment of 28 May 1985, at 67–68; *Saadi v UK* (Application 13229/03), Judgment of 29 January 2008, at 64.

[17] *Saadi v UK*, at 80.

[18] Section 9(1) and Sch 1, Part 1, paragraphs 30, 31 (asylum and international protection); 28, 29 (domestic violence); 32 (trafficking); 25 (detention); and 19(5)–(8) (judicial review).

Robert Thomas (2011: 113) has argued that, specifically in asylum appeals, due to their legal complexity and the linguistic and other difficulties faced by appellants, legal representatives generally enhance the ability to present their cases effectively, thus increasing the chances of success.[19] For those affected by legal aid cuts to immigration litigation, the effects are particularly painful. Immigration law clients are not only poor; they also often face linguistic and geographical barriers (Smith 1993).

Restrictions to immigration legal aid have had catastrophic effects on practitioners. Since a significant number of their clients are poor, specialist immigration law practitioners tend to operate in law centres or firms that have a high proportion of legal aid casework. Amid a marked increase in asylum applications in the early 2000s, the government introduced further eligibility requirements and fixed fees which pushed two major legal aid immigration law centres (the Immigration Advisory Service and Refugee Migrant Justice) into administration, leaving thousands of applicants unrepresented (Singh and Webber 2011: 3; York 2013: 131). These cuts were compounded by restrictions phased in by LASPO.[20] Following its implementation, the majority of immigration cases were no longer in scope for legal aid. Indeed, legal aid statistics reported a 45 per cent decrease in the immigration workload for 2013–14 in comparison with the previous year, a downfall that outstripped the drop in general civil legal aid workload (MoJ 2014a: 25, 2014b: 23).

The composite effects of these cuts have exacerbated the problem of poor quality of legal advice. Inadequate training, poor-quality representation and exploitation of clients remain the most acute and prevailing problems in immigration litigation (Thomas 2011: 114; York 2013: 126). As the immigration practitioners interviewed by Penny Smith complained, the slashing of legal aid funding opened up the field to 'crooks' and 'sharks', unregulated and untrained advisers who preyed on vulnerable, despairing clients (Smith 1993: 173). Similarly, the detainees interviewed by Mary Bosworth complained about the poor quality of services and corruption: 'My lawyer did not have a licence ... He kept my case for 6 months, wasting my time and got a lot of money' (Bosworth 2014: 145).

The extensive cuts to immigration legal aid can be conceived as one of the surreptitious facets of the so-called immigration exceptionalism, upheld by the line of jurisprudence reviewed above. A second pitfall of this jurisprudence is its assumption of a clear-cut and confined 'immigration context'. As Lord Bingham explained in *Belmarsh* (2004: 53, 55):

> The appellants were treated differently because of their nationality or immigration status. The comparison contended for by the Attorney-General might be reasonable and justified in an immigration context, but cannot in my opinion be so in a security context,

[19] Within his sample, Thomas (2011: 116) reported a higher success rate for represented appellants (31 per cent) in comparison to unrepresented clients (12 per cent).

[20] It entered into force on 1 April 2013.

> since the threat presented by suspected international terrorists did not depend on their nationality or immigration status … It is indeed obvious that in an immigration context some differentiation must almost inevitably be made between nationals and non-nationals since the former have a right of abode and the latter do not … The question is whether and to what extent states may differentiate outside the immigration context.

This assumption of discrete boundaries and independence between the immigration context and other contexts is untenable. Overt, lawful discrimination based on nationality and migration status in the immigration context has wider, spill-over effects beyond that context. The outsider status or foreignness, as Linda Bosniak has noted, 'shapes [the] experience and identity [of non-citizens] within the community in profound ways' (Bosniak 2008: 9). An example in point is the criminal justice realm. Given the increased intertwining between immigration and criminal law enforcement, immigration-related matters often percolate criminal justice proceedings. Issues apparently unrelated to the criminal liability of defendants—concerning their migration status, their liability for deportation or their extant asylum claim, for example—now feature prominently in the everyday work of the criminal justice system, which is increasingly called on to deal with foreign nationals. As such, decisions made elsewhere—where alienage is a lawful ground for dispensing differential treatment, including in the welfare and immigration spheres—can have profound effects for those accused of breaching the criminal law. In turn, a criminal conviction triggers a number of immigration consequences—the most serious of which is deportation. Hence, policy decisions in certain areas, particularly immigration law, have profound impacts elsewhere. An illustration of this is the situation of asylum claimants who are criminally prosecuted for entering the country illegally. Under domestic law, defendants in these circumstances may have a defence to the criminal charge provided certain conditions are met.[21] In these cases, knowledge and training on immigration and refugee law are crucial for successfully arguing a defence. Yet, as I have found, few criminal law practitioners are so trained, a factor indicated as one of the root causes of overturned convictions for various immigration-related crimes against refugees (Aliverti 2013: 92). According to the independent body that reviews cases involving potential miscarriages of justice, the number of such cases referred to it revealed a 'significant and potentially widespread misunderstanding or abuse of the law' (Criminal Cases Review Commission 2012: 15). Given the unavailability of specialised lawyers and the restricted access to legal aid funding for Criminal Cases Review Commission proceedings (Bird 2010), the cases that do reach it are a small minority. The drastic reductions in immigration legal aid funding will exacerbate this deficiency in legal representation, placing people at risk of miscarriages of justice.

Immigration legal aid cuts have detrimental effects on victims of crime. Domestic violence legislation provides that non-British, visa-holding victims of domestic

[21] See s 31 of the *Immigration and Asylum Act 1999*.

abuse are eligible for indefinite leave to remain, a determination that hinges on the criminal conviction of the abusive partner. In the context of the project Foreign Nations before the Criminal Courts: Immigration, Deportability and Punishment, I interviewed a domestic violence adviser who mentioned that it is increasingly difficult to find immigration lawyers to advise women on their eligibility for that status:

> [The migration issue] is a minefield … we have to refer to an immigration lawyer and it's really difficult because it is not clear-cut … with all the cuts that happened [to legal aid funding] then that has a knock-on effect on services that women can access … [A] few years ago you could easily get an immigration lawyer. Now, you know, you struggle to get one because it's funding, they've got no resources, they've got no money.

The need for expert legal representation is hence critical for non-citizens navigating legal systems with distinct rules, where consequences can be equally painful and serious, especially when they work together.[22] As in immigration proceedings, in the criminal justice system, non-citizens tend to rely on legal aid for a number of reasons. According to criminal law solicitors, foreign nationals tend not to have their own private lawyer, a 'family solicitor', and are more likely to rely on the pool of duty solicitors and lawyers doing legal aid work.[23] So too, as the majority of criminal defendants, they are predominantly poor. Legal aid is sometimes apparently easier to obtain for foreign nationals, according to one of my interviewees:

> Well, in a way they are much more likely to get legal aid because they are foreign nationals. They don't speak English, they haven't been before the courts before. Sometimes it is easier to get legal aid for a foreign national. (Solicitor, Birmingham Magistrates' Court)

Another lawyer agreed, mentioning that foreign nationals are more likely to fit into the Widgery criteria for legal aid funding because of linguistic difficulties and lack of familiarity with the domestic legal system.[24] These applications are assessed on two main grounds: the applicant's financial eligibility (the 'means' test) and the merits of the case (the 'interest of justice' test). One of the considerations for assessing the 'interest of justice' test is whether the applicant will be able to understand the court proceedings. Yet, given the lack of information about the

[22] The seriousness of deportation as a collateral consequence of a criminal conviction, and the right of the defendant to be advised by counsel about such risk, has been recognised as an aspect of constitutionally adequate representation by the United States Supreme Court in *Padilla v Commonwealth of Kentucky*, 559 US 356 (2010).

[23] In their research on the magistrates' court at Sheffield, Bottoms and McClean (1976: 146) reported that defendants with limited English tend to turn to lawyers, who are seen as 'an articulate voice in a strange environment'.

[24] The Departmental Committee on Criminal Legal Aid (the 'Widgery Committee') was set up to examine the provision of legal aid in criminal proceedings. In its report of March 1966, it established a set of rules that judges should consider when determining applications for legal aid, including in relation to the seriousness of the charge against the accused, whether the charge raises a substantial question of law, the ability of the defendant to defend himself, and the desirability of legal representation for protecting the interest of someone other than the accused (Zander 1966).

demography of legal aid beneficiaries based on citizenship, the reliance of foreign nationals on it is difficult to quantify.

V. Conclusion

Legal aid reform is not just about cost saving and austerity. Who gets to bear the burden of pain delivery measures reflects current social mores and hierarchies of deservingness. Policies and debates on how to distribute scarce resources point to the tensions between the right of individuals, on the one hand, and the wider public interest, on the other, particularly in the case of unpopular minorities. The limits of hospitality and tolerance towards those ruled out as undeserving are thus tested.

Recent debates around the residence test pose vexing questions about whose claims deserve to be publicly supported and under what premises. The High Court set a conclusive principle challenging the government's appeal to populist politics to exclude non-members. In doing so, it dismantled the argument relied upon by the government that the legal aid regime should shadow the national social security one in relation to the lawfulness of residence as a criterion for excluding beneficiaries. It is the legal accountability of 'outsiders'—and not their contributory capacity—that should be determinant in extending the protections recognised to legal residents. Yet, as I have shown, the ruling left unquestioned deep-seated assumptions about the state's prerogative to treat people differently on grounds of foreignness, and the popular sentiments on which those assumptions rely.

References

Aliverti, A (2013) *Crimes of Mobility: Criminal Law and the Regulation of Immigration* (Abingdon, Routledge).

—— (2014) 'Criminal Immigration Law and Human Rights in Europe' in S Pickering and J Ham (eds), *Routledge Handbook on Migration and Crime* (Abingdon, Routledge).

—— (2015) 'Enlisting the public in the policing of immigration' 55 *British Journal of Criminology* 215.

—— (2016) 'Researching the Global Criminal Court' in M Bosworth, C Hoyle and L Zedner (eds), *Changing Contours of Criminal Justice: Research, Politics and Policy* (Oxford, Oxford University Press).

Anderson, B (2010) 'Migration, immigration controls and the fashioning of precarious workers' 24 *Work, Employment & Society* 300.

—— (2013) *Us & Them? The Dangerous Politics of Immigration Control* (Oxford, Oxford University Press).

Bird, S (2010) 'The Inadequacy of Legal Aid' in M Naughton (ed.) *The Criminal Cases Review Commission. Hope for the Innocent?* (London, Palgrave Macmillan).

Bosniak, L (2008) *The Citizen and the Aliens. Dilemmas of Contemporary Membership* (Princeton NJ, Princeton University Press).

Bosworth, M (2012) 'Subjectivity and identity in detention: Punishment and society in a global age' 16 *Theoretical Criminology* 123.

—— (2014) *Inside Immigration Detention* (Oxford, Oxford University Press).

Bottoms, A and McClean, J (1976) *Defendants in the Criminal Process* (London, Routledge & Kegan Paul).

Cameron, D (2011) Full transcript: Speech on immigration, Institute of Government, *New Stateman*, 10 October 2011, available at: www.newstatesman.com/uk-politics/2011/10/immigration-british-work.

Chauvin, S and Garcés-Mascareñas, B (2012) 'Beyond Informal Citizenship: The New Moral Economy of Migrants Illegality' 6 *International Political Sociology* 241.

Cornelisse, G (2011) 'A new articulation of human rights, or why the European Court of Human Rights should think beyond Westphalian sovereignty' in M Dembour, M and T Kelly (eds), *Are Human Rights for Migrants? Critical Reflections on the Status of Irregular Migrants in Europe and the United States* (Abingdon, Routledge).

Criminal Cases Review Commission (2012) *Annual Report and Accounts 2011–12. HC 390* (London, The Stationery Office).

De Giorgi, A (2010) 'Immigration control, post-Fordism, and less eligibility: A materialist critique of the criminalization of immigration across Europe' 12 *Punishment & Society* 147.

Dembour, M (2003) 'Human Rights Law and National Sovereignty in Collusion: The Plight of Quasi-Nationals at Strasbourg' 21 *Netherlands Quarterly of Human Rights* 63.

—— (2012) 'Gaygusuz Revisited: The Limits of the European Court of Human Rights' Equality Agenda' 12 *Human Rights Law Review* 689.

Feeley, M (1979) *The Process is the Punishment: Handling Cases in a Lower Criminal Court* (New York, Russell Sage Foundation).

Fordham, M, Jaffey, B and Mehta, R (2013) *The Legality of the Proposed Residence Test For Civil Legal Aid. Joint Opinion*, available at: www.liberty-human-rights.org.uk/sites/default/files/pub-counsels-opinion-on-legality-of-proposed-residecy-test.pdf.

Goriely, T (1994) 'Rushcliffe Fifty Years on: The Changing Role of Civil Legal Aid within the Welfare State' 21 *Journal of Law and Society* 545.

—— (1999) 'Making the Welfare State Work: Changing Conceptions of Legal Remedies within the British Welfare State' in F Regan, A Paterson and T Goriely (eds), *The Transformation of Legal Aid: Comparative and Historical Studies* (Oxford, Oxford University Press).

HC Hansard (2013) House of Commons *Hansard*, 29 October 2013 (Col 60).

—— (2014) House of Commons *Hansard*, 18 March 2014 (Col 623).

HM Government (2010) *The Coalition: our programme for government* (London, HM Government).

Kennedy, S (2011) *The Habitual Residence Test. London: House of Commons. Commons Briefing Papers SN00416*, available at: researchbriefings.parliament.uk/ResearchBriefing/Summary/SN00416.

Khan, S (2014) 'Cutting legal aid is an easy gimmick—this is part of a pattern', *The Guardian*, 27 February 2014, available at: www.theguardian.com/commentisfree/2014/feb/27/cutting-legal-aid-reform-chris-grayling-justice-system.

Marshall, T (1950) *Citizenship and Social Class and Other Essays* (Cambridge, Cambridge University Press).

McBarnet, D (1981a) *Conviction. Law, the State and the Construction of Justice* (London, Macmillan Press).

—— (1981b) 'Magistrates' Courts and the Ideology of Justice' 8 *British Journal of Law and Society* 181.

McConville, M, Hodgson, J, Bridges, L and Pavlovic, A (1994) *Standing Accused. The organisation and practices of criminal defence lawyers in Britain* (Oxford, Oxford University Press).

Ministry of Justice (2011) *Reform of Legal Aid in England and Wales: the Government Response* (London, MoJ).

—— (2013a) *Residence Test: Equalities Analysis*, available at: consult.justice.gov.uk/digital-communications/transforming-legal-aid-next-steps/results/equalities-statement.pdf.

—— (2013b) *Transforming Legal Aid: Delivering a more credible and efficient system* (London, MoJ).

—— (2013c) *Transforming Legal Aid: Next Steps* (London, MoJ).

—— (2014a) *Legal Aid Statistics in England and Wales. July to September 2014* (London, MoJ/ Legal Aid Agency).

—— (2014b). *Legal Aid Statistics in England and Wales. Legal Aid Agency 2013–2014* (London, MoJ).

Newman, D (2013) *Legal Aid Lawyers and the Quest for Justice* (Oxford, Hart Publishing).

Patrick, R (2012) 'Work as the primary 'duty' of the responsible citizen: a critique of this work-centric approach' 6 *People, Place & Policy* 5.

Pratt, J (2006) *Penal Populism* (London, Routledge).

Ramsay, P (2012) *The Insecurity State: Vulnerable Autonomy and the Right to Security in the Criminal Law* (Oxford, Oxford University Press).

Roberts, J, Stalans, L, Indermaur, D and Hough, M (2003) *Penal Populism and Public Opinion: Lessons From Five Countries* (New York, Oxford University Press).

Schierup, C, Hansen, P and Castles, S (2006) *Migration, Citizenship, and the European Welfare State* (Oxford, Oxford University Press).

Singh, A and Webber, F (2011) 'Excluding migrants from justice: the legal aid cuts' *Briefing paper No. 7* (London, Institute of Race Relations).

Smith, P (1993) 'Reducing legal aid eligibility criteria: the impact for immigration law practitioners and their clients' 12 *Civil Justice Quarterly* 167.

Thomas, R (2011) *Administrative Justice and Asylum Appeals* (Oxford, Hart Publishing).

Thomson, G (1950) 'Legal Aid in Great Britain' 3 *The Western Political Quarterly* 28.

Wacquant, L (2014) 'Marginality, Ethnicity, and Penality. A Bourdieusian Perspective on Criminalization' in R Duff, L Farmer, S Marshall, M Renzo and V Tadros (eds), *Criminalization. The Political Morality of the Criminal Law* (Oxford, Oxford University Press).

York, S (2013) 'The end of legal aid in immigration. A barrier to access to justice for migrants and a decline in the rule of law' 27 *Journal of Immigration, Asylum and Nationality Law* 106.

Zander, M (1966) 'Departmental Committee Report: Legal Aid in Criminal Proceedings' 29 *The Modern Law Review* 639.

Treaties, Conventions, Principles, Directives, Rules and Legislation

Charter of Fundamental Rights of the European Union

European Convention for the Protection of Human Rights and Fundamental Freedoms

Immigration and Asylum Act 1999

Legal Aid Directive, Council Directive 2002/8/EC of 27 January 2003

Legal Aid and Advice Act 1949

Legal Aid and Solicitors (Scotland) Act 1949

Legal Aid, Sentencing and Punishment of Offenders Act 2012

Cases

A and others v Secretary of State for the Home Department [2004] UKHL 56 (HL)

Abdulaziz, Cabales and Balkandali v United Kingdom (Applications 9214/80; 9473/81; 9474/81), Judgment of 28 May 1985

Amuur v France (Application 19776/92), Judgment of 25 June 1996

Anakomba Yula v Belgium (Application 45413/07), Judgment of 10 March 2009

Carson and Others v United Kingdom (Application 42184/05), Judgment of 16 March 2010

Chahal v United Kingdom (Application 22414/93), Judgment of 15 November 1996

Padilla v Commonwealth of Kentucky, 559 US 356 (2010)

Public Law Project v Lord Chancellor [2015] EWCA Civ 1193

Public Law Project v Secretary of State for Justice [2014] EWHC 2365 (Admin)

R v Secretary of State for the Home Department, Ex parte Khawaja; R v Secretary of State for the Home Department, Ex parte Khera [1984] AC 74 (HL)

Saadi v United Kingdom (Application 13229/03), Judgment of 29 January 2008

Stec and Others v United Kingdom (Application 65731/01), Judgment of 12 April 2006

INDEX

Access to justice 4–5, 6–7, 18
Australia 4–5, 6–7
community lawyers 141–142
Indigenous people 17–18, 282–283
Aboriginal and Torres Strait Islander Legal Services (ATSILS) 270
field officers 278
resourcing 280–282, 283
complex needs as clients 273
language and communication 273–276
particular needs of women 278–279
providing cultural security 276–278
Indigenous Family Violence Prevention and Legal Services (IFVPLS) 270, 279
Indigenous Legal Needs Project (ILNP) 270, 279, 283
lack of knowledge or understanding of civil law 271–273
old and urgent story 269–271
England and Wales 4–5, 6–7
LASPO and mediation 17, 239–241, 250–251
access to appropriate dispute resolution process 247–250
access to court 244–247
access to law 241–244
principles for court efficiency, *see* View from the bench
video link from prison, *see* Video link technologies
voluntary advice services, *see* Citizens Advice Bureaux (CAB)
Advice agencies/services, *see* Legal advice in third sector
'Advice deserts' 2, 3, 17, 162, 223, 224
Alternative dispute resolution (ADR) 55, 127–128
Audiovisual communication technologies, *see* Video link technologies
Australia
access to justice, *see* Access to justice
growing inequality 26–27
legal aid, *see* Legal aid
view from bench, *see* View from the bench
Citizens Advice Bureaux (CAB) 16, 179–180, 192
changing times for advice 182–186
history of service 181–182
legal understandings 190–191
maintaining volunteers' attachments to advice 186–189
methodology 180–181
Civil legal aid
cuts to 16–17, 220–221
facilitating factors, lessons learned 226–227
austerity, civil legal aid and universal v non-universal benefits 227–229
public knowledge and understanding of civil law in England and Wales 231–232
public perceptions of legal aid lawyers/ civil justice system and cuts 229–231
future funding in England and Wales 233
answering question of what lawyers are for 235
'doing' lawyering, thinking creatively about provision of services 233–234
getting the message across, changing communication around civil law/ justice 234
impact 2, 16–17, 225
Legal Aid, Sentencing and Punishment of Offenders Act 2012 (LASPO) 222–224
legal profession 225–226
immigration and 'residence test', *see* Immigration and residence test'
Communication technologies, *see* Video link technologies
Community legal centres (CLCs) 3, 15–16, 43–44, 47–48, 51, 58, 157
community lawyers
broader vision for 'access to justice' 141–142
restriction on systemic advocacy 150–154
NSW Aboriginal Legal Service (NSWALS) 48
rise of 125–126
systemic advocacy 142–143, 157
CLC's response and future of 154–157
ending exploitation by door-to-door salespeople 147–148

family violence reform 143–146
forcing police to recognise and act on police racism 143–145
protecting CLC's role 149–150
restriction, community lawyers 150–154
tackling exploitative taxi driver conditions 146–147
women's access to VLA and consequences of cuts for justice system 265
Competitive tendering, *see* Tendering
Confidentiality
impact of video links 114–116
Criminal legal aid 14, 63–64, 80
competitive tendering scheme 72
'two-tier' system 72–74
decline of 68–74
fees 70
fixed 14, 71
pressure on 79
'real terms' increase 68
reduced 73, 74
Legal Aid Agency (LAA) 71, 78
primary objectives 78
'two-tier' competitive tendering scheme
analysis 73
delayed introduction 74
Legal Aid Board (LAB) 66, 78
Legal Services Commission (LSC) 66, 78
means test 71
Public Defender Service (PDS) 66–68, 79
rise of 64–68
Rushcliffe Committee 64, 65
uncertain future 74–79
Widgery Criteria 65

De-investment in legal aid 7
England and Wales 1
Discrimination
immigration legal aid and 'residence test' 288–289, 292, 295–296
'DIY law' 15
co-production and self-help 131
self-help and legal services market failure 131–132
self-represented litigants 132–134
court as help hub 134–135
making law accessible 125
de-legislation, alternative dispute resolution and self-help 127–128
de-professionalisation and plain language 126–127
rise of community legal centre (CLC) 125–126
neoliberalism, downstream consequences 128–130
technology and age of gifted amateur 123–125
undeserving legal client 135–136

England and Wales
access to justice 4–5, 6–7
legal aid 4–6
criminal legal aid, *see* Criminal legal aid
cuts 1–3
civil legal aid, *see* Civil legal aid
consequences 12–13
fee rates across services 1
House of Commons Justice Committee Report 2–3
de-investment 1
fixed-fee regime 1
Legal Aid, Sentencing and Punishment of Offenders Act 2012, *see* Legal Aid, Sentencing and Punishment of Offenders Act 2012 (LASPO)
reduction in firms 2
reforms 1–2

Face-to-face/interface communication, *see* Video link technologies

Human right to legal aid 16, 195–196, 213
criminal matters 199–200
human rights 196–197
legal aid 197–199
right to
reasoning 209–211
substantive 211–212
non-criminal matters
comparing criminal and non-criminal proceedings 200–202
conditions under which right to legal aid is engaged 208–209
emerging human rights jurisprudence 203
note on terminology 200
right to non-criminal legal aid
under ECHR 203–205
under ICCPR 205
under other treaties 206–208

Immigration and 'residence test' 18, 287–289, 300
discrimination 288–289, 292, 295–296
immigration exceptionalism, legal aid and justice 295–300
introduction of test ultra vires 292
judicial challenge 288, 290–295
legal aid in Britain 289–290
Inequality in Australia 26–27
women's access to legal aid in Victoria, *see* Women's access to Victoria legal aid (VLA)

Lawyer–client relationship 11, 15
audiovisual communication, *see* Video link technologies
face-to-face 15, 54–55

Legal advice in third sector 16
  study of impact of cuts on Liverpool City Region (Liverpool CR) 16, 161–165
    concluding remarks 174–176
    flexibility 171–172
    hampered response 172–174
    impact on services
      actions taken by agencies to help clients 166–168
      loss of funding for disbursements/ medical evidence 170
      loss of referrals 170–171
      quality 168
      reduced service provision 165–166
      unmet need 168–170
  voluntary services, *see* Citizens Advice Bureaux (CAB)
Legal aid, *see also* Civil legal aid; Criminal legal aid
  Australia 3–6, 13–14
    Access to Justice Advisory Committee (AJAC) report 53
    allocation of resources 4
    alternative dispute resolution mechanisms 55
    Australian Legal Aid Office (ALAO)
      development 48, 50
      establishment 14, 43, 48–50
      views regarding success of 50
    broader vision 47–51
      Commission of Inquiry into Poverty 50–51
      Sackville Report 50–51
    challenges facing system 23–38
    community legal centres (CLCs), *see* Community legal centres (CLCs)
    cuts 3–5
      consequences 12
      impacts 3
        disadvantaged 51
        indigenous communities, resourcing of ATSILS 280–282, 283
        women, *see* Women's access to Victoria legal aid (VLA)
      restoration of funding 4
      those targeted 9–10
    development 14, 43–59
    early arrangements 45–47
    focus on efficiency 51–55
    funding 24–25, 54
      purchaser-provider model 54
    history 43, 58–59
    Justice Statement 53
    legal aid commissions (LACs) 3, 43–44, 51, 53, 58–59
      alterations to governance arrangements 54
      fee caps 54
      means test 10
      'solution-orientation' approach 54
    legal aid impact statements 30
      challenge of 'joined-up' services 36–38
      family violence 31–33
        child protection 32
      law and order 30–31
      maintenance of efficient/effective mixed-model legal aid infrastructure 33–35
    legal aid services 25
      challenges 28–29
      changes to legal practice 26
      increasing demand 29–30
      potential and limitations 55–56
        Australian Legal Aid Innovations Research Project 55–56
    National Legal Aid Advisory Committee (NLAAC) 51
      Legal Aid for the Australian Community report 51
    National Legal Aid Representative Council 51
    National Partnership Agreement (NPA) on legal assistance services 27–28
    outline of system 23–24
    'solution-orientation' approach 51, 54
    women's access to legal aid in Victoria, *see* Women's access to Victoria legal aid (VLA)
  cuts 1–5
    civil legal aid, *see* Civil legal aid
    consequences 10–13
    Legal Aid Minister's comments 9
    study of impact on Liverpool City Region, *see* Legal advice in third sector
    susceptibility to/acceptance of 7–10
    Transforming Legal Aid consultation paper 9
  court efficiency, *see* View from the bench
  'DIY law', implications, *see* 'DIY' law
  England and Wales 4–6
    cuts 1–3
      civil legal aid, *see* Civil legal aid
      consequences 12–13
      fee rates across services 1
      House of Commons Justice Committee Report 2–3
    de-investment 1
    fixed-fee regime 1
    reduction in firms 2
    reforms 1–2, 288–289
      those targeted 9
        migrants, *see* Immigration and 'residence test'
  human right, *see* Human right to legal aid
  'residence test', *see* Immigration and residence test'

Legal Aid, Sentencing and Punishment of Offenders Act 2012 (LASPO)
- cuts to civil legal aid 222–224
  - legal profession 225–226
- implementation 7
- introduction 1
- mediation 17, 239–241, 250–251
  - access to appropriate dispute resolution process 247–250
  - access to court 244–247
  - access to law 241–244

Legal practice
- changes to 25–26, 33
- technologised 106

Legal profession, *see also* Legal practice; Private legal profession
- growth of 65
- impact on 5, 14, 68, 76
- LASPO and 225–226
- nationalisation of 46
- opposition to BVT 72
- public defender services, *see* Public defender service (PDS)
- reform of 53
- role of 51
- training
  - contracts 233
  - immigration and refugee law 298
    - inadequate training 297
  - plain language writing 127

Mediation, *see* Legal Aid, Sentencing and Punishment of Offenders Act 2012 (LASPO)

Migration, *see* Immigration and 'residence test'

Private legal profession 24, 43
- funding 34
  - competition for 33
- impact on 265
- legal challenge to establishment of ALAO 49
- publicly funded legal aid schemes 47
- role of 34

Public defender service (PDS)
- establishment 14
- opposition to 79
- piloting 66
- proposals for 65

Quality 67–68
- austerity, impact 297
- court system 89
- criminal court 94–95, 100
- representation 34, 112, 206
- services 54, 72, 79, 91, 168
  - assessing 57
  - assurance 63
  - criminal defence 76

'Residence test', *see* Immigration and 'residence test'

Self-help 56–57
- 'DIY' law, *see* 'DIY' law

Tendering
- best value tendering (BVT) 72
- competitive 14
  - introduction 53, 68, 71, 72
  - price-competitive tendering (PCT) 72
- third-sector agencies 174

Therapeutic jurisprudence (TJ) 14, 95, 97–100, 135
- application 95, 98
- managerialist objection 135

Third-sector advice agencies, *see* Legal advice in third sector

Video link technologies 15, 103, 116–117
- audiovisual links (AVLs) 105–106, 108, 116
- communication with lawyers from prison 109
  - AVL conferences
    - benefits 109–111
    - confidentiality 114–116
    - drawbacks 112–114
  - benefits of face-to-face conferences 111–112
- concept of 'access to justice' 107–108
- emergent prison portal 108–109
- legal matrix 104–105
- research methodology 103–104
- shifting paradigms of lawyering 105–107
  - Legal Aid NSW (LANSW) 105–106
  - Virtual Court 107

View from the bench 14–15
- case scenario 87–89
- court efficiency 89, 100
  - access to justice principles 92
    - active judicial case management, coupled with investment in early identification of representation pathway 93
    - adequate levels of legal aid funding based on evidence of legal need 92
    - funding structures promoting early resolution/matters going to full hearing 92–93
    - strategies to assist 'missing middle' 93–94
  - legal aid and 89–92
- role of lawyer
  - 'change agent' 97–98
  - defence lawyer in addressing underlying causes of offending 95–96
  - facilitating offender participation and 'voice' 98–99

facilitating self-determination and autonomy 96–97
maximising quality of criminal court 94–95
therapeutic jurisprudence (TJ) 95, 98–99
Voluntary advice services, *see* Citizens Advice Bureaux (CAB)

Women's access to Victoria legal aid (VLA) 17, 255–257, 267
broader consequences of cuts for justice system 264
impact on CLCs 265
impact on courts 264–265
impact on private legal profession 265
crisis in VLA funding in 2013 257
future of legal aid in family law 266–267
response from VLA 265–266
women unable to access legal aid 258–260
broader social and economic consequences for woman and children 260–261
financial hardship and poverty 262–263
homelessness 263–264
risk of future family violence and/or death 261–262